NEW DIMENSIONS OF INDIAN BANKING

NEW DIMENSIONS OF INDIAN BANKING

Ramashish Purvey

SERIALS PUBLICATIONS
NEW DELHI (INDIA)

First Published – 2010

ISBN: 978-81-8387-264-5

Published by

SERIALS PUBLICATIONS
4830/24, Prahlad Street, Ansari Road
Darya Ganj, New Delhi-110002 (India)
Phone : 23245225 Fax : 91-11-23272135
E-mail: serials@satyam.net.in

Dedicated

To

Reverend Prof. (Dr.)

Dev Muni Prasad

Former Pro-Vice-Chancellor

Veer Kunwar Singh, University, Ara

for Inspiring me with Innovative Ideas

Contents

Preface

The banking system has witnessed fast changes since 1991-92 through the process of Liberalization, Privatization and Globalization. These reforms have provided necessary platform to the banking sector to operate on the basis of operational flexibility and functional autonomy, thereby enhancing efficiency, productivity and profitability. Information technology, emerged as the integrator, assisting banks in the management of the process of transformation, has been taking place continuously. 'Electronic Banking' is the buzzwood in the field of present day banking. New technologies are unfolding the changing face of banking in the current competitive global environment with the goal to serve the customer in the best possible manner. In such a scenario, it is essential to keep these developments on track. The financial sector today is witnessing a convergence of Banking Insurance Business, Mutual Funds and other financial products. This is evident from the fact that more and more banks are giving one stop services.

World over, increasing competition in the banking field has generated a race to consolidate the industry and achieve greater scale as a necessary prerequisite for improving efficiency. History shows that the top managements of many banks have felt that the best way of increasing size by a relatively quick route is 'merging with another bank'. In the banking industry, internal growth is rather a slow process and, therefore, the easiest path is often mergers or takeovers. The policy debate on efficacy of 'mergers & acquisitions' (M&A) in Indian banking system was initiated by the Narasimham

Committee Report II (1998), which stated that "size has come to be regarded as a major source of strength. The trend towards convergence has also been driven by the move across the industry, towards 'Relationship Banking', that is to identify and meet all the needs of a customer through a single (or affiliated) institution". The Committee visualizes future of Indian banking sector with three to four large international banks and eight to ten national banks with widespread domestic presence. This necessitates quality working and better performance by the Indian banks with a view to cope with the operational efficiency of international banks.

With this background in mind, and realizing the importance of banking in economic development, more so in the coming times, I thought of bringing out a book on " New Dimensions of Indian Banking". The academic dream of such a book could be translated into reality only after organizing a U.G.C. sponsored national seminar (as Convener-Cum-Organizing Secretary) on "Indian Banking Today: Search for a Better Tomorrow", held under the aegis of Department of Commerce, Marwari College, Bhagalpur on 5-6 May, 2007. The themes of the seminar were devoted to various aspects of Banking in India with special concentration on New Dimensions of Banking. It is worth mentioning that the book (ed.) contains scholarly works/papers of those researchers, scholars, academicians, rural development practitioners, bankers and policy makers, who participated in the deliberations.

I take this opportunity to extend my sincere thanks to our present Vice-Chancellor, Dr. (Mrs.) Col. Prema Jha, who encouraged me in this endeavour. I express my sincere regards and gratitude to Dr. Nisha Rai, Principal, Marwari College, Bhagalpur, who encouraged me through out the academic work.

Almighty God has been so kind to me with His blessings that I got this great opportunity, in fact, the rarest of the rare. I wish to record my extreme gratitude to Prof. (Dr.) P.C. Patanjali, Former Vice-Chancellor, T.M. Bhagalpur University, Bhagalpur (Bihar) and V.B.S. Purvanchal University, Jaunpur (U.P.) & Prof. (Dr.) Deomuni Prasad, Former Pro-Vice-Chancellor, Veer Kunwar Singh University , Ara, for their invaluable guidance and consistent encouragement. Not only invaluable guidance, but also their blessings were so abundantly, rather most graciously and liberally showered upon me for undertaking this exercise.

I do gratefully record the help and guidance in completing this work, provided voluntarily and spontaneously by Prof. (Dr.) L.N. Bhagat, Former Registrar, Ranchi University, Ranchi (Jharkhand), Prof. (Dr.).) Mahavir Sah, Former Registrar, T.M. Bhagalpur University, Bhagalpur and Prof. (Dr.) Hira Lal, Former Principal, Marwari College, Bhagalpur.

I am also indebted to luminaries of the Commerce Faculty, like Prof. (Dr.) Sita Ram Sharma (Dean, Faculty of Commerce, T.M. Bhagalpur University, Bhagalpur and Head, Department of Commerce, Marwari College, Bhagalpur), Prof. (Dr.) R.K. Sinha (Head, P.G. Department of Commerce, T.M. Bhagalpur University, Bhagalpur), Prof. (Dr.) L.D. Shah (Head, Department of Commerce, Marwari College, Bhagalpur), Prof. (Dr.) A. Thakur (Director MBA, T.M. Bhagalpur University, Bhagalpur), Prof. (Dr.) A.K. Saha (Former Director, MBA, T.M. Bhagalpur University, Bhagalpur), and Prof. (Dr.) B.P. Singh, Faculty of Commerce, T.M. Bhagalpur University, Bhagalpur.

I express my deep sense of gratitude to Prof. (Dr.) Pulin B. Nayak (Director, Delhi School of Economics), Prof. (Dr.) G.C Agrawal (Former Pro-Vice-Chancellor, Allahabad university, Allahabad), Prof. (Dr.) Ram Prakash Mahto (Former State Education Minister, Govt. of Bihar, Patna), Prof. (Dr.) S.M. Jha (Head and Director, Faculty of Commerce & MBA Programme, L.N. Mithila University, Darbhanga), Prof. (Dr.) L.P. Singh (Co-ordinator, MBA Programme, L.N. Mithila University, Darbhanga) and Dr. Adesh Sharma (BRAC, University of Delhi) for effecting my long efforts in this regard to evident reality. Also I can't help mentioning the contribution of Dr. Shamim Ahmed, the director of Shree Satya Institute of Management, Moradabad, who has all along extended his helping hand to and stood by me in every weal and woe, starting with the writing of the literature to its publication.

En suite, my heartfelt thanks are also due to Prof. (Dr.) R.D. Sharma (Former Head and Dean, Faculty of Social

Sciences, T.M. Bhagalpur University, Bhagalpur), Prof. (Dr.) Balkrishna Jha (University Professor and Former Head, Department of Rural Economics and Co-operation & Hony Director, AERC for Bihar and Jharkhand, T.M. Bhagalpur University, Bhagalpur), Prof. (Dr.) Rajendra Prasad Singh (Head, University Dept. of Rural Economics and Co-operation, T.M. Bhagalpur University, Bhagalpur), who extended all co-operation and guidelines as and when required by me.

In making this magnum opus (academic) a success, the co-operation and assistance of Dr. Ranjan Kumar Sinha (Research Officer), Dr. Rajiv Kumar Sinha (Research Associate), Dr. S.D Mishra (Research Associate) of 'AERC for Bihar and Jharkhand', T.M.B.U., Bhagalpur, Dr. P.K Sinha, Department of Commerce, Marwari College, Bhagalpur, Dr. Mahesh Chandra Prasad, P.G. Dept. of Applied Economics & Commerce, Patna University, Patna and Dr. Indrajeet Prasad Roy, P.G. Dept. of Commerce, J.P. University, Chapra can never be underestimated in any way.

I express sincere gratitude to all noted scholars, who enthusiastically contributed their scholarly papers. These papers provide their deep insight into the themes concerned. No doubt, the papers included in this volume, have wide coverage containing their long applied experiences in the field of banking.

Mrs. Anju Panjiyar, my beloved wife, joined me in this endeavour and patiently shared every pain every moment from the very first day. I am highly indebted to her, my two sons, Anshu Raj and Ankur Raj, whose good sense of humour sustained me in this challenging work.

Last but not the least, I am grateful to the publishing firm M/s. Serials Publications, Ansari Road, Darya Ganj, New Delhi for bringing out the book in its present form within minimum possible time. My apologies to many others, whom I might have left out though not deliberately. It goes without saying that the usual disclaimers apply. I hope, this will prove to be a 'light house' for the scholars and practitioners wishing to have deep insight in banking issues.

Ramashish Purvey
Bhagalpur (Bihar)

List of Contributors

Santanu Bhaduri, Sel-Gr-Lecturer, Department of Commerce, Berhampore College, University of Kalyani, West Bengal.

Rajeshwari Kumari , Research Scholar, University Department of Home Science-Food & Nutrition, T. M. Bhagalpur University, Bhagalpur.

Ramashish Purvey , Faculty Member, Department of Commerce, Marwari College, Bhagalpur (T. M. Bhagalpur University, Bhagalpur)

R. P. Deshpande, Sr. Lecturer, B. V. Arts, Com. & Sc. College, Barivili (W), Mumbai.

Sitaram Sharma, Dean Faculty of Commerce, T. M. Bhagalpur University, Bhagalpur.

J. P. Sharma, Lecturer in Commerce, B. N. College, Bhagalpur, (T. M. Bhagalpur University, Bhagalpur)

Mahesh Chandra Prasad, Sr. Lecturer, Department of Applied Economics & Commerce, Patna University, Patna.

Shabnam Parween, Lecturer, Department of Economics, H.D. Jain College, Ara, V.K.S. University, Ara.

Madhuker Dikshit, Lecturer, Department of Sociology, N.D. College, Purnea, B.N. Mandal University, Madhepura.

Indrajit Prasad Roy, Sr. Lecturer, Department of Commerce, Rajendra College, Chapra (J.P. University, Chapra)

Binay Kumar, Sr. Lecturer, Department of Commerce, Rajendra College, Chapra (J.P. University, Chapra).

Shaheda Khanam, University Prof. & Head, University Department of Home Science-Food & Nutrition, T. M. Bhagalpur University, Bhagalpur.

Seema Dey, Lecturer, Department of Home Science, Marwari College, Ranchi University, Ranchi.

U. N. Singh, Reader in Commerce, Marwari College, Bhagalpur (T. M. Bhagalpur University, Bhagalpur).

Birendra Kumar Yadav, M.Com., Ph.D., T. M. Bhagalpur University, Bhagalpur.

Chandeshwari Tiwary, University Prof. & Head, Department of Economic, S.S.V. College, Kahalgaon, Bhagalpur.

Niranjana Jeswal, Head, Department of Commerce, S. M. College, Bhagalpur (T. M. Bhagalpur University, Bhagalpur).

Bijay Kumar Sinha, Lecturer, Department of Economics, PTPS College, Patratu, Hazaribagh.

Subhas Kumar, Head, Department of Commerce, Annanda College, Hazaribagh.

Md. Israr Hassan Khan, Head, Department of Commerce, D. A. V., P.G. College, Siwan, J. P. University, Chapra.

Md. Moazzam Nazri, Lecturer, Department of Commerce, Karim City College, Jamshedpur (Jharkhand).

Deepa Sharan, Lecturer, Department of Commerce, Jamshedpur Women's College.

Kishwar Ara, Lecturer, Department of Economics, Jamshedpur Women's College.

Shashi Kapur Das, Research Scholar, University Department of Commerce, T. M. Bhagalpur University, Bhagalpur.

B. K. Mohanty, Facutly of Commerce, B.H.U. Varanasi.

Navin Prasad, Head Department of Economics, P.T.P.S. College, Patratu, Hazaribagh.

Manmeet Singh, Reader, Medi-Caps Institute of Technology & Management, Indore,

R. K. Vyas, Reader, International Institute of Professional Studies, Indore.

V. K. Gautam, Director, International Institute of Foreign Trade & Research, Indore.

R. K. Srivastava, Sr. Lecturer, University Department of Commerce, B.R. Ambedkar, Bihar University, Muzaffarpur.

Parmanand Lal, M.Com., Ph. D., University Department of Commerce, B.R. Ambedkar, Bihar University, Muzaffarpur University,

P. Dubey, Lecturer, Department of Zoology, T. N. B. College, (T. M. Bhagalpur University, Bhagalpur).

D. M. Khondore, Reader School of Commerce & Management Sciences, S.R.T.M. University, Nanded.

Mohan S. Rode, Research Scholar, S.R.T.M. University, Nanded.

Sasanka Sekhar Bhaumik, Sel-Gr-Lecturer, Department of Commerce, Berhampore College, University of Kalyani, West Bengal.

Ashis Kumar Nandi, Sel-Gr-Lecturer, Department of Political Science Berhampore College, University of Kalyani, West Bengal.

Sanjay Kumar Gupta, Research Scholar, University Department of Commerce.

Anand Kumar, Lecturer, Department of Commerce, Allahabad Degree College, Allahabad (U.P.).

Raj Bihari Lal Srivastava, Lecturer, Department of Commerce, C.M.P. Degree College, Allahabad.

Gopal Kumar Singh, University Department of Commerce, T.M. Bhagalpur University, Bhagalpur).

Ashutosh Kumar, M. Com., University Department of Commerce (T. M. Bhagalpur University, Bhagalpur).

Surya Prakash, Research Scholar, Faculty of Commerce, BHU.

Sarika Sharma, Research Scholar, Faculty of Commerce, BHU.

B. B. Mansuri, Women's College, A.M.U., Aligarh

Badruzzama Siddiqui, Women's College, A.M.U., Aligarh

Ratna Shanker Mishra, Lecturer, Department of Vocational Courses, Faculty of Arts, B.H.U.

Amit Verma, Research Scholar, Faculty of Commerce, B.H.U., Varanasi.

Ajay Kumar, M.A. (Eco.) Ph.D., T. M. Bhagalpur University, Bhagalpur.

P. S. Tripathi, Reader, Department of Economics, D.B.S. College, Kanpur.

Shweta Dikshit, Research Scholar, Department of Economics, D.B.S. College, Kanpur.

K. C. Jha, Reader, Department of Commerce, Marwari College, Bhagalpur (T. M. Bhagalpur University, Bhagalpur).

P. C. Badalia, Reader, Department of Commerce, Marwari College, Bhagalpur (T. M. Bhagalpur University, Bhagalpur).

Manju Kumari, Research Scholar, University Department of Commerce, T. M. Bhagalpur University, Bhagalpur

Avnish Kr. Shukla, Research Scholar, Faculty of Commerce, B.H.U., Varanasi.

Pramod Kr. Verma, Research Scholar, Faculty of Commerce, B.H.U., Varanasi.

Amit Kumar, Research Scholar, University Department of Rural Economics & Co-operation, T. M. Bhagalpur University, Bhagalpur.

Sanjay Singh, Research Scholar, University Department of Commerce T. M. Bhagalpur University, Bhagalpur.

Lucy Kumari, Research Scholar, University Department of Commerce T. M. Bhagalpur University, Bhagalpur.

Jaishanker Prasad Singh, Lecturer, Department of Commerce, K.P. College, Murliganj (B. N. Mandal University, Madhepura)

Naveen Kumar Mishra, M.Com., Ph.D (T. M. Bhagalpur University, Bhagalpur).

Prabhat Kumar, Research Scholar, University Department of Commerce, T. M. Bhagalpur University, Bhagalpur.

Dipak B. Bhamare, Reader & Head Department of Business Administration, S.S.V.P.S. Arts and M.F.M.A. Com. College, Dhule, Maharashtra.

Jitendra Kumar, Sr. Lecturer, P.G. Department of Commerce & Business Management, H.D. Jain College, Ara, V.K.S. University, Ara.

Udita, Research Scholar, University Department of Rural Economics & Co-operation, T. M. Bhagalpur University, Bhagalpur.

Dimpal Rani, Research Scholar, University Department of Rural Economics & Co-operation, T. M. Bhagalpur University, Bhagalpur.

Md. Shahabuddin, Research Scholar, University Department of Commerce, T. M. Bhagalpur University, Bhagalpur.

Niru Kumari, Research Scholar, University Department of Commerce, T. M. Bhagalpur University, Bhagalpur

Kumari Madhulata, M.A. (Sociology), Ph.D. T. M. Bhagalpur University, Bhagalpur.

P.K. Sinha, Lecturer, Department of Commerce, Marwari College, Bhagalpur, T. M. Bhagalpur University, Bhagalpur.

Jitendra Kumar Singh, Research Scholar, University Department of Commerce, T. M. Bhagalpur University, Bhagalpur.

Piyush Kumar Singh, Research Scholar, University Department of Commerce, T. M. Bhagalpur University, Bhagalpur.

Ranjana Singh, Lecturer, Department of Economics, R.D.& D.J. College, Munger, T. M. Bhagalpur University, Bhagalpur.

Ajoy Kumar, Lecturer, Department of Commerce, J. M. College, Muzaffarpur, Bihar.

Murlidhar Mandal, Research Scholar, T. M. Bhagalpur University, Bhagalpur.

Sumit Prasad, M.Com., Ph. D., T.M. Bhagalpur University, Bhagalpur.

Ajit Kumar Thakur, Research Scholar, University Department of Rural Economics & Co-operation, T. M. Bhagalpur University, Bhagalpur.

1

An Overview of Growth and Development of Nationalized Banks in India

Santanu Bhaduri

Banking sector plays an important role in the ecomomic development of a country. Prior to nationalisation, the functions of banks were limited. The Indian banking registered tremendous growth in post-nationalisation era. The growth of Indian banking since independence can be divided into two distinct phases viz. 1947 to 1969 which witnessed the disjointed efforts made towards the regulation of the banking industry, and the post-1969 (nationalisation) period that marked a complete transformation from 'class banking' to 'mass banking'. It was in July, 1969 that following the recommendaions made by the Rural Credit Survey Committee, forteen major banks with aggreagate deposits of Rs. 50 crore and above were nationalised. Another 6 banks were nationalised in 1980. Thus, there were total 20 nationalized banks. But in the year 1993, the New Bank of India merged with the Punjab National Bank and the total of the public sector banks reduced to 19.Till than there are 19 public sector banks operating in india. At present, public sector banks comprise of the State Bank of India, its seven subsidiaries and the nineteen nationalised banks. These are shown in Table 1 and 2.

Table 1
State Bank Group

Name of the Bank	*Name of the Bank*
• State Bank of India	• State Bank of Travancore
• State Bank of Patiala	• State Bank of Bikaner& Jaipur
• State Bank of Surashtra	• State Bank of indore
• State Bank of Hyderabad	• State Bank of Mysore

All those banks in which the majority of shares are held by the Government of India are covered under the State Bank Group. The State Bank of India was established by statutory amalgamatio of the Imperial Bank of India and some major associated banks viz. the Bank of Surashtra, the Bank of Patiala, the Bank of Bikaner, the Bank of Mysore, the Bank of Rajasthan, the Hyderabad state Bank and the Travancore Bank. At present, there are a total of 8 banks under the SBI group including the State Bank of India and its 7 associates.

Table 2
Nationalized Banks

Name of the Bank	*Name of the Bank*
• Bank of Boroda	• UCO Bank
• Bank of India	• Allahabad Bank
• Punjab National bank	• Oriental Bank of Commerce
• Canara Bank	• Dena Bank
• Central Bank of India	• Vijaya Bank
• Union Bank of India	• Bank of Maharashtra
• Indian Overseas Bank	• Andhra Bank
• Indian Bank	• Punjab & Sind Bank
• Syndicate Bank	• Corporation Bank
• United Bank of India	

Nationalised banks are those banks in which the Government holds major or full stake. Except the Reserve Bank of India, which was nationalised in 1948, there was no other public sector bank till 1969. With the nationalisation of banks in July 1969, 14 banks, each of which had more than Rs. 50 crores in time and demand liabilities came in public sector. This was subsequently followed by the nationalisation of 6 more private sector commercial banks, each of which had crossed the deposit limit of 200 crores in June 1980. Thus, there were total 20 nationalized banks. But in the year 1993, the New Bank of India merged with the Punjab National Bank and the total of the public sector banks reduced to 19. Till than there are 19 public sector banks operating in India.

Since nationalisation, public sector banks have grown enormously, especially in unbanked and underbanked areas, in terms of the number of branches, volume of deposits, credit and priority sector advances etc.

After the introduction of financial sector reforms in 1991, there had been a massive increase in the number of private sector banks in India. Before 1991, therewere 25 private sector banks operating in the country. During the year 1995-1996, 9 private sector banks were issued licence and they commenced their operations. The list of old private sector banks is given in Table 3 & the new private sectoe banks is given in Table 4.

Table 3
Old Private Sector Banks

Name of the Bank	*Name of the Bank*
• The Vysya Bank	• The Dhana Lakshmi Bank
• The Federal Bank Ltd.	• Development Credit Bank Ltd.
• The Jammu & Kashmir Bank	• Bharat Overseas Bank Ltd.
• Bank of Rajasthan Ltd.	• City Union Bank Ltd.
• Karnataka Bank Ltd.	• The Banaras State Bank Ltd.
• The South Indian Bank Ltd.	• The Nadungadi Bank Ltd.
• The United Western Bank Ltd.	• Lord Krishna Bank Ltd.
• Bank of Madura Ltd.	• Bareilly Corporation Bank Ltd.
• The Catholic syrian Bank Ltd.	• Nainital Bank Ltd.
• The Karur Vysya Bank Ltd.	• The Ganesh Bank of Kurundwad Ltd.
• Tamiland Merchantile Bank	• The Ratnakar Bank Ltd.
• The lakshmi Vilas Bank Ltd.	• SBI Comm. & Int. Bank Ltd.
• The Sangli Bank Ltd.	

Table 4
New Private Sector Banks

Name of the Bank	*Name of the Bank*
• UTI Bank Ltd.	• Induslnd Bank Ltd.
• ICICI Bank Ltd.	• Global Trust Bank
• Centurion Bank Ltd.	• HDFC Bank Ltd.
• Times Bank Ltd.	• Bank of Punjab Ltd.
• IDBI Bank Ltd.	

Foreign Banks

Foreign Banks are those banks, which are registered or which have their headquarters in some other countries but they are operating in India. The presence of foreign banks in the country increased rapidly after the financial sector reforms, which were initiated in 1991. Table 5 shows the list of foreign banks in India.

Table 5
Foreign Banks

Name of the Bank	*Name of the Bank*
• ABN-AMRO Bank N V	• National Trust & Savings Association
• Abu Dhabi Commercial Bank Ltd.	• The Sakura Bank Ltd.
• American Express Bank Ltd.	• Banque Nationale De Paris
• Bank Muscat	• Citybank N A
• Bank of Ceylon	• Credit Lyonnais
• Bank of Bahrain & Kuwait	• ING Barings Bank N. V
• Bank International Indonesia	• S.A.O.G
• Barclays Bank Plc	• Standard Chartered Bank
• Credit Agricole Indosuez	• The Development Bank of Singapor Ltd.
• Dresdner Bank	• Hong Kong and Shanghai Banking Corporation Ltd.
• Oman International Bank	• Mashreq Bank P.S.C
• Societe General-The French & International Bank	• Bank of America
• The Sunitomo Bank Ltd.	• The Bank of Tokyo Mitsubishi Ltd.
• The Chase Manhattan Bank	• The Bank of Nova Scotia
• Arab Bangaladesh Bank	• State Bank of Nova Scotia
• International Saog	• Commerz Bank Ag
• National Trust & Savings Association	• Deutsche Bank

The policy of liberalization and globalization increased the competition among the banks in the ecnomy. Thus, the pace of development of the Indian banks lead to the branch opening and transformation of brick banking to electronic banking. Since the begining of 1991, there has been a sea change in the rule, organisation, scope and activity level of the Indian financial sector. The Indian banking industry has withessed a rapid growth after economic reforms from regulated to deregulated market economy and defined a new role for banks.

Structure of Shceduled Commercial Banks

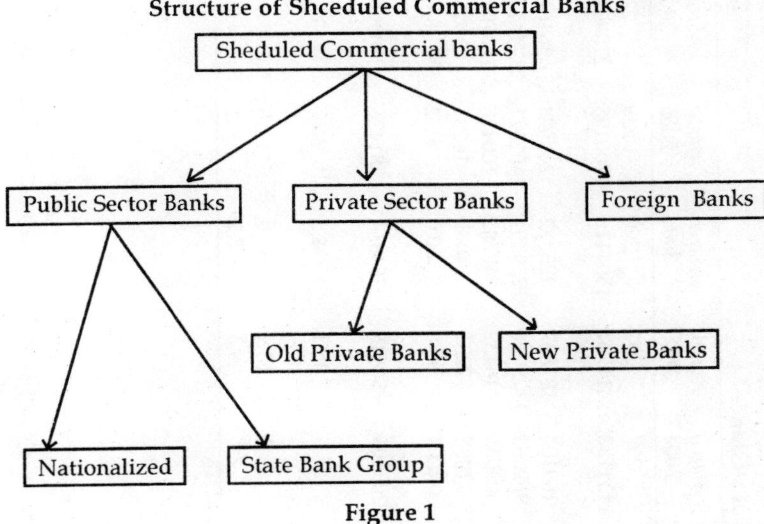

Figure 1

The Narasimham Committee (1991) had recommended several reforms in banking secotor such as reduction of reserve requirement, de-regulation of interest rates, introduction of prudential norms, allowing entry of private sector banks etc. The winds of changes gained momentum in the last few years such as globalisation and opening up of financial services under World Trade Organisation (WTO). It is expected that the banking sector eill undergo mergers and acquisitions, globalisation of operations, development of new technology and unversalization.

A comparative analysis of varous bank groups with respect to different variables has been taken. Important indicators of Scheduled Commercial Banks (SCBs) are analysed from 1969 to 2006. Table-6 shows SCBs at a glance. The number of commercial banks in India increased to 222 in March 2006 as compared to 89 in June 1969. India had just 89 commercial banks, both scheduled and non-scheduled at the time of nationalisation of banks. Over a period of time, it increased to 300 as on March 2001. After that the number gradually came down to 222, as on March 2006. The decline in number of banks is due to the merger and acquisition taking place in the banking industry at present.

Table 6

Scheduled Commercial Banks at a Glance

Indicators	*June 1969*	*March 1999*	*March 2000*	*March 2001*	*March 2002*	*March 2003*	*March 2004*	*March 2005*	*March 2006*
No. of commercial banks	89	301	298	300	297	292	290	289	222
Aggregate deposits of schedule commercialbanks	4646	722203	851593	989141	1131188	311761	1504416	1700198	2109049
(a) Demand deposits	2104	117423	145283	1594076	169103	187837	225022	248028	364640
(b) Time deposits	2542	604780	706310	829734	962065	1123924	1279394	1452171	1744409
Credit of SCB	3599	368837	454069	529271	609053	746432	840785	1100428	1507077
Dep.per Capita Dep. of SCBs	88	7359	8542	9770	11008	12253	14089	16281	19130
Dep. of SCBs as % of GNP at FC (constant parices)	15.5	50.3	53.5	56.0	54.4	58.8	60.0	60.2	66.3
SCBs Advs. to Priority Sector (INR in crore)	504	126309	155779	182255	205606	254648	263834	381476	509910
Share of Priority Advs. in total Credit of SCBs (in %)	14.0	35.3	35.4	31.0	34.8	35.1	34.5	36.7	35.3
Credit Deposit Ratio	77.5	51.1	53.3	53.5	53.8	56.9	55.9	62.6	70.1
Cash Deposit Ratio	8.2	9.4	9.8	8.4	7.1	6.3	7.2	6.4	6.7

Source: Statistical Tables relating to Banks in India, 2005-06, RBI.

Aggregate Deposits and Credit of Scheduled Commerical Banks

Moblization of deposits from the hitherto untapped source, particularly from the underbanked and unbanked areas, has been one of the prime objectives of the nationalisation of banks. The deposits of commercial banks have grown very fast in the post-nationalisation period. Sustained efforts were made by banks to induce people to keep a part of their savings as bank deposits.The average annual growth rate of bank deposits during the period 1971-80 has been to the order of about 50 per cent as against les than 20 per cent during the pervious decade, i.e. 1961-70 (Dutt and Sundram, 1991, p. 745). This tremendous rate of growth of bank deposits can be attributed to many factors. First, the rapid branch expanison by commercial banks during post-nationalisation period has been helpful in bringing banking services to the door steps of the people, thus motivating them to keep their savings in the form of bank deposits. Secondly, the government's plicy of deficit financing and creation of new money has had the effect of increasing the reserve base of the commercial banks. As a result, they indulged into multiple credit expansion which also led to a multiplication of their deposits.

Demand deposits of SCBs has increased from INR 2,104 crore in 1969 to INR 3,64,640 crore as on March 2006. However, time deposits of banks increased to INR 17,44,409 crore from INR 2,542 crore during the period concerned. The growth of time deposits in absolute term has been more than demand deposits. The high growth of time deposits over demand deposits is mainly due to higher interest rates being offered by the banks on such deposits as well as availability of tax benefits to certain deposits scheme. According to a study of CRISIL, growth of term deposits is due to the sensitivities of interest rate, while other deposits such as demand and saving deposits shows no sensitivities to interst rate movements.

The revised interest rate on *Domestic Term Deposits effective from the 16th August 2008* would be as under:

Table 7

Existing Interest Rates Duration	*Interest Rate (% p.a)*	*Revised Interest Rates w.e.f. 16th Aug 08 Duration*	*Interest Rate (%p.a)*
15 days to 45 days	4.75	15 days to 45 days	4.75
46 days to 90 days	5.25	46 days to 90 days	5.25
91 days to 180 days	7.00	91 days to 180 days	7.50
181 days to less than 1 year	8.00	181 days to less than 1 year	8.50
1 year to less than 2 years		1 year to less than 2 year	10.00
2 year to less than 3 years	9.50	2 years to less than 3 years	9.50
3 year to less than 5 years	9.00	3 year to less than 5 years	9.75
5 years and up to 10 years	9.00	5 years and up to 10 years	9.25

Note: Term deposits for maturity peirod of "7days to 14 days"will continue to be accepted for amounts of Rs. 1 crore and above and rates for the same will be advised by SME Department at corprate Centre. For a single term deposit of Rs. 15 lacs and above but less than Rupees One Crore,an additional 10 basis point over thecard rate will be paid as hitherto irrespective of the tenor of the deposit.

The private banks are also offering more or less the same rate of interest as offered by Public Sector banks (PSB). As a result of this, there is a growth in aggregate deposits of SCBs from INR 4,646 crore to INR 21,09,049 crore from June 1969 to March 2006.

Since nationalisation, there has been tremendous growth in the credit expansion of commercial banks. The banks are meeting the credit requirements of industry, trade and agriculture on a much larger scale than before just as bank deposits have expanded, bank credit too has expanded tremendously particularly since 1969. Along with the increase in aggregate deposits of SCBs, the credit of the banks has also increased from INR 3,599 crore in 1969 to INR 15,07,077 crore in the post-nationalisation period. Sustained efforts were made by banks to induce people to keep a part of their savings as bank deposits.The average annual growth rate of bank deposits during the period 1971-80 has been to the order of about 50 per cent as against les than 20 per cent during the pervious decade, i.e. 1961-70 (Dutt and Sundram, 1991, p. 745). This tremendous rate of growth of bank deposits can be attributed to many factors. First, the rapid branch expanison by commercial banks during post-nationalisation period has been helpful in bringing banking services to the door steps of the people, thus motivating them to keep their savings in the form of bank deposits. Secondly, the government's plicy of deficit financing and creation of new money has had the effect of increasing the reserve base of the commercial banks. As a result, they indulged into multiple credit expansion which also led to a multiplication of their deposits March 2006. The growth of credit has been largely due to the robust growth of the industrial sectors and the government decision to increase credit to the agriculture sector which led to rapid increase in bank credit.

In recent years bank credit has picked up smartly by around 20 to 21 per cent per annum. Some of the factors that have been responsible for the recent high rate of growth of bank credit are:

(i) rise in lendable resources of commercial banks as a result of large reduction in reserve requirements (i.e. CRR and SLR);

(ii) release of impounded cash balances under incremental cash reserce ratio (ICRR);

(iii) sharp increase in food credit mainly due to increased food procurement opeations and

(iv) increased demand for credit from public sector undertakings and the large increase in export credit. (Dutt and Sundaram, 1998, p. 746).

Priority Sector Advances

Extension of credit to hitherto neglected sectors (later termed as priority sectors) was one of the prime objectives of nationalisation of the top 14 banks in 1969, Soon after nationalisation the commerical banks were asked to accord priority to the financing of priority sectors which included agriculture, small industry and business and small transport operators, In couse of time, other priority sectors such as retail trade professional and self-employed persons, education, housing loans and consumption loans were also added to the earlier definition of priority sectors.The flow of credit to priority sectors increased to INR 50,991 crore in March 2006 as compared to INR 504 crore in June 1969. Credit flow to the priority sector is mainly to agriculture, small-scale industries and service sector. The share of priority sector advances to the total credit has increased to 35.3 per cent as on March 2006 compared to 14.0 per cent in June 1969. This increaseshows more than double the increase in the priority secotor advances to total advances over 35 years.

Credit-deposit Ratio

The credit-deposit (CD) ratio over a period of time has increased from 51.1per cent in March 1999 to 70.1 per cent in March 2006. The increase in demand for commercial credit and also food and non-food credit has led to an increase in total credit of SCBs over the last few decades and as a result of this, the CD ratio continued to increase.

Cash-deposit Ratio

The cash-deposit ratio during the period of nationalisation of bank in 1969 was 8.2 per cent and the same has declined to 6.7 per cent as on March 2006. The declining trend of cash-deposit ratio reveals efficient management of cash flow of SCBs during the period concerned.

A comparative analysis of some important indicators of five groups of banks from 1999-2000 to 2005-06. Interest income and interest expended as percentage of total assets from period 1999-2000 to 2005-06 of five groups of banks has been shown in Table 8.

It is observed from the table that, the interest income as percentage of total assetd goes on declining from 1999-2000 to 2005-06 across all the groups of banks. The interest expended as percentage of total assets has also declined during the period concerned, of the four groups of banks. The decline in interst income as percentage of total assets during 2005-06 was around 6-6.5 per cent as compared to 8-10 per cent during the year 1999-2000 for all groups of banks. Interest expended as percentage of total assets has also declined from 6-6.5 percnet

Table 8
Interest Income as Percentage of Total Assets

Name of the banks	1999-2000	2000-2001	2001-2002	2002 2003	2003-2004	2004-2005	2005-2006
Scheduled commercial banks	8.97	8.88	8.26	8.2	7.31	6.61	6.62
Public sector banks	8.92	8.85	8.72	8.34	7.45	6.79	6.63
Nationalised banks	9.06	9.09	8.78	83.9	7.44	6.91	6.73
Private sector banks	8.74	8.87	6.18	8.26	6.99	6.14	6.07
Foreign banks in India	9.93	9.27	8.56	7.68	6.74	5.94	6.07

Interest expended as percentage of total assets

Name of the banks	1999-2000	2000-2001	2001-2002	2002 2003	2003-2004	2004-2005	2005-2006
Scheduled commercial banks	6.25	6.03	5.70	5.51	4.44	3.78	3.84
Public sector banks	6.22	5.29	5.99	5.43	4.47	3.88	3.98
Nationalised banks	6.40	6.19	6.03	5.39	4.38	4.03	3.84
Private sector banks	6.58	6.54	4.60	6.29	4.78	3.80	3.76

Source: Hand Book of Sgtatistics of Indian Economy-2006, RBI.

in 1999-2000 to around four per cent in 2005-06 across the groups of banks. The decline in interest income and interest expended as percentage of total assets is due to decrease in the prime lending rate (PLR) of banks during the period concerned. As a result of this, interest income and interest expended has gone on declining.

Operating expenses include payment and provision for employees, rent, taxes and lighting, printing and stationery, insurance and others. Operating expenses as percentage of total assets of five groups of banks have been shown in Table-9 for the period 1999-2000 to 2005-06. The three groups of banks namely as SCBs, PSBs and nationalised banks have shown a decline in operating expenses as percentage of total assets from 1999-2000 to 2005-06. Private sector banks recorded their operating expenses as percentage of total assets less than SCBs, PSB and nationalised banks whereas foreign banks have shown more than the above four groups of banks during the period concerned.

Table 9
Operating Expenses as a Percentage of Total Assets

Name of the banks	*1999-2000*	*2000-2001*	*2001-2002*	*2002 2003*	*2003-2004*	*2004-2005*	*2005-2006*
Scheduled commercial banks	2.50	2.64	219	2.24	2.21	2.13	2.11
Public sector banks	2.53	2.72	2.29	2.25	2.21	2.09	2.06
Nationalised banks	2.57	2.76	2.40	2.33	2.21	2.18	2.02
Private sector banks	1.83	1.87	1.44	1.99	2.02	2.03	2.03
Foreign banks in India	3.22	3.05	3.00	2.79	2.77	2.88	2.79

Capital Adequacy Ratio

Commercial banks in India are expected to start implementing Basel-II norms with effect from March 2008. Implementation of BASEL-II will require more capital for banks in India to account for operational risk and accordingly, banks have to explore new ways of raising additional capital to meet BASEL-II norms. Capital adequacy ratio of all five groups of banks taken for analysis has increased from about 11.50 per cent in 2001 to 12.50 per cent in 2006. Foreign banks in India have had higher capital adequacy ratio during the period of 2001-2006 than other 4 groups of banks. This has been shown in Table 10.

Table 10
Capital Adequacy Ratio in Percentage

Name of the Banks	*2001*	*2002*	*2003*	*2004*	*2005*	*2006*
Scheduled commercial banks	11.40	12.00	12.70	12.90	12.80	12.40
Public sector banks	11.20	11.80	12.60	13.20	12.90	12.20
Nationalised banks	10.20	10.90	12.20	13.10	13.20	12.40
Private sector banks	11.90	12.50	12.80	13.70	12.50	11.70
Foreign banks in India	12.60	12.90	15.20	15.00	14.00	13.00

Source: Hand Book of Statistics of Indian Economy-2006, RBI.

The measure of non-performing assets (NPAs) explains the efficiency in allocation of resources made by banks to productive sectors. The problem of NPAs arises either due to bad management by banks or due to change in business cycle. The NPA as percentage of total assets has significantly reduced across all groups of banks from 1996-1997 to 2004-05 which is shown in the Table 11.

Table 11
Gross and Net NPAs of Scheduled Commercial Banks: Bank Groupwise

Year	*Scheduled Commercial Banks*	*Public Sector Banks*	*New Private Sector Banks*	*Foreign Banks in India*
1996-97	7.0	7.8	1.3	2.1
1997-98	6.5	7.0	1.5	3.0
1998-99	6.2	6.7	2.3	3.1
1999-00	5.5	6.0	1.6	3.2
2000-01	4.9	5.3	2.1	3.0
2001-02	4.6	4.9	3.9	2.4
2002-03	4.0	4.2	2.8	2.4
2003-04	3.3	3.5	2.4	2.1
2004-05	2.6	2.8	1.6	1.4

Source: Handbook of Statistics of Indian Economy-2006, RBI.

Non-performing Assets: As Percentage of Total Assets

With respect to the new private sector banks, the NPA as a percentage of total assets comparatively is lower than other three groups of banks. The SCBs and PSBs had around 7-8 per cent of NPAs during 1996-9 and it declined to around three per cent in the year 2004-05. In case of new private sector and foreign banks the percentage declined to 1.6 and 1.4 per cent respectively, during the year 20405.

The decline of NPAs implies that asset quality of banks registered significant improvements with rapid increase in the quantum of credit to the commercial sector. The robust industrial performance along with recovery shows a significant reduction on the levels of NPAs. A significant improvement in recovery of NPAs along with sharp increase in gross loans and advances led to a sharp decline in gross NPAs to gross advances ratio also. The setting up of the Asset Reconstruction Company Limited (ARCIL) also helped to a great extent in recovery of dues.

Other important indicators such as taking credit, aggregate deposits, total invstment and investment in Government Securities as percntage to GDP for the period from 1950-51 to 2005-06 for SCBs have been analysed and it has been shown in Table 12.

Table 12
Scheduled Commercial Banks-Ratio As Percentage to GDP

Year	Credit	Total Investment	Investment in Government Securities	Aggregate Deposits
1950-51	5.5	-	-	8.9
1960-61	7.8	-	3.3	10.1
1970-71	10.3	3.1	3.0	12.9
1980-81	17.6	9.2	6.4	26.4
1990-91	20.5	13.2	8.8	33.9
2000-01	24.2	17.6	15.1	45.7
2004-05	35.3	23.7	23.0	54.5
2005-06	42.7	20.3	19.8	59.7

Source: Handbook of Statistics of Indian Economy-2006, RBI.

The table reveals that the increase in percentage share of aggregate deposit to GDP has been more than credit percentage of SCBs. Thus, credit as well as aggregate deposits as percentage of GDP over a period of 50 years has gone on increasing.The credit as percentage of GDP increased to 42.7 per cent in 2005-06 over 5.5 per cent in 1950-51 and aggregate deposits increased to 59.7 per cent in 2005-06 over 8.9 per cent in 1950-51.

Table 13
Scheduled Commercial Banks Income

Year	*2000-01*	*2001-02*	*2005*	*2006*
Total Income	1,32,075	1,51,026	1,90,223	2,22,208
Interest Income	1,15,091	1,26,969	1,55,799	1,84,509
Other Income	16,984	24,056.16	3,44,24	3,76,99
Nationalised Banks (INR crore)				
Total Income	64,125.62	72,485.95	91,028	102,037
Interest Income	56,977	61,975.51	76,312	88499
Other Income	7,149.16	10,510.44	14,716	13538
SBI & Associate Banks (INR crore)				
Total Income	39,372	44,762	5,3532	58910
Interest Income	34,152	38,746.03	44052	49166
Other Income	5220.76	6,016	9480	9794
Foreign Banks in India (INR crore)				
Total Income	11,986.88	12,989.89	13.35	17435
Interest Income	9,469.51	9,699.64	9170	12235
Other Income	2,517.37	3,260.25	3865	5200

Income

Total income of a bank consists of interest income and non-interest income. Interest income is income from advances and investments and other income includes income earned in the form of commission, exchange and brokerage and income from profit on sale of investment etc. The interest income across the groups of banks has increased from 2001-02 to 2005-06 which is more than other income received by banks.SCBs had received comparatively higher total income than other nationalised banks, SBI & associate and foreign banks in India. The total income received by foreign banks in India is the lowest as compared to other banks as analysed during the period 200-01 to 2006. The income composition of banks has been shown in the Table 13.

Conclusion

There has been an increase in the number of SCBs in Post-nationalisation period but gradually the number has gone on declining and this has been due to the merger and acquisition taking place in the banking system. It is expected that in future a few mega banks will emerge and segment-wise banking function will take Place. It is also expected that with the consolidation of Regional Rural Banks (RRB), there would be only one RRB in each state to cater to the needs of rural masses.

The mega banks will have a national character and will make plethora of financial services available to their customers. There has been a significant change in the compostion of deposits, and term deposits have been on the higher side than demand deposits. Credit of banks in post-nationalised period has been showing an increasing trend. NPAs across the bank groups have been significantly declining. The decline in NPAs of new private sector banks and foreign banks in India is more than other groups of banks.

The share of interest income has been more than other income and total income across the different bank groups has also increased. The other important indicators which have been taken in the analysisamong the different groups of banks have also gone on declining. The share of deposits and credit in GDP over a period of time has witnessed a significant increase for SCBs. The Indian banking in future will become technology based banking.

References

Anand, A. (2007), 'Indian Banking Prospective', Bank of Baroda *Quarterly Economic Review*, January-March, p. 12-20.

Badade, K. & M. Katkar (2007), ' Beyond the Boundary', *Yojana*, July, p. 53-55.

Chaudhuri, S. (2002), 'Some Issues of Growth and Profitability in Indian Public Sector Bank', *Economic & Political Weekly*, June, p. 2155-2162.

FICCI (2006), Banking Conclave 2006.

Gupta, S. C. (2003), Banking Industry Vision 2010, IBA Commities.

Indian Banker (2006-07), Monthly Various Issues.

Ministry of Finance (2005-06), Economic Survey.

Ramasastri, A. S. & A. Samuel (2006), Banking Sector Development in India, 1980-2005: RBI, Occasional Paper, Vol. 27, No. 1 and 2.

Reserve Bank of India (2001-02), Report on Trend and Progress of Banking in India.

———(2005-06), Statistical Tables relating to Banks in India.

———(2006), Handbook of Statistics of Indian Economy.

Srivatava, R. M. & Divya Nigam (2007), 'Retail Banking in India', *Yojana*, July, p. 57-59.

Ahuja, Kanta (1977), "The Banking Sector After Reforms", *The Indian Economic Journal*, Vol. 44, No. 4, April-June, pp. 150-154.

Ambumani, V. and Niranjana S. (1999), "Social Objectives and Priority Sector Lendings," Conference Volume, *The Indian Economic Association*, IEA 82nd Conference, pp. 180-188.

Dharmambal, B. and Subramanjan, Chellam (1999), " An Analysis of Narasimham Committee Reports I and II in the Context of Banking and Financial Sector Reforms in India", Conference Volume, *The Indian Economic Association*, IEA 82nd Conference, pp. 164-171.

———(1993), "Narasimham Committee-Two Years After", *IBA Bulletin*, Vol. XV, No. 12, December, p. 8.

———(1995), "Restructuring Banks' Capital-Need for an Integrated Approach", *Economic and Political Weekly*, Vol. XXX, No. 9, March 4.

———(1996), "Banking Sector Reforms and Transparency", *Economic and Political Weekly*, Vol. XXXI, No. 12, March 23, pp. 745-751.

Majumdar, N. A. (1996), "Financial Sector Reforms: An Exercise in Introspection", *Economic and Political Weekly*, Vol. XXI, No. 12, March 23, pp. 727-731.

2

Indian Banking: Past, Present and Future

Rajeshwari Kumari

The world over, Banking system is the focal point in the financial set-up of any developing country. Banks are regarded as special in view of their specialized functions in the financial intermediation and payment system. In India too economic development has evolved around the banking system. With the advent of economic liberalisation since the mid-1991, the financial sector in general and the banking sector in particular has undergone phenomenal changes. New private sector banks with greater technology orientation have emerged. Automation of banking operations gained in importance. Competition in the market has increased. The public sector banks also embarked on computerisation of branches, networking of branch operations, introductions of new services such as Automated Teller Machines (ATMs), Telebanking Services, customer terminals and so on. Customer retention and more so, attracting and retaining high networth customer has come to occupy the center stage of banking environment.

During the same period, the software industry in India also began to grow culminating in the increase in purchasing power of the bourgeoisie class. The banks which were, more of less, averse to retail lending started seeing the enormous potential in earning from retail lending. This prompted banks to veer to segmentation banking from mass banking and further to customer specific business.

Banking in Retrospect

The banking sector, which plays a crucial role in the economic development of country, has undergone four phases during the past six decades since independence.

The period of six decades witnessed many macro-economic developments, monetary and banking policies and the external situation which influenced the evelution of Indian banking in different ways and in different periods. For this reason, it would be useful to analyse in some detail the evolution of Indian banking with reference to some distinct phases. The first phase covers the period from 1948 to 1968 and the second phasefrom 1969 to 1991. These two periods constitue the past. The perod of banking reforms beginning with 1992 and till the year 2002 may be regarded as the present or the current phase for the purpose of this analysis. It is the current phase which provides the basis for looking into the future of Indian banking system.

For the sake convenience, banking development in India can be classified into four phases:

First Phase: 1948-1968 Banking before Ntionalisation

It is useful to trace briefly the banking situation in India at the time of independence of the country in 1947. The country inherited a banking system that was patterned on the British banking system. There were many joint stock companies doing banking business, and they were concentrating mostly in major cities. Even the financing activity of these banks was confined to exports of jute, tea, etc.; and to traditional industries like textiles (jute, cotton) sugar. There was no uniform law governing banking activity. An immediate concern after the partition of the country was about bank brances located in Pakistan and steps were taken to close some of them as desired by that country. As a result of mushroom-like growth of banking companies, bank failures were very common in those days. In 1949 as many as 55 banks either went into liquidation or went out of banking business. Banking did not receive much attention of the policy makers and disjointed efforts were made towards the regulation of the banking industry.

After Independence

The first step was to create the legslative framwork appropriate for banking in a newly independent nation. The Banking Regulation Act passed in 1948 provided the legal framwork for the regulation of the banking system by the Reserve Bank of India (RBI). The Act, which came into force in March 1949 imposed certain discipline on the joint stock companies doing banking business in India. As a result, the banking industry came to be organised for the first time on certain uniform parameters. The Act prohibited the use of the word 'Bank' by financial companies which were not complying with certain minimum requirements i.e. a minimum paid-up capital and reserves. This stipulation, which came into force from March 1952, led to a process of weeding out financially weak banks.A number of banks went into liquidation.

The RBI, which was vested with greater powers of control over the banks, started collecting data from 1949 on various aspects of banking. There were 620 banking companies, big and small, scheduled and non-scheduled, operating mostly in state capitals and in urban centres. The total number of branches was 4,263. Total deposits and advances were Rs. 997 crore and Rs. 518 crore respectively. Investments were Rs. 376 crore. Imperial Bank of India was the biggest bank in those days with 433 branches. The present day subsidiaries of the State Bank of India were independent banking companies mostly in the former princely states. Besides the Indian banks, there were 15 Exchange Banks (foreign banks) with branches in big cities only; and they were dealing mostly with international banking i.e. financing the export and import of commodities

The banking system at the time of independence was deficent in many respects. The banks were largely urban-oriented and remained beyond the reach of the rural population. A large percentage of the rural population had to depend on the money lender as their main source of credit. Bank's rural penetration was grossly inadequate, as agriculture was not considered an economic proposition by banks in those days. Thus, the agricultural sector, the crucial segment of the Indian economy was not supported by the banking system in any form. Moreover, security oriented lending was the order of the day. Only 4 per cent of the total advances was made without any securiy. Another serious deficiency was that the focus of banks was entirely on short-term credit. There were no sources of long-term finance worth the name. There was no well developed capital market; nor was there any term-lending institution except for the Industrial Finance. Corporation of India set up in 1948.

Plan Era

With the introduction of economic planning in 1951, the need was felt for aligning monetary and banking activity with the requirements of planning. The first five-year plan observed that RBI as the Central Bank should create the machinery needed for financing development and ensure that the finance available flows in the directions intended. The objective was to widen and deepen the flow of agricultural and industrial credit.The thrust was on the rejuvenation of the rural economy and the banking system had to be geared to this. The branch expansion by banks and increase in rural credit including credit to the small-scale sector became imperative. The All-India Rural Credit Survey Committee appointed by the RBI reviewed the rural credit scheme in 1954 and brought out the maladies of the rural economy arising out of capital starvation. The Committee made a few major recommendations for improving the flow of rural credit. On the basis of its recommendations, the Imperial Bank of India was nationalised and renamed as State Bank of India (SBI) from July 1955. The new bank was charged with the responsibility of expanding its rural branch network within a time frame. Thus the first step was taken to induct the commercial banks into rural credit, which was till then reserved for co-operative credit agencies who were waging a battle against money lenders. As part of the process of geographical expansion of banking facilities to meet the credit needs of co-operatives, certain banking companies functioning in former princely states were converted in 1959 into subsidiaries of SBI, later came to be known as associate banks of SBI.

In 1960, the crash of Palai Central Bank in Kerala, shook the confidence of the public in the banking system; and the RBI came out with two schemes to stabilise the banking system. One was the establishment of the Deposit Insurance Corporation, to insure the deposits of small depositors. The second scheme was the compulsory mergers and amalgamations of banks of weak financial structure, with bigger and viable banks. Simultaneously, in terms of the Banking Companies (Amendment) Act, 1963, RBI acquired powers to: restrain control over the affairs of banks of particular groups of persons; regulate loans, advances and guarantees given by banks and to appoint/remove banks, executive personnel. In 1966, the co-operative banking system was brought within the statutory supervision and control of RBI. During these years Indian banks established overseas branches to increase their participation in external trade i.e. foreign exchange transactions.

There were some qualitative changes in the banking activity during these years . There was a shift in the financing of industries; there was a decline in the financing of textiles and sugar industries and with the emphasis of the Second Five Year Plan on heavy industry development, the financing of cement, chemicals, iron and steel and enginnering industries became prominent. Export financing also attracted attention, leading to the setting up of Export Credit Guarantee Corporation in 1964 to compensate exporters for the losses they might sustain. There was also some shift in the method of lending from security based to capacity-to-produce-and-sell criteria. A review of the ownership of bank deposits during this period revealed the nexus between business houses and banking companies, indicating the nature of control of banks by business houses.

On the Eve of Nationalisation

Even though Indian banking made considerable peogress both functionally and in terms of geographical coverage during this peirod, there were still many rural and semi-urban areas which were not served by banks. Moreover, large industries and big and established business houses tended to enjoy a major portion of the credit facilities, Vital sector like agriculture, small-scale industries and exports did not receive the attention they deserved. Therefore, the Government imposed in 1968 social control over banks by amending banking laws. The objectives was to achieve efficient distribution of banking resources in conformity with the requirements of the economy and to meet the needs of the priority sectors. In this process RBI acquired wider powers in matters of appointment of heads of banks, directors on the Boards of Banksand auditors.

The outcome of implementation of social control over banks is of interest. One is that the system of credit planning became an integral part of formulation of credit policy. Second, the introduction of the Lead Bank scheme was to make the banking system function as an instrument of development. Under social control the banking system including smaller banks started gaining strength as evidenced by the absence of voluntary or compulsory mergers of banks. Thus, social control was a milestone in the evolution of banking policy.

Second Phase: 1969-1991 Nationalisaton and After

This phase began in a sedate manner with the appointment in 1969 of the Banking Commission which was to recommend changes in structure procedures and policy for the Indian banking system. However, the Commission did not have much time to complete its task as it was overtaken by swift politico-economic developments, which culminated in the nationalisation, on July 19, 1969, of the 14 major indian scheduled commercial banks in the private sector. On April 15, 1980, six more private sector banks were nationalised, thus extending further the area of public contro over the Indian banking system. Nationalisation was seen as a major step to ensure adequate credit flow into genuine productive areas in conformity with plan priorities.

The objectives of nationalization of Banks were (i) lending to priority sector, (ii) helping weaker sections of society by granting ned based credit for asset generation at cheaper rates (purpose-oriented with consumption component for specified contingencies), (iii) extension of banking facilities to un-banked/under-banked areas, (iv) removal of control over banks by a few, (v) encouragement to new class of entrepreneurs and (vi) provision of adequate training to bank staff.

Nationalisation and After

The two significant aspects of nationalisation were therefore: rapid branch expansion and channelling credit according to priorities. In the wake of nationalisation the growth and development of the Indian banking system was phenomenal. By the end of the second decade of nationalisation, Indian banking was relatively sophisticated, with a wide network of branches, huge deposit resources and extensive credit operations. The outburst of banking activity during this period was such that it may be described as banking explossion.

Branch Expansion

In terms of the branch licensing policy laid down by the RBI the accent was on the opening of branches in rural and semi-urban areas, backward regions and under-banked states so that inter-regional disparities could be reduced. The details of the progress of branch network during the period is summarised in the table below:

Year	*Total No. of Branches*	*Rural Branches*	*Semi-urban Branches*
1969	8262	1833	3342
1980	32419	15105	8122
1991	60220	35206	11344

The total number of bank branches increased eight-fold between 1969 and 1991 and the bulk of the increase was on account of rural branches, which increased from less than two thousand in 1969 to over 35 thousand in 1991. The percentage share in the total number of branches of rural and semi-urban offices rose from 22 per cent and 4 per cent respectively in 1969 to 45 per cent and 25 per cent in 1980 and to 58 per cent and 18 per cent in 1991. A substantial part of the increase in branch expansion took place in the first decade after nationalisation. The share of rural and semi-urban branches together, in the total number of branches rose from 26 per cent in 1969 to 76 per cent in 1991. The impact of this phenomenal growth was to bring down the population per branch from 60,000 in 1969 to about 14,000. Thus, one of the objectives of nationalisation i.e. to make banking reach out to the small man in rual and semi-urban areas, may be said to have been served to a great extent. Even on the eve of banking reforms, the bank branch network was widespread. The total number of branches has gone up from a little over 8262 in the year 1969 to approximately 71,000 as at the end of March 2007. During the same period average population per branches has declined from 64,000 to around 15,000

Resource Mobilisation

One of the objectives of branch expansion was to mop up national savings both actual and potential and to channel them into investments according to plan priorities. The magnitude of resources mobilised by the banks during 1969 to 1991 is indicated below:

Rs. Crore

Year	*Total Deposits*	*Term Deposits*	*Saving Deposits*
1969	5173	3280	1524
1980	37988	19253	10937
1991	230758	128768	56902

Between 1969 and 1980, total deposits increased six-fold and between 1980 and 1991 the increase was five-fold. The substantial increase in total deposits was because of the rise in the term deposits and savings deposits, which represent the savings of the community. These two categtories of deposits recorded a six-fold increase in each of the periods 1969-1980 and 1981-1999. The share of time deposits was on an average 56 per cent of total deposits for the period 1969-1991 while the averge share of savings deposits was 27 per cent. It is noteworthy that deposits per bank office which was Rs. 0.6 crore in 1969 rose to Rs. 1.2 crore in 1980 and to Rs. 3.8 crore in 1991. This is the result of both widening and deepening of the branch network by banks.

Credit Operations

Given the objectives of ensuring adequate credit flow to genuine productive sectors and in accordance with plan priorities, banks resorted to extensive credit operations after nationalisaton.

This was made possible by the enlarged resource base of banks during the period. The RBI's credit policy over the years laid increasing emphasis on channelling of bank credit to preferred sector and borrowers of small means. Annual targets were laid down for lending to priority sectors of the society. It was also stipulated that a major portion of the deposits mobilised in rural and semi-urban areas should be deployed in respective areas i.e. credit deposit ratio.

The credit operaitons of banks during the period are summarised below:

(Rs. in crore)

	1969	*1980*	*1991*
Bank Credit	3729	25371	125592
Priority Sector	659	8501	45425
	(18)	(33)	(36)
Of which			
Agriculture	258	3584	18157
	(39)	(42)	(42)
SSI Sector	347	3229	18150
	(52)	(37)	(42)

Note: Figures in brackets are percentages to vertical totals.

Bank credit increased seven-fold between 1969 and 1980 and by five times between 1980 and 1991. The share of priority sector in total bank credit increased from 18 per cent in 1969 to 33 per cent in 1991. Within the priority group, the share of agriculture was 39 per cent in 1969, 42 per cent in 1980 and it remained at that in 1991. The share of SSi sector which was 52 per cent in 1969 showed a relative decline to 37 per cent in 1980 and was at 42 per cent in 1991. Bank advances per bank office was Rs. 0.4 crore in 1969 and it rose to Rs. 0.8 crore in 1980 and further to Rs. 2.1 crore in 1991. The 'total business' (deposits plus credit) of the Indian banking industry has gone up by more than seven times from INR 5984 billion in 1994-95 to INR 45372 billion in 2006-07. Fifteen years of financial sector reforms have strengthened the banks' balance sheet considerably.

Going by the rural spread of bank branches, deposits mobilised and credit extended, one could justifiably conclude that there was complete transformation from class banking to mass banking during the period.

Social Banking

An important banking development after nationalisation was the emergence of social banking i.e. the use of banking as an instrument for promoting socio-economic objectives. In the seventies, banking policy was reoriented for securing a progressive reduction in income inequalities, concentration of economic power and class disparities. For attaining the objectives of social banking, special institutions and schemes were sponsored by the Government of India and the RBI.

The introduction of the scheme for priority sector lending was followed by the establishment in 1971 of Credit Guarantee Corporation to provide guarantees against the risk of default in payment in respect of loans to various categories of small borrowers. This was intended to encourage banks to lend to these categories without hesitation. A number of innovations were made in the field of social banking and large volumes of credit were lent under programmes like 20-Point Economic Programmek, Integrated Rural Development Programme (IRDP), and programmes for self-employment of educated unemployed youth. Many of the poverty alleviation programmes in the nature of mass-lending shemes were adopted by the banking systems for financing.

Though banks penetrated into rural areas, planners were not satisfied with the amount of credit extended to weaker sections of the rural society. To ensure that the benefits of development percolated sufficiently to the needy, the Government of India came out with special programmes like Small Farmers Development Agency, the Marginal Farmers Development Agency and Agricultural Labourers Development Agency. It was felt that to cater to the needs of these target groups, a separate credit agency was necessary. The Narasimham Commttee which went into these problems in 1974, recommended the establishment of Regional Rural Banks (RRBs). Under the RRBs Act, 1975, banks in collaboration with central and state government set up RRBs in selected regions where the co-operative system was wea and where commercial banks were not very active.

An important aspect of credit policy during the period was the use of administered interest rates to direct the flow of funds to preferred sectors, small borrowers and weaker sections of the society. The aim was to make credit available at low cost to the identfied target groups.

Problems and Consolidation

The penomenal growth of the Indian banking system over the two decades prior to the reforms, gave rise to serveral problems which became more visible from the mid-eighties. The rapid and substantial growt rendered the banking system unwieldy. Besides, the constraints, both internal and external (to the banking system) under whic banks were functioning, exposed their several weakness. These were: low operational efficiency, inadequate capital base, high level of non-performing assets, low profitability, unhealthy balance sheets and unsatisfactory customer service. In short, the very viability of the banking system came in for scrutiny.

The period 1985-1991 may be regarded as a period of consolidation for the banking system. The process of consolidation called for action on several fronts. Individual banks were asked to prepare action plans covering organisation and structure, house-keeping, training, customer service, credit management, recovery of loans, productivity and profitability. The banks were asked to introduce, in a phased manner, modern technology in banking operations, following the recommendations of the Rangarajan Committee on computerisation in banks. Emphasis was laid on the financial viability of baks through improvement in profitability, strengthening the capital base of banks and allowing them flexibility in several areas of their operations.

Althoug the progress made by the banking system in terms of geographical and functional coverage, resources mobilised and credit deployed was laudable, it displayed all the characteristics of a repressed financial system.

Third Phase: 1992-2002 Regime of Reforms

The period 1992-2002 may be regarded as the present of the current phase in the evolution of Indian banking. Like the second phase (1969-1991) which began with a bang i.e. nationalisation of banks, the current phase also began with a radical departure from regulated banking towards market-oriented banking as result of the introduction of financial reforms especially banking reforms. India's economic reforms programme began as a response to the macroeconomic crisis that developed in early 1991. The crisis manifested itsef in rising inflations, high level fiscal deficit, low growth and unsustainable current account deficit, and the Gulfwar of 1990 precipitated the balance of payments crisis. Faced with the most serious balance of payments problems, Government of India initiated measures for stabilisation and structural adjustment, with far-reaching consequences.

The Reform Process

The main plank of economic reforms comprised (a) stabilisation of the economy so as to keep under control inflationary and balance of payments presures, (b) deregulation of the real and financial sectors and removal of the licence and permits system from all spheres of production and domestic trade, to promote competition, (c) liberalisation of international trade in various sectors to promote competition and efficiency by removing the high degree of protection enjoyed by the domestic industry and (d) integration with the world economy to attract capital and modern technology.

However economic reforms in the real sector of the economy would not succeed without parallel reforms in the financial sector. It hardly needs emphasis that a leberalised economy would be ill-served if the banking system remains highly sheltered or regulated, just as the banking system cannot become viable or sustainable in the longrun unless it adequately responds to the needs of the market-oriented economy.Thus, financial sector reforms were a necessary concomitant of liberalisation of industrial and trade policies.

Banking Reforms

The broad directions of the financial reforms were improvement in the overall monetary policy framework, strengthening financial institutions and gradual integration of the domestic financial system into the global economy. Within these broad goals of policy, banking reforms have the specific task of achieving: (a) a suitable modification in the policy framework within which banks operate, (b) improvement in the financial health and competitive capabilities of banks, (c) building financial infrastructure relating to supervision, audit and technology and (d) upgradation of the level of managerial competence and the quality of human resources. The banking reforms based on these specific tasks have two aspects; Macro-level policy changes and micro-level policy reforms. The former aims at removing external constraints on the banking system as a whole and thus creating a climate in which banks could function in tune with liberalisation. Micro-level reforms, on the other hand, are concerned with specifics of individual banks and banks as a whole to enable them to overcome internal constraints on their functioning.

Major Components of Reforms

The basis for banking reforms was provided by the Committee on financial System (Narasimham Committee) which made recommendations in November 1991; and these recommendations are a landmark in the evolution of banking policy in the country, as these transformed the Indian banking system from a highly regulated to a more market-oriented system. The major components of banking reforms are outlined in the following paragraphs.

Modifying the Policy Framework was the starting point. The pre-emption of banks resources by way of cash reserve ratio (CRR) and statutory liquidity ratio (SLR) was acting as an external constraint on their profitability. This constraint was relaxed in two ways. These two ratios together pre-empted as much as 63.5 per cent of banks resources in 1991. The average CRR was reduced to 7.5 per cent by May 2001. The SLR was also rationalised into a uniform ratio of 25 per cent of net demand and time liabilities (NDTL) of banks. The interest paid on eligible cash balance under CRR was raised to 6 per cent. Alongside, the Bank Rate was activated in April 1997 as an effective signal and as a reference rate.

There was also the deregulation of the administered structure of interest rates. The plethora of lending rates were rationalised and interest rates were made market-oriented for most of the transactions, the exceptions being the lending rates for small borrowers and interest rate on savings bank deposits. A continuous and careful step-by-step approach has been the main feature of deregulation of interest rates. To facilitate the use of open market operations as a monetary instrument, many policy changes were made in government securities market with reference to yields, sales procedures, network of dealers and maturity patterns. These were supplemented by measures to discontinue automatic monetisation of fiscal deficit by phasing out the issue of adhoc treasury bills.

The modifications in the policy framework carried out as part of the reforms have paved the way for greater reliance on indirect instruments of monetary control.

Improving the financial soundness of banks is the second major component. In an attempt to maintain profitability, banks developed a tendency to over-extend their lending by accepting debtors of low creditworthiness, which has come to be known as "adverse selection". In 1992, prudential norms and regulations were introduced, to ensure safety and soundness of banks and impart greater transparency and accountability in operations.

Prudential norms introduced relate to income recognition, provisioning for bad and doubtful debts and capital adequacy. Prudential norms have helped to serve two purposes. One, they have brought out the true position of the banking systems loans portfolio, and two the norms have helped to arrest its deterioration. The norms have been progressively tightened since their introduction.

Related to the improving of financial soundness of banks are the other measures such as recapitalisation of public sector banks on a selective basis by the Government, improved governance in banks and a certain amount of functional autonomy to the management of public sector banks.

Strenthening the institutional framework is another key element of banking reforms. A more competitive environment has also been created for banks so as to raise their efficiency and performance. Efficiency is not just operational or allocational efficiency but functional efficiency as well. Banks already face competition from non-banking finance companies (NBFCs), mutual funds and from within the industry itself. While existing banks have been allowed greater flexibility, new banks are now being set up in the private sector to provide increased competition. In January 1993, RBI announced guidelines for the entry of new private sector banks. Approvals have been given for the establishement of new foreign banks to set up their operations in India and existing foreign banks have been allowed to expand their branch network.

Strengthening of supervisory mechanism is essential for a sound banking system. There has to be an alert mechanism for monitoring compliance with prudential norms and directives of RBI and other regulatory agencies. The systems of external supervision has been revamped by the establishement of the Board for Financial Supervision, with the operational support of the Department of Banking Supervision of RBI. In the tune with international practices of supervision, a three-tier supervisory model comprising onsite inspection, off-site monitoring and a periodical external autditing based on CAMELS (capital adequacy, asset quality, management, earnings, liquidity and systems controls has been put in place.

Development finance institutions and non-banking finance institutions were also brought into the regulatory ambit of RBI. In terms of the Khanna Committee (1955) recommendations and the Amendment in 1997 of the RBI Act, a three-tier supervisory framework was introduced in respect of non-banking finance companies (NBFCs). The CAMELS approach has been made applicable to NBFCs also. A department of non-banking supervision has been created to exclusively supervise NBFCs only.

Narasimham Committee: 1998

The Government appointed a second high-level "Committee on Banking Sector Reforms" headed by Shri M. Narasimham, to review the implementation of the reforms recommended by th earlier committee and to look ahead and chart the reforms necessaryin the years ahead to make Indian banking strong and better equipped to compete effectively in a fast-changing environment.

The Committee in its report submitted in April 1998, made wide-ranging recommendations covering various aspects of banking policy, institutional, supervisory and legislative dimensions, The committee came out with recommendations with regard to : capital adequacy, asset quality; non performing assets (NPAs); directed credit; prudential norms; disclosure requirements; asset liability management; earnings and profitability; systems and methods in banks; restructuring including mergers and amalgamations; reduction of government and RBI shareholding to 33 per cent in the public sector banks; devising effective regulatory norms and the review of banking sector laws. These recommendations are being progressively implemented. In follow up of Narasimham Committee's (1998) reference to weak banks in the context of restructuring of banks, Verma commitee was appointed in 1999 with the specific task of identifying weak public sector banks, examining their problems and suggesting strategies for restructuring them. The recommendations of the Committee were approved in principle.

Reforms and Response

The progress of banking reforms in the last ten years has been impressive. The RBI made substantial progress in modifying the policy framework for reforms. The proportion of bank's resources pre-empted has been brought down. For instance, the SLR which was 37.4 per cent in March 1992 came down to 25 per cent in 2001. Similarly the CRR which was 15 per cent in January 1992 was brought down to 5.5 per cent in December 2001. The Bank Rate was reduced from 12 per cent in October 1991 to 6.5 per cent in October 2001. The interest rate regime has been rationalised and in the context of deregulation, banks have been given considerable operational flexibility and autonomy in April 2001, in determing the rates with the approval of their Boards. To restore the soundness of public sector of public sector banks, capital adequacy ratio was introduced in 1992 and this was accompanied by recapitalisation of banks by the Governement. Between 1992-93 and 1998-99 the Government contributed over Rs. 20,000 crore to the capital of public sector banks. New initiatives were taken to strengthen the supervisory system for banks by moving towards consolidated supervision and also towards risk-based supervision.

The response of the banks to the reforms has been impressive. The banks have been adjusting very well to the new environment, though gradually. As at the end of March 2001, 23 out of 27 public sector banks had capital adequacy in excess of 10 per cent, the prescribed ratio being 9 per cent. 15 nationalised banks fell into this category i.e. exceeding 10 per cent. There has been considerable reduction in non-performing assets (NPAs). The ratio of gross NPAs to gross advances which was 23 per cent in 1992-93 declined to 12.4 per cent by March 2001. Net NPAs to net advances was 6.7 per cent in 2001. Net profits of public sector banks amounted to Rs. 2095 crore in 2001 as against a net loss of Rs. 4705 crore in 1993-94. Deposits mobilised increased four-fold between 1992and 2000, the share of time deposits being 80 per cent in 2000. Credit deployed in 200 showed a fourfold increase over 1991. The share of credit to priority sector in total bank credit was a little over 30 per cent. In 1992-93, the first post-reform year, 12 out of 27 public sector banks reported net losses; by March 2001 only 2 banks recorded net losses. The striking feature of the banking system during 1991-2001 is its continuing branch expansion. By March 2001 there were 65,901 branches and the share of rural and semi-urban branches together was 70 per cent indicating the wide reach of the banking system. There is little doubt that the benefits of the banking reforms have been considerable.

Fourth Phase: Beyond 2002 New Challenges

The first phase of financial reforms laid the basis for a sound banking system. Considerable progress has been made in implementing the reforms and the banking system is now moving towards the second phase. Nevertheless, the Indian banking system faces several difficult challenges; therefore, the banks have to re-orient their strategies in the light of their own strengths and the kind of market in which they ae likely to operate. Some of the challenges are home-grown, e.g. high cost of doing business; level of non-performing assets; and low levels of customer satisfaction. some of the challenges are external e.g. phenomenal growth in the volume of capital inflows; integration of financial markets across the globe. In view of these domestic and international developments, it is necessary to chart out a path for the development of efficient banking in the new century. there are several areas of concern which need to be addressed.

New Dimension

Indian banks will have to operate in a deregulated competitive financial sector. competitive pressure is building up for Indian banks both from within and from outside. Competition is likely to intensify in the coming years within the industry, from NBFCs and from foreign entities. Competition is not just in terms of number of competitors but in terms of proliferation of innovations, specialised markets, cross-border trade in financial services and capital flows. Our reforms have made progress but we have not become competitive internationally. We cannot lag behind other countries and we have to transform the Indian banking system from being a largely domestic one to a truly international one; and this should enable to emerge as an interanational banking centre.

The worldwide revolution in information and communication technology (ICT) has become the biggest force of change in banking. It is a source of productivity growth and facillitates effective competition. ICT reduces costs, increases volumes and facilitates customised products. It plays an important role in the payments and settlement system. Technology has opened up new avenues in banking for discharging the same functions in a cost-effective manner: 24-hour banking, Telebanking; internet banking; E-banking. The process of technological changes is just beginning in Indian banking. Even the use of existing technology is at low levels.

Though RBI and the banks have been taking steps in the last few years, computerisation has been mostly directed towards accounting and related activities. Without emphasis on critical areas relevant to management and customer service and customised products. The Indian banking system will have to redouble its efforts to build the technological infrastructure not only to provide cost-effective and competitive customer service but also to achieve international recognition and status.

The level of non-performing assets (NPAs), though declining in recent years, continues to be high by international standards. NPAs have become a first charge on banks funds for provisioning and these affect banks performance by eating into their profitability. The most important condition for improvement in the profitability of banks is a reduction in the level of NPAs. In fact, it is a pre-condition for the stability of the banking system. The response to the efforts at debt recovery and restructuring of assets and other methods has been slow. The strategies for containing the problem of NPAs should emphasise the strict enforcement of prudential norms and requirements, transparency and disclosure and the need for legislation which will make the recovery process smoother. Reforms have to be supported by legal changes for enforceability of contracts. In any effort to build a banking system of international stature, reduction in NPAs should be the priority target.

Asset-liability mismatches expose the banks to various types of risks i.e. risks of illiquidity and insolvency; risks arising from gloabalisation and deregulation. Risk management is a continuous process of controlling assets and liabilities in terms of size, maturities and yields. As operations in the financial market become varied and complex, banks have to equip themselves with a variety of skills and appropriate technology. The RBI has issued guidelines to banks in April 1999, for asset-liability management which would help the bank management to meet the challenges. Banks are encouraged to prescribe risk parameters and establish effective control systems. Now the action lies entirely with banks. The general complaint that customer satisfaction is at low levels needs to be addressed in all seriousness. The effort should be not only to preserve the existing circle of clients, both corporate and individual, but also to enlarge the client base. Banks need to develop customer relationship, which has come to be known as "Relationship Banking". It is concerned essentially with maintaining relations with customers on a continuing basis. This is CRM and it is not just the relationship built around raising deposits and making loans, though that is important. CRM goes well beyond that.

Two important aspects of CRM are: one that it does not view customers in totality or in the aggregate and two the devising of banking products. Regarding the first, customers needs and demands and business styles vary; and it is necessary to consider segments of customers and build customer profiles to evolve strategies. As banking products are intangible, CRM involves personal selling. As for the second, once the need for segment approach is recognised, product differentiation becomes important. The present methods of evolving banking products and then looking around for customers for those products would not yield the desired results. In short banking products should be customer -based. Besides, the method of pricing products should also change from cost plus to product quality. To raise the level of customer satisfaction, banks will have to set up CRM groups or CRM departments.

HRD: Rigidities

Human resource development (HRD) is the most important needs for a service industry like banking. The banking industry being largely in the public sector, certain rigidities developed in HRD within the banking system. Apart from being the preferred employer for the edcated manpower, public sector banks followed a hierarchical structure, which gives preference to seniority over performance. Besides, the banks continued, until recently, their generalist orientation in the matter of recruitment. In the result, the best talent especially specialist, could not be attracted. The approach to human resources management in banks will have to change in tune with the fast-changing banking environment at home and abroad. While it is difficult to bring about radical changes in the staff structure in the near future, public sector banks can effect improvements in the existing practices of recruitment, training and redeployment. The focus must shift from generalist orientation of the staff to specialist orientation i.e. the ability to imbibe and absorb technology. Information technology is an area where HRD is now critical. There is also the urgent need for training for upgradation of different types of skills, for redeployment, for changing the mindset and attitudes. It is time that banks revamp their HRD departments and evolve appropriate policies to make the best use of their primary asset i.e. human resources.

There are issues in supervision and regulation with which the banks will have to be very much concerned in the days ahead. The banks should have to prepare for tightening of prudential norms as the new Basel Accord becomes effective. The earlierBasel Accord (1988) gave recognition mainly to credit or the principal risk. Since then a number of events have taken place including the East Asian crisis, which brought to light the inadequacy of the 1988 arrangement, as it did not recognise market risks and operational risks. It also did not distinguish between different types of exposures with different dimensions of risk. According to the New Capital Accord, baks would have to provide capital in terms of "Economic Capital" rather than the minimum regulatory capital. The concept of economic capital covers all risks embedded in the banks balance sheet. Again in terms of the accord, supervision involves moving from the transaction-based approach to a risk-based approach, to determine the level of risk that each bank is exposed to. Bank managements will therefore have to develop internal capital evaluation according to their risk profile. Risk weights are being constantly revised to take into consideration additional sources of risk.

Corporate Governance

Corporate governance is assuming greater importance in the banking sector today as a result of certain unhealthy developments in recent years. The main focus in corporate governance is how to enhance shareholder value; and this needs to be achieved in a legal and ethical manner leading to contribution to business prosperity. The major ingredients of good corporate governance would be accountability at all levels, transparency and enhancing the image of the organisation in the eyes of the public. Corporate governance underlines the belief that the public good should be placed above the private goods and that corporate resources cannnot be used for personal benefit. Ethics is part of good governance. Ethics apart, good governance is concerned with observing rules and regulations, guidelines and clean corporate practices. Public sector banks have to pay considerable attention to corporate governance in the context of deregulation, prudential norms, risk-based supervision and globalisation. As part of the ongoing reforms, bank managements and their Boards have been given greater autonomy. It is very important that greater vigilance over adherence to prescribed rules, norms and regulations is exercised. It is only then that autonomy for banks would be meaningful.

The response groups in the banking system are banks, RBI, the Government and the customers; and the onus is on them to raise Indian banking to international standards.

Conclusion

Banking Industries, the worldover, has been going through a process of transformation during the last many years. This is clearly evident from the changes that have occured in the financial markets, institutions and products. Indian banking sector has made significant progress in recent years. The prudential norms, accounting and disclosure standards and risk management practices, etc. are keeping pace with global standards. The financial soundness and enduring supervisory practices pursued by RBI have made our banking system resilient to global shocks. While the banking system has done fairly well in adjusting to new market dynamics, the greater challenges lie ahead. Financial sector would be opened up for greater international competition under WTO. In addition free trade agreements (FTAs) such as with Singapore may also have an impact on the shape of bankig industry. Banks need to prepare for these changes proactively by adopting best global practices, systems and procedures so as to develop the most resilient, competitive and dynamic financial system.

References

Mehra Dalip (1999), Indian Financial System and Commercial Bankiong.

Samal B. (2001), "Indian Banking System: Phases of Transition", *IBA Bulletin*, Vol. XXIII, No. 3, Special Issue March.

Alexander Georga Smith (2003), "Acquiring a Cutting Edge", *Business Standard,* Banking Annual, October.

Arora Kalpana (2003), Indian Banking-Managing Transformation Through Technology, *IBA Bulletin*, Vol. XXV, No. 3, Special Issue, March.

Murty N. R. Narayana (2003), "Reinventing Banking in India", Bank Quest, *The Journal of The Institute of Banking & Finance,* Vol. 74, No.3, July-September.

Srivastava, R. M. (1998), "Management of Indian Financial Institutions", Himalaya Publishing House, Mumbai.

Trivedi, A. K. (2003), "Managing Transformation", *IBA Special Bulletin,* March.

Uppal, R. K. & Kaur Rimpi (2006), "Banking Sector Reforms in India: A Review of the Post 1991 Development", New Century Publications, New Delhi.

Pai D. T. (2001), "Indian Banking-Changing Scenario", *IBA Bulletin,* Vol. XXIII, No. 3, Special Issue March.

Shroff Dr. Firdos T. (2004), "Impact of Technology on Banking", *IBA Bulletin,* Vol. XXVI, No. 1, Special Issue, January.

Toor, N. S. (2002), Information Handbook for Bankers, Section 4.1 to 4.11.

Velayudham Dr. T. K. (2002), "Developments in Indian Banking: Past, Present and Future", Bank Quest, *The Journal of the Indian Institute of Bankers, Platinum Jubilee* Special Issue, October-December.

3

Indian Banking Today and Tomorrow

Ramashish Purvey

The Indian banking industry has now entered a new phase wherein challenges, both within the banking sector and from the economy, have to be catered. The present paper discusses the issues contemporary in nature, which have critical significance for the banking system as of today and will have a deep impact in shaping the future of the Indian banking scenario.

The old world of Banking has, no doubt, changed considerably. The forces of free trade between countries' dominance of *short-term/ long- term profit making market forces,* globalization and technology have, ultimately, resulted in increasing integration of economies across the world. Today, banks have to *no more compete locally,* but globally also. It is important for Banks to adopt to this new and challenging environment. In the words of Karen Kaiser Clark: *Life is change, growth is optional,* choose wisely.

Coming back to the past, the Indian Banking system is unique and, perhaps has no parallels in *the Banking history of any country in the world,* It is interesting to capture the historical emergence of the Indian Banking over the last 54 to 55 years, in terms of *organization, functions, resource mobilization, socio-economic role, problems and solutions.* The period of about five and half decades witnessed several *macro economic* developments monetary and banking policies and the external situation, which directly or indirectly influenced the evolution of Indian Banking in different ways and in different periods. For this reasons it would be proper to analyze in summarized form the evolution of Indian banking with reference to some *distinguished or clear-cut demarcated phases.* The first phase covers *the period from 1948 to 1968 (pre-nationalization phase).*

Development/changes/trend of banking businesses have to be seen experienced during *the second phase from 1969 to 1991.* These two periods include the post. *The period of banking reforms beginning with 1992 could be marked as the post-reform phase (1991-2005).*

As a matter of fact, *the Banking Regulation Act, 1948* provided the legal framework for the regulation of the banking system by the Reserve Bank of India. With the introduction of *economic planning in 1951,* the need was left for aligning monetary and banking activity with the requirements of planning.

In the period between 1969 -1990, the growth of banking sector was on account of massive branch expansion and Government driven thrust on outreach. The banking outreach increased enabling more and more people to access the system. As a result, the average population per branch, which was at 64,000 in 1969, came down to 16,000 by 1990. Business volumes exploded. However, merely manifold expansion in business volume will not serve the purpose in its totality.

During this period, M. O.F. and RBI had issued detailed guidelines on almost all aspects of bank management to be followed by the banks. *Development through credit was the central theme.* Business mix of the banks closely reflected the policies and priorities of the Government. During the period, banking industry recorded a growth rate of 18 per cent. The sector was characterized by uniform salaries, similar rates of interest (neither capital nor risk driven), similar products, similar volumes and even similar repayment periods. As regards providing satisfaction to customers, choice of bank was more an issue of proximity of the branch than terms of credit or variety of service. It means *the growth was policy /demand driven.*

Emerged Changes

Issues such as *profitability and financial stability* cannot be commented upon as *uniform prudential accounting norms were not in place.* It will be in the fitness of thing to note that almost immediately on the introduction of uniform prudential norms, banks showed an NPA of nearly 30%.

Many changes could be witnessed in early 90's. Firstly; (i) the introduction of prudential norms (ii) capital adequacy, and (iii) deregulation of interest rates were announced by *the Regulators.* The second issue that impacted India's stride in *IT on banks.* The third important change was the entry of new highly capitalized private sector Banks which heralded real competition for the Banking sector. ICICI Bank, HDFC Bank, Times Bank and Global Trust Bank started not only with IT driven initiatives, but were able to manage more than 65% of their business through outsourcing, when most of the Indian public sector banks are not being easily able to achieve excellence on some of its performance parameters with their large number of permanent employees (having traditional mindset and old knowledge), there is no merit in avoiding rejecting to get some of its customers' related works and other business activities performed through outsourcing.

Fourthly, introduction of ATMs and variety of cards substantially changed the way banking was known in the country.

Fifthly, as regards competition from out-side banking sector, other financial players of similar nature showing powerful presence in the market and from outside the banking sector, this period saw a substantial reduction in the role of *NBFCs.* However, the lack of competition from *NBCFs,* was more than made up by the opening of *insurance and mutual fund sector.* Keeping in view, much tougher competition for funds, it was high time for public sector Banks to wakeup.

During the last decade (1995-2005), more pronounced improvements in regard to delivery channels of both privet sector and public sector banks, were witnessed. Risk taking ability has become so important that Rick Management skills have become a crucial driver of business growth. Issues, such as: branding, cross selling segregation of clients into high net-worth and retail, efforts for reduction in cost, capacity building of staff by way of providing them latest technical training and upto date theoretical knowledge understanding the competitor's business plans.

Understanding impact of globalization etc. have started vying for the attention of the bank managements. Last but not the least, proper size has also assumed importance. On the regulatory front greater thrust on containing (i) inflation, (ii) better liquidity management and (iii) policies conducive for business growth have also been witnessed during the period. Guidelines on risk management and capital requirement in terms of Basel – II have already been put in place. Despite these regulatory and business promoting strategies, it is discouraging that in terms of outreach, product access by consumers is uneven across the country. It could be seen that most of the recent innovations are available to the urban and semi-urban centers and not across the country. In overall sense, payment system has improved.

Today Indian Banking can be compared well with its Asian counterparts, particularly in terms of Asset quality and profitability. There is no denying the fact that non- performing loan ratio has been contained. Exposure Management has improved. Reserve Bank of India, in its latest Report on currency and Finance (2006-07), has indicated that the Regulatory and Supervisory indicators are satisfactory and Basel–II. Mile stones have been road mapped. Need for an additional capital of Rs. 60,000 crores has been indicated during he next five years. So innovation and performance will be the success mantra for banks. Concludingly, (i) Regulatory design and policy measures, (ii) Management initiatives in changing and upgrading organizational structure and efficiency are the three pre–requisites that will decide the future shape of the banks.

Review Based Obsrvations

Issues such as profitability and financial stability cannot be commented upon as uniform prudential accounting norms were not in place. It will be in the fitness of thing to note that almost immediately on the introduction of uniform prudential norms, banks showed an NPA of nearly 30 per cent (Sinor, 2003) observed that NPA had shown a perceptible decline, both in terms of gross number and net number. Banks, however, need to look at their revenue streams more closely to ensure that volatility is substituted by sustainable growth in income. With its tremendous market potential, India is fast becoming the play ground to be explored for increasing value accretions. This is simultaneously true for the banking sector also. 'To tap the opportunities in the financial markets' is the need for the Indian Banks for repositioning themselves. And the marriage of technology and banking will hold the key for Indian banks in order to keep pace with changes in the global scenario. "Technological advancements together with changing demographic profile and heightened customer's expectations are creating a new, efficient economic environment and driving the changes in every sphere-observed purwar (2006). In this context, Jack Welch suggested "Right marketing strategy and trained manpower for credit plus approach for ensuring customers delight, which is the pre- requisite for customer success.

Highlighting the significance of latest training modes in banking industry, Nair (2006) ascertained: "When the whole gamut of banking is under going a metamorphosis, with the conditional frontiers being either removed or expanded by the Central Bank of the country, training, one of the vital features of Human Resource Development, cannot be left behind to stay in the traditional path without venturing into new ways and means in tune with the vagaries of the market. With the size and complexities of present day business leading to the corporate form of organization, share ownership and operational management of enterprises get significantly distanced and consequently, accountability and governance issues assume greater importance. Sir Adrian Cadbury (1993) and William G. Bowen (1994), rightly confirmed. In effect therefore, Corporate Governance has to do with power and accountability ". Deloitte D. Tohmatsm (2003), was of the view that "good Corporate and financial governance supported by comprehensive, open, transparent internal and external communications are the major pillars among the top priorities of banks.

Basel–I framework for capital adequacy, which was introduced in 1988, was designed to establish minimum levels of capital for internationally active banks. India Implemented the Basel- I framework spread over three years with effect from 1999 -93. Basel - II accord incorporates a new capital standard for banks. This was released by the Basel committee in June, 2004 for implementation starting in January, 2007 in a group of 10 countries.

Showing the way for indemnification caused due to Basel–I provisions, Chidambaram (2006) cautioned. "Implementation of Basel- II will require more capital for banks in India to account for operational risk, which is not captured under Basel-I, and the capital charge for market risk prescribed recently. Professor Narayan (2006) stated that the worries that existed in 2003 with regard to Basel–II implementation, were then, to be completely resolved. Based on study done by Internal Ratings Based (IRB) Approach, it was revealed that a 20 per cent reduction in regulatory capital was possible, which would largely depend on asset quality and portfolio composition of each bank. "Basel- II implementation is not a one time affair, it will be an on-going process". Opined Saran (2006). The same was termed by him as an exercise in Change Management by exhorting the banks to expedite their Core Banking implementation.

Study conducted by ICRA (2006) forestalled that the additional capital requirement on account of operational risk (using Basic Indicator Approach), to be in the range of Rs. 20,000 crores (but likely to be over Rs. 42,000 crores by March 2010 as per Union Finance Minister. Therefore, Indian Banks must attempt the Advanced Measurement Approach (AMA) to reduce the capital charge on account of operational risk. Alan, Greenspan (2006) suggested a Liquidity At Risk Rule that takes into account the foreseeable risks that a county could face in the event of: (a) Near absence of a purely non-interventionist exchange rate policies and (b) cost benefit grade off in the quantity of reserve accumulation .

Betokening better strategy for achieving the foundation of three pillars of Basel–II, Chidambaram (2006). Opined its implementation should lead to enhance financial stability through better Risk Management systems in banks, better banking supervision in member countries, and improved market discipline."

Niall, S. K. Booker (2006) observed with certitude that financial service sector was, then, characterized by product and service offerings that are largely commoditised. The key differentiation that would help banks stand out from the crowd, would be strong brand innovation and service quality.

One of the main recommendations of the Committee under the Chairmanship of Dr. N.L. Mitra (constituted by the Reserve Bank of India), is Development of Best Practices Code (BPC) by all Banks. (Prasad, Sina (2004) . It is worth mentioning that banks are supposed to evolve best practices to uphold the Principle of Corporate Governance in view of the extant guidelines.

Highlighting the distinctive advantages of Consolidation and Mergers, Chidambaram (2006) observed, "Key drivers of consolidation include revenue growth from larger customer base, efficiencies in operations, optimal deployment of excess capital, stabilization of asset quality, need to upgrade technology and offer a comprehensive bouquet of products, savings in cost and shrinking margins. I caution every one that with the implementation of Basel- II norms from March 2007, weaker banks may have no option, but to merge with banks with excess capital".

Leeladhar, V. (2006) rightly remarked having espoused for consolidation and core competencies. "We are slowly but surely moving from a regime of large number of small banks to small number of large banks. The new era is going to be one of the consolidation around identified core competencies".

Challenges

Some of the challenges which the Indian banks will have to face in future are as follows:

- The major challenges would be the shaping up of the banks, internally as well as externally. Internally it will be with re spect to target markets and customers, business models and risk management. At external level, consolidation with changes in landscape due to mergers and acquisitions (M&A).

- Since the dynamics of the rural markets are changing and rural markets are their forte, the PSPs would have to change their strategies to take advantage of their penetration in rural sector.
- Consolidation of banks is a necessity to face the international challenge. India needs to have a small number of large banks rather than large number of small banks, large in terms of assets, volume of business and profits. Hence, mutual discussion among banks will be essential for consolidation.
- Human resource will play a big role in transformation of the banking industry ion India in the post 2009 era. Specialization of work and specialized workforce will rule and show the door to general banking. Re-skilling of the existing staff and recruitment of skilled persons will have to be undertaken. The total employment of the banking industry will expand and not shrink with increase in the business.
- The easy way to learn the best global practices of banking is either by imparting training to staff by deputation overseas or by hiring top class management from abroad so that the staff members have some exposure of global financial markets. One more way is that the Indian banks may acquire banks abroad to learn best practice, earn substantial profits, hire top class management, raise money on global financial markets and grow. Presence of foreign competition is one of the ways to improve performance.
- With India moving towards full capital convertibility, the banking industry will have the role of managing foreign exchange risks. Now, India has a cushion of huge forex reserve, which can help in case of sudden withdrawal of funds. Full rupee convertibility would

provide banks an opportunity to increase their overseas borrowings and expand their potential source of funds.

- The India banks have to reduce the cost of services, improve corporate governance and innovate. The Indian banking would have to give up the restrictions on capital availability, restrictions on credit deployment, restrictive labor laws and weak corporate governance.
- Customer centric approach needs to be followed by the banks. These banks need to be efficient in providing services, have flexibility and become polite so as to cater to the needs of the customers.
- Risk due to innovative products will have to be managed by the Indian banks. Indian has seen risks in other fields and Indians are also risk takers. The Indian banks will easily learn the trade of managing upcoming risks.
- Technology will be of prime importance to the Indian banks, as the foreign banks are already techno-savvy. Indian banks need to have a well-maintained computerised database, with constant upgradation of their technology to suit the new generation techno-savvy customers. Data warehousing and data processing will have to be given due importance.
- Credit rating framework, credit assessment centres and credit bureaus will have to be developed.
- Back-office operations and front-office work have to be segregated so as to manage handling large number of customers.

Are Indian banks ready for Challenges?

The Indian banks can transform these challenges into opportunities for managing change by initiating several measures, some of which are enumerated below in this concluding section:

- Adoption of global best practices in the form of risk management techniques, new business models, new operating models, etc;
- Technology upgradation through core banking solutions;
- Skill development to the new generation banking techniques.
- Synchronization and harmonization of planning process of various business and operative models with technology as the base and accordingly upgrade skill of manpower;
- Augmentation of capital to meet the requirement of new credit growth.

The Indian banks are all set to meet the challenges as they are already well-structured in their expertise and experience gained in fulfillment of post-reforms requirement. There should not be any doubt why Indian banks cannot meet the real challenge being thrown up in future.

To Conclude, banks could be financial intermediaries for any thing (without posing itself to be a purely 'profit making organization' avoiding customers' interests) that the customer might be wanting within the regulatory and other legal parameters defined. Banking in that sense could be as imaginative as any body's fertile imagination provided *the future strategies are framed properly, trapped timely and adopted efficiently.*

References

Banking Industry–Vision 2010.

Marketing of Banking Services by-I.I.B.

An Anthakrishnan, G. (2004), " *I.B.A. Bulletin*", April.

Sir Adrian Cadbury (1994), in Reflections on Corporate Governance, Earnest Sykes Memorial Lecture, March 11,1993, in London. Quested by William G. Bowen in Inside The Board Room, John Wiley & Sons.

Dr. Bala Subramanian, N. (2004), "Corporate Governance Imperatives in Banks: Some National and International Perspectives", *IBA Bulletin* (September).

Restoring Confidence is an Imperative for Banks in Top Ten Issues, Global Banking Industry Out look (2003), Deloitte Jouche Tohmatsu.

Sinor, H.N. (2003), " *I.B.A. Bulletin*", August.

The Indian Banker (September, 2006).

Ranjan, Nitesh (2006), "Understanding Foreign Exchange Reserves," The Indian Banker, June.

Booker, Naill S.K. (2006), "USP in Marketing Bank Products", The Indian Banker, May.

Dr. Singh, Sukhdev (2006), "Performance of Banking Sectors, in Comparison to Benchmarks," The Indian Banker, April.

Prasad, Sina (2004).

Leeladhar, V. (2006).

Murthy, N. R. Narayana (2003), " Reinventing Banking in India", BANK QUEST (*The Journal of Indian Institute of Banking & Finance*), July-September .

Dr. Velayudham, T. K. (2002), "Developments in Indian Banking: Past, Present and Future" BANK QUEST, October-December.

Bhaskaran, R. (2006), BANK QUEST, April-June.

Kulkarni, V. N. (2006), "The Indian Banker", October..

Purwar, A. K. (2006), "Indian Banking Breaking Through, Old Moulds", The Indian Banker, January.

Darshan , N. V. (2006), " The Growth of Banks As Financial Super Markets", *Ibid,* October.

Nair, S. Nagappan (2006), " Employee Training Initiatives in Banks- A Future Perspective", *Ibid,* January.

Chidambaram, P. (2006), Address of the Union Finance Minister, Govt. of India at the 59th Annual General Meeting of the I.B.A., "The Indian Banker, July, p. 18-22.

4

Globalisation and Changing Perspective of the Banking Sector

R. P. Deshpande

Globalisation

Globalisation covers a wide spectrum expending international trade, growth of multinational business rise in international ventures, movement of labour and increasing interdependence through capital flows and information. Today market are no longer synonymous with geographical co-ordinates, Countries do not produce at home but the world is perceived as a global village where resources are best utilised a source and value additions done there.

Financial services are at the centre of the present trend in globalisation. On one hand increasing integration of economies and markets is making global banking is reality while, on the other global banks are the drivers behind global trade and corporate globalisation, Deregulation of capital markets in both developed and developing counties in the 1990's has resulted in larger and free flow of capital with flows across counties becoming significant the provision of financial services on a global scale is gaining importance. In fact international banking is key component of the global economy it is central to the flow of capital around the world through provision of Loans, supply of financial advice and involvement in securities market.

Globalisation of Services

The financial services sector is not only the largest sub-sector in the service sector, but it is also the fastest growing sub-sector both in the developed and the developing economies. In addition to overall output, it also contributes significantly to employment generation. In the backdrop of ensuring efficient financial services in future, India has deregulated and liberalized the financial sector in particular. Simultaneously, the scope for India's international trade in financial services is growing substantially, through aided by the development in new technologies, especially in telecommunications and increase in foreign investment. With full implementation of the financial services agreement (FSA) under the world trade organization, the entire spectrum of banking and all other financial services including insurance would function subject to multilateral trade rules.

The FSA under the aegis of the GATS provides the multilateral legal framework for 95 per cent of world trade in financial services. Over the last decade, International trade in financial services has increased at a more rapid pace than the growth in the domestic financial sector, Be sides, the markets have deepened and widened significantly with the introduction of more players and more instruments. Although the developed countries continue to dominate the scene of trade in financial services, yet the developing countries are increasingly integrating themselves, introduction more of innovations and becoming echnologically more capable.

Internationalization of Financial Services

Internationalization of Financial Services can be defined as "eliminating discrimination in the treatment between foreign and domestic financial services providers as well as removing barriers to the cross-border provision of financial services".

The FSA under the auspices of GATS does exactly both; and hence a country by signing the FSA consciously promotes internationalization of its financial services sector.

Banking Scene

Banking scenario has changes rapidly since 1990's. The decade of 90's has witnessed a sea change in the way banking is done in India. Technology has made tremendous impart in banking. Anywhere banking and any time banking have become reality.

Foreign banks and the new private sector banks have embraced technology right from the inception of their operations and therefore, they have adopted themselves to changes in the technology easily. Where as the public sector banks (PS Bs) and the old private sector banks have not been able to keep pace with these developments. In this regard, one can city historical, political and other factors like culture and working relations as the main constraints.

Introduction of prudential norms and liberalization of the economy has infused serve competition posing several challenges in the banking PS B's and old private banks have lost quality manpower as well as quality advances to their counterparts in foreign banks and now private sector banks.

Indian Banking Sector and WTO

India's commitment in banking under the FSA are relatively at a lower side, reflecting its gradual and cautious approach, which was any way visible during the process of negotiation. Among the twenty countries in the Asia Pacific region for which the liberalization indices are available, India ranks 12th in deposit taking and 15th in lending. arranged in the descending order. The indices were much below the regional as well as the world averages.

Nevertheless, India's move to sign the FSA could be said as strategic and timely, as by now India had already implemented several reform measures in the financial sector in general and the banking sector in particular.

Bank-level Issues

1. It is apparent from the net profit equation that banks should manage spread, burden and NPA to remain profitable as well as safe and sound.
2. The focus should be on burden management. This would require evolving strategies for increasing other income and decreasing operating expenses:
3. The standards of corporate governance in banks should be further strengthened to build competency.
4. Bank should institute well-orchestrated human resource development policies with a degree of specialization, to meet their specific needs.
5. Banks should strengthen their internal control mechanisms through simplification of documentation procedures and building efficient interoffice communication channels.
6. Foreign branches of Indian banks should be used not only to facilities exports and ethnic business but also to bring in foreign investment and transfer of technology to India.
7. Banks should explicitly plan for the profitability of their overseas office. The annual accounts of banks should state how much profit has been earned from overseas operation.
8. To materialize the proposal to allow offshore banking units to be set up in the special economic zones.

Challenges to Indian Banking

While globalisation bring in opportunities and rewards it also widens the parameters of risk. Indian banks have shown good resilience in facing the pressures of Globalisation but many challenges still remain including the resources both financial and technical.

Competition

The banking sector today faces unprecedented competition pressure fuelled by the twin forces of deregulation and technology. These forces are shaping technical changes in the global financial services industry, leading to consolidation on global financial services industry, leading to consolidation on a global scale and secular shift towards a "Universal Banking" frame work. Evolution & new generation Internet-based technology platforms, compiled with the trend towards customer-centric business models in the financial services industry, has blurred the perimeter of conventional banking.

Non-performing Assets

Even after the introduction of assets classification and prudential norms a large number of banks are saddled with a high proportion of non-performing assets. Such proportion is growing in the non-directed portfolio of lending of commercial banks. The Debt recovery tribunals do not also help much in the reduction of NPA's.

Overseas Banking

Indian banks have also made their presence overseas through it is still limited. There are about 123 branches of Indian banks located abroad. Expansion overseas of Indian banks so for has been mainly in countries with relatively high concentration of Indian. International standing of a bank is linked awing other factors, to the assets size and soundness of the bank. Together these reflect the risk-bearing capacity of the bank, a feature which is highly desirable for a global bank.

Capital Adequacy

Soundness of a bank in turn is reflected by the capital base and the capital adequacy ratio there of India has accepted the basic fromework of the minimum capital adequacy standards of Basel committee of banks for international settlements (BIS) in this connection all public sector banks have achieved minimum capital adequacy of a per cent prescribed by system has taken various steps to upgrade the soundness of Indian banks including recapitalization of the weaker banks from time to time.

All in all banks should strive to achieve significant in their productivity, efficiency and profitability. The area of challenges that ahead would be:

- Restructuring and recognizing banks set-up towards thinner and leaner administrative office.
- Closing down and/or merging of unlivable branches particularly in urban and metropolitan branches.
- Forging of strategic alliances to take advantage of the geographic spread of branch network of banks.
- Type of customer concentration with a view to developing niche market suitable for each banks consistent with its ethnos and culture.
- Develop new products and services that would meet the emerging customer needs.
- Professionalizing management structures that would meet the emerging customers needs.
- Public sector banks should be allowed to access both domestic and foreign capital.

Measures to Overcome

The forces of deregulation, globalisation and advancing technology have greatly increased the competitive pressures in the banking industry banks are functioning under competitive pressures from within the banking system from non-banking institutions as well as from the domestic and international financial markets. In highlighting this paradigm shift, the following measures can be taken to overcome the problems of Indian Banking System.

Reorganization and Restructuring

The financial sector reforms have brought in the much needed competition in the market place. Opening up of banking sector to global players would see. banks facing global competition. The pressure on capital structure is expected to trigger a phase of consolidation inn the banking industry Banks could achieve consolidation through different ways. Mergers and acquisitions could be one way to achieve this. In recent years, market led mergers between private banks have taken place it is expected that this process would gain momentum in the coming years.

Technology in Banking

Technology will bring fundamental shift in the functioning of banks it would not only help them bring improvements in their internal functioning but also enable them to provide better customer service. Entry of ATMs has changed the profile of front offices in bank branches. Customers no longer need to visit branches for their day to day banking transaction–E-banking and internet banking have opened new avenues in convenience banking.

Product Innovation

With increased competition in the banking industry the net interest margin of banks has come down over the last one decade. Banks will look for fee based income to fill the gap in interest income. As banks strive to provide value added services to customers, the market will see the emergence of strong investment and merchant banking entities. Product innovation and creating brand equity for specialized products will decide the market share and volumes. Banks will play an active role in the development of derivative products & will offer a variety of hedge products to the corporate sector and other investors.

Risk Management

Risk is inherent in any commercial activity and banking is no exception to this role. In the regulated banking environment, banks had to primarily deal with credit or default risk. Building up a proper risk management structure would be crucial for the banks in future. Measurement of risk exposure is essential for implementing hedging strategies. Credit risk, Market risk and Operational risk are the three major parameters in risk management systems for banks.

Human Resource Management

The key to the success of any organization lies in how efficiently the organization managers its human resources. The public sector banks are striving hard to keep pace with the technological changes and meet the challenges of globalisation.

In order to meet the global standards and to remain competitive bank will have to recruit specialists in the various fields such as Treasury management, Credit risk management IT Services etc. in keeping with the segmentation and product innovation.

Conclusion

Banking sector has apparently responded well to the financial reforms in India. Banks can look back with satisfaction at having responded effectively to the challenges posed before them from time to time. Banks have adjusted their systems of functioning venture into new areas improve efficiency levels by inclusion of trained and skilled manpower and restructured their organization, Indian market with its enormous pot will be a centre of interest of the world community and Indian banks have to find their places in this competitive scenario.

Financial reform is here to stay. It led had to expansion in international money capital and securities markets banks role in pivotal in each of these areas It is for Indian banks to position themselves competitively in international scenario. The complexity of operations and sophistication of financial products calls for development of new skills and expertise. However a combination of factors including regulatory support and technological up gradation will enable Indian banks to achieve their global aspirations.

Gearing up to face the challenges of globalization, commercial banks are marching ahead in the right direction by building of risk management system, technological up gradation human resource development, product innovation and by adopting creative thinking and innovative methodology.

References

Meera Lal (2003), "Economic Reforms in India", Himalaya Publishing House Mumbai.

Narendra Jadhav (1996), "Challenges to Indian Banking Macmillan India Ltd.", New Delhi.

Uma Kapila (2005), Indian Banking and Financial Sector Reforms Academic Foundation New Delhi.

IBA Indian Banker January 2007.

5

Challenges and Prospects of Indian Banks in Post-Globalisation Era

Sitaram Sharma & J. P. Sharma

The process of globalisation has resulted in much upheaval in the Indian financial structure and the past decade has witnessed much painful introspection over the philosophy and strategy of financial system. One of the offshoots of globalisation has been the testing of business acumen of financial institutions and by extension, of the viability of their financial institutions themselves just as they test the viability of their financial lendings. But, financial institutions cannot entirely operate on loss or profit considerations, human welfare is equally, if not more important.

In India, we had strengthened the banking sector to face the pressures that may arise out of the frontiers of globalisation by adopting the banking sector reforms. It is evident that we took to reforms in early ninties, strengthened the banking system, opened up in calibrated manner, which followed the twin governing principles of allowing the competition to sink in and tone up the efficiency and service quality. The entire reform process - the concept, pace and sequencing, was undertaken in such a manner that change was achieved in a non-disruptive progress and consultative process manner. The market participants and the regulator act in tandem to bring about resilience in the financial system, shoring up the confidence levels, which are imperative for tapping the fruit of globalisation.

Banking in India

Indian banking system has recorded rapid progress. This was possible mainly due to planned economic growth, increase in money supply, growth of banking habit, control and guidance by the Reserve Bank of India. Rapid economic growth presupposes rapid expansion of commercial banks. Initially the banks were conservative and opened up branches mainly in metropolitan cities and other major cities. Branch expansion gained momentum after the nationalisation of commercial banks and the introduction of lead Bank Scheme.

Table 1

Progress of Scheduled Commercial Banks in India

Year	*Total No. of Branches*	*Rural Branches*	*Rural Branches as percentage of the total*	*Population per Bank office*
1969	8,260	1,860	22	63,800
1991	60,650	32,750	54	14,150
2003	66,640	32,270	48	15,000

Source: Economic Survey, 2003-04, Govt. of India.

Table 2

Expansion of Bank Deposits and Credit of all Scheduled Commercial Banks in India

Year	*Number of reporting Banks*	*Bank Deposits (Rs. crores)*	*Bank credit (Rs. crore)*
1990-91	271	1,92,540	1,16,300
2000-04	297	9,62,620	5,11,430
2003-04	288	15,01,930	8,35,380

Source: RBI Bulletin, August 2004.

From Table 1, it is clear that the total number of branches of all commercial banks increased from 8,260 in 1969 to 60,650 in 1991, recorded growth of above seven times, But, it was only a fraction during 1991 to 2003. Another remarkable matter was that the rural branches as well as rural branches as percentage of the total decreased from 32,750 and 54 in 1991 to 32,250 and 48 in 2003 repectively.

From the Table 2, it is clear that the bank deposits rncreased from Rs. 1,92,540 crores in 1991 to Rs. 9,62,620 crores in 2000-01 and Rs. 15,01,930 crores in 2003-04 i.e. over a period of 12 years from 1990-91 to 2003-04, the growth of deposits in India of all scheduled commercial banks was 780% (about 7.8 times). Table : 2 shows that the bank credit increased from Rs. 1,16,300 crores in 1990-91 to Rs. 5,11,430 crores in 2000-01 and Rs. 8,35,380 crores in 2003-04 i.e.over a period of 12 years from 1990-91 to 2003-04, the growth of credit in India of all scheduled commercial banks was about 619% (i.e. about 6.2 times), but it was lower than the growth ot deposits.

Banking in a deregulated environment has become more challenging than in the bygone era marked by administered interest rate and other regulations. The biggest challenge for the banking system operating in a deregulated environment is that it should reorient its focus, operations and outlook which are far more different from the regulated era. The challenges facing the Indian banking system are mainly grouped in the following areas, though they are closely related to each other.

The Corporate Governance in Banks

In a regulated environment, the overall parameters within which the banking system had to operate was delineated in much detail by the RBI or the Government. The main job of the banking system was to implement the guidelines/ circulars/schemes given to them. In a deregulated environment, the Boards of banks are vested with more authority and responsibility to conduct the operations of banks in a most efficient manner and hence the need to upgrade the quality of the management. The Board has to act in a new mould and that involves shift in the mindset and parameters.

In the budget for 2000-01, the Government announced its intention to reduce its stake in nationlised banks to a minimum of 63 per cent of the equity capital. The entry of competent investors from the quality market into the banks' Boards would infuse professional approach to management of banks. Banks have to go a long way in introducing the principles of corporate governance which focuses on the maintenance and improvement of return for the shareholders and also the interest of the stakeholders like, employees, consumers, debtors and creditors, etc. Continuous efforts are on at the international level to evolve acceptable standards are codes, also known as international best practices for corporate governance.

The Use of Technology

The strides made in the area of Information Technology (IT) and its convergence with computers have virtually transformed the face of the world into a global village. Banking is no exception. Rather, the impact of IT in the banking system has altered the frontiers of banking beyond recognition. The main objective of the IT is to improve customer service, house keeping, employees productivity, decision making process, risk management, etc. Further, all the product innovations in the banking industry is through using networking technology in the form of e-cards like, ATM, debit card , credit card, smart card, etc.

Another area which IT has impacted is the payment and settlement system. Now, the instant funds transmisson from one corner of the country to another corner has been made possible through networking at a much reduced marginal cost. Since, the payment and settlement system is the backbone of the financial and other economic systems, it improves the allocational efficiency of the banking system. In the context of branch banking adopted as a predominant mode of banking, the networking can solve the complexities associated with branch banking specially in regard to generating adequate and timely information on the various activities of the different branches located in the remote corners of the country. IT can be made use of to make informed decisions backed by adequate data rather than groping in the dark.

However, implementation of IT plans in banks involves huge capital outlay at the initial stage and the sustained availability of trained manpower. In response to the entry of private sector banks who are armed with sophisticated technology. Some of the public sector banks have made adequate progress in the usage of technology within a very short period. However, banking system as a whole is yet to make adequate progress. Networking at least of the urban and metropolitan branches accounting for more than fifty per cent of the turnover is still in a nascent stage. Further, computerisation is achieved on a stand alone basis without much standardization of the software which may pose compatability problems later.

Human Resources Development

After the advent of IT which re-engineered the whole process of banking, the time lag usually associated with a number of traditional activities (e.g. realisation of outstation cheques, cash disbursement through ATM, etc.) has come down drastically. Another impact of the IT is that it enables banks to trim its hierarchy. It is also realised that the key to improve the bottom line in the changed scenario is through relationship banking characterised by enhanced of staff to cope up with the rapid changes presently sweeping the banking system. In this regard, the continuous infusion of fresh talents from the market and gradual reduction in the unproductive work force through devising and implementing voluntary retirement schemes assumes special significance. The gains achieved by banks in reducing the excess staff through evolving attractive voluntary retirement schemes remains to be consolidated. After shedding the excess flab which made the organisation unwieldy, customer satisfaction. The sustained viability and profitability of banks hinges, therefore on the adaptability the whole process of recruitement and retention of skilled work force needs to be focused by evolving an appropriate incentive system which rewards performance. In the changed scenario, recognition and provision of appropriate skill based training assumes paramount importance.

Shrinking Interest Rate Spread

One of the important consequences of introducing competition amongst the institutions and products is that the spread available to the market players between the deposit and lending rate is becoming smaller and smaller with the intensification of competition over a period of time. The spread between the deposit and lending rate reduced from as high as 7-8 per cent in 1991-92 to 1.5 to 4 per cent in 1999-2000. However the interest rate spread should be adequate to cover the administrative and establishment cost, provision for bad quality assets and adequate return on capital employed. In the midst of competition, charging of higher rate of interest than that of the competitors would result in adverse selection leading to further accumulation of NPAs in future. The only way left to cover such charges would be to achieve increased turnover through improved customer satisfaction at a reduced cost. Banks also need to venture more in the fee-based business. This calls for improved operational efficiency resulting from increased income and economy in the expenditure. The IT related products and services are being looked upon as holding the key for improved operational efficiency. Hence, the need for putting in place appropriate systems and procedures based on IT related products and services demands urgent attention of the banks.

Risk Management and Capital Adequacy Norms NPA Management

Though the level of Non Performing Assets (NPA) either as a per cent of bank credit or a per cent to total assets appears to have come down, in absolute terms, it remains substantially large at Rs. 60,841 crore at end-March 2000. The role played by the Debt Recovery Tribunals for expending the process of recovery has also not been encouraging. Legal reform to expedite the recovery of debt is underway but it may take some more time to crystallise. The results of efforts being made by the RBI for recovery of NPA by constituting Settlement Advisory Committee and compromise settlement is yet to be seen. However, banks need to tone up their administrative machinery for appropriate credit appraisal, follow up so that the emergence of fresh NPAs is minimised.

Risk Mangement

After the policy guidelines in regard to appropriate risk management in banks was made available from the RBI, significant progress has ben achieved by banks by putting in place a separate risk management system suited to the requirements of individual banks. However, the effectiveness of such a system depends crucially upon the capability of banks to identify, measure, monitor and control such risks. Efforts are being made at the international level to devise appropriate standards and codes so that the implications of different types of risks associated with banking is properly understood and acted upon. Risk management calls for a scientific approach and needs to be clearly understood both by the management and machinery at the middle and grass root levels. Apart from the above, risk management demands improved management information system to support the decision making with wider information base.

The 1988 capital accord of the Bank for International Settlement prescribed capital adequacy norm depending upon the riskiness of the portfolio of the banks. After the recognition of the implications of credit risk, market risk and operational risks embedded in the portfolios of the Balance Sheet, the earlier accord received a lot of criticism as it basically provided for credit risk alone. The amendment to the above accord made in 1996 allowed banks to provide for trading and market risks. The revised capital accord consultative package released in June 1999 intends to provide more risk sensitivity framework, also called three pillars approach consisting of minimum capital requirement, supervisory review process and market discipline. Another notable development in this regard is that banks at the international level regard the regulatory requirements of capital as the minimum and they try to maintain what is known as 'economic capital' which would be enough to cover all types of risks associated with the operations of banks and identified by the individual banks. In the Indian context, providing for additional capital on a continuous basis is going to prove as a daunting task.

Importance of the Treasury Management

To enable the process of securitisation, the restriction on banks on the extent of investment on preference shares, debentures and bonds were removed. Banks have to take decisions in regard to their deployment either in the form of conventional credit or through investments of the commercial sector. However, the successful management of the investment portfolio is a more complicated task as compared to the credit management. The efficiency of the treasury management should act as a sort of defence mechanism so that the value of the investment is insulated against market shocks.

The Integration of Treasury and Forex Management

After the emergence of the close linkages between the money and forex market, it is being realised that there should be an integrated management of treasury and forex operations as any lack of co -ordination might lead to taking up untenable positions either in the forex market or in the money market.

Internet Re-organisation of Banks

With a view to meeting the above challenges, banks have to re-engineer the whole process of their operations and redraw their organisational chart with appropriate specification of the roles in a transparent manner so that the role conflicts at different levels and lack of relegation of powers to the lower level is overcome. The easiest way to sub-optional performance can be laid through concentration of power in a few hands at the top rung of the hierarchy. The formation of separate committee with responsibilities of overall policy making, implementation in regard to Asset-Liability Management, Credit Management and the other risk management are generally being adopted by various banks as a feasible solution to the various methods of enabling decision making process.

Conclusion

To sum up, the finacial sector reform has catapulated the Indian banking system from its highly regulated and protected environment to a liberalised environment. This has encouraged individual banks to take initiatives and make innovations, focussing their business on viability and profitability, keeping in mind at the same time the increased customer awareness and competition. Increased capital adequacy in tune with international norms and above all provision of economic capital will definitely pose a major challenge to banks in India. Introducing appropriate technology and updating it periodically, strengthening the human resources management and above all, evolving appropriate norms for Corporate Governance, it should be possible for banks in India to address the various emerging issues suitably.The global challenges which banks face are not confined only to the global banks. These aspects are also highly relevant for banks, which are part of a globalised banking system. Further, overcoming these challenges by the other banks is expected to not only stand them in good stead during difficult times but also augurs well for the banking system to which they belong and will also equip them to launch themselves as a global bank.

References

Kalra, S. and Singh, K. (2000), "Economic Viability and Equity Issues in Financial Institutional Reforms: A Study of Regional Rural Banks in Punjab," *Indian Journal of Agricultural Economics,* Vol. 55, No. 4.

Majumdar, N. A. (1999), 'Reviving Rural Credit', *Economic and Political Weekly,* June 19-25.

Mishra, M. N. (1996), 'Rural Banking for Rural Poor', *Yojana,* Vol. 29, No. 24, January.

Puhazhendhi, V. and Joy, N. B. (1999), 'Rural Credit Delivery, Performance and Challenge Before Banks,' *Economic and Political Weekly,* January 16-23.

Rao, C. S. (2002), Economics of Rural Banking: Anmol Publication Pvt. Ltd., New Delhi.

Reddy, Y.V. (2000), 'Future of Rural Banking', *RBI Bulletin,* January.

RBI (Different Issues), Report on Trend and Progress of Banking in India, Reserve Bank of India Bulletin, Mumbai.

Satish P. and Gopal Krishna, S. K. (1997), 'Viability of Rural Banking,' *Economic and Political Weekly,* Oct. 18-24.

C. R. Gopalsundaram, "The Emerging Challenges for Banking Industry".

6

Indian Banks: Gearing up for Growth in the Era of Liberalisation

Mahesh Chandra Prasad

The process of economic reforms in India initiated in 1991 seems irreversible. There is enough evidence that the Government is withdrawing, though gradually, as a controller and licenser of private activity and allowing competition and market forces to guide investment decisions. The new Government at the centre, which assumed office in May 2004, has given enough indications, through its Common Minimum Programme (CMP) [Later rechristened as National Common Minimum Programme (NCMP)] and the 2004-05 budget proposals presented to Parliament on July 8, 2004, that it intends to proceed further with the economic reforms programme under way. The economic reforms process has encompassed all areas of the economy. The wide-ranging reforms, initiated and implemented since 1991, have induced greater efficiency and competitiveness in all spheres of economic activity and placed the economy on a higher growth path.

Obviously the banking sector is no exception to this. The reform process has placed banks under increasing pressure to improve performance including the quality and content of their business. Under globalization of economy, the competition from inside and outside has also put pressure on banks to improve customer service by all means like adoption of technology and work for image building. Banks need to substantially increase customer service with the help of technology and by using MIS.

RBI, keeping these in mind, has taken many step to fulfill the customers' expectations with the help of technological developments in the banking business. It constituted committees like Dr. Rangarajan Committee, Sarat Committee etc. mainly to study the issues relating to adoption of modern technology in banking business. In the light of the recommendations of these committees, RBI accepted as a policy to implement the adoption of technology in a phased manner. Further, RBI is playing a productive role enabling all banks to benefit from the technology.

Tomorrow is not going to be like today. There is no doubt that the technology revolution is going to be dominant in banking business. These charges have already had profound impact on banking sector and will continue to have in the days to come. Modern technology in banking business is an effective trump card in attracting business and it also renders better customer service. Under globalisation scenario, decision-making becomes highly complex and beyond the manual capacity. An efficient information system covering the entire network of branches and technology to analyse the information on a continuous basis have become essential inputs for a successful bank. In other words, a successful bank is one having far more efficient Management Information System (MIS) and strong technology than its competitors.

Technology is an ever growing process. E-Commerce and internet banking are two recent examples. The Information Technology products are also becoming more user-friendly and cost-effective to adopt.

Banks as Financial Intermediaries

The banks of a country are the channels for transferring resources from the surplus sectors to deficit sectors. Financial intermediaries play an important role in the growth process by encouraging saving and investment and by improving the allocative efficiency of resources. In India, the main conduits of credit are commercial and co-operative banks, development finance institutions (DFIs) and non-banking financial companies (NBFCs). Banks and NBFCs provide short term credit whereas DFIs specialise in extending medium-term and long-term loans.

A financial system refers to the whole gamut of institutional arrangements which help to mobilise financial surpluses of an economy and transfer them to areas of financial deficit. The financial system is the linchpin of a modern industrial economy. The financial system promotes savings by providing a wide variety of financial assets to the general public. Savings collected from the household sector are pooled together and allocated to various sectors of the economy for raising production levels. If the allocation of credit is socially equitable, it can help the uplift of the weaker sections of society and contribute to the speedy development of the backward regions of the country.

Prior to reforms, the mutual fund industry suffered from lack of competition and was dominated for long by one institution, namely the Unit Trust of India. Similarly, financial markets were characterised by barriers to entry, control over pricing of financial assets, high transaction costs and restrictions on movement of funds from one market segment to another.

Commercial Banks in India can be classified in a variety of ways. These are Scheduled and Non-scheduled Banks, Indian and Foreign Banks, Public Sector and Private Sector Banks and Regional Rural Banks.

Co-operative banking sector in India comprises urban co-operative banks and rural co-operative banks such as state cooperative banks and district central co-operative banks. They have an extensive branch network and reach out to people in remote areas. They have traditionally played an important role in creating banking habits among the lower and middle-income groups and in strengthening the rural credit delivery system.

Development Finance Institutions–The financial institutions, though outside the banking sector, are no less important. They include IDBI, IFCI, ICICI, UTI, LIC, GIC, NABARD, NHB (India level) and SFCs, SIDCs (State level).

Non-banking Financial Companies are financial intermediaries, which provide a variety of services including equipment leasing, hire purchase, loans, investments and chit fund activities. This sector comprises a heterogeneous lot of privately-owned, small sized financial intermediaries.

Mutual funds are an ideal medium for investment by small investors in the stock market. Mutual funds pool together the Investments small investors for participation in the stock market.

Assessment of Indian Banking

The RBI observed, "Financial sector reforms have been successful in bringing significant improvement in various market segments. Reforms have helped in improving the depth, liquidity and efficiency of markets. The money market is now reasonably developed with an array of instruments. The character of the Government securities market has changed from a captive market to a broad-based market. It has also become deep and liquid, which has enabled the RBI to pursue its monetary policy through market-based instruments. Various reform measures have resulted in sharp growth of the foreign exchange market. Reforms have also been successful in creating, by and large, orderly conditions in the market. The capital market has become a safer place for investors as various risks involved at various stages of trading and settlement have been either completely eliminated or reduced considerably.

Prior to reforms, the Indian Government determined the quantum, allocation and the price of credit, a situation called by some as financial repression. The banking sector suffered from lack of competition, low capital base, inefficiency and high intermediation cost. Ever since the bank nationalisation of 1969, the banking sector had been dominated by the public sector along with a high degree of financial repression characterised by administered interest rates and allocated credit.

Reforms in respect of the banking as well as non-banking financial institutions have focused on creating a deregulated environment and ensuring free play of market forces. Reforms in financial markets have focused on more transparency, introduction of new instruments, free pricing of financial assets and improvement in trading, clearing and settlement practices.

With a view to providing greater choice to customers and promote competition, the RBI is more liberal in permitting the entry of new private banks and foreign banks. Over the reforms period, the financial system has experienced tremendous growth in the sophistication and size of non-bank intermediation. Financial repression has eased substantially with the deregulation of interest rates and substantial removal of credit allocation. As a result of the policy changes made during the 1990s, the private sector has made significant progress in finance. It has a dominant position in securities intermediation and a new presence in the banking and insurance sector.

Banks Bring Big Fortune

The banking stocks emerged as the biggest gainers on the bourses, outperforming all other sectors as well as the benchmark Sensex and added more than Rs.45000 crore to their shareholders' wealth during the 1000 point journey to the 13000 milestone. The Bombay Stock Exchange's bankex index, which consists of 18 banking stocks, including giants like SBI, ICICI Bank and HDFC Bank has soared by more than 23 per cent when the market first hit the 12000 level (October 2006).

In contrast, the benchmark Sensex has added just about 8 per cent during the past 4 months–the time it took to more from 12000 to 13000, while indices of sectors like auto, pharmaceuticals, FMCG, metal as well as the PSUs, midcap and small-cap segments, lost value during this period.

Even today, banking index outperforms all the sectoral and segment indices with a gain of 1.9 per cent driven by smart gains in stock like ICICI bank, HDFC Bank and Allahabad

Bank. The State Bank of India, UTI Bank, Bank of India, Kotak Bank and Vijaya Bank also closed in the positive territory during previous months. The robust gains registered by banking stock in the recent past have been driven by impressive quarterly results, strong credit growth and capital raising initiatives. The credit growth story, softening yield on investment and positive impact on valuations from enhanced hybrid capital are among the major drivers of the banking sector rally.

Thus, the banking sector is in a process of rapid transformation. Reforms are continuing as part of the overall structural reforms aimed at, improving the productivity and efficiency of the economy. The role of an integrated financial infrastructure is to stimulate and sustain economic growth.

The Indian banking sector has grown and has displayed stability for the last several years, even when other markets in the Asian region were facing a crisis. This stability was ensured through the resilience that has been built into the system over time. The financial sector has kept pace with the growing needs of corporate and other borrowers. Banks, capital market participants and insurers have developed a wide range of products and services to suit varied customer requirements. The Reserve Bank of India has successfully introduced a regime where interest rates are more in line with market forces.

Banks have combated the reduction in interest rates and pressure on their margins by constantly innovating and targeting attractive consumer segments. Banks have also played an important role in promoting foreign trade of the country. And given the economic take off that India is currently experiencing, it is no wonder that this sector will be one of the biggest contributor to India's global position in the future.

Bank Loans: Buy your Dreams, Now!

Bank loans have made it possible that those desires are fulfilled without our having to shell out cash immediately from our pocket. All we have to do is fill a form, part with few personal details and voilal. We have ready cash in our hand. We can choose to pay back the money with interest in equated monthly installments (EMIs) spread over a period of time, say two, three or five years. Combine this with not having to produce any guarantors or collateral security and we have a really good deal in our hands. Whether it is for our personal requirement, or for the dream car or house we wanted to buy, there are loans for everyone, to suit individual needs and occasion. We could also get a lower rate of interest or a special rate of interest if our company has a tie-up with the bank. The buy now-pay later credit culture that loans endorse has fuelled the growing need in people to spend beyond their means and acquire things they have always secretly dreamt of obtaining for themselves and their families.

Thus, bank loans are a one-stop shop for all our requirements today. Starting out with minimum advantages for the person, loans have come a long way. In terms of categories, Personal, Housing and Auto loans are the most commonly availed and these three categories have evolved with the years to provide increased benefits to customers.

Assessment Bank Credit–Credit has grown at 30 per cent for the past two years and promises to do so in the current year as well. The RBI has indicated that it would like to see credit growth lowing down to 20 per cent. What risks does rapid credit growth pose and how should policy makers respond?

The IMF's World Economic Outlook has a chapter on credit booms in emerging markets that sums up the issues. Credit can grow rapidly for three reasons: financial deeping, normal cyclical upturns and excessive cyclical movements. Only the last qualifies as a 'Credit boom' that is potentially destabilising.

Credit Typically Grows Faster than GDP as an Economy Develops–That is what financial deepening is all about. It can also grow faster than GDP because firms' investment and working capital needs fluctuate with the business cycle. The problem arises when asset prices get magnified. For instance, when stock prices shoot up, a firms' net worth rises sharply. Banks may then be tempted to lend more. When asset prices collapse, banks find themselves in trouble.

The World Economic Outlook (WEO) also identifies a number of warning signs: a surge in capital inflows, a consumption or investment boom, a sharp rise in stock prices, a worsening of corporate leverage and an increase in banks' external borrowings. The first three are in evidence in India but not the last two.

Although household credit has grown rapidly in emerging markets in recent years, it remains low in relation to GDP. For emerging markets, the ratio of household credit to GDP averages 18 per cent; for emerging markets, the figure is 58 per cent. This difference is reflected in penetration rates for various segments : consumer credit, housing loans, credit cards etc. In taking a view on rapid credit growth, it is important to track exposure to sensitive sectors such as real estate (which comprises loans to developers, not individuals), capital market and commodities. These sectors together accounted for just 3.5 per cent of advances in the Indian banking sector in 2005.

Conclusion

Banks need to substantially increase customer service with the help of technology and by using MIS. Technology is an ever growing process. E-Commerce, ATM, Phone Line Banking and Internet banking are recent examples. The Information Technology products are also becoming more user friendly and cost- effective to adopt. In order to operate banks successfully and face competition, they have a good information system, technology and skills for decision-making, improved customer services and friendly attitudinal pattern of the personnel at all levels.

No organisation can become great or achieve prosperity without its people developing a sense of self discipline, humanistic motive, an enlightened membership awareness and capacity and willingness to do hard, efficient, co-operative work. Before the Banking Industry can reap the Internet advantages fully, the employees should be trained with proper tools depending upon the nature of the job they have been assigned to undertake. Various skills for the computerisation should be brought out in the banks with the advanced technology.

Apart from the training programme for the staff members, the awareness programme for the customers should also be a part of the banking operation. Thus, due to the technological revolution and to meet out the banking services in the new environment like, Internet, E-mails etc., trained manpower should be established in all the banks both in the rural and urban Banking Sector.

Elsewhere in USA and UK, Banks are merging with non-banks and with securities and insurance firms. Whereas in Central European Economies, Australia, Japan and Latin American countries, the reason for banking disintermediation respectively are investment funds, pension funds, postal saving schemes and tax by government on bank withdrawls. Tougher capital regulations have helped to preserve the funding advantage that some large companies have in accessing international capital markets on their own. And the growth so far can be seen with the declining share of banks deposits in the global finance from 45 per cent in 1980 to 30 per cent in 2006, with corresponding increase in the debt and equity securities. So, the banks have been forced to find additional sources of revenue including new ways of intermediating and fee-based business.

Higher operating cost is a major obstacle affecting the profitability of banks. The financial viability of bank can be enhanced by keeping a control on operating cost through higher labour productivity, updated technology, low cost funds and restructuring of unremunerating branches.

Changing financial scenario have opened up opportunities for banks to expand their global presence through self expansion, strategic alliances etc.

The financial sector reforms have brought Indian financial system closer to global standards. The process of strengthening the banking system has to be viewed as continuous one.

References

A. Banerjee and S.K. Singh (2001), *Banking and Financial Sector Reforms in India*, Deep and Deep Publications.

D. Kaith (1981), *Human Behaviour at Work*, Tata McGraw Hill Publishing Company Ltd., New Delhi.

D. S. Sangwan (2005), Human Resource Management in Banks, *IBA Bulletin,* June.

F. Cherunilam (1995), *Business Environment,* Himalaya Publishing House, Bombay.

J. Bhagwati (2006), IMF & World Bank: In a Time Warp, *Business Standard,* September 14.

L.G. Kulkarni (1994), HRD in Indian Banks, *IBA Bulletin,* January.

M. Arunachalam (1995), Motivation–What, Why and How, *The Hindu,* December 27.

N. Panchanathan (1998), Problem Solving Approach for Global Marketing Functions–An HRD Base, *Indian Journal of Training and Development.*

Reserve Bank of India, *Report on Trend and Progress of Banking in India,* 2004-05.

S. Guruswamy (2001), *Banking in the New Millennium*: Issues, Challenges and Strategies, Kanishka Publishers.

S. Jain (1995), *Quality of Work Life,* Deep & Deep Publishing House, New Delhi.

Sharad Kumar (1996), *Human Factors Contributing to* Organizational Effectiveness–with Special Reference *to Indian Banks, SBI Monthly Review,* Vol. XXXV, No. 12, December.

The Corporate Internet, World Bank Publications, 1998

The Hindu, February 19, 1998

The Hindu, September 30, 1998

The Indian Journal of Commerce, Vol. 59, No. 1, January-March 2006.

The Indian Economic Journal, Vol. 53, No. 1, April-June 2005.

V. Raghunathan (2006), *Banks vs. MFI vs. Moneylenders, The Economic Times,* September 30.

7

Performance of Indian Banks in Post–Reform Period

Shabnam Parween & Madhuker Dikshit

In the era of liberalization, Privatization and globalization Banking sector has become backbone of Indian economy. Now a days banking sector, being an integral part of Indian financial system has undergone dramatic changes reflecting the ongoing economic and financial sector reforms. Banking sector has playing a vital role in development of Indian agriculture and industries. Presently Banking has become Important part of economy & society. Banking industry which was highly regulated in pre-reform period is reorienting itself to face new challenges emerging in the financial sector globally. Basic factors responsible for performance of public sectors banks were stringent regulation, poor recovery process and above all lack of competition.

Objectives

- To review the financial sector reforms with special refer ence to the Indian banking sector,
- To conduct a comparative appraisal of financial performance of Nationalised Banks, state Bank Group private sector Bank & Foreign Bank in India during post reform era.

- To analyze the comparative performance of Banking sector in India.
- To suggest some measures and recommendations to improve the performance of Indian Banks.

Research Methodology

Data used in this paper are secondary in nature. They have been collected from the report on Trend and progress of Banking in India. 2004-05 and from the bulletin of The Indian Banker special issue "Database on Indian Banking"–06. For making analysis possible of financial performance of banking sector, Key financial performance indicators have been used. Namely Net interest income as % to Assets, operating profit as % to Assets, capital Adequacy Ratio (CDR), Return on Assets (ROA), Net NPA to net Advances, Business per employee, profit per employee, For these purpose percentages, tables and graphs have been used.

Performance of Banking Sector in post Reforms Period

In the post reform period, the performance of banking sector has been reasonably well. For the purpose of analyzing the performance of banks in India, banking sector is categorized into foreign sector banks, Indian private sector banks, Nationalised banks and SBI Group. For making comparative analysis seven key indicators of financial performance like Return an assets (ROA), operating profit as % to assets, Net interest income as % to assets, Net NPA to net Advances, Business per employee, profit per employee, and capital Adequacy Ratio (CDR) has been selected from the time period of 2001-02 to 2004-05.

Return on Assets (ROA)

Return on assets is defined as the ratio of profits after tax to average asset. It refits the efficiency with which banks deploy their assets. Table 1 Shows that ROA of foreign banks is comparatively higher than the other domestic Indian banks. Nationalized banks have very poor Return on Assets this is because. Private and foreign banks emphasis mare on earning income from non traditional source of income by selling diversified third party product for which no capital is required.

Table 1
Return on Assets

Banks	*2000-2001*	*2001-2002*	*2002-2003*	*2003-2004*	*2004-2005*
Nationalised Banks	0.33	0.69	0.98	1.19	0.89
State Bank group	0.55	0.77	0.91	1.02	6.67
Private Sector Bank	0.76	0.68	0.90	0.95	0.84
Foreign Bank in India	0.94	1.32	0.87	1.51	1.29

Source: IBA bulletin special Issue March 2003 & 2006.

Net NPA to Net Advances

Table 2 shows that the Nationalized banks, state bank group and private sector banks are more exposed to high potential losses in case of defaults. Net NPA to net Advances is 1.82 of foreign banks as compared to 7.01% of Nationalized banks in the year 2000-01. we can also show in the above given table that during the last five years all the banks are able to bring down the net NPA percentage. Implementation of the Securitization and Reconstruction of Financial Asset and Enforcement of security Interest Act 2002 (SAPFAEST Act.) has contributed positively to wards the reducing level of NPA in banks.

Table 2
Net NPA to Net Advances

Banks	*2000-2001*	*2001-2002*	*2002-2003*	*2003-2004*	*2004-2005*
Nationalised Banks	7.01	6.01	4.74	3.13	2.24
State Bank group	6.27	5.45	4.12	2.71	1.41
Private Sector Bank	5.44	5.73	4.95	2.84	3.28
Foreign Bank in India	1.82	1.89	1.76	1.49	0.86

Source: IBA Bulletin Special Issue March 2003 & 2006.

Operating Profit as % to Assets

Table 3 high lights that operating profit as % to assets of Foreign Banks are comparatively high than the Nationalised banks, State bank group & private sector Banks the above given table also shows that the during the last five year except year 2004-05 the operating profit as % to Assets is going up in all banks highest % is 3.64 for the Foreign banks in year 2003-04 and lowest is year 2000-01.

Table 3
Operating Profit as % to Assets

Banks	*2000-2001*	*2001-2002*	*2002-2003*	*2003-2004*	*2004-2005*
Nationalised Banks	1.29	1.83	2.34	2.70	2.20
State Bank group	1.42	1.94	2.27	2.62	2.43
Private Sector Bank	1.78	1.76	2.65	2.63	1.80
Foreign Bank in India	2.80	3.25	3.17	3.64	2.97

Source: IBA Bulletin special Issue March 2003 & 2006.

Net Interest Income as % to Assets

State banks group has gat very well Net interest income as % to Assets during the last five year which is reflected in the Table 4. In this time Foreign banks are not performing well. Foreign banks are continuously declining their percentage though all the banks are also losing their fate in this indicator there was 9.09% for the Nationalised banks in the year 00-01 and 6.91% in year 2004-05.

Table 4
Net Interest Income as % to Assets

Banks	*2000-2001*	*2001-2002*	*2002-2003*	*2003-2004*	*2004-2005*
Nationalised Banks	9.09	8.78	8.39	7.43	6.91
State Bank group	8.47	8.62	8.26	7.46	7.02
Private Sector Bank	8.87	6.17	8.26	6.99	6.14
Foreign Bank in India	8.28	8.47	7.75	6.74	5.95

Source: IBA bulletin special Issue March 2003 & 2006.

Business Per Employee

Table 5 reflects that foreign banks are generating two times higher business per employee as compared to their counter part Indian private sector banks and public sector banks. Foreign banks employ personnel with professional skill and experience and these are generally in less number while in case of public sector banks, they are overstaffed, moreover lack of promotional and incentive policies are the main reasons of poor performance of per employee business generation. The above given table shows that Foreign banks are generating to the tune of Rs. 940.29 lacs p.a. as compared to Nationalised banks which they are getting business per employees at Rs. 308.21 lacs p.a. in year 2004-05.

Table 5
Business Per Employee (Rs. in Lacs)

Banks	*2000-2001*	*2001-2002*	*2002-2003*	*2003-2004*	*2004-2005*
Nationalised Banks	159.93	197.29	220.80	25.74	308.21
State Bank group	159.68	181.52	205.11	233.56	409.32
Private Sector Bank	305.66	400.80	399.69	522.76	576.78
Foreign Bank in India	817.59	959.87	861.97	986.77	940.29

Source: IBA bulletin special Issue March 2003 & 2006.

Profit Per Employee

Table 6 shows that Foreign banks are generating very high profit per employee as compare to other Indian banks. Nationalized banks get profit per employee below one lack. Where Foreign banks are getting profit per employee around 11 to 15 lacs. The above given table reflects that foreign banks generating to the tune of Rs. 11.52 lacs as compared to Nationalised banks which they are getting profit per employees at Rs. 0.92 lacs and state banks group at 2.04 lacs and private sector banks at 3.85 lacs p.a. in year 2004-05.

Table 6
Profit Per Employee (Rs. In Lacs)

Banks	*2000-2001*	*2001-2002*	*2002-2003*	*2003-2004*	*2004-2005*
Nationalised Banks	0.32	0.51	0.65	0.78	0.92
State Bank group	0.77	1.21	1.59	2.00	2.04
Private Sector Bank	3.20	2.57	3.79	4.14	3.85
Foreign Bank in India	N.A.	12.17	15.45	14.35	11.52

Source: IBA bulletin special Issue March 2003 & 2006.

Capital Adequacy Ratio (%)

Capital Adequacy ratio is a measure of a banks financial health. The Ratio is provided by equity plus reserves over total assets. It reflects the soundness of a financial institution. As it shown in the Table 7 in the year 2004-05 the capital adequacy ratio of foreign banks is 14% as compared to Nationalised banks and state bank group where it is 13.20 and 12.40 respectively. Above given table shows that there were no much difference in capital adequacy ratio in all the banks.

Table 7
Capital Adequacy Ratio (Rs. in Crore)

Banks	*2000-2001*	*2001-2002*	*2002-2003*	*2003-2004*	*2004-2005*
Nationalised Banks	10.20	10.90	12.20	13.10	13.20
State Bank group	12.70	13.30	13.40	13.40	12.40
Private Sector Bank Old	11.90	12.50	12.80	13.70	12.50
Private Sector Bank New	11.50	12.30	11.30	10.20	12.07
Foreign Bank in India	12.60	12.90	15.20	15.00	14.00

Source: Report on Trend and Progress of Banking in India 2004-05.

Recommendations and Suggestions for Public Sector Banks

The forgoing analysis reveals that though there is phenomenal development in various banking sectors yet the public sectors in particular is still lagging behind major thrust areas such as asset quality, business per employee capital adequacy requirements, and profitability etc. Some suggestions and recommendations for improvement in performance of public sector banks are given below.

Check on Operating Cost

Higher operating cost is a major obstacle affecting the profitability of public sector banks. The financial viability of public Sector banks. The financial viability of Public Sector Banks can be enhanced by keeping by keeping a control on operating cost through higher labor productivity, updated technology, low cost funds and restructuring of unremunerating branches.

Rationalization of Staff Cost

In public sector banks, the proportion of wage bill is significantly higher as compared to private sector banks and foreign banks and in turn ratio of business per employee and profit per employee is quite low in comparison to other banks. Though public sector banks have tended to rationalized staff cost by VRS schemes, but employees per cost of Public Sector Banks has risen due to the changing composition of the staff and increased provisioning to wards superannuation liabilities. The manpower for each branch should be determined by customer profile. Network of branches and the level of computerization while ensuring to retain the best talent in the organization.

Human Resource Development

Human resource development is a critical factor which can play major role in enhancing business per employees and profit per employee. Public Sector Banks are lagging behind in Human Resource Development practices as compared to foreign and private sector banks. Public Sector Banks should devise continuous and compulsory training and development program in their organizations to inculcate professional work culture, and interpersonal skills. Efforts should also be made for making the staff technology savvy.

NPA Reduction and Deployment of Funds in Quality Assets

Asset quality reflects the soundness of financial institutions. Public Sector Banks should disburse their funds in quality asset to reduce NPA level. As the risk profile of banks lending is more diversifying, it is essential on the part of banks to pay adequate attention to quality of lending so that credit expansion could be on sustainable basis building upon higher profitability while ensuring financial stability.

Technology Up Gradation

Information technologies have become a business driver along with business enabler. Banks are increasingly adopting technology as a platform for their product offering so as to differentiate themselves from competition. Foreign Sector banks and infrastructure easily to adapt from the inception to operations. Public Sector Banks required considerable investment on computerization of branch networks and their operations to get quick and greater access to information.

Devise Effective Risk Management With Sound Internal Control System

As asset portfolio is diversifying, greater specialization in the technical aspects of lending and credit valuations is necessary. Strong internal control and supervision mechanism can play an important role in ensuing quality of assets and reduction in NPA lever. For financial stability, an efficient and sound risk management system is a pre-requisite. With better risk assessment capabilities, banks will be able to shed their risk averse attitude and extend more finance to unbaked segments of agriculture, industry and services. Banks must undertake an assessment of risk involved in retail banking segment and apply adequate risk management techniques.

Market Driver Approach and Customer Relation Management

Public sector banks are required to become market driven and innovative in product offering with customer oriented outlook which include factors such as extension of working hours, net banking tele-banking which enable the customers to transact as per their convenience. Public sector banks have an edge over the foreign banks in terms of their extensive reach through branch network and wide customer base. But to keep this wide customer base is a major challenge which public sector banks are facing. Sincere efforts are required to improve service orientation and customer's friendly approach in customers dealing in the public sector banks. Banks may create the database of new customers' through referrals of existing customers and using the same for increasing the customer base of bank.

Conclusion

Banking sector in India has given a positive and encouraging responses to the financial sector reforms. Entry of new private banks and foreign banks has shaken up Public sector banks to competition. The financial sector reforms have brought India financial system closer to global standards. With the India increasingly getting integrated with the global financial world, the Indian banking sector has a still long way to go to catch up with their counter parts.

References

Das, A. and Ghosh, S. (2004), Corporate Governance in Indian Banking: An Empirical Investigation, *Economic and Political Weekly*, March 20.

Nandwana N. M. (2004), Performance of Public Sector Banks, 2003-04, Central Bank of India, *Economic Bulletin*, p. 5-7.

Reserve Bank of India (2004-05), Report on Trend and Progress of Banking in India.

Economic and Political Weekly, March 2006 Various Articles, Vol. XLI, No. 11.

Goiporia M. N. (1991), "Commercial Banks: Performance and Prospects", in Ghonasgi, B.D. and Anagol, Malati (ed.)'s Financial System of India, Himalaya Publishing House, Bombay, pp. 61-67.

Hegde, Y. S. and Rajeshwari (1993), "Diversification in Banking-The Strategy and Response", *IBA Bulletin* (Special Issue) 15(1), January, pp. 87-90.

Mithani, D. M. (1993), "Some Reflections on Profitability of Commercial Banks", in Bhuleshkar, A.V. and Mithani, D.M. (ed.) Indian Banking in Transition : Structural Reforms, Anmol Publications, New Delhi.

Patel, I. G. (1994), "Some Reflections on Financial Liberalization", *The Journal of the Indian Institute of Bankers*, Vol. 65, No. 1, January-March, pp. 15-18.

Rangarajan, C. (1991), "Banking and Profitability", *Reserve Bank of Indian Bulletin*, Vol. XLV, No. 2, February, pp. 215-217.

———(1992), "Banking and Profitability", in Chaudhary, C.M. (ed.)'s Dynamics of Indian Banking, Printwell, Jaipur, pp. 35-46.

———(1993), "Changing Phase of Banking in India", *Pigmy Economic Review*, Vol. 38, No. 8, March, p. 1.

8

Banking Sector Reforms in India

Indrajit Prasad Roy & Binay Kumar

Commercial banking system in India comprises of the scheduled and non-scheduled commercial banks. The scheduled commercial banks are further classified as public sector and private sector banks. The public sector bank consists of State Bank of India and its seven Associate Banks and Nineteen nationalised banks. Apart from the other Indian scheduled commercial banks, the foreign banks are also included in the private sector banks.

The commercial banking system in India consists of 274 commercial banks and 4 non-scheduled banks in 1989. Of the 274 scheduled banks, 2 are foreign banks that specialise in financing foreign trade but also compete for domestic businesses. The largest scheduled bank is the State Bank of India (SBI) constituted by nationalising the Imperial Bank of India in 1955. The State Bank acts as the agent of the Reserve Bank. The subsidiaries of the State Bank act as the agents of the State Bank to transact government business as well as undertaking commercial functions. Other largest 14 banks with aggregate deposites of more than Rs. 500 million were nationalised in 1969 and 6 banks were nationalised in April 1980. The 28 Public sector banks account for about 90% of deposit and bank credit of all scheduled commercial banks.

Financial markets in India comprise of the credit market, money market, foreign axchange market, debt market, capital market and informal markets, which are well developed. Some of the less developed and integrated markets in India are the household finance markets. Agriculture finance markets, Non-Banking Financial Companies (NBFCs) market, and the insurance markets.

Objectives

One of the objectives of nationalisation of the banks in 1969 was to extend the reach of banking services to all parts of the country and to mainstream the neglected sectors of society. Since 1969 there has been a major significant spread of the banking habit and the banks have been the major mobilisers of savings in the economy. Despite significant achievements by the banking industry, the operational efficiency was unsatisfactory and characterized by low profitability, ever growing non-performing assets and relatively low capital base.

Most of the nations around the world, irrespective of their economic frame work and political idelogy, initiated restructuring through liberalisation. The elaborate reommendations of a committee of Financial System popularly known as Narasimham Committee made in November 199a are of great significance in this connection. It has placed great emphasis on the steps needed to improve the financial health of Indian Banks and to make them efficient, market oriented, vibrant, dynamic and globally competitive with the gradual implementation of financial sector reforms such as accounting practices and procedures of international tandards, capital adequacy norms, asset classification, Provisioning for bad debts, entry of private and foreign banks etc.

The winds of freedom and change sweeping across the financial sector due to reforms, have thrown open several challenges to the banks. The most important changes that have overtaken the nations banking industry relates to the fact that the competitive for as are sought to be introduced consciously in the financial services sector in general and banking industry in particular though the policies of interest rate deregulation and more particularly through a new liberal policy move to open doors wider to facilitate the entry of foreign banks and new private sector banks.

First Stage of Reforms

In India, the first phase of reforms in the banking sector was initiated since the formal announcement of the Union Budget of 1991-92 based on the recommendations of Narasimham Committee Report. A considerable ground has been covered in putting a place in financial system which can be meet the requirements of a more competitive and open economy. From 1992 there was an accelerated programme of banking sector reforms. Firstly, a concerted effort was made to more to market related rates of the interest. Secondly, the pre-emptions by way of the Cash Reserve Ratio (CRR) and the Statuory Liquidity Ratio (SLR) were reduced. Thirdly, there was a total freeing of deposit and lending rates with only very limited controls. Fourthly, following the Basic Committee standards prudential norms were prescribed for capital adequacy, income recognition and provisioning. Fifthly, the banks were required to observe stricter disclosure norms. Sixthly, the regulatory/ Supervisory system was strengthened by the setting up of a Board for Financial supervision. Lastly, institutional Strengthening was undertaken to ensure the progressive development and integration of the securities, money and forex markets.

In India, by and large the financial reforms have proceeded in four major directions. First, setting the policy conditions right and removing the operational constraints of the financial system. The second directional change sector through reform measures such as relaxation of entry and exit norms, reform has been the strengthening of market institutions and allowing greater freedom to financial intermediates. The fourth element of reform concerns the safety aspect of financial system.

In this research paper an attempt has been made to analyse the response of the banking sector to the changes unleashed in the country as a part of economic reform process in general and financial sector reform in particular. The structures and systematic changes that are strategically being brought about by RBI and Government in terms of the Narasimham Committee's recommendations played significant role in smooth transition of banking sector to the reform process, one has to keep in mind that the banking system consists of a few distinct response groups-namely the government and the regulatory authority Reserve Bank of India, the managements of bank employees and above all the customers.

Measures Taken by Government

The Government of India has initiated the reforms process by appointing the Narasimham Committee whose report become the magnacarta of the financial sector reforms. The Government can claim due credit for (a) dismantling the iron gates of entry of new banks both domestic and foreign especially in the private sector, (b) its willingness to dilute its overall equity stake in the nationalised banks upto 33 per cent, (c) establishing over the country, (d) merger of a weaker and non-viable banks whether in public sector or private sector (New Bank of India was merged with Punjab National Bank) and (e) introducing bank Ombudsman Scheme for redressing the grievances of customers.

Measures Taken by Reserve Bank of India

Reserve Bank of India also took major steps like market based interest rate structure both for deposits and advances, phased reduction of statutory pre-emptions like CRR and SLR, introducing internationally acceptable accounting norms for arriving at the bank's income and quality of assets, notably the income recognition, asset classification and provisioning norms.

1. *SLR*–The statutory Liquidity Ratio has been brought down in a phasesd manner to 25 per cent.
2. *CRR*–The Cash Reserve Ratio has reduced to 8 per cent with effect from 1st April 2000 which is significant step taken by RBI.
3. *Prudential Norms:* (i) As pere the RBI Guidelines, the minimum capital Adequancy Ratio of 9 per cent

should be maintained by the indian banks since March, 2000 according to Basle Committee recommendations. Most of the public sector banks have achieved the minimum capital adequacy norm of 9 per cent.

(ii) Income recognition norms are Primarily based on the principle of record of recovery rather than any subjective consideration. The income from NPA's is not recognised on accrual basis but is booked as income only when it is actually received.

(iii) In the light of the Narasimham Committee recommendations, the RBI has redefined the NPA's and advised the banks to classify their advances into four broad groups viz., standard, sub-standard.

4. *NPAs*–An asset becomes non-performing when it ceases to generate income for the bank. Previously a non-performing asset (NPA) was defdined as a credit facility in respect of which the interest or installment of principal has remained past due for a specified period of time which was reduced from four quarters to two quarters in a phased manner.

Due to the improvements in the payment and settlement system, recovery climate, upgradation of technology in the banking system etc; it has been decided to dispense with past due concept, with effect from March 31, 2001. Accordingly, as from that date, a non-performing assets (NPA) is an advance where:

(a) Interest and/or installment of principal remain overdue for a period of more than 180 days in respect of term loan.

(b) The account remains out of order for period of more than 180 days, in respect of an overdraft/Cash Credit(OD / CC).

(c) The bill remains overdue for a period of more than 180 days in the case of bills purchased and discounted.

(d) Interest and/or installement of principal remains overdue for two harvest seasons but for a period not exceeding two half years in the case of an advance granted for agricultural purposes, and

(e) Any amount to be received remains overdue for a period of more than 180 days in respect of other accounts.

With a view to moving towards international best practices and to ensure greater transparency, it has been decided to adopt the 90 days overdue norms for identification of NPAs, from the year ending 31st March 2004.

Banks are required to classify non-performing assets further into following three categories based on the period for which the asset has remained non-performing and the reliability of the dues :

(i) Sub-Standard Assets,
(ii) Doubtful Assets, and
(iii) Loss Assets

An advance is to be classified as sub-standard if it remains NPA upto a period of 18 months and will be classified as doubtful if it remains NPA for more than 18 months. An account can be classified as loss without any waiting period where the dues are considered uncollectible by the bank or internal or external auditor or RBI inspectors but the amount has not been written off wholly.

RBI has suggested that the Net NPAs of banks should be below 5 per cent. The Gross NPAs of PSBs were 19.5 per cent and Net NPAs were 10.7 per cent in the year 1994-95 which were reduced to 11.54 per cent and 6.16 per cent respectively in 2001-02.

Response of Banks and Employees

Coming to the rsponse of bank managements, results for the financial year 1994-95 encouragingly indicate that all public sector banks except one have show operating profits as against a very gloomy picture of 1992-93 and 1993-94. This is all the more creditable as the profits are worked after adopting the international accounting norms for income recognition, asset classification and provisioning.

In the case of most public sector banks business per employee and profit per employee have shown improvement in the recent period. The change in the attitude and helpful moves taken by the trade unions in facilitating to bring in higher productivity especially technology adoption etc., is perhaps significant in this context. The branches of PSBs are fastly computerizing and adopting e-banking, e-commerce techniques. The balance sheets of banks in India are to some extent transparent and further steps are taking to expose more transparency in them. Few banks urging the RBI to reduce their sake of more than 51 per cent capital with them.

Narasimham Committee II

The Committee on Banking Sector Reforms popularly known as Narasimham Committee II submitted its report in March, 1998. Its mandate was to review the record of financial sector reforms since 1991, implimented on the basis of the recommendations of the committee on financial system 1991 and to suggest measures of strengthening the banking system.

Second Generation Reforms

Narasimham Committee II (1998) rcommended second generation reforms which include:

(a) Capital adequacy requirements should take into account market risks and CARAR to be raised to 10 per cent from the present 9 per cent by 2000 and 10 per cent by 2002.

(b) Risk weight for a Government guaranted account must be 100 per cent and NPA level should be brought down to 5 per cent by 2000 and 3 per cent by 2002 and an asset should be classified as doubtful if it is in the substandard category for 18 months instead of the present 24 months and gradually to replace it by international norm of 90 days.

(c) Banks should avoid ever greening of their advances and there should be no further re-capitalization by the government.

(d) Government guaranteed accounts must also be categorized as NPAs under the usual norms.

(e) Banks should up date their operational manuals which should form the basic document of internal control systems.

(f) Recruitment of skilled manpower directly from the market be given urgent consideration and to rationalize staff strengths, an appropriate VRS must be introduced.

Banking sector have reacted positively in implementing these reforms. These reforms have enhanced the overall efficiency and viability of the banks which have resulted in the entry of new players in the field in the form of new generation private sector banks and foreign banks. These banks entered in the market with the high technical and professional capabilities with quality service like HSBC, HDFC, ICICI etc. The public sector banks with an international presence have forced to reanalyze their performance and approach. After the implementation of reforms and freeing from regulatory clutches, they have improved significantly over the last decade. State Bank of India stands 82nd ranking in the top 1000 banks in the world.

Conclusion

Banking sector in India has given a positive and encouraging response to the financial sector reforms. Entry of new private banks and foreign banks has shaken up public Sector Banks to competition. Changing financial scanerio have opend up oppertunities for banks to expand their global presence through self expansion, stretagic alliances etc. Banks are diverting their focus on retail banking so as to obtain access to low cost funds and to expand into relatively untapped potential growth Areas. Banking sector is set to witness the emergence of financial super markets in the form of universal banks. They are providing a suite of services from retail to corporate banking (a large segment) and industrial lending to invertment banking, besides providing personal financial services which is the highest growth segment. The financial sector reforms have·brought Indian financial system colser to global standards. The process of strengthening the banking system has to be viewed as continuous one. With the India increasingly getting integrated with the global financial world, the Indian Banking Sector has a still long way to go to catch up with their counter parts. Saying of a renowned Philosopher Jiddu Krishna Murthy "Challenges are new but responses continue to be old"– aptly applies to the banking industry.

References

Banerjee, Amalesh and Singh, S. K. (2001), 'Banking and Financial Sector Reforms in India'Deep and Deep Publications, pp. 338-360.

Prasad, L. S. N. (2003), 'Indian Economy: Retrospect and Prospects', Serial Publications, Delhi, pp. 170-234.

Das, A. and Ghosh, S. (2004), Corporate Governance in Indian Banking: An Empirical Investigation, *Economic and Political Weekly*, March 20.

Guruswamy, S. (2001), Banking in the new Millennium Issues, Challenges and Strategies. Kanishka Publishers, pp. 92-117.

Reserve Bank of India (2004-05), Report on Trend and Progress of Banking in India.

The Indian Journal of Commerce,Vol. 59, No. 1. Jan.-March, 2006, pp. 96-105.

The IndianJournal of Commerce, Vol. 52, No. 2, April-June 1999, pp. 42-49.

9

Financial Sector Reforms in India: An Analysis

Shaheda Khanam & Seema Dey

Reforms in the financial sector play an important role in the process of overall economic development of the country. Liberalisation of this sector is one of the significant strategies of structural adjustment programmes. Major stability in monetary and fiscal mechanism is supposed to chief prerequisite for financial sector reform. As stabilisation process is a long-term assessment, financial sector reforms have to be developed in the midst of macro-economic instability. The magnitude of instability has coined the problems of this sector so seriously that the policy-makers have no option except to attach them to the process of adjustment. Before opening the door of our economy to global competition, it is indispensable to have our domestic economy restructured and the financial sector reform is a forward step in this direction.

As regards its implementation planning, there are three stages of reform of this sector. The first stage is the stage of improvement of institutional framework by reducing direct loans and adjustment in the rate structure of interest of the banks. The second stage relates to the establishment of new institutions in the financial and capital markets and to start the entry of new units and foreign institutions in the domestic financial markets. And, the third stage is mainly concerned with the initiatives of deregulation in the mechanism of interest and removal of control on capital flow and movements. In this way, the implication of financial sector reform in the context of money market, corporate and banking sector is thoughtfully adjudicated here in this paper.

The present paper has been divided into four headings. The first is an introductory sketch of the issue of reforms of financial sector, second deals with the brief survey of innovative steps taken in the field of financial sector reforms, third part is an explanation of effective policy options as to how the process of planning of implementation could be made more accurate and effective and the last part is a presentation of concluding observation of the study.

Innovative Steps Initiated

The initiatives for financial sector reforms have been taken under the NEP which constitutes an important component of the overall structural adjustment process. Financial sector reforms which basically mean the improvement of efficiency and productivity of the financial sector raise a variety of issues.

Now the first question that arises is why does Indian financial sector necessitate a reform? Historically, the financial system in India was long characterised by control on entry and expansions, administered interest rates and allocation of credit for specific sectors with varying degrees of interest rate concessions. In case of commercial banks, both the deposit rates and lending rates were regulated. Unit recently, the rate at which corporate entities could borrow in the form of debentures was also regulated. The main aim of administered structure of interest rates was to enable certain priority sectors to obtain funds and concessional rate of interest. However, the quality of services rendered by the financial sector was not satisfactory and suffered from several drawbacks such as, low productivity and efficiency, deterioration in portfolio quality, low capital base of commercial banks, poor services to customers, sickness in financial institutions, systemic sickness and inability, lack of adequate modernisation, traditional information technology and lack of sense of responsibility. All these problems compelled the policy makers to think of introducing an agenda of financial sector reforms. The rationale for reform was that "the spirit of competitive efficiency that we are trying to bring about in the real sectors of the economy should cover the financial sector also, if adjustment in the real sector has to be meaningful and, secondly, can the financial sector can undertake this task only if the systems are healthy and profitable, it would need a considerable measure of operational flexibility and functional autonomy", (narasimham, 1991).

On the basis of the recommendations of the Chakravarty Committee (1985) and the Narasimham Committee (1991), a list of deregulatory steps of reforms were taken in the financial system of India whose gist is as under:

The first step of reform of financial sector involve setting up of SEBI (Stock Exchange Board of India) which has prepared a framework of comprehensive rules and regulations covering various aspects of the Stock Market and intermediaries operating therein with a view to improving trading practices, rules of disclosure and other measures of protection of investor's interests.

Secondly, the mutual funds for the private sector were freed to operate under the rules and regulations of SEBI.

Thirdly, there was a plan to set up a National Stock Exchange to allow screen-based trading and electronic clearing and settlement systems.

Fourthly, the pension funds, the mutual funds, etc. of foreign investors were allowed to make investment in the capital markets under the rules and regulations of SEBI.

Fifth, the statutory Liquidity Ratio (SLR) was brought down to 36.75 per cent and finally to 34.75 per cent in three successive reductions during the latter months of 1993. The SLR on increment deposits was brought down from 30 to 25 per cent.

Sixth, in addition to reduction in SLR, the Reserve Bank of India discontinued incremental Cash Reserve Ratio (CRR) of 10 per cent from April 1992. The base CRR, which had remained stagnant since July 1989, was reduced by one percentage point from 15.0 per cent to 14.0 per cent in two steps during April-May 1993. On account of the deposits which was at 63.5 per cent in 1991-92 declined to 45 per cent in the first half of 1992-93 Seventh, the number of lending categories was brought down from over 50 in 1989 to only 3 in December 1993.

Eighth, the existing private sector banks were allowed to expand without fear of nationalisation and new private sector banks were allowed to be set up provided they conformed to RBI guidelines for such banks.

Ninth, the minimum lending rates were brought down in four stages, from 20 per cent in October 1991 to 16 per cent in June 1993 and to 15 per cent in October 1993.

Tenth, a sizeable portion of fixed deposit was freed from interest rate control effective from April 17, 1993. The new limits for raising Certificates of Deposits (CDs) without any interest rate ceiling from this date were set equal to 10 per cent of the fortnightly average outstanding aggregate deposits in 1991-92.

Last, new accounting and prudential norms related to income recognition, provisioning and capital adequacy, in line with accepted international standards, were implemented in course of 1992-93. This was to ensure that the books of banks would reflect their true financial position which is a pre-requisite for effective monitoring and improving performance.

In this way the process of financial innovation involved in creating new instruments and techniques by unbundling and repackaging the characteristic to suit the changing requirements of structural adjustment particularly the needs of borrowers and investors.

But the task of reforming the financial sector is not so easy and now the process is on critical threshold. The monetary authorities have been increasing the area of discretionary decision making for banks and if the current busy session of credit policy is an indicator, the process of further deregulation will continue. But it is a moot question, what has been the result of the reforms so far and where do the banks stand? With the application of the new prudential norms, more particularly, the revised provisioning requirements, the real worth of assets of the banking system has emerged. Provisioning is a prior claim on profits and after making such claims, albeit not fully, many nationalised banks have dipped into the red. However, few strong banks after meeting their provisioning needs, adequately have shown profits, For instance, some subsidiaries of SBI and Canara Bank have made 100 per cent provisions, while PNB at 76 per cent and SBI at 55 per cent, have made adequate provisions. The provisioning norms will become stringent in the current year. It is reported that Government is likely to allocate Rs. 5700 Crore provided in the 1993-94 budget among the 19 banks subject to the latter signing the Memorandum of Understanding (MoU) with the RBI. But since many of the banks have made only minimum provisions during 1992-93, there will be large carry over to the next year, necessitating further contributions from the government.

The persistent slow-down in the industrial sector and further deterioration in some sub-sectors, may lead to further increase in Non-Performing Assets (NPAs), larger provisioning during the current year and further enhancement in the margin of losses for banks. Bank officials have a dislike for NPA and this combined with the capital adequacy requirements, they have been wary of creating new loan assets while the pressure of the government officials for creating new loan assets is quite apparent. The surplus liquidity with the banks have kept the Treasury Managers busy with investment of such funds in Government securities with Zero-risk and assured return. That the RBI has conceded to this particular situation is fully evident from the busy session of credit policy which aims at increasing the credit flows to the commercial sector. The Tandon and Chore Committee norms for working capital management have almost been given a go-by and it devolves on banks to bring about more professionalism in assessment of the credit needs of the borrowing client (Kurup, 1993).

Liberalisation of interest rate regime is an important aspect of financial reforms. There is progressive freeing of interest rates and banks have been given freedom to accept CDs to any extent while the borrowers have been given the further option of choosing alternative forms of finance in the forms of CPs. Complete freeing of interest rates is dependent on a host of factors, most important being achievement of macro-economic stability. This, therefore, may take more time and will hinder the smooth running of this package of reforms.

In a major turnaround, banks have been permitted to undertake a course of rationalisation of their branch network. They are free to close down unviable urban, metro and semi-urban branches. However, after due permission from the RBI and the respective State Government, such branches in rural areas with more than one branch may be closed. But such action of bank will create a confusion and resentment among the rural people which ultimately will have to be faced by the banks.

As a forerunner to the process of system restructuring, the New Bank of India has been merged with Punjab National Bank. This is the first step of merging two nationalised banks, one being the smallest and loss-making and another a large and profitable bank. Within the 'Shut-period' of 15 days, normalcy has been achieved and the bank has been able to provide uninterrupted service to the customers. Since the overall impact of the merger would be known only in the longer-run, whether more such mergers will take place is anybody's guess. The scheme of merging of loss-making bank with a profit-oriented bank is nothing but an attempt to put the latter into an infectious zone of sickness.

Though the reforms are broad enough in contents, many vital areas still remained untouched. For instance, the reconciliation of profitability with social responsibility still remains a challenge. The crucial area of functional autonomy for nationalised banks has not been taken into account. The rural credit structure needs thorough revamp while suitable changes will also be required in the supervisory practices. Without paying proper attention to these problems of financial sector, the pace of success of reforms will be slow (Kurup, 1993).

Suggestions

Now the question arises as how to make this package of reforms more effective in financial sector. In this connection, a list of following viable suggestions may be forwarded for consideration.

In the first place, the gap between the conditions of domestic financial markets and international financial markets should be minimised.

Second, steps should be taken to strengthen the domestic financial resources.

Third, the package of Directed Credit Programmes of the commercial banks in India should not be held responsible solely or even largely, responsible for the deterioration in the profitability, efficiency and productivity of the India Commercial banking system, as was pointed out by the Narasimham Committee, but on the contrary, the concepts of growth of the banking system should be redefined in the context of the requirements of the financial infrastructure of a developing economy.

Fourth, the success of institutional development would depend on the nature of social conflict in each country. Labour is the engine of economic growth which has to be included in the national economic decision-making process. Hence, the labour unions should be made to shoulder the burden of social responsibility of complementing their real influence over social and political like in our country.

Fifth, it is suggested that the RBI should raise the interest rates of FDR to mop up the funds from small and medium investors.

Sixth, in the interest of our socio-economic requirements, loan melas and waivers should be stopped and autonomy be granted to banks. In the name of financial viability and obsession with high profitability, the needs of vital sectors of agriculture and small scale sector should be assigned more roles.

Seventh, the financial system should not be considered in isolation in formulating development strategy for economic development. Financial policies can be more effective in almost all development activities of the country.

Eighth, the banking sector reforms must be enforced strictly and should be based on the assessment of facts of reforms enunciated by Narasimham Committee.

Ninth, the reforms in Capital Market should reflect the true health of the economy and steps should be taken to ensure that the security scams do not take place in future.

Tenth, the market participants must be alert to respect the concept of integrity of credit and the ethics of financial system. As banks are losing the principle active intermediately role, perhaps, a larger number of private banks and mutual funds would lead the entire scam.

Last, the reforms must be sensitive to the social needs and ground realities, can not translate into action by 'analytical obsoletism' alone but be in the context of aspirations and needs of vast mass of population and be guided by the consideration of safeguarding their interest.

Conclusion

On the basis of above observations we may conclude that the initiatives of reforms, as adopted, are conducive to improve the functions of intuitional financing agencies by rendering their services to the needy people at grass roots level, particularly the vulnerable sections of the society. Improvement in the conditions of profitability in an accomplishment of target for the future financial viability of public sector commercial banks by raising operating income on the one hand and reducing loan loss risk on the other. This reform of financial sector is a guarantee of non-repetition of any scandal or security scam in the country in future because the powers of SEBI have already been enhanced and its functions are also transparent. By adopting such package of reforms in the financial sector, the issue of strengthening monetary policy like the Open Market Operations as an instrument of credit control, are effective and the problem of debt management has become easy and adjustable. Moreover, placement of check on reduction in SLR and CRR which has come to an unsustainable stage has become an effective tool to improve banks' profitability and operational flexibility. The most striking achievement of the financial sector reform has been that 1991-92 to 31.71 per cent in 1995-96.

The priority sector lending, one of the important props of this reform, has witnessed a sizeable increase in credit. The total bank credit of all PSBs steadily increased from Rs.1,08,918.57 crore in 1991-92 to Rs.1,69,038.46 crore in 1995-96. In this way, it is vivid from the foregoing analysis that the financial sector reform, as done by the Government of India in 1991, is much responsive to the correction of ills of the monetary and financial system of the country.

References

Government of India, Report of the Committee on the Financial System, New Delhi, November, 1991.

Public Sector Commercial Banks and Financial Sector *Reform: Rebuilding for a Better Future,* Discussion Paper, New Delhi, December 1993.

Malhotra, R. N. (1994), *Reforming the Financial Sector,* Eleventh Dr. C.D. Deshmukh Memorial Lecture, New Delhi, January, at India International Centre.

Narasimham, M. (1993), *Financial Sector Reforms: The Unfinished Agenda,* The A.D. Shrooff Memorial Lecture, Bombay, September.

Patel, I. G. (1993), 'Liberalisation : What Banks Can Do?" *Hindustan Times,* December 20.

Rangarajan, C. (1993), Banking Sector Reforms' *Reserve Bank of India Bulletin,* March.

Brahmananda, P. R. (1992), "Towards a New Adjustment and Reform Rationale, *Indian Journal of Applied Economics,* 1, 3 and 4 April-September.

Bhat V. V., 'On Restructuring Financial System', *EPW, XXVII,* February 8, 1992. 'On Improving the Effectiveness and Efficiency of the Financial System in India', *EPW,* October 12, 1991.

10

Working and Performance of Indian Banks During Post Reform Era

U. N. Singh & Birendra Kumar Yadav

It is now a widely accepted fact that during recent years a significant transformation has been witnessed by the Indian banking system. Before the institution of financial sector reforms, Indian banks operated in the highly controlled, thoroughly monitored and over regulated environment with regard to different parameters, such as: (i) Branch location, (ii) Deposite and lending rates and (iii) deployment of credit. Further in view of the social and political obligations of the democratically elected government of India, to be fulfilled mainly through the banking sector, profitability was not considered as an important yardstick of their performance. The main thrust of banking activities had been on social banking right from the time of nationalization of 14 major scheduled commercial banks in 1969. Enhancing the branch network in rural and semi–urban areas (on priority basis) was emphasized accordingly. In addition to these, several other responsibilities, viz; financing the fiscal deficit and facilitating the development of some specific sectors as reflected in 'high and increasing prescription of SLR 'and the banks also included' direct lending'. By and large, banking remained concentrated in the public sector and functioned in a highly regulated environment.

Financial Sector Reforms

'The Financial sector Reforms' of the country, particularly introduced for up gradation and a qualitative change in the banking sector include:

(i) Deregulation of interest rates,

(ii) Capital adequacy norms,

(iii) Internationally accepted prudential accounting norms for income recognition,

(iv) Assets classification and provisioning of NPAs

(v) Entry of new private and foreign banks,

(vi) Reducing Government's stake in the equity of banks etc. These have, of course, changed the character of banking.

Commercial character of banks with profit making motive on the top is now being adopted in varying degree by one all banks. They play their role within the prescribed regulatory framework and fast changing economic environments that is emerging in the post liberalization and globalization era. To enhance the quantum of profit and profitability by securing larger deposits for earning higher incomes through interests on loans/advances have become the buzz words. Profitability has become the parameter that give a competitive edge for banks in the market-oriented system. Banks are going to the capital market to augment their capital base besides emphasizing on internal generation of surplus and without attractive profitability track record they cannot attract investors in domestic as well as overseas capital market. In this way, profitability at the corporate level has become a dominant indicator for assessment of the OPERATIONAL EFFICIENCY of a bank.

According to the recent "Trends And Progress Of Banking In India" of the Reserve Bank of India, commercial banks in the country will become stick unless they increase the profitability of their operations by improving the quality of their lending. Not only this, if the banking industry is to survive in the country, it is imperative that the effectiveness and profitability of the bank branches/unit are improved.

Internet Banking: A Step Towards Globalization

In India, INTERNET BANKING is slowly taking roots. A number of bank have already taken banking portals allowing their customer to access facilities, like: obtaining information, querying on their account, etc. it is not long before more number of banks would start using Internet as a delivery channel in view of the tremendous cost saving that it would provide. Rough estimates confirm (assuming the TELLER COST) at Rs. 1 per transaction put ATM transaction cost bat 45 paise. The more cost conscious banks in the country are therefore, actively considering the use of the internet as a channel for providing services. Fully computerized banks, with better management of their customer base are in a stronger position to cross-sell their products through this channel.

Challenges before PSBs and Globalization

In tune with the liberalization if Indian economy, a number of initiatives were to introduce reforms in the banking sector of India as well. In this context, with a view to breath fresh surviving volition and infuse a sense of competition with ability to complete other financial institutions 'both formal and informal' and innovation in the banking sector, the recommendation of the two committee under the Chairmanship of Shri M. Narsimham, former Governor of the Reserve Bank of India, were implemented to a great extent.

The SLR requirement was brought down to 25% from the high level of 389.50% prevailing prior to the introduction of reform measures. Simultaneously, the prices of governmental borrowing from the banking system were tuned to market rates of interest and bitter complain made by the banking system oftenly about pre- emption started finding.

Investment in government securities more attractive. As a result of it, many banks now have a government securities more attractive. As a result of it, many banks now have a government securities portfolio much more than what is actually needed for their SLR requirements. The CRR was also brought down from the high level of 25% on incremental demand and time liability to 5.5%$ and the rate of interest on balances over CRR of 3% was raised to 6.5% at the Bank Rate. Liquidity of the banking system were achieved as substantial improvement as a result of these two measures. Reserve bank of India was earlier empowered to decide the rates of interest on deposits among banks, giving the best possible deal to customers. The threat of survival of different banks in India starts fro here in the form of challenges of increasing share of (i) old private sector Banks, (ii) New Private Sector banks and (iii) Foreign Banks in the total assets of Scheduled Commercial Banks.

Challenges of Declining Share of Public Sector Banks

Out of the total assets of Scheduled Commercial Banks (SCBs), Public Sector Banks (PSB's), no doubt, have continued to occupy predominant position (80.2% of the total assets) followed by Foreign banks (7.5%), Old private sector banks (7%) and New private sector banks (5.3%). But, discouraging scenario of the aspect is that there has been a steady decline in the share of PSBs in the total assets of SCBs during 1995-96 to the end of March, 2000(1999–2000). It declined by 5.09% during the period (from 84.5% of 1995–69 to 80.2% in 1999–2000). On the other hand, share of old private sector banks witness an increase of 12.09% i.e., it went up from 6.2 % of 1995–96 to 7% in 1999–2000. An all time high increase of 278.57 % in the share of New private sector banks to total assets of SCBs was observed (it went up from 1.4% to 5.3%) during the

Table 1
Share of Different Bank Groups in the Total Assets of Scheduled Commercial Banks (in per cent)

Year	*Public Sector Banks*	*Old Private Sector Banks*	*New Private Foreign Banks*	*Foreign Banks*
1995-96	84.5	6.2	1.4	7.9
1996-97	83.0	6.6	2.2	8.2
1997-98	81.7	6.9	3.2	8.2
1998-99	81.0	6.9	4.0	8.1
1999-2000	80.2	7.0	5.3	7.5
Percentage change over the year 1995-96	(-) 5.09	12.90	278.57	(-) 5.06

period. Share of foreign banks also showed upward trend from 1995– 96 to 1997–98. In the last two years it declined marginally from 8.2% to 8.1% and 7.5% during 1998-99 and 1999–2000 respectively. However, final fall comparison to 1995–96 (7.9%) Was of 5.06%, i.e. less than that of PSBs.

Table 2
Trend in Bank's Profitability
(Net Profits as a Percentage of Total Assets) (in per cent)

Year	*Public Sector Banks*	*Old Private Sector Banks*	*New Private Foreign Banks*	*Foreign Banks*	*All Scheduled Commercial Banks*
1995–96	(-) 0.07	1.06	1.85	1.58	0.16
1996-97	0.57	0.91	1.73	1.19	0.67
1997-98	0.77	0.81	1.55	0.97	0.82
1998-99	0.42	0.48	1.03	0.69	0.47
1999-02	0.57	0.84	0.97	1.17	0.66
Percentage change over base year	914.28	(-) 20.75	(-) 47.57	(-) 25.95	312.5

Better Profitability Performance of PSBs and SCBs

Date related to trends in bank's profitability of Public Sector Banks (net profit as percentage of total assets) clearly reveal a very high and encouraging increase of 914.28% increase in case of public sector banks during the post reform period from (-)0.07% of 1995-96 to 0.57% in 1999-200. All scheduled commercial banks also witness a significant increase in 312.5% during the period (from 0.16 to 0.66%). These figures undoubtedly show its competitive advantages/better position over Old private sector banks, New private sector banks and foreign banks. Net profits of these two types of private banks and Foreign banks showed declines of (-) 20.75% (-) 47.57% and (-)25.95% during the period 1995-96 to 1999-2000 (i.e., it slided down from 1.06% to 0.84%, 1.85%, to 0.97% and 1.58% to 1.17%) respectively (Table 2). Profitability trend/scenario of banks in India, thus confirms that PSBs and SCBs have been moving forward very successfully to face the challenges of globalization.

Superior Customer Service: Need for Survival

In the phase of globalization, Indian banks have been operating in a highly competitive business environment. Average population per bank branch can be used for gauging the extent of competition among banks in India. In 1969, the average population per bank branch was estimated at 64,000 which dropped to 15,000 in 1997 and this ratio was as low as 6000 people per branch in some areas (RBI). A given population is since being created to and served by more banks, the saving of the population get distributed among various banks which leads to compel banks for competitive to secure good quantum of deposits. Similarly, banks are also faced with competition on the advance front. With the slowing down of economy banks are oftenly fearful in making investments for bankable projects. Established corporates having funding requirements are offered to be assisted by a large number of Banks, and as a result, they are in a position to dictate interest rates. More and more corporates are able to access loans at sub prime lending rates as low as 7.5% per annum.

In a competitive scenario mentioned above, banks offering superior Customer Service to their depositors and to their borrower will only survive. Superior customer service will be the only differentiating factor among banks offering very similar products in the future. Customer will continue to patronize only those banks that can provide excellent service. In order to ensure superior customer service, bank will only those banks that can provide excellent service. In order to ensure superior customer service, banks will have to introduce easy procedures and processes that provide excellent quick service and better service including insurance coverage to their customer/depositors.

Structural Strength of Indian Banking: Present Position

Expansion of banks/financial institutions in regard to its number and operational performance at different tiers/level also provide mighty back up to face the challenges of globalization. No doubt, the policy developments have resulted in a rapid increase in the total number of bank since

1969. The commercial banking group consists of 27 public sector banks, 31 Private sector banks, 42 Foreign banks and 196 Regional Rural Banks. Public sector banks are further classified in two categories:

(i) Nationalised Banks (19 in number) and State Bank of India and its associates (08) with 23 old private sector banks and 08 new Private sector banks, Private Sector Banks (as a whole) have major role to play. Apart from Scheduled commercial banks, 67 Scheduled Co-operative Banks (along with supporting network of 51 Scheduled Urban Co-operative Banks and 16 scheduled State Co-operative Banks) have been working in our country. In this way, 290 (including 27 PSBs, 196 RRBs and 67 Scheduled Co-operative Banks) have been operating to survive against the challenges being posed by all in total 73 Nos. (including 31 Private sector banks and 42 foreign banks) belonging to non public sector banks category. Thus, the strength of covering wider area of the nation by these Scheduled Commercial Banks and Urban and State Co-operative Banks can be exploited in a better way by encouraging the employees and officers of all cadres to consider the depositor's account holder and other type of bank customer to be GOODESS of PROSPERITY and accordingly behave with positive response and attitude to satisfy their banking needs.

Increasing NPAs: Threat to Indian Banking

According to a report on TREND AND PROGRESS OF BANKING IN INDIA, gross non-performing assets (NPAs) of Scheduled commercial banks as a percentage of gross advances increased from 14.4 % at end of March, 1999. There has been an improvement in the performance of the scheduled commercial banks during 1999-2000 as this percentage declined to 12.8 % as the end of March 2000. However, in absolute terms, the gross NPAs increased from Rs. 50,815 crore as at the end of March 1998 to Rs. 60,841 crore at the end of March, 2000. Net NPAs increased from Rs. 23,761 crore to Rs. 30,152 crore during the same period. It means there increases of 19.7 % and 26.8 % in gross NPAs and net NPAs respectively during the above period.

Thus, during 1999-2000 also there has been an increase in the non- performing assets of the banking industry despite various steps taken by the banks which must be a matter of concern and immediate policy initiative to be taken by them.

It will not be out of order to mention here that the banking system still continues to show weakness in its solvency. It is true that banks have, by and large, reached the capital adequacy ration, but neither it is an evidence of the strength of banks, nor a source of satisfaction unless bank's assets achieve the *Quality Standard* and become liquid and safe from the point of view of recovery in time. Delayed recoveries result in assets and liabilities mismatch in the sense that technically assets liabilities may match, but assets become non- performing and liabilities have to be redeemed. This type of mismatch also runs into insolvency. However, opportunity before Indian banking system does also exist in the form of market of the order of more than, Rs. 50,000 crore which can be converted into a *Credit Default Protection Instrument.* In case of default by the loanee even after several offers to repay their outstanding in easy installments, this instrument can be traded in the market.

It is worth mentioning here that an increase in non-performing assets result in low amounts of bank's profits because of provisioning margining etc. Banks have to make provision for non performing assets and this will result in a decline of the market capitalization of these banks due to change in perception of the investor. Almost all the banks have recorded loss in their market worth. There has been deterioration in market capitalization also. In this situation, it becomes pertinent for the banks to make all possible efforts (including departmental pressure, legal and filing of certificate case) to hedge their loans and advances so that their quality of assets remain intact.

Reduction of PSBs NPAs: Need of the Hour

One of the most important dimension of the banking sector reforms was reduction of the Non- performing assets (NPAs).

In fact, the whole effort to bring an overall improvement in the banking sector to make it sustainable with a view to face the challenges and forces of globalization would collapse if the banks are not able to contain and reduce their NPAs. It will be impossible for a bank with high NPAs to be either vibrant or competitive. Actually NPAs are the assets that do not yield any return. It is like owning a vast field where nothing grows through the field was purchased at high rates.

Technically, NPAs consist of three categories of assets (i) Sub-standard (ii) Doubtful and (iii) Loss AS per the new norms for recognition, identification and classification of assets (changed with effect from March 31, 2001) assets classified as NPAs for a period upto two years belong to sub- standard category, while doubtful assets are those that remain NPAs for a period beyond two years. Loss assets are those which are identified as such either by banks themselves or internal/ external auditors or RBI, but not written off.

According to the Economic survey (2002–2003), gross NPAs of the public sector banks were of the order of Rs. 56,507 crore at end of 2001-02. Private sector banks had gross NPAs of Rs. 11,672 crore and Foreign banks were having NPAs Rs. 2,726 crore. Total gross NPAs of the banking sector, thus amounted to Rs. 70,905 crore. Having calculated it in terms of percentage to gross advances, it was estimated at 10.4 per cent. This means that banking sector does not earn any return on an investment of Rs. 70,905 crore. In this regard, it can be treated as positive effort of Union Government that the successive Finance Ministers have been to fight this menace of growing NPAs.

It is a positive trend that these efforts are resulting into declining NPAs in percentage terms. Gross NPAs as percentage of gross advances were 12.7% in 1999-2000. It came down to 11.4 % in 2000–01 and 10.4% in 2001-02. Similarly encouraging trend could be observed in terms of net NPAs to net advances during the period 1999-2000 to 2001-2002. Net NPAs as percentage of net advances by the banking sector marginally came down from 6.8 per cent in 1999- 2000 to 6.2% in 2000–01 and it further declined by 0.7% to touch the lower level of 5.5% in 2001-02. These data related to declining NPAs, no doubt suggest that the Banking sector reforms are on the right track, though the pace of reduction of NPAs does not allow the banking sector to relax, but promotes bank management policy makers and the government to gear up its efforts for the development of the sector as a whole. There was a significant decline in the non-performing assets (NPAs) of SCBs in 2003-2004, despite adoption of 90 days delinquency norm from March 31, 2004. The gross NPAs of SCBsa decline from 4.0 per cent of total asset in 2002-03 to 3.3 per cent in 2003-04. The corresponding decline in net NPAs was from 1.9 per cent to 1.2 per cent. Both gross NPAs decline from Rs. 68,717 crore in 2002-03 to Rs. 64,787 crore in 2003-04, net NPAs decline from Rs. 32,670 crore to Rs. 24,617 crore in the same period. There was also a significant decline in the proportion of net NPAs to net advance from 4.4 per cent in 2002-03 to 2.9 per cent in 2003-04. The significant decline in the net NPAs by 24.7 per cent in 2003-04 as compared to 8.1 per cent in 2002-03 was mainly on account of higher provision(upto 40 per cent) for NPAs made by SCBs. The decline in NPAs in 2003-04 was witness across all bank groups. The decline in net also increased. Measures taken to reduce NPAs include reschedulement, re-structuring at the bank level, corporate debt restructuring, and recovery through Lok Adalats, Civil Courts and Debt Recovery Tribunals and compromise settlements.

Suggested Measures

Keeping in view the changed character of banking in India after the financial sector reforms in terms of : (i) Deragulation of interest rates, (ii) Capital adequacy norms, (iii) Internationally accepted prudential accounting norms for income recognition, (iv) Assets classification and provisioning of NPAs (v) Entry of new private and foreign banks and (vi) Reducing Government's stake in the equity of banks, all scheduled commercial banks, should introduce the facilities of tele banking along with the provisions of DAY-AND NIGHT SERVICE including SUNDAY also by recruiting four sets of employees/officials each required to work for six hours only on appreciable CONSOLIDATED HONORARIUM basis. To

Items	*Gross NPAs (Rs. Crore)*			*Percentage to gross advances*			*Percentage to total assets*		
	2001-02	*2002-03*	*2003-04*	*2001-02*	*2002-03*	*2003-04*	*2001-02*	*2002-03*	*2003-04*
Bank Group									
1. Public	5647	5409	5153	11.1	9.4	7.8	4.9	4.2	3.5
Sector	3	0	8	9.6	8.1	5.8	4.4	4.0	2.8
2. Private	1166	1178	1035	5.4	5.3	4.6	2.4	2.4	21
Sector	2	2	5	10.4	8.8	7.8	4.6	4.0	3.3
3. Foreign	2726	2845	2894						
4. SCBs	7086	6871	6478						
(1+2+3)	1	7	7						

Items	*Gross NPAs (Rs. Crore)*			*Percentage to Net advances*			*Percentage to total assets*		
1. Public Sector	2795	2486	1886	5.8	4.5	3.0	2.4	1.9	1.3
2. Private Sector	8	7	0	5.7	5.0	2.8	2.5	2.3	1.3
3. Foreign	6676	6882	4857	1.9	1.8	1.5	0.8	0.8	0.1
4. SCBs	920	921	900	5.5	4.4	2.9	2.3	1.9	1.2
(1+2+3)	3555	3267	2461						
		4	0	7					

face the challenge of open competition from foreign banks and other private domestic banks, commercial banks in the country will have to improve its quality of lending through providing very high number of 'secured loans/advances; particularly to salaried and even to farmer or other property holders against the mortgage of their landed property/houses other collateral requirement should be minimum, of course at lower rates of interests (keeping in view the purpose of the loan and economic, social/academic dignity of the loanee). After providing basic training regarding use of INTERNET banking to bank employees all branches of PSBs cost should introduce INTERNET BANKING in different phase as its PER TRANSACTION cost is estimated at only 10 paise in comparison to Rs. 1 for TELLER, 45 paise (ATM), 35 paise for PHONE BANKING and 20 paise for DEBIT CARDS.

Despit major share of 80.2% of the PSBs in total assets of Scheduled Commercial Banks, its declined trend (by 5.09%)

during 1995-96 to 1999-200, in comparison to increases of Old and New private sector banks from 12.09-278.57%) respectively and a comparatively low decline of Foreign banks (5.06%) will have to be seriously checked by enhancing the quantum of total deposits through announcing attractive incentive on short and long term deposits.

Keeping in view the highly competitive business environment, Indian bank will have to improve its customer service by specially instructing employees and officers of all cadre to maintain timeliness, courtesy, and assurance for discharge of obligation in letter and spirit (considering the importance of customer's valuable time). Level of customer's service may also be enhanced by positioning well trained and knowledgeable employees (fully acquainted with all bank related matters) on the front desks of banks so that all queries of new prospects or old account holders are satisfied/ answered at one table/window.

Better performance of all the public sector banks, RRBs and Scheduled Co-operative Banks (290in number) over Private sector banks and Foreign banks (73 in number) could be achieve by bringing an overall attitudinal change in the working culture of the employees and officials of these Banks through making them individually responsible for the closure of accounts of the depositors mainly due to bad behavior or non co-operative attitude of particular employee/official/ Branch Manager of the concerned bank, BANK Employees Association should also be warned against coming forward to protect such erring employees/officials.

19.7% increase in gross NPAs and 26.8% increase in net NPAs during March 1998 to March 2000 (for scheduled commercial banks in India) should be effectively checked and reduced by (i) Ensuring timely recoveries by keeping in regular touch with the loanees, (ii) Mismatch of assets liabilities be minimized, (iii) Converting potential market of Rs. 50,000 crore in India into a credit default protection instrument, (iv) By checking deterioration of Market Capitalization, and (v) By creating pressure on big business houses and politicians to repay their bank loans with interests and other outstanding.

Higher gross amount of NPAs in case of Public sector banks (Rs. 56,507 crore at the end of 2001–02) has to be effectively reduced by evolving ways and means to check it after having searched the cause responsible for such NPAs through survey based reports. Service of reputed and established Research Institution/Economic Research Center AEERCs may be sought for this purpose on consultancy basis.

Above steps (if taken seriously) with firm wiliness, will create wide prospect for the Indian Banking sector enabling it to face the emerging challenges of globalization. And this is the urgent need of the hour too.

References

Swamy, B. N. Anantha (2001), "Bank Quest", *The Journal of the Indian Institute of Bankers*, Vol. 72, No. 3, (July–September), p. 3-22.

Pagaria, M. L. and Yadav, Ram Jass (2002), "Bank Quest", *The Journal of the Indian Institute of Bankers*", Vol. 73, No. 3, July–September, p. 24-29.

Raman, K. A. V. (2003), "Better Housekeeping for Banks, "*IBA Bulletin*, Vol. XXV, No. 8, August, p. 31-32.

Sukthankar, Vaideheee (2002), "IT Act, 2000 Scope and It's Impact on the Banking Industry", *IBA Bulletin*, Vol. XXIV, No. 4, April-June, p. 22-31.

Varghese, K. Cherian (2002), "Policies and Reforms in Banking", *Bank Quest, The Journal of The Institute of Bankers*, Vol. 73, No. 2, April–June, p. 36-40.

Mundargi, Kishore (2003), "Re-Orienting Structure: A Model for Indian Banks", *IBA Bulletin* Special Issue, March, p. 77.

Samal, B. (2003), "EVA: A Key Performance Mesure", *IBA Bulletin* Special Issue (March), p. 57.

Khan, M. Y. (2002), "The Market Potential of Credit Deviates in India", *Bank Quest*, Vol. 71, No. 2 April–June, p. 4-16.

Shekhar, Chander "Reduction of NPAs Key to Banking Reforms", *Yojana*, (October–2003), p. 11-13.

11

Growth Oriented Financial Reforms in India

Chandeshwari Tiwary

Prior to the gulf crisis of 1991, greater stress was laid on the public sector for its planned development. It resulted in serious financial constraints in opening the closed Indian economy to the international economy. The important constraints are-government dominance in financial activities, ownership of banks, automatic monetization of fiscal deficit large pre-emptions, administered interest rates etc. Financial reforms started in India lately and gradually since 1990's decade with various recommendations and measures enabling the environment for operative financial units for commercial view. The ownership has been diversified. Public sector banks were charged for their lapses and government share holding reduced to 33% for private participation but strengthened with various remedial measures. Private and foreign banks were allowed and encouraged to establish units for competition. The administered interest rates were deregulated. Domestic financial markets were strengthened to compete with the international financial markets. The financial doors have been opened for international investments and technologies. Money markets, capital markets, equity markets, bond markets, bill markets, foreign exchange markets, stock markets and others, have been strengthened and developed under the successful regulatory and supervisory leadership of the Reserve Bank of India. As a result, the public sector banks improved their working status with more autonomy, increased profits and reduced non-performing assets (NPAs) within operational code and discipline. Various guidelines have been issued for consolidation, good governance, prudential norms, liberalisation efficiency, know your customer (KYC) etc. The manpower resources, asset quality, credit delivery etc., have also been improved leading to low cost with improved infrastructural framework. The present capital adequacy of Indian banks based on Basel II is comparable to those at international level. India is today on a sound footing with continuous reforms leading to 9.2% real GDP growth rate.

India is a developing country with 9.2% GDP growth rate and aspiring to aim at 10 to 11 per cent GDP growth rate in 11th five year plan and onwards. For this, the nation must have a strong and developed financial sector domestically and globally. Reforms in financial sectors after gulf crisis (1991) and onwards are highly appreciable but more have to be done for fast economic development making the nation a developed one by 2020, the target cherished by the Honourable President of India.

This paper deals with (I) historical background for the need of reforms in Indian financial sector, (II) reform measures and their features, (III) Impact of reforms, (IV) Constraints of the financial sector and (V) Future strategies for reforms in this sector.

The financial sector of the pre reform era essentially catered to the needs of planned development in a mixed economy framework. The public sector had a predominant role in economic activity leading to large developmen expenditure met by long terms finance at fine and low rates of interest below the market rates for private sector. The govtionary effects of such large scale monetisation. The existence of a complex structure of interest rates arising from economic and social concerns of providing concessional credit to certain sectors resulted in "cross subsidisation" which implied that higher rates were charged from non-concessional borrowers. The regulation of lending rates led to the regulation of deposit rates to keep cost of funds to public sector banks at reasonable levels so that the spread between cost of funds and return on funds is maintained.

All these led to various benefits to the government and the country. The post nationalisation phase witnessed significant branch expansion of public sector banks to mobilise savings and to increase bank credit to agriculture, small scale industries and exports. But the directed and concessional availability of bank credit to these privileged sectors caused distortions in the interest rates mechanisms as well as it also adversely affected the viability and profitability of these banks. Their very performances were questioned in markets. Their lack of recognition of the importance of transparency, accountability and prudential norms in the operations of the banking systems led also to a rising burden of non performing asset's (NPA's). Many criticised the de facto joint family balance sheet of government, RBI and commercial banks (mainly PSB's) because the transactions between the three segments were mainly governed by plan priorities rather than sound principles of financing inter-institutional transactions leading to loss of transparency of accountability and of incentive to measure or seek efficiency.

The Indian financial sector thus needed reforms under the principles of liberalisation, privatisation, globalisation, disinvestment, commercialisation, competition and others without forgetting the national goal of economic development with social justice under the constitutional umbrella of Indian government and RBI for the public interests/customers. The Industrial policy of 1991opened the above doors for financial reforms too by removing "Licence Raj" and by allowing private sector and foreign capital to grow and prosper and to compete with the public sector banks and other financial and monetary institutions. Accordingly, various measures were initiated and undertaken to create an enabling environment and framework for reforms in financial sector. The important among them are the followings:

(1) The administered of interest rates were liberalised and deregulated. This important reform process has

imparted greater efficiency to resource allocation with prudential regulation, market behaviour, financial opening and above all the underlying macroeconomic conditions.

(2) Since the onset of reforms, there has been a change in the ownership pattern of banks. The legislative framework governing public sector banks (PSBs) was amended in 1994 to enable them to raise capital funds from the market by way of bank issue of shares. Many public sector banks have accessed the market since then to meet the increasing capital requirements and until 2001-2002, government made capital injections out of the budget to bail out public sector banks to totalling about 2 per cent of GDP. Moreover, the government has reduced the minimum government ownership in nationalised banks from 51per cent to 33 per cent, without altering their public sector haracter.

(3) Reforms have altered the organizational forms, ownership pattern and domain of operations of financial institutions (FIs) on both the asset and liability fronts. They have led the intensification of the competition for resources for both banks and FIs. At the same time, with banks entering the domain of term lending and FIs making a foray into disbursing short term loans, the competition for supply of funds has also increased. Besides, FIs have also entered into various fee based services like stock-broking, merchant banking, advisory services and the like.

(4) Consolidation in the banking sector has been another important reform process. For it, the guidelines for merger between non-banking financial companies and banks, as well as between private sector banks have been issued making a major initiative towards universal banking. The RBI enabled the reverse merger of large development financial institutions (DFIs) with the commercial banking subsidiaries. Currently ICICI,

NBFC, HDFC and IDBI are doing well. These merger principles and guidelines are equally applicable to the public sector banks.

(5) One of the major objectives of baking sector reforms has been to enhance efficiency and productivity through competition. For this, guidelines have been laid down for establishments of new banks in the private sector and the foreign banks have been allowed more liberal entry. Foreign direct investment in the private sector is now allowed more than 74% subject to conformity with guidelines issued from time to time. PSBs still lag behind private sector banks.

(6) Impressive institutional and legal reforms have been undertaken in relation to the banking sector. Board for Financial Supervision (BFS) for undivided attention to supervisions, a Board for Regulation and Supervision of Payment Settlements systems (BPSS), the Credit Information Companies (Regulation), Government securities Bills and others have been constituted to enhance the operational efficiency and to facilitate the banking works under RBI's regulation and supervision.

(7) A set of prudential measures aimed at imparting strength to the banking system as well as ensuring safety and soundness through greater transparency, accountability and public credibility have been undertaken.

(8) All cases of penalty and directions are to be placed in the public domain for enhancing the transparency and disclosures.

(9) Moreover, the regulatory framework in India is increasingly focusing on ensuring good governance through "fit and proper." Owners, directors and senior managers of the banks including private banks are required to comply with governance principles laid down by the SEBI–the securities markets regulator.

(10) Capital adequacy norms are in line with the Basel committee standards and from the end of March 2000, the prescribed ratio has been raised to 9 %.

(11) The banking sector reforms have also emphasized the need to review the manpower resources and rationalize the requirements by drawing a realistic plan so as to reduce the operating cost and to improve the profitability even leading to outsourcing.

(12) The annual policy statement of May 2004 also flagged major areas requiring urgent attention specially in the areas of ownership, governance, conflicts of interest and customer protection through UK mechanism of know your customer (KYC) system.

(13) The annual statement of 2005 laid greater emphasis on depositor's interest compared to borrowers. The banks should be obliged to provide banking services to all segments of the population - pensioners, self employed and those employed in unorganised sector on equitable basis.

(14) It has also been emphasized that domestic compulsions must be in harmony with global developments. Global developments especially relating to Basel II must be respected. The commercial banks in India will start implementing Basel II with effect from March 31, 2007.

(15) At present, the RBI holds shares in a number of institutions. The further reform agenda is to divest the RBI of all its ownership functions for better financial, monetary and stable management of its own spheres of regulator, supervisor and debt manager with autonomy flexibility.

(16) Since the outset of reforms, various effective measures have been undertaken to improve the functioning of money market, capital market, government securities market and foreign exchange market, credit delivery and others.

(17) And others.

Thus various measures have been undertaken for the financial sector reforms in India but their features are of great interest such as:

(a) they were not driven by any crisis,

(b) nor they have been an out come of multilateral aid,

(c) the design and details of the reforms were evolved by domestic expertise, always keeping in view the international experiences,

(d) the government preferred that public sector banks manage the over-hung problems of the past rather than clean up the balance sheets with support of the government,

(e) it was also felt convenient that there is enough room for growth and healthy competition for public and private sector banks as well as foreign and domestic banks based on the twin governing principles of non-disruptive progress and consultative process under the disciplined leadership of the RBI and the democratic policy.

The financial sector reform measures have major impact on the overall efficiency and stability of the banking system in India. The present capital adequacy of Indian banks is comparable to those at international level. There has been a marked improvement in the asset quality with the percentage of gross non-performing assets (NPAs) to gross advances for the banking system reduced from 14.4 per cent in 1998 to 7.2 per cent in 2004. The reform measures have also resulted in an improvement in the profitability of banks. Indian banks are said to be well placed today with better equipped manpower, reduced operating cost and high profits. During the last five years as per the report of the RBI, the business per employee for public sector banks were more than double to around Rs. 25 million in 2004.

The third quarter review of annual monetary policy 2006-2007 and related financial review reports are worth commendable:

(i) Real GDP increased by 9.2 per cent,

(ii) The momentum of economic activity has been sustained with some set backs in the agricultural sector,

(iii) The industrial activity has picked up,

(iv) Business confidence picked up.

(v) Financial markets more or less remained stable and orderly except some volatility.

(vi) Capital flow (Mainly FDI) to India remained sizable during 2006-2007.

(vii) Foreign exchange reserves rose to US $ 178.1 billion by January 19, 2007.

(viii) Global financial markets have been reasonably stable.

(ix) The India Rupee appreciated vs the US Dollar during the quarter ending December 2006.

Thus, putting India on a bright future is all due to the above first phase and second phase reform measures. Although, India's banking sector is more developed than many emerging market economies even more than China, still our financial and banking sectors have the following problems and demerits.

(1) The level of house hold sectors lending is well below other Asian Emerging Market economies (EMs) like Korea, Thailand, Malaysia and Taiwan.

(2) Private sector is not fully developed in India leading to underdeveloped structure of Indian Financial sector. In Order to achieve a more efficient allocation of capital, market rather than the government has to play more of a role in deciding who gets credit and how much.

(3) Hung Q. Tran in his article of July 16, 2006 while comparing Chinese economy with the Indian, has rightly remarked that

(a) Market liquidity is poor in India as in other EMs.

(b) Corporate governance practices are weak in India. It still lacks share holder activism that can take up corporate governance related issues

(c) India lacks a deep and liquid corporate bond market because the bond market in India have been historically dominated by the government sector.

(4) Many liberal experts criticise that Indian Rupee is not fully convertible. The Committee on Fuller Capital Account Convertibility has submitted its plan to the RBI, chalking out the path to a fuller rupee convertibility for capital account transactions.

(5) A stable international financial system is a vital ingredient to promoting sustained economic growth which is lacking due to uncertainties in international economies. The IMF has also an important role to play in our financial stability.

(6) India faces a daunting challenge on the fiscal and structural fronts.

(7) Jalan, ex-governor of RBI has rightly criticised the heavy burgeoning fiscal deficit of the central government causing high inflation.

(8) Jalan has also rightly warned that beyond a point it is not simply feasible for banks and financial institutions to increase the share of government securities in their overall asset portfolio without affecting their own viability and the viability of the productive sector of the economy.

It is therefore, felt that the concerned authorities must pay their attentions for the solution of the above problems making and ensuring India a more prosperous and developing country to achieve its destiny of a developed economy at international level. Let us conclude by hoping that in case of any adverse and unexpected developments, the financial and monetary sectors should respond swiftly with all possible measures, as appropriate to the evolving global and domestic situation impinging on inflation expectations and the growth momentum.

References

Uppal, R. K. & Kaur, Rimpi (2006), Banking Sector Reforms in India: A Review of Post-1991 Development, Eastern Book Corporation.

Vasudev, C. M. (2006), Monetary Policy and Banking Sector Reforms, *www. financialexpress.com.*

Dreze Jean and Amartya Sen (eds.) (1995), *India: Economic Development and Social Opportunity,* Oxford University Press.

Jalan, B. (2001), 'Banking and Finance in the New Millennium', *RBI Bulletin,* February, 215.232.

Rangarajan, C. (2000), "*Perspectives on Indian Economy–A Collection of Essays*", UBS Publishers' Distributors Ltd.

Reddy, Y. V. (2000), Monetary *and Financial Sector Reforms in India, A Central Banker's Perspective,* UBS Publishers, New Delhi.

Reserve Bank of India (1997), *Report of the Committee on Banking Sector Reform,* Chairman Shri M. Narasimham.

Tarapore, S. S. (2002), Twists *and Turns in Financial Reforms,* UBS Publishers.

Third Quarter Review of Annual Monetary Policy for the Year 2006-07, Reserve Bank of India, *www.rbi.org.in.*

12

Financial Sector Reforms and Public Sector Banks

Niranjana Jeswal

The performance of banking sector in post reform era and to ensure greater accountability and market discipline. Narsiman committee II (1998) recommended second generation reforms which is include.

- Capital adequacy requirements should take into account market risks and CARAR to be raised to 10% from the present 9% by 2000 and 10% present by 2002.
- Risk Weight for a Govt. guaranteed account must be 100% and NPM. Level should be brought down to 5% by 2000 and 3% by 2002 and an asset should be classified as Doubtful if it is in the sub- standard category for 18 months instead of the present 24 months and gradually to replace it by international norm of 90 day.
- Bank should avoid ever greering of their advances and there should be no further re-capitalization by the government.
- Govt. Guaranteed accounts must also be categorized as NPAS under the usual norms.

- Banks should up date their operational manuals which should form the basic document of internal control systems.
- Recruitment of skilled manpower directly from the market be given urgent consideration and to rationalize staff strengths, an appropriate VRS must be introduced.

Banking sector have reacted positively implementing these reforms. These reforms have enhanced the overall efficiency and viability of the banks which have resulted in the entry of new players in the field in the forms of new generation private sector banks and foreign banks. These banks entered in the market with high quality service like HSBC , HDFC, ICICI etc. these public sector banks with an international presence have forced to reanalyze their performance and approach. After the implementation of reforms and freeing from regulatory clutches, they have improved significantly over the last decade. State Bank of India stands 82nd ranking in the top 1000 banks in the world.

Objectives

- To review the financial sector reforms with specia l reference to the Indian banking sector.
- To conduct a comparative appraisal of financial performance of public, private and foreign banks in India during post reforms era.
- To suggest some measures and recommendation to improve the performance of public sector banks.

Diversification of Banking Activities

We may summarize latest trends and development in on world that is diversification of Banking Activities. RBI has permitted commercial banks to engage in diverse activities such as security related transactions, foreign exchange transaction, leasing and cross selling etc. in the present scenario banks in all sectors are concentrating on diversifying their operations to nontraditional banking business such as insurance, underwriting brokerage besides providing lending and deposited services. Declining in interest margins and other factors like customer expectations have been instrumental in making banks diversifying their portfolios. They are diversifying their operation to tap and untapped market like retail product segment by expanding geographically and stressing heavily on retail banking and e-banking. Moreover low no minimum capital based required for these services have boasted this trend.

Customer Relationship Management

With the intensified competition the outlook of banks towards customer has undergone a big change. Especially in public sector banks where they are gradually shifting their emphasis on customer orientation from account orientation. With the help of CRM mechanism bank are making a positive endeavor to ensure enhancement in the profitability ratio by cross selling more products to the existing customers. Private sector and foreign sector banks are head of public sector banks in this respect. Although their customer coverage base is low as compared to public sector but they generate steadily high business from cross selling and up selling because of effective customer relation management.

Performance of Banking Sector in Post Reforms Era

In the post reforms period, the performance of banking sector has been reasonably well. For the purpose of analyzing the performance of banks in India, banking sector is broadly categorized into foreign sector banks, Indian private bank sector. Nationalized banks and SBI & Associate. For making comparative analysis seven key indicators of financial performance like return of assets (ROA), Capital Asset risk weighted ratio, NPA to net profitability of banks and off balance sheet operations of scheduled commercial banks has been selected from the time period of 1994 to 2004-05.

Return on Assets (Roa)

Return on assets is defined as the ratio of profits after to average asset. It reflects the efficiency with which banks deploy their assets.

Table 1 show that ROA of public sector banks exceeded that of private and foreign banks except in the year 1996-97. In addition to this, over all ROA declined in 2004-05. the decline being the biggest in case of private sector banks followed by foreign sector bank and public sector banks. This is because private and foreign banks emphasis more on earning income from non-traditional source of income by selling diversified third party product.

Table 1

Return on Assets

Banks	*2004-2005*	*2003-2004*	*2002-2003*	*2001-2002*	*2000-2001*	*1999-2000*	*1998-1999*	*1997-1998*	*1996-1997*
Foreign Banks	0.55	1.07	1.01	-0.5	-23.43	0.34	0.62	0.71	1.1
Indian Private Banks	0.13	0.75	0.83	1.18	-31.43	1.25	0.95	1.43	1.49
Nationalized Bank	0.9	1.27	1	0.68	0.42	0.53	0.54	0.66	0.58
SBI Associates	0.83	1.34	1.15	0.95	0.66	0.85	0.65	0.15	0.76

For which minimum or no capital base is required profit from securities, foreign transaction and brokerage commission services contribute significantly in fee based income of these banks.

Capital Risk Weighted Assets Ratio

Capital Risk Weighted Assets Ratio is a measure of a bank's financial health. The ratio is provided by equity plus reserves over total risk weighted assets. It reflects the soundness of a financial institution. As it is shown in the Table 2 in the year 2004-05 the capital risk weighted asset ratio of foreign banks is 41.11% as compared to private banks and public sector banks where it is 13.49 and 12.85 respectively. This suggests that foreign banks have greater incentive to lend prudently and remain well capitalized than the three other kinds of banks. The balance sheet of foreign banks appear to be more structurally sound than those of domestic and public sector banks based on this ratio as compared to new generation private bank and public sector banks. It is noteworthy that advance component of foreign banks is quite low as compared to public sector banks with wide coverage both in terms of quantity and geographical expansion.

Table 2
Capital Risk Weighted Assets Ratio

Banks	*2004-2005*	*2003-2004*	*2002-2003*	*2001-2002*	*2000-2001*	*1999-2000*	*1998-1999*	*1997-1998*	*1996-1997*
Foreign Banks	41.00	42.3	53.49	45.22	33.11	31.50	44.22	39.72	62.58
Indian Private Banks	13.49	13.51	12.17	9.6	12.37	12.72	12.14	12.21	12.48
Nationalized Bank	12.85	13.18	12.21	7.5	10.98	11.14	10.95	10.53	8.67
SBI Associates	12.15	13.02	13.09	9.8	12.43	11.95	11.89	12.55	10.44

NPAs of Schedule Commercial Bank

Capital adequacy and Assets quality are two crucial parameters which reflect the soundness of a financial institution. In the Indian context both these parameters have shown a significant improvement over the years while the level of non-performing assets (NAPA), both in gross and net terms has, declined, the capital adequacy ratio has improved steadily. Reflecting the combined impact of increase in the capital position and improvement in assets quality, net NPLS to capital ratio, which is a worst case scenario measure, declined, steadily from a high level of 71.3 per cent at end of March 1999 to 22.8 per cent at end March 2004 and further to 15.5 per cent by end March 2005.

Though in post reform era, performance of public sector banks had improved in terms of ROA and reduction in NPA level, butthey differ significantly from new private sector and foreign bank in terms of operation issues, organizational culture, mindset and human resource issue etc. the overall performance of public sector banks appears comparable with foreign bank and new generation private sector banks. In general, foreign banks performed better in terms of cost, earning efficiency and in generating business per employee. However public sector banks in terms of return on assets (ROA) and net NPS as a percentage to net advances.

Recommendation and Suggestion for Public Sector Banks

The forgoing analysis reveals that though there is phenomenal development in various banking sectors yet the public sectors in particular is still lagging behind major thrust areas such as asset quality, business per employee, capital adequacy requirements and profitability etc. some suggestion and recommendation of improvement in performance of public sector banks are given below.

Check on Operating Cost

Higher operating cost is a major obstacle affecting the profitability of public sector banks. The financial viability of public sector banks can be enhanced by keeping a control on operating cost through higher labor productivity, updated, technology, low cost funds and restructuring of unremunerating branches.

Rationalization of Staff Cost

In public sector banks the proportion of wage bill is significantly higher as compared to private sector banks and foreign banks and in turn ratio of business per employee and profit per employee in quite low in comparison to other banks. Though public sector banks have tended to rationalize staff cost by VRS schemes but employee per cost of public sector banks has risen due to the changing composition of the staff and increased provisioning towards super annulations liabilities. The manpower for each branch should be determined by the customer profile network of branches and the level of computerization while ensuring to relation the best talent in the organization.

Human Resource Development

Human resource development is a critical factor which can play major role in enhancing business per employee and profit per employee. Public sector banks are lagging behind in Human resource development practices as compared to foreign and private sector banks. Public sector banks should devise continuous and compulsory training and development program in their organizations to inculcate professional work culture, and interpersonal skills.

Technology Up Gradation

Public sector banks required considerable investment in computerization of branch network and their operations to get quick and greater access to information.

Market Driven Approch and Customer Relation Management

Public sector banks are required to become market drivers and innovative in product offering with customer oriented outlook which include factors such as extension of working hours, net banking, tele-banking which enable the customers to transact as per their convenience. Public sector banks have an edge over the foreign banks in terms of their extensive reach through branch network and wide customer base. But to keep this wide customer base is a major challenge which Public sector banks are facing.Sincere orientation and customer's friendly approach in customers dealing in the Public sector banks. Banks may create the database of new customers through referrals of existing customers and using the same for increasing the customer base of bank.

Improvement in Credit Delivery Mechanism

It is also a major thrust area where Public sector banks are required to pay attention.

Conclusion

Banking sector in India has given a positive and encouraging response to the financial sector reforms. Entry of new private banks and foreign banks has shaken up Public sector banks to competition, changing financial scenario have opened up opportunities for banks to expend their global presence through self expansion, strategic alliance etc. banks are diverting their focus on retail banking so as to obtain access to low cost funds and to expand into relatively untapped potential growth areas. Banking sector is set to witness the emergence of financial supermarkets in the form of universal banks. The financial sectors reforms have brought Indian financial system closer to global standards. The process of strengthening the banking system has to be viewed as continuous one. With the India increasingly getting integrated with the global financial world, the Indian banking sector has a still long way go to catch up with their counter parts.

References

Banerjee, Amalesh, and Singh, S. K. (2001), "Banking and Financial Sector Reforms in India, pp. 3.38-360, Deep and Deep Publication.

Nandwana N. M. (2004), Performance of Public Sector Banks, 2003-04, Central Bank of India, *Economic Bullentin*, p. 5-7.

Reserve Bank of India (2004-05), Report on Trend and Progress of Banking in India.

Sangwan D. S. (2005), Human Resource Management in Banks, *IBM Bulletin*, June, pp. 9-15.

Sengupta, Arjun K. (1994), "The Financial Sector and Economic Reforms in India (Sir Purshottamdas Thakurdas Memorial Lecture 1994)", The Indian Institute of Bankers, Mumbai.

Shetty, J. V. (1994), "Banks and Financial Services", *The Journal of the Indian Institute of Bankers*, Vol. 65, No. 3, July-September, pp. 111-115.

Shetty, Vasudeva S. (1994), "Priorities in the Next Decade", *IBA Bulletin*, Vol. XVI, No., January, pp. 48-50.

Singh, Shrawan Kumar (1999), "Banking Sector Reforms Some Issues (with Emphasis on Problem of NPAs)" Conference Volume, The Indian Economic Association, IEA 82nd Conference, pp. 171-179.

13

Financial Sector Reforms with Special Reference to Indian Banking Sector

Bijay Kumar Sinha & Subhas Kumar

The Indian financial system is quite old with a rich and varied evolutionary experience. The growth and development of an economy is a reflection of the growth and development of its financial system. More efficient a financial system, the more stronger an economy.

The path of growth of the financial system in any developing economy including India can be classified into three different phases, broadly described as under

- Active State Intervention
- Liberalisation Partial
- Liberalisation total

The first phase is one of active state intervention mainly with a view build up institutional infrastructure so that the economy will be in a position to catch up with the developed countries. This phase commenced immediately after the independence viz. 1950s in our country. Naturally, this phase is marked by a fast growth of the financial system, creating in the process number of pitfalls and aberrations. This gave rise to the second phase when the focus shifted to building up of rationalisation and simplification in the whole system. This phase we would say lasted till 1990s. The third phase effective from 1990s could be viewed to herald the beginning of the era of globalisation in our economy. Over a period of time, the government thought to being with liberalisation of the sector, more specifically from 1991, after the Narasimham Committee Recommendation were announced. And now, the country is poised towards total liberalisation of the financial sector. In this phase, maximum autonomy is provided to institution with a view to enable them to develop their own effective self regulation.

Financial system can be bifurcated into two broad categories.

(a) Organised Sector

(b) Unorganised Sector.

In the former category, we have a nationalised banking structure, Cooperative banks and developments banks established under various enactments as well as the private sector. All these entitles are subjects to control by the governments/RBI.

The second category includes money lenders, indigenous bankers, pawnbrokers, traders etc. Besides, a number of non-banking financial companies, not fulfilling the criteria notified by the Reserve Bank of India also came under this category.

In the initial phases viz. 1950s, more specifically immediately after independence, the financial system merely comprised money lenders, who did the lending from their own resources. Then came the chit funds. This was followed by the indigenous bankers, who collected deposits and lent loans. The evolution next reached the cooperative banking structure. The next phase was characterised by joint stock banks established under the companies Act. There were some failures of these banks with the result that 'consolidation' took place. Then there was the advent of Commercial banks and the process of nationalisation. Development banks and specialised financial institutions appeared on the scene subsequently. Merchant Banking also came to occupy an important place. And now, with the conscious and on the performance of the public sector banks. Financial liberalization in relation to banks involves two aspects. There is the first task of rehabilitation of weak banks, mainly the public sector ones whose creditable record in branch expansion, encouragement of saving and service to the weak and the neglected has been increasingly rubbished by the virus of internal and external abuse. The second aspect relates to creative conditions of effective and free competition. On the basis of the aforesaid facts, the Indian Banking can be analysed in the following context.

The benefits of nationalisation are far too significant to be ignored while the benefits should be retained, the rigorous arising out of various pressures that have been build upon banks should be softened and where necessary, eliminated. Privatisation if resorted to, should be on a selective basis, but retained in a large measure. The benefits from nationalisation, the tendency towards populist measure, to placate and build up political support has weakened the system perceptibly for the genuine benefits of nationalisation to be of sustaining nature, the banking system should be insulated from political pressure.

Better customer service is more a function of motivated, will equipped and trained manpower than anything else. What is required today is not the privatisation of banks but the modernisation and professionalisation of banks,

Narashimham Committee has recommended restructuring of Banking system along the following lines (a) 3 - 4 large banks which could become international, in Charter, (b) 8 -10 National Banks (c) Rural Banks including RRBs. It also recommends against further nationalisation of Banks. The Committee also recommended abolition of Branch licensing for opening of branches within the country. It also recommended liberal entry of foreign banks and permit joint ventures between Indian permit joint ventures between Indian and foreign banks. The committee also recommended that foreign operate ones of Indian Banks should be rationalised.

Presently a Bank is divided into zones and zones into Divisions and Divisions into Branches. The Divisions and zones perform almost the same functions monitoring the working of the branches and reporting to the corporating to the corporate working the branches and reporting to the corporate office. Clubbing together both the Divisions and Zones makes not only sense but also saves times, money and manpower.

The Banking sector in India is now in a position to handle every critical situation. So it is to come to give full autonomy to Indian Banking. But more than that their calibre compares very well the advanced countries and meets with the International standards. Today they are matured enough to handle the things themselves carefully and efficiently within the overall objectives. There should be a good mechanism of control and inspection. In private sector banks, all the top most positions like the CMD and ED are filled up by the owners themselves. Therefore, there should not be any hesitation to impart functional autonomy.

There has been eight fold increse in the number of Commercial Banks branches since June 1969 till day (It rose from 8262 in June 1996 to 66186 in June 30, 2002). But this was not enough, because even the average popultion per branch is higher than the developed country.

Hence the following measure are to be taken to strengthen the branch expansion.

(i) First of all the branch pattern of the bank should be materially changed in respect to both number and location. Emphasis should be given to open new branches in that area, where the average population per office is higher than the state average.

(ii) Semi Urban area of the State should not be neglected in respect opening of branches and there should be balanced development of banking facilities in the rural and semi urban areas.

(iii) Branch should not be opened in haste only to achieve the targets rather they should be opened with advanced planning for recruitment acquisition of premises, training of staff etc.

(iv) Government should provide infrastructure facilities such as transport accommodation security arrangements etc.

In recent period the main cause of law profitability of the banks is to having increase in Non performing Assets of Banks. NPAS are such type of loan which are disbursed by the banks or financial institutions but can not recovered by the bank either partially or wholly i.e., principle amount and the interest in a given stipulated span of time. The gross NPAs of SCBs increasing Rs. 7164 crores to Rs. 70,905 crores (in 2001-02) and net NPAs increased by Rs. 3084 crores to Rs. 35546 crores. This is the major problem before SCBs. Hence, it is essential to recover it. For this following measures are to be taken:

(i) A recovery cell should be created in each branch of a Bank.

(ii) Recovery should be made on easy instruments.

(iii) The government should cooperate banks in recovery of loans.

(iv) Legal action should be taken against defaulters.

(v) Along with comprehensive restructuring by injecting modern technology and adopting business strategy based on skill competency and adoption of non fun activities.

These banks have not been successful to the stiff challenges faced, due to the constraints, both internal as well as external, in working of the top managements.

Thus, to strengthen such banks, the following valuable suggestions have been recommended by Verma Committee:

(a) mergers of closure of Banks

(b) change in ownership

(c) undertaking comprehensive operational, financial and systematic restructuring.

After nationalisation there hs been phenomenal increase in the deposits of commercial branches that of SBI. Total deposit of commecial Bank in India increased about 300 times in June 1969 to June 2006. The tremendous increase in the value of deposits has been mainly due to opening of more branches in rural areas and various deposit mobilisation scheme introduced by bank after Nationalisation. Largest rural having being tapped by the Banking system which are encouraging trends for the banking system of the state. However, there has been a number of difficulties in the mobilisation of deposits by Banks. Deposits are the basic of entire Banking system.

Following measures can be taken to increase the volume of deposits and bank credits.

(a) Launching of saving campaign such as wide propaganda and publicity in rural as well as urban areas.

(b) Starting of deposit prize scheme by linking deposits with lottery like the postal deposit prize scheme.

(c) Preparation of an annual district plan for deposit mobilisation.

(d) Fixing an attractive interstate.

(e) Avoidance of undue delaying graviting credit and simplification of loan procedure.

(f) Check on diversion of deposits from rural branches to urban and metropolitan branches.

Improved consumer service is the most vital factor of the Banks. In this regard RBI constituted under the Chairmanship of Sri M.N. Goiporia, on making recommendation for consumer service improvements in banks. The main recommendations of the committee were as given ahead.

(a) Expansion of banking hours for all workers excluding cash payment.

(b) Re adjustment of Bank opening time for staff so as to ensure start of work at bank counters well in time.

(c) Spot deposit of outstation cheques of Rs. 5,000 instead of existing 2,500 in Bank accounts.

(d) Increase in Bank interest are on saving accounts.

(e) Providing tax benefit on Bank deposit amounts.

(f) To ensure optimum use of powers available with bank staff. The recommendation of Goporia Committee are still under consideration of the Government and the RBI.

Computerisation is a positive step to bring banking growth. Computerisation is essential even to keep pace with the ever-changing need and behaviour of the business environment. To inspire a rate Bank of trust in Banking the Bank should believe in excellency, punctuality and strive for the quality. The judicious use of computer would not only bring savings in cost but would also fulfill the aspiration of employees as well as customers with an explosive increase in the activities of Banks and wide geographical coverage, a minimum degree of computerisation has become essential in the following functions of the Banks are to be performed fficiently.

(a) Service to customers both depositors and borrowers.

(b) Update maintenance of various general ledger accounts and reconciliation of transactions among branches.

(c) Generate required data for control and monitoring.

The Bank will have the information right at the time it desires, by computerisation, such as:

(a) Customer satisfaction

(b) Prompt transaction handling across the counter.

(c) On-line transaction validation and update.

(d) Customer account statements and balance incurring atpress of the button

(e) Standing instruction as transfers, credit payments.

(f) Any MIS report required for the Bank can be generated within a minute.

(g) One can handle multi currency in multi currency ledger.

(h) On line interactive transaction, update instant validation and automatic posting and updating.

(i) On line documents printing instant printing of documents etc. deposits, pay orders and deposit receipts.

(j) Inter connection of all Taluka, Village level branches to main branch through computers using concept of INTERNET.

(k) By using INTERNET and modem one can do intra branch transaction (IBT) within a minute.

(l) Reduced fraud through enhanced security, vendor control and net work management.

Conclusion

Banking industry is the nerve centre of the Indian economy and it is playing crucial role in the growth and development of the nation. However today the industry is at the cross roads. The biggest challenge before it is to improve its image.

References

Desai, Banking and Financial System, International Book House, Shakti Nagar, Delhi.

Hukku, V. N. (1968), Commercial Banking in Public Sector in India, *The Indian Journal of Commerce,* XXI, 4, 27 Dec.

Kurup, N. P. (1969), The Story of Indian Banking, Published in *Yojana,* August, 24.

Khalkhate, D. (1994), Indian Banking Institution and Reform Sequencing, Mimco, Washington, D. C.

Patel Urjit, R. (1997), Emerging Reforms in Indian Banking, *Economic and Political Weekly,* A Sameeksha Trust Publication, Vol. XXXII, No. 42 October 19-24, Delhi.

Journal and Reports

Economic and Political Weekly, March 4 -10, 2000.

Government of India, *Economic Survey,* 2001 -02, 02-03, 03-04, 04-05.

The Journal of the Indian Institute of Bankers, Mumbi, April-June 2005.

Yojana, August 24, 1969, November, 30, 1991, April, 1998, & March 2003.

The Indian Economic Journal, Bangalore.

14

Banking Sector Reforms in India: A Glimpse

Md. Israr Hassan Khan & Md. Moazzam Nazri

It is said 'A bank is what a Bank does'. Many authors like Walter Leaf Kinely, Herbert L. Hart etc. tried to define the word in their own way which fit to that time Banking Regulation Act 1949 also explain in detail about Banks, Banking and function u/s 5(a) and 5(c).

Why Reforms

Banking industry played an important role in the restructuring of national and world economic. So management of working of Banks becomes very critical and important in such situation reform is essential.

'Reform is the real economy need to be supported by an efficient financial sector capable of mobilizing the savings of the community and allocating them to the most productive users. In many countries in the world there is at this stage a need for major reforms of financial sector, which invariably holds important changes for Banking Industry. The main areas of the banking sector reforms are:

1. Monetary and credit policy issues relating to reserve requirements, interest rates, refinancing facilities, etc.
2. The prescription of prudential norms relating to assets classification and income recognition.

3. Adequate provisioning for bad and doubtful assets.
4. Introduction of a capital to risk-weighted assets ratio system for banks (including foreign banks).
5. Establishment of strong supervisory system.

Objective

The objective of banking sector reforms is to improve the competitiveness and operational efficiencies of the banking sector.

Changing banking, scenario in India is causing e-Banking strategies. The reason to start is the way creates more customer contact than any other area of the bank. Due to the explosion in communication technology in 1990, because of emergency of computer network e-commerce has become a Buzz work, which includes e-banking, e-marketing e-shopping etc.

The need for banking sector reforms arose from the fact that although banking sector made rapid strides in terms of functional and geographical coverage, its operational efficiency (characterized by low profitability high and growing non-performing assets and relatively low capital base) was at very low ebb. Due to lack of proper disclosure norms led many banks to keep.

Their teething problem under cover. Besides, these internal factors, there more certain external factors like high levels of preemption in reserve ratio, administered structure of interest rates and direct credit allocations to certain schemes and sectors at distorted interest rates that were responsible for the banking crisis as well. On the basis of the recommendations of the Narasimham committee, the first phase of financial sector reforms was initiated in 1992 and the second phase of reforms based on the recommendations of the Committee on the Banking Sector Reform (CBSR) of 1998. The major reform measures have been taken and their effects are broadly outlined here bellow.

Reduction in SLR and CRR

The vital external constrain bearing on the profitability and functioning of commercial banks was massive preemption of bank resources to finance government's budgetary needs. These included high-level Statutory Liquidity Ratio (SLR) and high-level Cash Reserve Ratio (CRR). This ratios come down from 54 per cent to less than 35 per cent since the implementation of finical sector reforms. While the effective CRR, which was as high as 16.5 per cent, has been come down to 9.75 per cent, the SLR has been gradually coming down from an average effective rate of 37.4 to 25 per cent in same years. The fall of these ratios had the effect of both augmenting loanable resources of the bank and improving profitability.

Credit Control Policy

Micro regulations of credit delivery which take the form of selective controls have largely been dispensed with and consequently, there is greater freedom for both banks and borrowers. The loans and advances meant for priority sectors have been enlarged and interest rates have been deregulated. The major area of concern is credit for government sponsored programmes involving subsidies. These are very serious problems of co-ordination and recovery in such directed credit programmes. There is an urgent need for procedural simplifications of credit extended to small - scale industries and exports. The Reserve Bank of India is sincerely looking after these things nowadays.

Rationalise Rate of Interest

In India banking system the deregulation of the structure of administered interest rates has been one of the vital reform measures. Prescription of rates of all term deposits and condition for premature withdrawal have been completely dismantled .lending rates for different types of deposits have been slowly and gradually abolished . However differentiated interest rates ceiling prescribed for foreign currency denominated deposit from non-resident Indian is continuing. The deregulation of interest rate structure has given a high degree of freedom to banks in determining deposit and lending rates.

Transparent Guidelines

Competition is sought to be fostered in financial sector also by permitting new private sector bank and more liberal entry of foreign banks. Local branches are encouraged to foster competition in rural and semi-urban areas. However, it must be noted that the reforms process is yet to embrace cooperative and regional rural banks and local banks. Except in maturity pattern of assent and liabilities, movements in provision account and NPA's transparency have been enhanced to meet instructional standards. RBI's annual publication "Trend and progress of Banking in India," presents detailed information on individual banks to have comparative information on the performance of individual banks.

CBSR Prudential Norms

With a view to improving the financial health and credibility of banks, capital adequacy ratio has been marked up and no risk weights have been assigned to different government approval securities. In this regard recommendation of CBSR prudential norms comparable to instructional standards have been initiated in relation to capital adequacy income recognition and asset provisioning. International norm of ninety days has been introduced for income recognition, except income on assets which is not received within 30 days after due date. A significant decision taken in relation to asset classification is the treatment of asset guaranteed by the state government as non-performing assets under certain circumstances.

Recovery of Debts

The recovery of debts due to banks and financial institutions Act, 1993 was enacted for setting up of dedicated tribunals for expeditious adjudication and recovery of debts. A few Tribunals have been set up in a number of cities and an Appellate Tribunal has also been set up in Mumbai.

Recapitalization

The implementation of the new norms under the reform measures will lead to a considerable impairment of capital in some of the nationalized banks which have to be recapitalized. Hence, the government has been making provision for such recapitalization since the budget of 1993-94.

Access to Capital Market

The nationalized banks have been allowed direct access to capital market to mobilize funds from the citizen of India although they will continue to keep in the control of the government which will retain fifty one per cent of the equity in their own hands.

The Progress of the Reforms

The Narasimham committee had proposed wide-ranging reforms for

(i) Improving the financial viability of the banks.

(ii) Increasing their autonomy from government direction.

(iii) Restructuring non-viable banks.

(iv) Allowing a great entry to the private sector in banking.

(v) Furthering operational flexibility and competition among the financial institutions.

(vi) Liberalizing the capital market&

(vii) Setting up of proper supervisory system.

The reform process in banking sector which began in India with the adoption and implementation of the recommendations of the Narsimham's Committee. To reform the banking sector on the lines of Narsimham Committee, the bank have to introduce various structural changes in respect of mergers, amalgamations, acquisitions and takeover. It is needed to think on those lines to compete with international bank in the world market. The reforms will be successful of the banking sector can reduce drastically the percentage of non-performing assets. In order to make the reforms operational and functional, banks should come forwards with innovative programmes so that the economic restructuring measures can lead the economy to attain high level of economic growth and development.

Conclusion

On the basis of above observation we may conclude that the initiatives of reforms, as adopted , are conducive to improve the functions of institutional financing agencies by rendering their services to the needy people at grass roots level, particularly the vulnerable section of the society. Improvement in the conditions of profitability is an accomplishment of target in the future financial viability of public sector commercial banks by raising operating income on the one hand and reducing loan loss risk on the other. This reform of financial sector is a guarantee of non-repetition of any scandal on security scam in the country in future because the proves of SEBI have already been enhanced and its functions are also transparent by adopting such of reform in financial sector, the issue of strengthening monetary policy like the, open market operation as an instrument of credit control, are effective and problem of debt management has become early and adjustable. Moreover, placement of check on reduction in SLR and CRR which has come to an unsustainable stage has become an effective tool to improve banks profitability and operational flexibility. The most striking achievement of the financial sector reform has been that the enhancement of rate of net profit in recent years. The banking reform since 1992 based on the recommendation of Narsimham's Committee 1991 aimed at transforming the regulated and directed public sector banks into the banking operations characterized by open competition, operational efficiency and functional discipline Commercial banks thus need to become conscious as reported by RBI, that they are entering a challenging environment and will have to redefined their position in the financial industry. New ways and methods will have to be determined in order to successfully respond to the new challenges particularly, the growing demands from customers for high quality services. The banking reforms initiated in 1992 and later reviewed in 1998 may provide impetus to banking operational efficiency and profitability.

References

G. Chandrasekhar Rao and D. Krishnamoorthy, "Financial Sector Reform in India and Impending Financial Fragility", p. 78.

Reddy, Y. V. (1999), "Financial Sector Reform Review A Prospects Reserve Bank of India Bulletin", p. 33.

King, Robert G. and Ross Lerine (1993), "Finance and Growth: Schumpeter may be Right", *Quarterly Journal of Economics,* Vol. 108, p. 37.

Rangarajan, C. (1999), "Rationale of Reforms in the Financial Sector", *The Indian Economic Journal,* 46 No. 3, p. 5.

Asli Demmirgue-kunt and Enrica Detragiache (1999), "Financial Liberalisation and Financial Fragility", p. 306.6. Baidysnath Pd. Singh and Gangadhar Das, "Financial Sector Reform in India: Functional Realities and Prospects," p. 87.

Government of India, Report of the Committee on Financial System, p. 30.

Reserve Bank of India Bulletins.

15

An Analysis of Banking Sector Reforms in India

Deepa Sharan & Kishwar Ara

The entire world has undergone a change. The most important of these changes is that various economies of the world have moved towards capitalism either from their past communism or socialism. Communist country like China is inviting foreign direct investment. The developed and developing nations opened up there economies to the market forces resulting in free flow of trade among countries. India, in tune with the global trends undertook reform processes popularly known as liberalization, privatization and globalization in the early nineties. For the introduction and implementation of these reforms an efficient and competitive banking system was necessary. Over the years, Indian banking and the financial system has made impressive progress in terms of both geographical spread and functional reach. The banking sector reforms were started in India in 1992. The Narasimham Committee has set the stage for far-reaching changes in the financial system, by making several key recommendations relevant to monetary management; including reduction of statutory reserve requirements, regulation of interest rates, cutting down directed lending, promting competitiveness etc.

India faced a serious economic crisis in 1991. There was a steep fall in the country's foreign exchange reserve to about $1billion, equal to the value of only two week's imports. There was a large fiscal deficit close to 10% of GDP and an unsustainable external balance with current account deficit at 3% of GDP. In tune with the changes in economic policies and with the implementation of financial sector reforms, the banking sector in India has undergone a sea change over the last fifteen years.

The landmarks in banking reforms were the introduction of prudential norms, partial deregulation of interest rates, reduction in directed lending, SLRand CRR and also the entry of private sector banks. The initial reforms in 1992-93 aimed at bringing in transparency in banking system. Introduced in April 1992, the prudential norms involved a new look at asset classification, income recognition, provisioning of bad debt, capital adequacy etc. Income is now viewed in terms of realization rather than on accrual basis.

Expansion of Banking Sector in Pcst Reform Period

The major recommendations of Narasimham Committee were accepted and implementation was started straight away by the Govt., in spite of stiff opposition from bank unions and political parties in the country. These reforms include reduction in CRR and SLR, setting up new private sector banks and deregulation of interest rates.

The above table shows that in 22 years(1969 to 1990-91)after the nationalization of banks in 1969 there was 640per cent increase in the number of branches, the most spectacular progress was in rural areas i.e. about 2340 per cent increase. It is pointed out that the single striking feature of the post-nationalization banking scene is the rapidity with which the branches network has multiplied itself. The rate of branch expansion has been unparalleled anywhere else in the world. In the post reform period (1990-91 to 1999-2000) the number of branches showed an increase of only about 8 per cent. The number of rural branches has shown a decline. The share of rural branches as percentage of total branches has declined

Table 1
Expansion of Banking (1969, 1990-91 to 2000-01)

As on 31st March	*Total no.of branches*	*Rural branches*	*Rural branches*	*Bank deposits*	*Bank credit as % of ratio total*	*Credit deposit*
1969	8187	1443	17.6	4822	3467	0.72
1990-91	60597	35216	58.1	219539	133745	0.61
1991-92	60690	35218	58.0	233086	142211	0.61
1992-93	61235	35301	57.6	27068	165836	o.61
1993-94	61852	35379	57.2	317918	180017	0.57
1994-95	62264	35008	56.2	375864	222507	0.59
1995-96	62849	33092	52.7	426073	263533	0.62
1996-97	63534	33008	52.0	492227	282237	0.57
1997-98	64267	32890	51.2	592068	328637	0.56
1998-99	65118	32856	50.5	7011871	389460	0.55
1999-00	65521	32719	49.9	822133	469032	0.57

Source: Dr. D. Dakshina Murthy, Banking Sector Reforms–The challenges ahead

from 58.1 per cent in 1990-91 to 49.9 per cent in 1999-2000. There has been an increase in bank deposit and bank credit.

Table 2
Movement of CRR and SLR

Period	*CRR*	*SLR*
1990-91	15	38.5
August 1998	11	25
March 1999	09	25
March 2001	08	25
May 2001	7.5	25
October 2001	5.5	25
June 2002	5.0	25
December 2006	5.50	
April 2007	6.50	

Source: Dr.D.Dakshina Murthy, Banking Sector Reforms–the challenges ahead.

The table shows that the reserve pre-emption have been gradually brought down to boost profitability of bank. The CRR, which was 15 per cent in 1991-92, has been gradually reduced over the years and was at 11 per cent in August, 1998, and it was further reduced to 5 per cent in June 2002. The base

SLR which stood at 38.5 per cent in 1991-92 has been reduced to a statutory level of 25 per cent, which is the minimum stipulated under the Banking Regulation Act 1949. Decrease in the rate of interest, CRR and SLR has resulted in a sharp increase in bank credit, which in turn increased inflation. To tame inflation the RBI hiked CRR to 6.50 in April 2007 from 5.50 per cent in December 2006.

Private Banks in India

All the banks in India were earlier private banks. They were found in pre independence era to cater the banking needs of the people. But after nationalization of banks in 1969 public sector banks came to occupy dominant role in the banking structure. Private sector banking in India received a fillip in 1994 when reserve bank of India encouraged setting up of private banks as part of its policy of liberalization of the Indian banking industry. Entry of new private banks required a minimum paid up capital of Rs.100 crores. Housing Development Finance Corporation Limited (HDFC) was amongst the first to receive an 'in principle' approval from the RBI to set up a bank in private sector.

Private Banks have played a major role in the development of Indian banking industry. They have made banking more efficient and customer friendly. In the process they have jolted public sector banks out of complacency and forced them to become more competitive. Now the public sector banks are working in conditioned atmosphere. The autonomy and the freedom of management have enabled them to strip their excess fat and trim to size. The new private sector banks have increased their market share. The profitability of the new banks also remains the highest. Major private banks in India are:

1. Bank of Rajasthan
2. Bharat Overseas Bank
3. Catholic Syrian Bank
4. Centurian Bank of Punjab
5. Dhanalakshmi Bank
6. Federal Bank

7. HDFC Bank
8. ICICI Bank
9. IDBI Bank
10. IndusInd Bank
11. ING Vysya Bank
12. Jammu & Kashmir bank
13. Kranataka Bank
14. Karur Vysya Bank
15. Kotak Mahindra Bank
16. SBI Commercial and International Bank
17. South Indian Bank
18. United Western Bank
19. UTI Bank
20. YES Bank

Voluntary Retirement Scheme (VRS) as Banking Reform Measure

Adoption of Banking Sector Reforms forced the public sector enterprises to get rid of surplus or no-longer needed employees. The Narasimham Committee recommended that the banks have the authority of redeployment of staff, cut in operating cost and reduction of manpower. The main objective of VRS is bringing down the cost of operations in the Public sector banks. The banking of new Millennium is more technology based than people based. Ms. K.R Chitra in her article on Voluntary Retirement Scheme pointed out that by the end of the first decade of the new Millennium, the public sector banks will not need their entire clerical workforce along with the first line supervisory officers, as their functions will be taken over by technology.

Following the recommendation of Narasimham committee all public sector banks, except Corporation bank, have carried out VRS between November 15, 2000 and March 31, 2001. It was estimated that out of 8.63 lakh employees in 27 public sector banks, 2.5 lakh were surplus. Out of the total strength 1, 26,714 or 14 per cent applied for VRS. About 80 per cent of the number of applications were accepted, and the staff relieved under VRS until December 31, 2001 were 1, 01,300. This constituted 11.7 per cent of the total staff strength.

Voluntary Retirement Scheme in the first round led to major benefits for the bank's balance sheet. A study of Business India finds that employee's cost in the banks has largely fallen after VRS. Some bankers agree that it is difficult to arrive at a direct relation between a decline in employee cost and an increase in profitability but still they admit that VRS had a major role in higher profits posted by a number of banks.

Decline of Credit to Agriculture

It is pointed out by the Narasimham Committee that the productivity and efficiency of the financial sector industry is declining. The major responsible factors identified by the Committee for this decline were directed investments and credit programmes of the govt., as well as rapid branch expansion. To maintain the competitive efficiency of banks the distortions in allocation of resources was to be removed and profitability as well as portfolio quality of the banking system were to be restored. Keeping this in mind there had been changes in the sect oral flow of credit.

Table 3
Sectoral Share and Rate of Growth of Bank Credit

	Agriculture		*Industry*		*Tertiary Sector*		*Total Bank Credit*
Period	*Share in Total Credit*	*Average Annual Rate of Growth*	*Share in Total Credit*	*Average Annual Rate of Growth*	*Share in Total Credit*	*Average Annual Rate of Growth*	*Rate of Growth*
1972-79	9.1	15	45.2	5.8	43.9	18	11.7
1980-89	13.3	9.8	35.9	7.2	50.8	6.5	7.2
1990-99	12.4	0.5	46.7	5.7	40.9	1.8	3.4
1992-99	11.8	1.2	46.9	5.8	41.3	4.9	4.9
1992-99	11.8	6.6	42.9	6.1	45.3	7.8	6.8

Source: RBI, Statistical tables relating to banks in India.

The above table captures the period-wise trend in the share and rate of growth of bank credit in the three broad economic sector, viz., agriculture, industry and tertiary. During the 1970s, agricultural and tertiary sectors witnessed higher rate of growth of bank credit than the industrial sector. However, during 1990s, the rate of growth of credit to both agricultural and tertiary sectors has considerably slowed down. There has also been a decline in the rate of growth of credit to the industrial sector during this period, but this is still higher at 5.8 per cent than the total credit expansion at 4.9 per cent. The reason for an industrial sector getting a larger share of the bank credit in the post-reform period was the bank's perception that the loans to industrial sector are less risky than those to the agricultural and tertiary sector.

The reforms in India are halting and hesitant. The weak and worsening economic performance must raise the question in some mind; do the reforms have some lasting damage to the growth process? It is admitted that the reform process can not be entirely painless. While there are achievements, there are pitfalls as well. There has been an increase in the ratio of deposits to national income in the post reform period. There has also been an increase in the rate of growth of bank credit. The banks have invested in govt. securities a much larger proportion of their deposits than is warranted by the prescribed SLR.This has mainly been due to the persistently large budget deficit run by the Central and State govt. The deregulated environment has not resulted in any marked improvement in the efficiency of PSBs with the exception of the few. Govt. and political interference in the decision making of the banks are the problems that plagued the PSBs.

After examining the existing evidence on the cost and benefit of priority sector lending in India, it has been argued that credit policy in this regard needs to be re-appraised and geared towards more specific objectives. The objectives could be defined locally on the basis of bank –industry exchange that could guide the banks as to which firm or industries are to be financed. Lending to agriculture in general and to the small and marginal farmers in particular needs to be enhanced beyond the prescribed levels.

References

Dr. D. Dakshina Murthy, Banking Sector Reforms: The Challenges Ahead, Serials Publication, New Delhi.

Dr. Noor Basha Abdul, Indian Banking Sector Reforms: An Appraisal, Serial Publications, New Delhi.

Business Telegraph, 2nd April 2007.

Ms. K. R.Chitra, Voluntary Retirement Scheme Implemented by Public Sector Banks, website RBI.

16

Banking Sector Reforms in India

Shashi Kapur Das

Banking sector Reforms in India was initiated in 1992 on the basis of the recommendations of the Committee on the Financial System headed by Mr. M. Narasimham. Several of these recommendations were implemented during the first phase of reform and the second phase of reform began after the Committee on Banking Sector Sector Reform also headed by Mr. M. Narasimham submitted its reports in 1998. The two Reports of Mr. M. Narasimham Committee have been instrumental in bringing about a major shift in the approach to the development of the banking sector in India.

The basic aim of banking reform is to establish a sound and viable banking system, which would help the development of the real economy. The objective of promoting efficiency in the real economy cannot be fulfiled unless there is reform of the financial sector as well. As pointed out by the Committee on Financial System, "Economic Reforms in the real sectors of the economy will, ..., fail to realise their potential without a parallel reform of the financial sector, in order, broadly speaking, to enhance the efficiency of financial intermediation. Financial sector reform is, therefore, a necessary concomitant of trade and industrial policy liberalization so that the competitive spirit and efficiency that we are seeking to bring about in the real economy would cover the critically important financial sector and be further sustained by it."

These reforms have brought out structural changes in the financial sector, eased external constraints in the working, introduced transparancy in reporting procedures, restructuring and recapitalization of banks and have increased the competitive element in the market.

Reforms

First, in the reform process, competitive environment has been created since such an environment is necessary for improving the efficiency and productivity of the banking system. Competitive environment was lacking in the pre-reform period because of the existence of administered interest rates, restriction on the entry of foreign banks and denial of opportunity for licensing of any new private banks. With the removal of adminiistered interest rates and starting of new private sector banks and liberalized policy in respect of entry of foreign banks into the Indian banking sector and starting of more branches by the existing foreign banks, competitive environment in Indian banking has been created which is supposed to contribute to the improvement in the efficiency of the banking sector in India.

In tune with the Narasimhan Committee I recommendation, RBI has relaxed norms for issuing license to new banks with objective to induce greater competition and operational efficiency in the Indian banking system. Many new private sector banks have been set up out of which YES Bank is the latest offering. Further RBI/GOI has decided to permit foreign banks operating in India to open new branches and also adopt subsidiary route to do business. As competition mounted, Public Sector Banks, which operated on the comfort of sovereign guarantee, are forced to keep pace with private sector counter parts by upgrading their work process through technology and also becoming customer focused. Banks are replicating the story clearly seen in telecom and aviation. Nationalized banks have witnessed the most significant decline in their share of assets from 52.5% at the end of March 97 to

46.7 per cent at the end of March 04 whereas market share of private sector banks increased from 2.4 per cent from March 1997 to 12.5 per cent in March 2004.

RBI has recently notified 'roadmap for presence of foreign banks in India and guidelines on ownership and governance in private banks.' As per ceht roadmap, foreign banks wishing to establish a presence in India for the first time could either choose to operate through branch presence, or set up 100 per cent subsidiary (WOS) following the 'one mode presence criterion' In phase-I, foreign banks already operating in India will be allowed to convert their existing branches to WOS. In phase-II, WOS of foreign banks will be accorded full national treatment, including opting for going public, subject to 26 per cent of the capital being held by resident Indians at all times. RBI has also allowed some flexibility in individual stake and subject to RBI approval this stake can exceed 10 per cent. Opening up of the financial sector from 2009, under WTO, would see a number of global banks taking large stakes and control over banking entities in India. They would bring with them capital, technology and management skills.

The minimum prescribed Govt. equity has been brought down to 51 per cent. The Standing Committee on finance has cleared the proposal to bring down the government stake in PSBs from 51 per cent to 33 per cent but GOI has decided to keep government equity to 51 per cent minimum. The State Bank of India Act 1955 and Nationalization act of 1970 have also been amended to enable the banks to access the capital market for debt and equity. RBI has also permitted banks to raise long term funds through bond for infrastructure finance to overcome problem of assets liability mismatch and is also considering to permit banks to issue preference shares and to remove cap 10 per cent of voting rights imposed under secton 12 of banking Regulation Act, 1949. The Finance Minister announced in budget proposals 2005 to bring comprehensive bill to amend Banking Regulation Act 1949 and to address all concerns to tackle the problem of banking sector (particularly co-operative banks). GOI has also announced more managerial autonomy for public sector banks - freedom of action on merger and acquisition, managing and closing down unviable branches, crafting HR policies on recruitment, tranfer and promotions, sanction of differential pay to employees linked to performance and creating additional post of General Mangers.

Second, the Committee on Financial System made a strong case for a re-examination of the relevance of the directed credit programme and argued in favour of a gradual phasing out of this programme on the following grounds:

1. "Directed credit programmes have led to stagnation of credit markets and introduced an element of inflexibility in bank operations."
2. Availability of credit to traditional sectors of medium and large industry is affected and this has deleterious effect on the growth of industrial investment and production.
3. Agriculture and SSIs are now fairly well developed and their requirements can be met on the basis of commercial judgment of banks.

The committee also opposed concession in the retes of interest on priority sector lending on the ground that it is timely and adequate availability of credit rather than the cost of credit that is really important. It recommended that the priority sector should be reduced from 40 per cent to 10 per cent of total bank credit. Such a recommendation was obviously not acceptable to the Government that there is need for continued and adequate flow of credit to the rural sector from the point of view of food security, employment generation and encouragement to dry land farming. The Committee on Banking Sector Reforms, i.e. Second Narasimham Committee gave up the idea of phasing out the directed credit programme and recognised the need for its continuation. It said, "The Committee has noted the reasons why the Government could not accept the recommendation for reducing the scope of directed credit under priority sector from 40 per cent to 10 per cent. The Committee recognised that the small and marginal farmers and the tiny sector of industry and small business have problems with regard to obtaining credit and some earmarking may be necessary for this sector. Under the present dispensation, within the priority sector 10 per cent of bank credit is earmarked for lending to weaker sections. A major portion of this lending is on account of Government sponsored poverty alleviation and employment generation schemes. The Committee recommends that given the social needs of this sector, the current practice may continue."

Despite the rejection of the recommendations of the Committee on the Financial System in respect of directed credit policy and the recognition of the need for continuation of the directed credit programme by the Committee on Banking Sector Reforms, some changes have taken place in respect of directed credit in the reform era as a result of which the concept of directed credit is diluted. The definition of directed credit in the pre-reform period included agriculture, small scale industries, small road and water transport operators, small business, retail trade, state-sponsored organizations for SC/STs, educational loans granted to individuals by banks under their schemes and credit schemes for weaker sections. The definition of priority sector has been enlarged in the reform era and now it includes:

1. Loans to traditional plantation crops viz. tea, coffee, cardamom, etc. irrespective of size of holding.
2. Educational loans upto INR 20 lacs for studies abroad and INR 10 lacs for studies in India will qualify as priority sector advances.
3. Loans for housing up to Rs. 5 lakhs.
4. Loans to transport operators up to ten vehicles.
5. Advances to dealers of drip/sprinkler irrigation system and agricultural machinery.
6. Investmens made by banks in special bonds of SIDBI, NABARD, NHB, NSIC, HUDCO, SFCs, SIDCs and REC and contributions to Rural Infrastructure Fund.
7. Banks' investment in bonds issued by Rural Electrification Corporation (REC) for financing its Systems

Improvement Scheme under Special Project Agriculture (SI-SPA).

8. Advances to NBFCs for on-lending to truck operators satisfying priority sector norms.
9. Advances up to Rs. 10 million to software industry.

Though the stipulation that 40 per cent of total bank credit should go to priority sector continues, the target is not a rigid one. The requirement is that if the target is not reached, an amount equivalent to the shortfall should be invested in NABARD/SIDBI and that means banks need not lend to commercially non-viable activities. With several profitable avenues included in the priority sector and in the absence of compulsion to reach the priority sector lending target, opportunity is provided to banks to extend loans on commercially viable terms. Though these changes are welcome from the point of view of enabling banks to operate on commercially viable terms, availability of bank loans for agriculture, SSIs and weaker sections is bound to suffer. According to the Annual Report of the RBI, in 1990-00, the share of the priority sector advances constituted only 34.3 per cent of the incremental credit as against the norm of 40 per cent. A dip in the expansion of credit for the SSI sector has indicated that there is no healthy distribution of bank credit sectorally. The SLR requirement has been brought down from 38.5 per cent in 1991-92 to 25 per cent and CRR has been brought down from 15 per cent in 1991-92 to 5 per cent. There is proposal in Union budget of 2005 to scrap legislative minimum cap on SLR of 25 per cent and cap on CRR of 3 per cent to give RBI more discretion. The measure will enable banks to have more funds for lending.

In the wake of the failure of the target-oriented approach, the emphasis has shifted to enhancement of the role of NGOs and self-help groups. While the priority sector lending should continue, the emphasis should be on lending at commercial rates, effective utilisation of credit and prompt repayment. The Committee on Banking Sector Reforms has rightly recognised the importance of micro-credit institutions. It has recommended that "Banking policy should facilitate the evolution and growth of micro-credit institutions, including Local Area Banks which focus on agriculture, tiny and small scale industries, including such specialist institutions as may be prompted by NGOs for meeting the banking needs of the poor." The micro-credit movement is catching up and its coverage must be further expanded.

Third, all lending rates except for lending to small borrowers up to Rs. 2 lakhs and a part of export finance has been de-regulated. Banks have been given freedom to price their loan above or below Bank Prime Lending Rate (BPLR) subject to transparent guidelines and credit policy. Banks have introduced floating and fixed interest rate products and are more aggressive in their offering. RBI has also made lending rate disclosure mandatory for banks to announce Benchmark PLR after taking into consideration (a) actual cost of funds, (b) operating expenses and (c) mimimum margin to cover regulatory requirement of provision, capital charge and profit margin.

Fourth, prudential norms such as capital adequacy, income recognition, asset classification and provisioning standards adopted in the reform era are of global standards and they aim at strengthening the safety and soundness of the banking system. Adequate capital is one of the pre-requisites for the efficient working of banks. In the pre-reform period there were no capital adequacy requirements and some banks were seriously undercapitalized. The Committee on Financial System rightly said that "the ratio of capital funds in relation to a bank's deposits or its assets is a well recognized and universally accepted measure of the strength and stability of the institutions." Based on the Basel Committee international norms, it prescribed capital to risk asset ratio of 8 per cent and recommended that this should be reached in a phased manner. Most of the banks comply with this ratio now. The Committee on Banking Sector Reforms suggested that there should be further increase in the capital adequacy ratio to 9 per cent. Thus. the earlier argument that the banks owned by the Government need not prescribe capital adequacy ratios has been rejected and the commercial element in the banking sector owned by the Government is recognized. But further capital infusion cannot take place through recapitalization by the Government and the public sector banks have to raise funds in the market, the success of which depends on the conditions in the stock market and the soundness of the concerned banks.

To ensure transparency in financial statements of banks, the Committee on Financial System recommended that interest should be recognized only on actual basis and not on accrual basis and accordingly now "banks cannot recognize income on assets where income is not received within two quarters after it is past due." The Committee on Banking Sector Reforms called for further improvement by adopting the international norm of ninety days instead of two quarters. Another measure for ensuring transparency is the new prescription given for asset classification into eight health code categories was there in the pre-reform period, the classification was not objective and it was left to the discretion of each bank. But after the introduction of reforms, all advances have to be classified into four broad groups, namely, (a) standard, (b) sub-standard (non-performing for a period not exceeding two years), (c) doubtful (instalments overdue for a period exceeding two years), and (d) loss assets (loss has been identified, but the amount not written off).

Further, provisioning standards, which were left to the discretion of banks in the pre-reform period, have been enhanced and tightened after the introduction of reforms. Banks have to now make 10 per cent general provision on outstanding substandard advances, 100 per cent provision on unsecured portion of doubtful debts, 20 per cent to 50 per cent provision on secured portion of doubtful assets over a three year period and 100 per cent on loss assets. The Committee on Banking Sector Reforms has recommended that even Government guaranteed advances should be brought under the new provisioning standards.

Fifth, in the reform process, the supervisory system has been streamlined and this is another important step towards establishing a sound banking system. In the pre-reform period, the RBI supervisory strategy consisted of only on-site inspection. But after the reform, both on-site inspection and off-site surveillance are followed. A Board for Financial Supervision has been set-up within the Reserve Bank of India. Under on-site inspection, total operations and performance of banks are assessed. Capital adequacy, Asset quality, Management, Earnings, Liquidity and Systems (CAMELS) are evaluated under on-site inspection. The financial condition of banks is monitored to identify banks, which show financial deterioration under off-site suveillance. Thus, the supervisory system has been strengthened with the introduction of these new measures.

Sixth, for strengthening the recovery process, the Committee on Financial System recommended the establishment of Debt Recovery Tribunals and accordingly Recovery of Debts Due to Banks and Financial Institutions Act was passed in 1993 which provided for the establishment of the tribunals for facilitating expeditious adjudication and recovery of debts. But in reality, the tribunals have not helped the recovery process much. The Committee on Banking Sector Reforms reviewed the working of Debt Recovery Tribunals and identified certain shortcomings and recommended that the tribunals should be vested with the powers of attachment before judgment to make them more effective. RBI's Working Group to Review the Functioning of DRTs also made certain recommendations for improving the working of DRTs and amendment to the Recovery of Debts Act has been brought anout on the basis of the recommendations of the Working Group. An expert group has also looked into legal lacunae. Debt Recovery Tribunals, which have not been effective so far, are expected to do better in future. It is widely recognized that the legal system is defaulter-friendly and that the recovery process will not improve unless their is a change in this.

Securitisation and Reconstruction of Financial Assets and enforcement of Security Interest Act 2002 allows setting up of Asset Reconstruction Companies (ARC) by banks with unprecedented powers to take over the management of a defaulting company or take over and sale distressed loan. The Act provides for 60 days notice to borrower to discharge the liability in full failing which a bank can take possession of mortgaged/hypothecated assets and sale them for liquidation of dues. ARCs set up under Securitisation and Reconstruction of Financial Assets and Enforcement of Security Interest Act have been empowered to take over NPA from banks, engage in innovative corporate finance such as merger, sale of brands or plants, inject new capital, convert distressed companies into new companies and even take out an IPO. ARC will have to work within RBI guidelines and subject to registration/license from RBI. ARCs should have minimum owned funds of Rs. 100 crores and have to maintain minimum capital adequacy of 15 per cent at all times. Several players have applied to RBI for registration in order to commence business. The major ones are, Assets Reconstruction Company (India) Ltd. (Arcil) and Assets Care Enterprise (ACE). First ARC known, as ARCIL has been registered as private sector entity with 51 per cent equity in the hands of private sector banks. It is registered with RBI under section 3 of the SARFESAI Act, 2002 as Securitisation and Reconstruction Company, which commenced business from August 29, 2003. The compay is an associate member of IBA. In its one and half year operation, ARCIL has acquired 362 bad loans of Rs. 16,500 crores. ICICI bank is the biggest seller of bad loan to ARCIL. It sold 134 cases of Rs. 8450 crores followed by SBI which sold 181 cases of Rs. 2468 crores.

Seventh, in view of the diverse financial and non-financial risks confronted by banks in the wake of the financial sector deregulation, RBI has put the risk management system in place. Banks have been asked to adopt sophisticated techniques like VaR, Duration and Simulation model-based approaches as also credit risk modeling techniques as part of risk management measures. RBI has issued detailed guidelines for Risk Based Supervision (RBS) and have advised banks to develop internal capital assessmtne processes in accordance with their risk profile and control environment which will sbjected to review and supervisory intervention by RBI as necessary. The emphasis will be on evaluating the quality of risk management and the adequacy of risk constainment. The transaction based internal/external audit would be replaced by Risk Based Internal Audit (RBIA) system.

Eight, an adequate institutional and legal framework is in place in India for effectively implementing a code of sound corporate governance in banks. The status have built in legal provisions that prohibit or strongly limit activities and relationships that diminish the quality of corporate governance in banks. As a major step towards strengthening corporate governance in banks, banks have been asked by RBI to place before their Board of Directors the Report of the Consultative Group of Directors of banks and FIs (Dr. Ganguly Group) set up to review the supervisory role of Boards of banks. The recommendations include the responsibility of the Board of Directors, role and responsibility of independent and non-executive directors, etc. With number of banks now listed on stock exchange and accountable to shareholders, it is necessary to focus on corporate governance in letter and spirit as quality of decision making will be crucial in enhancing share-holders' value.

Nineth, one more issues that needs to be addressed is the performance of weak banks. The presence of weak banks is a threat to the stability of the banking system. The Working Group on Weak Banks headed by Mr. Verma has suggested the criteria for identifying the weak banks and the measures to be undertaken for strengthening these banks. It has suggested a four-pronged strategy consisting of operational, organizatioal, financial and systemic restructuring in the first stage and privatisation or mergers in the second state. Privatization or merger appears to be a better option. The Committee on Financial System had recommended that the entire banking system should be restructured in such a way that there would be 3 or 4 large banks of international charachter, 8 or 10 national banks, local banks and rural banks. But this recommnedation has not been implemented so far. Such a restructuring might provide an answer to the problem of weak banks.

The branching policy advocated by the Narasimham Committee I and II also needs careful examinationa. Both advocated that unremunerative rural branches which are responsible for high level of NPAs and low profitabilty should be closed down or in other words, the presence of the public sector banks in the rural sector must be reduced and their place should be taken over by the local area banks and institutions promoted by NGOs. It is doubtful whether this approach would be helpful to the rural economy. It is, viable rural branches, an attempt should be made to restructure them so that they may become viable. It is also being argued that it is possible to draw lessons from Indonesian experience in this regard. What helped the transformation of non-viable Indonesian rural bank branches into viable ones was the introduction of measures like deregulation of interest rates, autonomy, accountability, incentives and proper training for staff, hiring of local staff for keeping the costs low, treating each branch as a separate profit centre with its own balance sheet, computerisation, etc. Similar measures can be tried in India instead of resorting to closing down of non-viable rural branches. In any case, it is necessary to ensure that the rural economy is not starved of credit.

In sum, the reform measures introduced so far have laid the base for a sound and viable banking system. But the problems of the banking sector are far from over. The main areas of concern are profitability, adequacy of capital, non-performing assets, functioning of the supervisiory system, adequate flow of credit to the rural sector and SSIs and human resource development in the banking sector.

References

Government of India (1998), Report of the Committee on Banking Sector Reforms.

Jalan, B. (2000), "Agenda for Banking in the New Millennium", *Reserve Bank of India Bulletin*, March.

Reserve Bank of India (1991), Report of the Committee on the Financial System.

Reserve Bank of India, Report on the Trend and Progress of Banking in India (various years).

Reserve Bank of India (1999), Banking Sector Reform, Annexture I, *Reserve Bank of India Bulletin*, March.

Ahluwalia, M. S. (1999), India's Economic Reforms; An Appraisal. India in the era of Economic Reform, Oxford University Press.

17

Banking Sector Reforms– An Emergng Dimension of NPA Management

B. K. Mohanty

NPAs are those assets which do not yield any return. NPAs i.e. are the loans where borrowers are not able to pay their interest/principal on due dates. After all high NPAs impose an additional cost on performing assets. Which now have to carry the burden of a higher rate of interest to make up for the loan implied in NPAs not paying interest. Moreover, while high NPAs are definitely a cause for concern, low NPAs are no guarantee against banking distress.

In Malaysia Bank Negura, tightened the definition of NPA as per the directive issued by IMF and the Banks were compelled to put a squeeze on credit which further aggravated the financial crisis. IMF study finds a strong correlation between severe financial crises and hasty financial sector reform. In Korea even when there is lowest NPA financial crises have been marked.

An NPA was defined "as a credit facility where interest has remained past due for a period of four quarters ended March 31st 1993. Three quarters ended March 31st March 1994. Two quarters ended March 31st 1995.

Technically, NPA consists of three categories of assets– substantial, doubtful and loan assets. The definition of the above classification of assets vary from time to time. As per the new norms for recognition, March 31, 2001, assets classified as NPAs for a period up to two years belong to sub standard category, while doubtful assets are those that remain NPA for a period beyond two years. Loan assets are those which are identified as such either by Banks themselves or auditors or RBI but not written off with a view to moving closer to the international practices. Further more the time gap of classification of an asset as "doubtful" is also sought to be reduced from 18 months to 12 months effective from March 31, 2003.

Problems

Credit risk is an important factor imposing on financial entities. The solvency crises of financial systems such as the American savings and loan crises in the 1980s, the Nordic Banking crises at the beginning of the 1990s and more recently the banking sector problems in Japan and Turkey, been a consequence of accumulation of problem loans overtime.

NPAs are basically a factor of today's state of industry and the bad legal system for recovery of loans. But there is a mistake that critics are making.

Internationally, the collaterals are taken into consideration for calculating the final NPA figure. In our country (India) this is not the case and though we move a provision for shortfall of collaterals we do not subtract the collaterals on our books before calculating NPAs. In India most of the loans are balanced by securities. If these securities are taken into account, our NPA levels will be amongst the lowest.

Banking is a risky business because commercial banks maximum depends upon the depositors from the public. The public depositors are payable on demand and if these banks first to pay the public money at the time of demand naturally the entire banking system will collapse. According to Martin Wolf a "London Financial Times", the assets on which the bank invest their money may not be able to realize sufficient amount of cash at the time of demand because the assets are subject to various kinds of risk– (1) Market risk (Changes in Assets value)–

(2) Credit risk break down of the payment system and forex risk (forex devaluation) another risk also arise due to political interference and fraud. Any one of these could give rise to NPAs. Prudent bankers try to minimize there risks by taking informed decisions technical experts in financial forecasting and market forecasting help in solving these NPA problems to a greater extent.

Prudential norms in respect of loan classification vary widely across countries. Countries follow varied approaches. As an example, in UK do not require banks to adopt any particular form of loan classification and they do not give much emphasis on the number of classification categories that bank should follow. On the other hand United States of America follow a more descriptive approach wherein loans are classified into several categories based on a set of criteria ranging from payment experience to the environment in which the doctor evolves.

The problem of calculating the real NPA is that till now there is no universally accepted definition the RBI has its own definition to call banks to recognize NPAs only 180 days after then become past due as against the developed country norm of 45-90 days. As a result cross country comparison are not very meaningful. Even within the same country. NPA estimate differs in a number of ways which leads to misleading the true NPA figure.

Loan classification may be based upon two criteria (i) Subjective criteria (ii) Objective criteria. Subjective criteria includes features like insufficient working capital, absence of adequate financial infrastructure and the line. On the other hand objective criteria include the number of days as loan is past due and more broadly the current condition of the debtor. Other criteria include an accurate assessment of the expected probability of default.

Previously the norms was if the interest was not paid during the last two seasons of harvest (covering two half years) after it became past due.

RBI has tightened the provisioning norms in respect of advances granted for agricultural purposes. NPA of agricultural sector has been increasing due to the prescribed norms of RBI. RBI introduced that an advance granted in agricultural purposes shall be treated as NPA if the interest/ investment is in arrear for more than two quarters from the date the interest/investment are due for repayment.

Generally Banks provide agricultural advances either as term loans or as crop loans. According to them in case of crop loans interest is paid along with principal on the due date. The due date is synchronized with the harvest period. As per the new norms the agricultural advances will be reduced ultimately as NPA will increase. Further bank argues that "agriculture is a gamble of monsoons" so this approach of calculating NPA may not be ideal.

In one side RBI has been advocating increasing agricultural advances, and on the other side, tightening the prudential norms for advancing in loans.

Recent Changes of Definition

The definition of priority sector lending has been continuously changing according to the financial sector reforms and monetary policy measures of 2004-05. The mid term review committee headed by Prof. V.S. Vyas. The recommendations of the committee has been accepted by the RBI and implemented.

In order to further enhance credit flow to build up storage facilities, it is proposed that–loans to storage units, including cold storage units which are designed to store agricultural produce irrespective of their locations would be treated as indirect agricultural finance. Priority sector according to new economic reform policy announced in 2004-05 investment by banks in securitized assets representing direct (indirect) lending to agriculture would be treated as their indirect (indirect), lending to agriculture under priority sector. Presently agricultural loan above Rs. 10,000/- banks are free to keep margin and security taking into account the importance of flow of credit to agriculture particularly to small borrowers. Who may not provide collateral security. According to the new RBI norm now it has been mentioned that security requirement for agriculture loan up to Rs. 50,000/- and in case of agri-business and agri-clinics with up to rupees five lakhs the banks can wive the security margin.

Revised NPA Norm for Agricultural Advances

In terms of earlier guidelines, an specified direct agricultural advances were treated as NPA when Internal/interior statement of principal remain unpaid after it has become due for two harvest seasons but for a period not exceeding 2.5 years. It has been decided on June, 2004 effective September 30,2004, that loans granted for ST duration and long term duration crops would be treated as NPA it's the installment of principal or interest thereon remains overdue for two crop seasons and one crop season, respectively. NPA's would be done in the same banks which at present is the 90 days delinquency norm.

Provisioning Norms

As per the earlier guidelines, banks were advised to make a provision of 50% in respect of the secured portion of NPA included in 'doubtful' for more than three years category. On a review, it has been decided in June 2004 to introduce a graded higher provisioning on the secured portion of NPAs ranging from 60% to 100% over a period of 3 years in a phased manner with effect from 31st March, 2005.

However, in respect of an advances classified as doubtful for more than 3 years on or after April 1, 2004 the provisioning requirement would be 100%. The provisioning requirement for unsecured portion of NPAs under the above category will continue to be 100%.

A borrower is treated as willful defaulter if he (i) Diverts the income to other channels (ii) no botheration of legal action (iii) fear of not getting fresh loans after repayment of loan.

Suggestive Measures and Steps taken by Banks for Reducing NPA

One time settlement/compromised scheme–the guidelines issued on January 29, 2003 for compromise settlement are as follows:

1. Compromise settlement of NPAs can be made up to rupees 10 crores.
2. The guidelines will cover all NPAs in all sectors which have become doubtful or loss assets as on 31st March, 2000 with outstanding balance of Rs. 10 crores.
3. The guidelines also cover NPAs classified as substandard assets as on 31st March, 2000.
4. The guideline will be applicable to cases to which the banks have initiated actions under the "securitization and reconstruction" of financial assets and enforcement of security interest (SARFAFSI) Act, 2002 and also cases pending before courts.
5. The last date of receipt of application from borrowers under the scheme was Sept. 30, 2003 and their processing should be completed by Dec. 31, 2003. Guidelines for OTS scheme for loans up to Rs. 50,000/- to small and marginal farmers has been extended up to March 31, 2003.
6. In May, 2003 the time limit for processing of applications received under the raised guidelines for compromise settlement of chronic NPAs of Public sector banks, upto Rs. 10 crores was extended to December 31, 2003. Based on the requests received for further extending the time limit for operation of the guidelines and in consultation with Government of India, the time limit for receiving applications was further extended upto July 31, 2004.

Lok Adalats

Banks were advised by RBI to participate Lok Adalat convened by DRT (Debt Recovery Tribunal) or DRATS (Debt Recovery Appellate Tribunals) for resolving cases involving rupees 10 lakhs or above to reduce the stock of NPAs. As on June 30, 2003, 2,72,793 cases were filed amounting Rs. 1193.3 crores and amount recovered was from 87,907 cases was Rs. 190.5 crores. The number of cases filed by commercial banks with Lok Adalats stood at 485046 involving an amount of 2.43 crore.

The number of cases decided was 2051032 involving an amount of Rs. 974 crore, and the recoveries effected in 159316 cases stood at Rs. 328 crore as on March 31, 2004.

SARFACSI Act 2002

Recovery management of NPAs has become a keyword for the banking industry in recent years in the Indian context several initiatives have been taken by RBI to reduce the NPAs of banks. As a consequence NPA of SCBs have declined. The public sector banks and financial institutions have been advised to take action under the act and report compliance to RBI. These guidelines, inter-alia prescribe the financial assets which can be sold to SCS/RCS by banks/FIS. Proceedings due for such sales, prudential norms for the sale transactions and related disclosures. The declined in NPA has been marked except in 2000-01, in line of this declining trend NPA declined sharply in 2002-03 reflecting impact of earlier measures towards NPA reduction and the enactment of the SARAFAESI Act. ensuring prompt recoveries without intervention of court or tribunal.

CDR Mechanism

A scheme of corporate debt restructuring (CDR) was developed in India based on international experience and detail guidelines on the same were issued for implementation by banks and financial institutions in 2001. The objective of the mechanism has been to ensure timely and transparent mechanism for restructuring the corporate debt of viable entities. The features of CDR scheme are as follows–

1. It will cover multiple banking accounts with outstanding exposure of Rs. 20 crores or above.
2. It is a voluntary system based on debtor-creditor agreement (DCA) and inter creditor agreement (ICA).
3. The system have a 3 tire structure (i) CDR standing forum (Policy making body) (ii) CDR empowered group (the functional group), (iii) The CDR cell (the secretariat to the CDR system).

4. The revised guideline provides the exceeding system for lenders who do not wish to commit additional financing or wish to sell their existing share.
5. "Stand Still" agreement binding for 90 days or 180 days by debtors or creditors respectively under which both sides committee not to take recourse any legal action during the "stand still period".

Basing on the recommendation made by high level group and in consultation with the Government, a revised schemd of CDR was finalized and forwarded to banks in Feb. 2003. The number of cases and value of assets restructured under the CDR mechanism stood at 94 and Rs. 64,017 crore, respectively, as on June 30, 2004. The major beneficiaries were iron and steel, refinery, fertilizers and telecommunications industries, accounting for more than two-third shares of value of assets restructured.

Recommendations of Working Group (Wilful Defauters)

The willful defaulters know how to connive, manipulate and influence the officials of the lending institutions. Such defaulters may also instigate others not to repay on the assurance that they will help them in case of any difficulty because of such defaults. To prevent all such practices the new policy has made classification of borrowal accounts and the redressal mechanism into two distinct process (i) identification of defaulters as willful with clear cut reasons and (ii) providing an opportunity to the borrowers to make a representation before being classified as a willful defaulter.

A committee has been formed head by the chairman Shri S. S. Kohli, which issued further guide lines on July 29, 2003 to banks and FIS who are required to form a committee of higher functionaries headed by the Executive Director for classification of borrower accounts as willful defaulters, and create to form a committee headed by chairman and Managing Director for giving a hearing to borrowers who represent then they have been wrangles classified as willful defaulters.

The grievance of the borrower concerned is to be corroding thoroughly through two district processes viz. (i) Identification of default as 'wilful' based as the prescribed norms through a committee approach and (ii) suitably advising the borrower about the proposal to classify him as willful defaulter along with the reasons therefore. The concerned borrower would be provided 15 days time. A final declaration as willful defaulter would be made any after a view is taken by the committee as specific representation.

Board for Financial Supervision

Several important issues were discussed in the meetings of BFS during 2003-04 as regard NPA's, provisioning, disclosure and ratings. The major areas of concern included– (i) The need for obtaining proper securing and transparency in application of interest rates for housing loans (ii) fixing the limit an exposure of banks with respect to gross advances rather than capital funds as is being done presently (iii) the case for exclusion of new economy businesses. Like IT, Service sector, retail trade, while applying 15% ceiling on unsecured advances (iv) the systemic impact of cross holdings of subordinated debt and equities across banks and financial institutions (v) impact in financial position of banks of marking to market cent-per-cent of investments.

Risk based supervision is being taken up an co-pilot basis from the year 2001. The recommendations of the report of consultative group as the role of directors of bank and financial institutions regarding corporate governance were conveyed to banks for implementations.

Debt Recovery Tribunals

The amendments made in 2000 to the DRT act and the rules reformed there under have strengthened the functioning of DRT's as the recommendation of the RBI, Government has since setup a working group headed by additional secretary, Govt. of India, to improve the functioning of DRT's. As on June 30, 2004 i.e. of 63,600 crores (involving Rs. 91,926 crore) filed with DRTs by the banks 27,956 cases. (involving Rs. 25,358 crore) have been adjudicated by them. The amount recovered so far through the adjudicated cases as placed at Rs. 7845 crore.

Asset Re-construction Companies (ARCS)

To solve the problem of bad loans, several institutions have initiated steps towards establishment of ARCS, which take over non-performing loans of banks and FIS at a discounted rate, and manage and dispose such assets. The RBI has granted certificate of registration to three ARCS so for out of which ARCIL has already started its operations so far ARCIL has acquired NPAs worth Rs. 9,631 crore from banks and FIS at a price of Rs. 2089 crore. In order that ARCS have a sound capital base and a stake in the management of the NPA acquired, the requirement of owned fund for commencement of business has been stipulated as not less than 15% of the asset acquired on Rs. 100 crore, whichever is less.

Credit Information as Defaulters and Role of Credit Information Bureau

Credit information covering data supplied as suit filed defaulters in the financial system is being under taken by CIBIL with effect from March 2003; and the data can be assessed as CIBIL website. The RBI had issued instructions to banks and FIS to obtain the cases of all their borrowers for pooling of data for development of a comprehensive credit information system. In order to give further thrust in the matter of operationalization of CIBIL, the RBI advised banks to review the measures taken at their board level and report compliance to the RBI about the same. It was reported by a major nationalized bank that they have submitted credit information relating to 80% of their eligible borrowers after obtaining necessary consent. Banks have been urged to make persistent efforts in obtaining consent from their borrowers in order to establish efficient credit system, which would help in enhancing the quality credit decisions and improving the asset quality of banks.

From Table 1 it has been revealed that, up to June 2003 all scheduled commercial banks have issued 33,736 no. of notices amounting an outstanding amount of Rs. 12,147.2 crores out

Table 1
Bank-wise Details of Progress under SARFAEST Act
(As at end–June 2003) (Amount in Crores)

Name of the Bank	*Notices issued*	*Amount out-standing*	*Recovered cases*	*Amount recovered*	*Percent of amount recovered to amount out-standing*
Allahabad Bank	1,579	514.8	610	21.9	4.2
Andhra Bank	401	73.9	118	9.5	12.8
Bank of Baroda	125	429.5	19	7.8	1.8
Bank of India	1,241	405.8	692	34.3	8.4
Bank of Maharashtra	332	52.7	61	2.6	4.9
Canara Bank	1,011	350.5	393	34.5	9.8
Central Bank of India	2,617	1,204.9	395	39.1	3.3
Corporation Bank	247	155.0	98	18.5	11.9
Dena Bank	348	358.6	147	32.3	6.2
Indian Bank	1,007	425.8	240	19.5	4.6
Indian Overseas Bank	1,879	509.9	747	29.4	5.8
Allahabad Bank	1,579	514.8	610	21.9	4.2
Andhra Bank	401	73.9	118	9.5	12.8
Bank of Baroda	125	429.5	19	7.8	1.8
Bank of India	1,241	405.8	692	34.3	8.4
Bank of Maharashtra	332	52.7	61	2.6	4.9
Canara Bank	1,011	350.5	393	34.5	9.8
Central Bank of India	2,617	1,204.9	395	39.1	3.3
Corporation Bank	247	155.0	98	18.5	11.9
Dena Bank	348	358.6	147	32.3	6.2
Indian Bank	1,007	425.8	240	19.5	4.6
Indian Overseas Bank	1,879	509.9	747	29.4	5.8
Oriental Bank of Commerce	2,217	427.5	1,184	41.9	9.8
Punjab National Bank	3,015	711.8	1,086	39.3	5.5
Punjab & Sindh Bank	1,102	499.0	509	23.0	4.6
Syndicate Bank	1,226	156.9	480	17.2	10.9
Union Bank of India	1,601	757.2	524	22.6	2.9
United Bank of India	148	14.1	54	1.8	13.0
Uco Bank	1,130	88.4	138	4.6	5.2

Contd...

Name of the Bank	*Notices issued*	*Amount out-standing*	*Recovered cases*	*Amount recovered*	*Percent of amount recovered to amount out-standing*
Vijaya Bank	1,988	239.9	638	26.4	11.0
State Bank of India	7,141	3,974.0	1,037	48.0	1.2
State Bank of Bikaner & Jaipur	606	114.5	217	3.9	3.4
State Bank of Hyderabad	827	282.5	102	9.8	3.5
State Bank of Indore	403	68.6	123	6.6	9.6
State Bank of Mysore	344	102.1	34	4.6	4.5
State Bank of Patiala	807	126.0	210	4.4	3.5
State Bank of Sourastra	325	70.8	59	3.6	5.1
State Bank of Travancore	69	32.5	31	2.1	6.6
Total	33,736	12,147.2	9,946	499.2	4.1

Source: Reserve Bank of India (2003), Annual Reports 2002-03, Mumbai Reserve Bank of India (2002), Report on Trend & Progress of Banking in India (2001-02), Mumbai

of which 9,946 cases were recovered amounting Rs. 499.2 crores representing 4.1% of the total outstanding amount. More than 10% of the total outstanding amount have been recovered from the borrowers of Andhra Bank, Corporation Bank, Syndicate Bank, United Bank of India and Vijaya Bank. Lowest 1.2% recovery has been made by State Bank of India. Highest recovery of 13% has been made by the United Bank of India. As on June 30,2004, 27 Public Sector banks had issued 61,263 notices involving outstanding amount of Rs. 19,744 crore, and had recovered an amount of Rs. 1748 crore from 24,092 cases.

From Table 2 it has been seen that in 2003 there were 71 cases reformed to CDR forum and the number increased to 135 in 2004. Similarly the final scheme approved which was 41 increased to 94. The amount of the final scheme approved which was stood that 38,638 crore increased to 64,071 crore nearly double the amount of the year 2003. This is an indication that CDR mechanism has performed well in solving the NPA problem.

Table 2
Progress Under CDR Scheme

	No. of Cases		*Amount Involved*	
Particulars	*2003*	*2004*	*2003*	*2004*
Cases reformed to CDR Forum	71	135	53,736	72,139
Final Scheme Approved	41	94	38,638	64,107
Rejected	18	30	7,252	5,445
Pending	12	11	7,846	2,677

Source: Report on Trend & Progress of Banking in India (2003-04).

Table 3 revealed that the Gross NPA to total assets of public sector banks which was stood at 5.95% in 1999-2000 reduced to 4.21% in 2002-03 and further reduced to 3.50% in 2003-04 similarly the net NPA to total assets which was stood at 2.94% reduced to 1.94% in 2002-03 and further reduced to 1.28% in 2003-04. From 1999-2000 to 2003-04 both gross NPA to total assets and net NPA to total assets have shown a declining trend which indicates that steps have been taken byn banks in realizing the NPA amount.

From Table 4 it has been remarked that the gross NPA as percentage of advances of public sector banks which was stood at 13.98% in 1999-2000 reduced to 9.79% in 2003-04. Similarly the net NPA to gross advances which was stood at 7.42% in 1999-2000 reduced to 3.98% in 2003-04. Almost all the years the advance percentage of public sector banks have been showing a declining trend. This shows that public sector banks have taken some conservative policy in advancing the loan amount to the borrowers and have taken active steps in realizing the outstanding amount advanced in the past.

From the Table 5 it has been observed that the presentation of standard assets have been showing in increasing trend during the period from 2001 to 2004 whereas substandard assets, doubtful assets and loss assets percentage have been showing gradual declining trend. Similarly the total NPA percentage which was stored at 12.4% in 2001 reduced to 7.8% approximately 5% in 2004 which indicates that substantial improvement has been made in the recovery positions of the banks after the reformation process. Similarly in the year 2004 no public sector

Table 3

Non Performing Assets as Percentage of Total Assets Public Sector Banks (Per Cent)

	Gross NPA/Total Assets					*Net NPA/Total Assets*				
Name of the Bank Group	*99-20*	*20-01*	*01-02*	*02-03*	*03-04*	*99-20*	*20-01*	*01-02*	*02-03*	*03-04*
Nationalized Bank	6.00	5.44	5.21	4.66	3.85	3.15	2.95	2.69	2.17	1.40
State Bank Group	5.88	5.11	4.39	3.48	2.91	2.60	2.35	2.00	1.58	1.09
Public Sector Banks	5.95	5.31	4.89	4.21	3.50	2.94	2.79	2.42	1.94	1.28

Source: Report on Trend & Progress of Banking in India (2003-04). Nationalized banks consists 19 banks and State bank group consists 8 banks. Public Sector bank is a combination of nationalized banks and SBI groups i.e. 19 + 8 = 27 banks.

Table 4

Non Performing Assets as Percentage of Advances Public Sector Banks (Per cent)

	Gross NPA/Total Assets					*Net NPA/Total Assets*				
Name of the Bank Group	*99-20*	*20-01*	*01-02*	*02-03*	*03-04*	*99-20*	*20-01*	*01-02*	*02-03*	*03-04*
Nationalized Bank	13.91	12.16	11.01	9.72	8.21	7.80	7.01	6.01	4.77	3.13
State Bank Group	14.08	12.73	11.23	8.68	6.98	6.77	6.27	5.45	4.12	2.71
Public Sector Banks	13.98	12.37	11.09	9.36	7.79	7.42	6.74	5.82	4.5	2.98

Source: Report on trend & progress of Banking in India (2003-04).

Table 5

Classification of Loan Assets of Public Sector Banks (Amount in Crore)

	Standard Assets Assets		*Substandard Assets*		*Doubtful*		*Loss Assets*		*Total NPA*	
Year	*Amt.*	%	*Amt.*	%	*Amt.*	%	*Amt.*	%	*Amt.*	%
2001	3,87,360	87.6	14,745	3.3	33,485	7.6	6,544	1.5	54,774	12.4
2002	4,52,862	88.9	15,788	3.1	33,658	6.6	7,061	1.4	56,507	11.1
2003	5,23,724	90.6	14,909	2.6	32,340	5.6	6,840	1.2	54,089	9.4
2004	6,10,435	92.2	16,909	2.6	28,756	4.3	5,876	0.9	51,541	7.8

Source: Report on trend and progress of banking in India (2003-04).

bank was reported above 10% and upto 20% of NPA. During the study period from 2000 to 2001 no public sector bank was found remaining above 20% NPA bracket (Refer Table 6).

Table 6
Distribution of Public Sector Banks by Ratio of Net NPA as Net Advances

Year	*Upto 10 Per cent*	*Above 10% & upto 20%*	*Above 20 Per cent*
2000	22	5	NIL
2001	22	5	NIL
2002	24	3	NIL
2003	25	2	NIL
2004	27	NIL	NIL

Source: Report on trend and progress of banking in India (2003-04).

From the perspective of regulating and supervisory process, the capital to risk weighted assets ratio (CRAR) constitutes the most important indicator for assessing soundness and solvency of banks. The CRAR of the majority of the banks in public sector was well above the regulations stipulation. (Refer Rable 7). Among public sector bank groups CRAR as at March 2004 was higher than the March, 2003 levels.

Table 7
Public Sector Banks CRAR (As at End of March) (Per cent)

	Years						
Bank Group	*1998*	*1999*	*2000*	*2001*	*2002*	*2003*	*2004*
Nationalized Banks	10.3	10.6	10.1	10.2	10.9	12.2	13.1
State Bank Group	14.0	12.3	11.6	12.7	13.3	13.4	13.4
Public Sector Banks	11.6	11.3	10.7	11.2	11.8	12.6	13.2

Source: Report on trend and progress of banking in India (2003-04).

It has been revealed from the Table 8 that highest percentage i.e. 17.6% of NPA was recorded in the small scale industries sector and total priority sector NPA percentage remaining lower than the total non-priority sector during the year 2004. Priority sector NPA remained 47.5% where as it was 51.2% in non priority sector. This shows that banks have taken active steps in realizing the loan amount from the priority sector. (refer Table 8).

Table 8

Sectorwise Non-performing Assets of Public Sector Banks (As at end of March 2004) Amount in crore

	Agriculture		Small Scale Industries		Others		Priority Sector		Public Sector		Non Priority Sector	
Name of the Bank Group	*Amt.*	*% to total*	*Amt.*	*% to total*	*Amt.*	*% to total*	*Amt.*	*% to total*	*Amt.*	*% to total*	*Amt.*	*% to total*
Nationalized Banks	4739.71	13.55	6557.38	18.74	5407.70	15.46	16704.78	47.74	390.14	1.12	17894.78	51.14
State Bank Group	2500.59	16.50	2280.54	15.04	2354.42	15.53	7135.55	47.07	220.09	1.45	7802.97	51.48
Public Sector Banks	7240.30	14.44	8837.92	17.62	7762.11	15.48	23840.33	47.54	610.23	1.22	25697.75	51.24

Source: Report on trend and progress of banking in India (2003-04).

Table 9 shows the NPA in advances to weaker section of the society of the public sector banks. In the year 2004 the total percentage of priority section NPA was 47.5% (refer Table 8) of which 19%. NPA in advances remained in the weaker sections. More than one forth of the NPA remained in the weaker sections. Highest 34.83% of NPA was recorded by

Table 9
NPA in Advances to Weaker Section under Priority Sector, Public Sector Banks (As at end of March, 2004) (Percentage)

Name of the Bank	*Percentage of NPA to total Advance*
Allahabad Bank	18.32
Andhra Bank	6.31
Bank of Baroda	16.15
Bank of India	26.53
Bank of Maharashtra	30.19
Canara Bank	16.04
Central Bank of India	34.83
Corporation Bank	14.41
Dena Bank	19.57
Indian Bank	23.13
Indian Overseas Bank	3.60
Oriental Bank of Commerce	9.97
Punjab National Bank	0.00
Punjab & Sindh Bank	23.49
Syndicate Bank	12.30
UCO Bank	20.48
Union Bank of India	21.89
United Bank of India	13.68
Vijaya Bank	11.18
State Bank of Bikaner & Jaipur	10.50
State Bank of Hyderabad	4.59
State Bank of India	31.24
State Bank of Indore	6.42
State Bank of Mysore	9.07
State Bank of Patiala	12.56
State Bank of Sourastra	6.64
State Bank of Travancore	13.33
Total	18.90

Source: Report on trend and progress of banking in India (2003-04).

Central Bank of India. SBI and Canara Bank was ranked 2nd and 3rd respectively in the NPA advances to weaker sections under priority sector. No doubt public sector banks have performed well in advancing a sizable portion of their loan amount towards the betterment of the weaker sections but steps should be taken for the realization of the NPA for the future.

Table 10 shows the total priority sector advance made by Public Sector banks from 2000-03. The total priority sector advance in 1969 when 14 commercial banks were nationalized was stood 14.12% and increased to 42.5% in March 2003. From the year 2002-03 (Except 2003) an increasing trend has been found. Out of the total priority sector advance agricultural sector received the first choice of the banks and 1969 the agricultural sector advance which was stood at 5.4% increased to 15.4% in March, 2004 and more importance has been giving in providing finance towards direct agricultural sector as compared to indirect sector. Table no. 10 shows the total priority sector advance made by public sector banks from 2000-03. The total priority sector advance in 1969 when 14 commercial banks were nationalized was stood 14.12% and increased to 42.5% in March 2003. From the year 2002-03 (except 2003) an increasing trend has been found. Out of the total priority sector advance agricultural sector received the first choice of the banks and 1969 the agricultural sector advance which was stood at 5.4% increased to 15.4% in March 2004 and more importance has been giving in providing finance towards direct agricultural sector as compared to indirect sector.

Recommendations

Due to the various reforms a measures reduced to the minimum level of approximately 3%. However, for the better management of the NPA for the future the following recommendations have been suggested.

Introduction of Weather Insurance

The farmer faces two kinds of risk i.e. (i) price risk and (ii) volumetric risk. Price risk is the risk which the farmer bears with him till the harvest is over, and it price falls at the harvest

Table 10
Advances to the Priority Sectors by Public Sector Banks (Rupees in Crores)

	No. of Accounts in takes						*Amount outstanding rupees in crores*					
	June 1969	*Mar 2000*	*Mar 2001*	*Mar 2002*	*Mar 2003 @*	*Mar 2004 @*	*June 1969 @*	*Mar 2000*	*Mar 2001*	*Mar 2002 @*	*Mar 2003 @*	*Mar 2004 @*
Agriculture	1.7	160	188	161	168	177	162 (5.4)	45296 (14.3)	53571 (15.7)	63082 (15.9)	73507 (15.3)	86187 (15.4)
Direct	16	157	185	157	164	174	40 (1.3)	34247 (10.6)	38137 (12.2)	44908 (11.3)	51799 (10.8)	61957 (11.1)
Indirect	0.1	3	3	4	4	3	122	11049 (3.5)	15434 (4.5)	18174 (4.6)	21708 (4.5)	24230 (4.3)
Small Scale Industries	0.5	22	20	22	17	16	257 (8.5)	46045 (14.6)	48400 (14.2)	49743 (12.5)	52988 (11.1)	58278 (10.4)
Other Priority Sector Advances	0.4	81	80	83	79	88	22 (0.7)	30816 (9.7)	40791 (12.1)	53712 (13.5)	71448 (15.0)	94959 (17.0)
Total Priority Sector Advances	2.6	265	288	269	268	286	441 (14.6)	127478 (40.3)	149116 (43.7)	171185 (43.1)	203095 (42.5)	245672 (44.0)
Net Bank Credit	-	-	-	-	-	-	3016	316427	341291	396954	477899	558849

@ Data are provisional

Industry of Advances to setting of Industrial estate, funds provided to RRBs by sponsored banks loans to software industries, food and agricultural processing sector, self help group and venture capital.

Note: Figures in brackets represent percentage in Net Bank Credit.

time there is a loss. Similarly, volumetric risk is the risk where the farmer is unsure of the quantity that will be produced from his end. Even though the price risk is covered by the exchange, he may not be able to deliver the promised quantity. So the farmer's liability increases. These type of risk, can be covered by taking suitable insurance policies. Now there arrived a 'weather derivative' where weather index can be calculated and can be expressed in rupee terms. So banks should insist the insurance companies to come forward for the rescue of the poor farmers by which banks NPA can be reduced to a greater extent.

Change in the Banking Regulation Act

The farmers may not understand the commodity derivative market or have too little knowledge of the system of operation.So, here the banks could play a leading role by aggregating the produce for farmers and hedging through their central office treasuries. Suitable changes in the banking regulations act are required.

Creation of Value Chain Process

Credit instruments should not merely focus on primary production but an augmentation of the entire value chain such as food processing, or value addition for commercial crops. The above value chain process will help in counter balancing one year's loss suffered by the farmers by means of which loans can be repaid in time and bad debt can be reduced to a greater extent.

Commercialization of Agriculture

In India fragmentation of land holding is the main cause for the bad debt. Larger size of land will no doubt increase the productivity and it is easier to apply the modem scientific method of technology. So better financial benefit can be achieved if we insist on dividing the *yield* among the holders of land proportionately. This will ensure a sizeable income and help to the farmers in repaying the old debt promptly.

Flexible Delivery System

We need rural branches which can offer flexible working hours to suit the requirement of farmers. More opening of rural evening bank branches are to be insisted upon as the farmers can get sufficient time for discussing their problems with the bank officials.

Change in the Recruitment Process

We also need staff having sympathy towards rural people. We need a set of people who are reconciled to work in rural areas. Recruitment of staff in a rural cadre which will be eligible for urban posting until they reach the level of senior manager may be insisted upon to have a proper monitoring system for the recovery of the outstanding advance amount.

Rural Infrastructure

Apart from finance, attention has to be paid to improve rural infrastructure. Roads and electricity are basic ingredients for development. Storage facilities by way of godowns and cold storages can also help the farmer in getting better price realization for agricultural produce. The benefit of technology need to be extended to rural areas.

Adoption of Micro Financial Services

Since the huge demand for rural poor for micro financial services can be satisfied by formal credit agencies, it is necessary to adopt an integrated approach for providing training, credit and necessary production as well as market infrastructures to its members so that they can become credit worthy clients and can go from the lower step of the ladder i.e. from a marginal worker to the micro entrepreneur, ladder on the upper step.

Conclusion

We should not forget the bulk of NPA of banks are a baggage of the past which can not be reduced immediately. RBI has been taking measures for reducing NPA of banks from time to time while retaining flexibility to take specific measures promptly and efficiently as per the evolving circumstances warrant. The RBI should consult the legal and accounting aspects with the apex bodies of the concerned department. So that the banking sector in our country can equally complete with that of the banking sector of the foreign countries. Legal and accounting standard reforms should precede the banking sector reforms which will ultimately help achieving an ideal financial sector reform.

References

Agrawal, A. N. (1995), Problems of Development & Planning–Vani Educational Books.

Rajasekhar H. (2003), Commercial Banking and Finance, Kitab Mahal.

Jain Gopallal (2003), Rural Economy and Society, Kitab Mahal.

Naresaiah, M. L. (2003), Globalization and Economic Growth, Kitab Mahal.

Dr. Balishter (1990), Loan Waiver Scheme–Consequences and Possibilities, *Yojana,* Vol. 34, Oct. 16-31.

Gupta Anil (1990), Loan Waiver Justified, *Yojana,* Vol. 34, October, 16-31.

Sekhar Chander (2003), Reduction of NPA–Key to Banking Reforms, *Yojana,* Vol. 47, October, No. 10.

18

Non-performing Assets and Declining Profitability of Banks

Navin Prasad & Bijay Kumar Sinha

In the current scenario higher non performing assets culminating into banking crisis along with low profit margins on the one hand and challenges from young banks and seems foreign banks offering diversified banking services are tailored according to needs of customers and are compatible with their financial stability.

Banking crisis exists if non performing assets touched 10 per cent of banking assets, banking problems result in large scale nationalisation of banks or extensive bank failures or emergency measures such as deposit freeze, prolong bank holidays or deposit guarantees introduced in response to crisis. A severe banking crisis were called when there were banks runs or other substantial portfolio shifts, collapse of financial firms or massive government intervention to prevent bank failures.

The NPAs are the assets that do not yield any return. The RBI norms are that loans in respect of which principle or at least interest repayment are not made for 90 days fall in the NPAs category. In India, NPAs of banks have shown as increase of Rs. 7739 crores which form 15.9% of gross advances which rose by Rs. 48556 crores in 1998-99 as compared to 6.9% in 1997-98 and net non performing assets increased from 2.9% to 8.9%.

The ratio of gross NPAs to gross advances of Scheduled Commercial Banks declined from 15.7% as at end March 1997 to 10.5% as at March 2002. At present it is still around 10 %.

The degree of vulnerability of Banks can be estimated by studying net profit coverage ratio of NPAs. It is revealing to note that in 1997-98, net profit of scheduled commercial banks covered only 27.0 per cent of NPAs but in recent times, this coverage ratio declined to 17 per cent. In case of public sector and old private sector banks, net profit covered 14 per cent and 13 per cent of NPAs, respectively. However, new banks performance was good as their net profits more than covered the NPAs, All new banks net profits provided more than 100 per cent coverage. Thus despite the efforts made by RBI, incidence of NPAs could not be reduced. Even if capital adequacy ratio is taken into account, net profit ratio and capital adequacy ratio together fall short of full coverage of NPAs. The position is not good in case of old private banks.

In order to provide little more insight, bank wise status of non performing assets in relation to few other indicators like business per employee, profit per employee, return on assets, income other than interest and interest income, one more important in the present scenario.

The business per employee would indicate extent of productivity or in a way extent of excess employment in relation to non performing assets. It may also be noted that the banks with relatively lower business an employee reported higher non performing assets ratio and lower profit per employee than the banks with higher business per employee. For instance, business per employee was the lowest in UCO Bank, Central Bank of India and United Bank of India. These banks reported either loss in terms of profit per employee or the lowest profit alongwith high ratio of non performing assets. Some banks like Andhra Bank and Syndicate Bank with lower non performing assets and higher business per employee among the low business group banks reported higher profits per employee. On the other hand Corporation Bank followed by Oriental Bank of Commerce and bank of Baroda reported higher business per employee and very low non performing assets indicating higher profits, per employee and better rate of return.

Hence, higher business per employee resulted in higher profits and lower NPAs. Inspite of the fact that interest income and other non interest income were quite comparable, low business banks reported very low profit ratio and profits per employee.

Bank's profits are low and inadequate for certain other resources also. First, interest spreads for banks have been narrowing, second, the credit side of balance sheet has become less profitable than before due to competition and banks hesitation to loan. Today, large corporations can borrow directly from the market by issuing commercial paper at rates below what banks can offer. Third, operation costs are increasing because banks are introducing technological innovations to make their operations more efficient or convenient. Fourth, personnel costs are rising as banks are hiring aggressive, marketing oriented people and try to retain specialized employees expected to be lured away by competitors.

SBI and its 7 associate banks have recorded steady rise in net profits . But as per per cent of total assets, however, net profit of SBI Group has been really low which is 0.6 per cent only. In the case of the 19 nationalised banks viz. other public sector banks, profitability is always been quit low. During 1992-93 and 193-94 these public sector banks posted huge losses to the tune of Rs. 3,648 crores and Rs. 4,779 crores respectively. These losses were due to securities scam were and also the result of decades of non commercial orientation, directed lending, loan waivers and rising trend in non performing assets. In 1995-96 too these banks again posted losses to the tune of Rs. 1,160 crores. Since then, all public sector banks have recorded substantial improvements in both operating and net profits. As per per cent of total assets, net profit of the 19 nationalised banks stood at 0.3 per cent.

As percentage of total assets, net profit of private sector banks was better than that of the nationalised banks which is 0.6 per cent.

The profitability of the foreign banks has always been excellent. But in 1992-93, these banks were caught up in the securities scam and suffered a huge loss of Rs. 842 crores. But soon these banks recovered and have posted impressive profit regularly, year after year. Net profit as per cent of total assets stood at 0.9 per cent.

A comparison of profitability of different kinds of banking systems in India brings out clearly the relatively low profitability of public sector banks. Three of the public sector banks were deeply in the red for many years. It is possible to defend the low profitability and poor financial condition of public sector banks by referring to their deep commitment to social obligations "imposed" by the Government: as for instance, opening rural branches, setting up and subsidising regional rural banks, financing IRDP and other poverty alleviation programmes at commissional rates of interest, priority sector lending to the extent of 40% of the total credit, etc. These arguments hold good, to a large extent, to the private sector scheduled commercial banks too but these are making more profits than public sector banks. In the case of foreign banks which have offices mainly in metropolitan areas and in some selected permitted cities, the social obligations may not apply. But the other constraints on revenues such as high SLR and CRR apply to them also. Still they manage to make huge profits.

Banks are commercial organisations and they have to undoubtedly look for profits besides fulfilling social obligations. In fact, profit is an index of their operational efficiency. It, therefore, becomes necessary for banks to prepare profit budgets both at micro as well as macro levels. Profit budget should become part and parcel of overall planning process at corporate level.

Therefore it is pertinent to analyse the reasons for declining profitability in recent times.As a result of increasing emphasis on social goals banks have to lend funds at lower rates of interest. Around 20% of loanable funds are lent to priority sectors at concessional rates of interest. Priority sector advances today constitute 40% of total bank credit whose average yield is 11%.

In recent period the main cause of law profitability of the banks is to heaving increase in Non performing Assets of banks. The ratios of gross and net NPAs of commercial banks to advances and total assets have been declining across all bank groups. Gross NPAs of public sector banks at 11.1% of gross advances and 4.9% of total assets are higher than those of private sector banks and foreign banks in India.

Reserve Bank of India has recently conducted a study to ascertain the contributory factors of high level of NPAs in banks covering 800 top NPA accounts in 17 banks . The study revealed that the following major factors are contributing to the loans becoming NPAs.

- Diversion of funds for expansion, diversification, modernization, undertaking new projects and for helping associate concerns. This is coupled with recessionary trends and failure to tap funda in the capital and debt markets.
- Business failure (product, marketing etc.) inefficient management , strained labour relations, inappropriate technology / technical problems ,product obsolescence, etc.
- Recession, input/ power shortage, price escalation,, accident, natural calamities , etc. beside externalization problems in other countries leading to non-payment of overdues.
- Time/cost overrun during project implementation stage.
- Government policies like changes in excise duties, pollution control orders ctc.
- Willful default ,siphoning off of funds, fraud/ misappropriation, promoters', directors' disputes.
- Deficiencies on the part of banks like delay in release limits and delay in release of payments/ subsidies by Government.

Many companies have sought to address their NPAs management problems by creating dedicated outfits for acquiring and managing NPAs. An Asset Reconstruction Company (ARC) is a special purpose limited liability company which (i) acquires problem assets of banks and financial intermediates and (ii) subsequently sells these to other buyers. Beginning with the Narasimbham Committee Report in December 1991, there have been consistent recommendations for setting up ARCs in India . Narsimham II reiterated this point. More recently, the M.S.Verma Committee Report on Weak bank has again made a case for Asset Reconstruction Companies.

It is to be noted that given the inadequacies of SICA, BIFR, DRTs, foreclosures and other recovery process, an ARC may find it difficult to lead a viable existence . Therefore, simultaneously we need to make radical changes in bankruptcy and recovery laws and procedures.

As an interim measure, banks have opened specialized rehabilitation and recovery branches to focus on BIFR cases and high value accounts, specially in "doubtful" and "loss" categories.

To tackle chronic NPAs in priority sector, RBI has recently come out with a one time measure- constitutions of 'Settlement Advisory Committee' (SACs) by banks. This is to promote compromise settlement in small sector viz., SSI, small business including , trade ,agriculture and personal segments . Bankers need to appreciate the fact that compromise settlement is an effective and accepted non- legal remedy for recovery in chronic NPAs accounts . For encouraging compromise settlements imparting necessary knowledge , refining negotiating skills and reorienting attitude to operating functionaries are some prerequisites.

There has been a suggestion of passing the non performing assets to asset management company, which can be promoted by the Government and can be managed by the experts from private sector. This step may shift the burden from banks to some other agency and may clean the balance sheet of weak banks but the problem of non performing assets will not disappear unless we change the legal structure and make the borrowers punishable with recovery provisions. Another way could be to promote multiple agencies to provide protection to the banks by accepting the obligation of making the recovery of loans on commission basis. An instrument like 'Credit Protection Instrument' can be created which can be bought by these agencies. Privatisation of banks to full extent can also improve the position of banks, but one may have to frame anti resources concentration laws to frustrate those who would like to monopolize the banks' funds. Moreover, banks may like to include depositors in their board, as these are people who suffer more at the time of crisis.

In conclusion, it can be stated that the surest way of containing NPAs is to prevent their occurrence. The tenets of this policy lie in the following:

(i) proper risk management systems be put place in the banks.

(ii) Strong and effective 0credit monitoring

(iii) An open and co-operative working relationship between banks and borrowers that would allow exchange of confidences and initiation of corrective action early.

But to manage effectively the existing NPAs , the banks must adopt a structured NPAs Management Policy for guidance of operating functionaries. Finally, an effective legal framework will be needed to bring recovery suits to their logical conclusion and effect recoveries , within a reasonable time frame. Compromise settlements should be explored as an effective non-legal option for recovery.

References

The Journal of the Indian Institute of Bankers, April-June 2000.

Yojana, D.A.V.P. Govt. of India October, 2003, November 2006

RBI Report on The Trend and Progress of Banking in India 2003-04.

Journal of Banking Studies, April 2003, July 2005.

Report of the Committee on the Financial System, 1991

Economic Survey, 2001-02, 2003

19

Non-performing Assets: An Unavoidable Burden on Banking Industry in India

Manmeet Singh, R. K. Vyas & V. K. Gautam

The basic functions of Commercial banks are the accepting of all kinds of deposits and lending of money. In general there are several challenges confronting the commercial banks in its day today operations. The main challenge facing the commercial banks is the disbursement of funds in quality assets (Loans and Advances) or other wise it leads to Non-performing assets. Financial stability is considered as *sine qua non* of sustained and rapid economic progress. Among various indicators of financial stability, banks' non-performing loan assumes critical importance since it reflects on the asset quality, credit risk and efficiency in the allocation of resources to productive sectors. A common perspective is that the problem of banks' non-performing loans is ascribed to political, economic, social, technological, legal and environmental. The complete elimination of such losses is not possible, but banks can always aim to keep the losses at a low level. Non performing Assets (NPAs) has emerged since over a decade as an alarming threat to the banking industry in our country sending distressing signals on the sustainability and insurability of the affected banks .The issue of NPAs has been discussed at length for financial system all over the country and the problem of NPAs is not only affecting the banks but also the whole economy. In fact high level of NPAs in banks is nothing but a reflection of the state of health of the industry and trade.

Literature Review

A comparative study of non performing assets of India in the global context examines the causes and solutions for handling NPA across five countries (India, China, Japan, Korea and Thailand). The results indicate that all Asian countries had weak legal mechanisms for asset disposal and all the countries made extensive usage of government guarantees and funding to try and solve the problem .However, causes of the NPA varied significantly across countries with real estate, directed credit and lack of prudential norms being the critical factors (Reddy, 2002). In a seminal summit (Muniappan, 2002) addressed the issue of management of NPAs. He emphasized the rigourous and appropriate credit appraisal system to avoid the problem at the initial stage and lenders and the borrowers both should realize there role and responsibilities.

The problem of NPA can be resolved if the root of NPA which exists at the micro level (Bank level) are dealt with effectively. Economic Value of Equity (EVE) and EVE at Risk (EVER) if mandatorily disclosed on a monthly basis in banks which will make the deficiencies visible and it will eliminate them. (Sharma and Mor, 2003). To resolve the China Non-Performing Loans (NPL) position, Securitization tops the list of innovative financing techniques besides the initial disposable methods ranging from loans sales to debt-for- equity swaps (Chen, 2004). Even China's huge NPL burden was largely as a result of two functions: (a) sustained losses at the state owned enterprises (b) the lack of commercial credit culture at major financial institutions (Xu, 2005).

(Bhaumik and Jenifer, 2005) Another study, examined the behaviour of banks' in the context of emerging credit markets particularly India. The results indicate that the credit market behaviour of banks is largely influenced by past trends, presumably limiting significantly the ability of the new and dynamic firms and sectors to grow rapidly. Regulations also have an impact on bank lending in India by way of priority sector norms of RBI, these norms make banks less willing to disburse credit. The researchers also find evidence that the second generation of reforms in India, the thrust of which was the enablement of banks to clear NPA off their balance sheets, had a positive impact on the credit disbursal of the banks. In a similar study on the trend and sectoral composition of NPA of public sector banks in India, study revealed that gross and net NPAs have gone down gradually and quality of portfolio of the PSBs has improved quite impressively over the period (Reddy, *et. al* 2006).

Rationale of the Study

The financial sector reforms ushered in the year 1991 have been well calibrated and timed to ensure a smooth transition of the system from a highly regulated regime to a market economy. The financial sector reforms have brought in the much-needed competition in the market place. The competition to the existing banks came mainly from the techno-savvy private sector banks. In the coming years, it is expected to see greater flow of foreign capital to come into the Indian banking sector. Opening up of banking sector to global players would see banks facing global competition. Due to increased competition, the net interest margin of banks has come down over the last one decade. Liberalization with globalization will see the spreads narrowing further to 1-1.5% as in the case of banks operating in the developed countries. In this banking scenario, if the quality of the assets is not monitored, it may turn into NPAs and net profit margin may worsen further.

Objectives of the Study

- To assess the magnitude and trend of NPAs in cross country perspective and in various bank groups like Public Sector Banks, Private Sector Banks and Foreign banks operating in India.
- To assess the causes and steps taken for recovery of NPAs.

Methodology

During the study, secondary data was collected and collated from various journals, well known magazines, 'Report on Trend and Progress of banking in India', and various issues of RBI. Besides that; certain dominions were also amplified for better understanding and uniformity. Same was interpreted and after deliberate analysis, the findings with recommendations were made and the same are given in the succeeding paragraphs.

Meaning of Non Performing Asset (NPA)

NPA is defined as a credit facility in respect of which the interest and/or installment of principal has remained "past due" for a specified period of time. With a view to moving towards international best practices and to ensure greater transparency , the '90 days' overdue norm for identification of NPAs has been adopted, from the year ending 31st March, 2004 (Earlier the period was 180 days).Thus if either interest or installment is overdue for more than 90 days then the account would become NPA. Interest or installment, which is due on 30th December, 2005 would be overdue for more than 90 days as on 31st March, 2006 and the account would become NPA. However, if the same was due on 31st December, 2005, then the account would not become NPA as on 31st March, 2006.

An account has to be classified as an NPA on the basis of record of recovery rather than security charged in favour of bank in respect of such account. Thus, an account of a borrower may become an NPA if interest charged to that particular borrower is not realized despite the account being fully secured.

Magnitude and Trend of NPAs

Cross-Country Perspective

Globally, the level of non-performing loans is estimated at about US $1.3 trillion during 2003, of which the Asian region accounts for about US $ 1 trillion, or about 77 per cent of global NPLs (Table 1). Within Asia, Japan and China have NPLs at about US $ 330 billion and US $ 307 billion thus, together accounting for 49 per cent of global NPLs. Other hot spots of NPLs in the Asian region are Taiwan (US $ 19 billion), Thailand (US$ 18.8 billion), Indonesia (US $ 16.9 billion) and Philippines (US $ 9 billion). India's NPLs of the financial sector as a whole is reported at about US$ 30 billion, which works out to a little over 2 per cent of global NPLs.

Table 1
Global Non-Performing Loans: 2003*

Countries	*NPLs (US $ billion)*	*Share in Global (per cent)*
Japan	330	25.4
China	307	23.6
Taiwan	19.1	1.5
Thailand	18.8	1.5
Philippines	9.0	0.7
Indonesia	16.9	1.3
India	30	2.3
Korea	15.0	1.2
Total	746	57.4
Asia	1000	76.9
Germany	283	21.8
Turkey	8.0	0.6
Global	1300	100.0

* NPLs of all financial institutions.
Source: Global NPL Report 2004, Ernst and Young.

In terms of the ratio of NPLs to total assets of banking sector, there is evidence that the performance of the Asian region is far lower than Europe and US (Table 2). The trend in the NPL ratios of select countries, particularly the emerging countries of East Asia, during the last five-six years provides an interesting insight about the impact of structural reform on the accumulation of non-performing loans by banks. In emerging countries like Thailand and Indonesia, structural reform after the Asian crisis had an immediate impact of removing the accumulated excesses from the financial sector and consequently induced a sharp reduction in NPAsRatio in Thailand, the NPLs ratio declined by about 25 percentage points from about 43 per cent in 1998 to about 18 per cent in

2003. In a similar manner, the NPAs ratio in Indonesia declined by about 30 percentage points from about 49 per cent in 1998 to 19 per cent in 2003.

Table 2
Ratio of Non-Performing Loans to Total Loans (%)

Countries	*1998*	*1999*	*2000*	*2001*	*2002*	*2003*
United Kingdom	3.2	3.0	2.5	2.6	2.6	2.2
United States	1.0	0.9	1.1	1.4	1.6	1.3
Japan	5.4	5.8	6.1	6.6	8.9	7.2
France	6.3	5.7	5	5	5	4.9
Germany	4.5	4.6	5.1	4.9	5	-
Greece	13.6	15.5	12.3	9.2	8.1	8.4
Italy	9.1	8.5	7.7	6.7	6.5	-
Russia	17.3	13.4	7.7	6.3	6.5	6.1
Turkey	6.7	9.7	9.2	29.3	17.6	14.2
Argentina	5.3	7.1	8.7	13.2	17.5	22.7
China	–	28.5	22.4	29.8	25.5	22.0
India	14.4	14.7	12.7	11.4	10.4	8.8
Indonesia	48.6	32.9	18.8	11.9	5.8	-
Korea	7.4	8.3	6.6	2.9	1.9	2.3
Malayasia	18.6	16.6	15.4	17.8	15.9	14.8
Philippines	11.0	12.7	14.9	16.9	15.4	15.2
Thailand	42.9	38.6	17.7	10.5	15.8	15.5
Srilanka	16.6	16.6	15	16.9	15.7	13.9
Bangladesh	40.7	41.1	34.9	31.5	28	-
Pakistan	23.1	25.9	23.5	23.3	23.7	20.7

Source: Global Financial Stability Report, April 2004, IMF), Trends in India.

The following table shows the quantitative details of the NPAs of Scheduled Commercial Banks in India and it shows *a decreasing trend* of Gross and Net NPAs as a percentage of Advances and to total assets.

SCB-All Scheduled Commercial Banks, PSB—Public Sector Banks, Old Pvt. B—Old Private Sector B, New Pvt. B—New Private Sector Banks, Foreign B—Foreign Banks in India.

Analysis of the Tables (3 and 4): At the end of March 2006, the ratio of net NPAs to net advances of public sector banks and old private sector banks was less than 2% at the bank group level. Net NPA ratio of new private banks and foreign banks were 0.8% As at end-March2006, 66banks (as against 51 last year) out of 84 (as against 88 last year) had net NPAs to net

Table 3
Bank Group-Wise Gross and Net NPAs of Scheduled Commercial Banks (as at end-March)

(Amount in Rs. Crore)

Bank group/ year	*Gross Advances (Amt.)*	*Gross NPAs (Amt.)*	*Gross NPAs %to gross Advance*	*Gross NPAs % To Total Assets*	*Net Advances (Amount) Total Assets*	*Net NPAs (Amount)*	*Net NPAs % to Net Advances*	*Net NPAs % to*
SCB 1998	352697	50815	14.4	6.4	325522	23761	7.3	3.0
1999	399436	58722	14.7	6.2	367012	28020	7.6	2.9
2000	475113	60408	12.7	5.5	444292	30073	6.8	2.7
2001	558766	63883	11.4	4.9	526329	32468	6.2	2.5
2002	680958	70861	10.4	4.6	645859	35554	5.5	2.3
2003	778043	68717	8.8	4.1	740473	29692	4.0	1.8
2004	902026	64785	7.2	3.3	862643	24396	2.8	1.2
2005	1152682	59373	5.2	2.5	1115663	21754	2.0	0.9
2006	1551378	51816	3.3	1.9	1515669	18529	1.2	0.7
PSB 1998	284971	45653	16.0	7.0	260459	21232	8.2	3.3
1999	325328	51710	15.9	6.7	297789	24211	8.1	3.1
2000	379461	53033	14.0	6.0	352714	26187	7.4	2.9
2001	442134	54773	12.4	5.3	415207	27969	6.7	2.7
2002	509368	56473	11.1	4.9	480681	27958	5.8	2.4
2003	577813	54090	9.4	4.2	549351	24877	4.5	1.9
2004	661975	51538	7.8	3.5	631383	19335	3.1	1.3

Contd...

(Amount in Rs. Crore)

Bank group/ year	*Gross Advances (Amt.)*	*Gross NPAs (Amt.)*	*Gross NPAs %to gross Advance*	*Gross NPAs % To Total Assets*	*Net Advances (Amount) Total Assets*	*Net NPAs (Amount)*	*Net NPAs % to Net Advances*	*Net NPAs % to*
2005	877825	48399	5.5	2.7	848912	16904	2.1	1.0
2006	1134724	42106	3.7	2.1	1106128	14561	1.3	0.7
OldpvtB 1998	25580	2794	10.9	5.1	24353	1572	6.5	2.9
1999	43049	3784	13.1	5.8	26017	2332	9.0	3.6
2000	35404	3815	10.8	5.2	33879	2393	7.1	3.3
2001	39738	4420	11.1	5.2	37973	2770	7.3	3.3
2002	44057	4851	11.0	5.2	42286	3013	7.1	3.2
2003	51329	4550	8.9	4.3	49436	2548	5.2	2.5
2004	57908	4393	7.6	3.6	55648	2142	3.8	1.8
2005	70412	4200	6.0	3.1	67742	1859	2.7	1.4
2006	85154	3740	4.3	2.5	81980	1368	1.6	0.9
NewPvt.B 1998	11173	392	3.5	1.5	11058	291	2.6	1.1
1999	14070	871	6.2	2.3	13714	611	4.5	1.6
2000	22816	946	4.1	1.6	22156	638	2.9	1.1
2001	31499	1619	5.1	2.1	30086	929	3.1	1.2
2002	76901	6811	8.9	3.9	74187	3663	4.9	2.1
2003	94718	7232	7.6	3.8	89515	1365	1.5	0.7
2004	119511	5961	5.0	2.4	115106	1986	1.7	0.8

Contd...

(Amount in Rs. Crore)

Bank group/ year	*Gross Advances (Amt.)*	*Gross NPAs (Amt.)*	*Gross NPAs %to gross Advance*	*Gross NPAs % To Total Assets*	*Net Advances (Amount) Total Assets*	*Net NPAs (Amount)*	*Net NPAs % to Net Advances*	*Net NPAs % to*
2005	127420	4582	3.6	1.6	123655	2353	1.9	0.8
2006	232536	4042	1.7	1.0	230005	1793	0.8	0.4
Foreign B 1998	30972	1976	6.4	3.0	29652	666	2.2	1.0
1999	31059	2357	7.6	3.1	29492	866	2.9	1.1
2000	37432	2614	7.0	3.2	35543	855	2.4	1.0
2001	45395	3071	6.8	3.0	43063	800	1.9	0.8
2002	50631	2726	5.4	2.4	48705	920	1.9	0.8
2003	54184	2845	5.3	2.4	52171	903	1.7	0.8
2004	62632	2894	4.6	2.1	60506	933	1.5	0.7
2005	77026	2192	2.8	1.4	75354	639	0.8	0.4
2006	98965	1927	1.9	1.0	97555	808	0.8	0.4

Source: Report on Trend and Progress of Banking in India, Various Issues, RBI.

Table 4
Distribution of Scheduled Commercial Banks by Ratio of Net NPAs to Net Advances As at End-March (Number of Banks)

Bank Group	*2002*	*2003*	*2004*	*2005*	2006
Public Sector banks	27	27	27	28	28
Up to 2%	0	4	11	19	23
Above 2% and up to 5%	11	14	13	7	5
Above 5% and up to 10%	13	7	3	2	0
Above 10%	3	2	0	0	0
Old Private Sector Banks	21	20	20	20	19
Up to 2%	2	2	2	4	11
Above 2% and up to 5%	2	4	9	12	7
Above 5% and up to 10%	12	12	7	4	1
Above 10%	5	2	2	0	0
New Private Sector Banks	9	9	10	9	8
Up to 2%	1	2	4	5	6
Above 2% and up to 5%	3	2	5	3	2
Above 5% and up to 10%	5	4	0	1	0
Above 10%	0	1	1	0	0
Foreign Banks	*42*	*36*	33	*31*	29
Up to 2%	24	19	22	23	26
Above 2% and up to 5%	4	3	2	2	0
Above 5% and up to 10%	1	6	3	2	0
Above 10%	13	8	6	4	3

Source: Report on trend and Progress of banking in India, 2006, RBI.

advances ratio less than 2%. Only 4 banks, 3 of which were foreign banks, had net NPAs ratio higher than 5% as compared with 13 in the previous year.

Asset Classification Standard Asset: The Account Is Not Non- Performing And Does Not Carry More Than Normal Risk Attached To The Business.

Having identified assets as NPA, banks are required to classify them further into:

(a) *Sub-Standard Asset*-A sub-standard asset is one, which has remained NPA for a period of less than or equal to 12 months.

(b) *Doubtful Assets*-An asset is classified as doubtful if it has remained in sub standard category for a period of 12 months.

(c) *Loss Assets*-A loss asset is one where the loss has been identified by the bank or internal or external auditors or RBI inspection but the amount has not been written off wholly. (SCB-All Scheduled Commercial Banks, PSB—Public Sector Banks, Old Pvt. B—Old Private Sector Banks, New Pvt. B— New Private Sector Banks, Foreign Bank—Foreign Banks in India).

Analysis of the Table 5

Decline in NPAs ratio was observed all categories, Substandard, doubtful and loss assets. In two categories (loss and doubtful), NPAs declined in absolute terms. NPAs in substandard category in the year 2006 increased marginally in case SCBs. More or less the same trend was observed all bank groups in the year 2006 in absolute terms, except old private sector banks, in which case sub standard assets declined and new private banks, in which case loss assets increased marginally in the year 2006.

Factors Contributing to NPAs

According to a recent study conducted by the RBI, the underlying reasons for NPAs in India can be classified into two heads namely, Internal Factors and External Factors.

Internal Factors

Internal factors that contribute to NPA in the order of prominence are; Diversion of funds for expansion/diversification/ modernization or for taking up new projects, Diversion of funds for assisting or promoting associate concerns, Time or cost overrun during the project implementation stage, Business failures due to product failure, failure in marketing etc., Inefficiency in management, Slackness in credit management and monitoring, and In appropriate technology or problems related to modern technology.

External Factors

External factors that contribute to NPAs are; Recession in the economy as a whole, Input or power shortage, Price escalation

Table 5

Classification of Loan Assets of Scheduled Commercial Banks-Bank GroupWise (As at end-March)

(Amount in Rs. Crore)

Bank group/ year	*Standard Assets (Amt.)*	*Std. Assets (%)*	*Sub –Std Asset (Amt)*	*Sub-Std Asset %*	*Doubtful Asset (Amt)*	*Doubtful Asset %*	*Loss Asset Amt*	*Loss Asset %*	*Total NPAs (Amt)*	*Total NPA (%)*	*Total Advances (Amt)*
SCB 1998	301881	85.6	17428	4.9	27146	7.7	6242	1.8	50815	14.4	352696
1999	340714	85.3	19928	5.0	31350	7.8	7444	1.9	58722	14.7	399436
2000	414917	87.2	19594	4.1	33688	7.1	7558	1.6	60840	12.8	475757
2001	494716	88.6	18206	3.3	37756	6.8	8001	1.4	63963	11.4	558679
2002	609972	89.6	21382	3.1	41201	6.0	8370	1.2	70953	10.4	680925
2003	709260	91.2	20078	2.6	39731	5.1	8971	1.1	68780	8.8	778040
2004	837130	92.9	21026	2.3	36247	4.0	7625	0.9	64898	7.2	902027
2005	1093523	94.9	14016	1.2	37763	3.3	7382	0.6	59161	5.1	1152684
2006	1499431	96.7	14826	1.0	30105	2.0	7016	0.4	51947	3.3	1551378
PSB 1998	239318	84.0	14463	5.1	25819	9.1	5371	1.9	45653	16.0	284971
1999	273618	84.1	16033	4.9	29252	9.0	6425	2.0	51710	15.9	325328
2000	326783	86.0	16361	4.3	30535	8.0	6398	1.7	53294	14.0	380077
2001	387360	87.6	14745	3.3	33485	7.6	6544	1.5	54774	12.4	442134
2002	452862	88.9	15788	3.1	33658	6.6	7061	1.4	56507	11.1	509369
2003	523724	90.6	14909	2.6	32340	5.6	6840	1.1	54089	9.4	577813
2004	610435	92..2	16909	2.5	28756	4.4	5876	0.9	51541	7.8	661975
2005	830029	94.6	11068	1.3	30779	3.5	5929	0.7	47796	5.4	877825
2006	1092607	96.2	11453	1.0	25028	2.2	5636	0.5	42117	3.7	1134724

Contd...

(Amount in Rs. Crore)

Bank group/ year	Standard Assets (Amt.)	Std. Assets (%)	Sub-Std Asset (Amt)	Sub-Std Asset %	Doubtful Asset (Amt)	Doubtful Asset %	Loss Asset Amt	Loss Asset %	Total NPAs (Amt)	Total NPA (%)	Total Advances (Amt)
Old Pvt B 1998	22786	89.1	1402	5.5	1068	4.2	324	1.3	2794	10.9	25580
1999	25195	86.9	1920	6.6	1463	5.0	401	1.4	3784	13.1	28979
2000	31447	88.8	1577	4.5	2061	5.8	347	1.0	3985	11.2	35432
2001	35166	88.7	1622	4.1	2449	6.2	413	1.0	4484	11.3	39650
2002	39262	89.0	1834	4.2	2668	6.1	348	0.8	4850	11.0	44112
2003	46761	91.1	1474	2.9	2772	5.4	321	0.6	4567	8.9	51328
2004	53516	92.4	1161	2.0	2727	4.7	504	0.9	4392	7.6	57908
2005	66212	94.0	784	1.1	2868	4.0	549	0.8	4201	6.0	70413
2006	81414	95.6	710	0.8	2551	3.0	479	0.6	3740	4.4	85154
New Pvt. B 1998	10781	96.5	365	3.3	9	0.1	19	0.2	392	3.5	11173
1999	13199	93.8	737	5.2	128	0.9	6	0.0	871	6.2	14070
2000	21870	95.9	560	2.5	294	1.3	92	0.4	946	4.1	22816
2001	29905	94.9	963	3.1	620	2.0	11	0.0	1594	5.1	31499
2002	70010	91.2	2904	3.8	3871	4.9	41	0.0	6816	8.8	76826
2003	87487	92.3	2700	2.9	3675	3.9	856	0.9	7231	7.6	94718
2004	113560	95.0	1966	1.6	3665	3.0	321	0.3	5952	5.0	119512
2005	122577	96.2	1449	1.1	3061	2.4	334	0.3	4844	3.8	127421
2006	228504	98.3	1717	0.7	1855	0.8	460	0.2	4032	1.8	232536
Foreign Bank 1998	28996	93.6	1198	3.9	250	0.8	528	1.7	1976	6.4	30972
1999	28702	92.4	1238	4.0	507	1.6	612	2.0	2357	7.6	31059

Contd...

(*Amount in Rs. Crore*)

Bank group/ year	*Standard Assets (Amt.)*	*Std. Assets (%)*	*Sub-Std Asset (Amt)*	*Sub-Std Asset %*	*Doubtful Asset (Amt)*	*Doubtful Asset %*	*Loss Asset Amt*	*Loss Asset %*	*Total NPAs (Amt)*	*Total NPA (%)*	*Total Advances (Amt)*
2000	34817	93.0	1096	2.9	798	21	721	1.9	2615	7.0	37432
2001	42285	93.1	876	1.9	1202	2.6	1033	2.3	3111	6.9	45396
2002	47838	94.5	856	1.7	1004	2.0	920	1.8	2780	5.5	50618
2003	51288	94.7	995	1.8	944	17	954	1.8	2893	5.3	54181
2004	59619	95.1	990	1.6	1099	1.8	924	1.5	3013	4.8	62632
2005	74705	97.0	715	1.1	1035	13	570	0.7	2320	3.0	77025
2006	96907	98.0	946	1.1	670	07	441	0.5	2057	2.0	98965

Source: Report on Trend and Progress of Banking in India, Various Issues, RBI.

of input, Exchange rate fluctuation, Accidents and natural calamities, Changes in Government policies relating to excise and import duties, pollution control orders etc., and Government loan waiver scheme.

Other Factors

Apart from the above factors, there are certain other factors which are responsible for standard assets becoming NPAs. are; Liberalization of the economy and the consequent pressures from liberalization like several competition, reduction of tariffs, removal of restriction etc., Poor monitoring of credits and the failure to recognize early warning signals shown by standard assets,. Promoters over optimism in setting up large projects, Sudden crashing of capital markets and the failure to raise adequate funds, Granting of loans of certain sectors on the basis of Government's directives rather than commercial imperatives, Mismatch of funding i.e. using loans granted for short terms for long term transactions., High leveraging and high cost of borrowing, and Commitment of willful defaults sensing that the legal recourse available to collect debts is very slow.

Institutional and Legal Measures for Recovery of NPAs

1. Setting up of Lok Adalats, Debt recovery Tribunals (DRTs), asset reconstruction companies, settlement advisory committees, corporate debt restructuring mechanism etc. for quicker recovery, restructuring Promulgation of Securitization and Reconstruction of Financial Assets and Enforcement of Securities Interest (SARFAESI) Act and its subsequent amendment to ensure creditor rights.
2. Setting up of Credit Information Bureau for information sharing on defaulters as also other borrowers.

During 2005-06, ARCIL acquired 559 cases of NPAs from 31banks/Fis with total dues amounting to Rs.21126 crore. The portfolio of assets acquired by ARCIL was diversified across major industry segments, which were generally performing well in the stock market.

Table 6
NPAs Recovered by SCBs Through Various Channels

(Amount in Rs. crore)

Item	*2004-05*			*2005-06*		
	No of cases referred	*Amount involved*	*Amount recovered*	*No of cases referred*	*Amount involved*	*Amount recovered*
Lok Adalats	185395	801	113	181547	1101	223
DRTs	4744	14317	2688	3524	6123	4710
SARFAESIAct	39288	13224	2391	38969	9831	3423

Table 7
Details of Financial Assets Acquired by Assets Construction Company (India) Ltd (ARCIL) (As on March 31, 2006)

(Amount in Rs. Crores)

Banks /Fis	*No of cases*	*Principal debt involved charges*	*Interest and other*	*Total dues purchased*
Public sector Banks	322	3638	3917	7555
Old Pvt. Banks	34	186	150	336
New Pvt. Banks	152	5037	4727	9764
Financial Institutions	51	1460	2011	3471
Total	559	10321	10805	21126

Source: Report on Trends and Progress of Banking in India, 2006, RBI.

Findings of the Study

The Standard Assets has increased over the period in all the Scheduled Commercial Banks in India due to decrease in the NPA level (Table 5). Three foreign banks are having a high level of NPAs (Net NPAs to Net Advances) of more than 10%. The major cause for NPAs was poor credit appraisal system and diversion of funds (Muniappan, 2002). The problem can be tackled through debt for equity swaps, use of Securitization (Reddy, 2002) (Chen, 2004) and (Chaudhari, 2005).The recapitalization of Banks through public issue and risk based regulations are the effective means to control the issue of NPAs in India.

Conclusion

It needs to be realized that there no quick-fix solutions in tackling the NPA problem. A lasting solution to the viscous problem of NPAs can be achieved when financial institutions put in place a sophisticated system of credit assessment and an integrated risk management mechanism, backed by a prompt and efficient legal framework. In a situation of liquidity overhang, banks in their attempt to book fresh business and maximize returns may go in for selection of assets which may later turn to be cases of adverse selection, resulting in NPAs. However, if the banking system is equipped with balanced prudential norms, these problems can, to a large extent, be minimized, if not avoided. This calls for organizational restructuring, improvement in managerial efficiency, skill up-gradation for proper assessment of creditworthiness and attitudinal change towards legal action.

References

Bhide, M. G., Prasad, A. and Ghosh Saibal (2001), Emerging Challenges in Indian Banking, Working Paper No. 103, Centre for Research on Economic Development and Policy Reform.

Bodla, B. S. and Verma, R. (2005), Credit Risk Analysis and Management in Banks, *The Journal of Indian Management & Strategy* Vol. 10, No. 4, October-December, pp. 17-22.

Chaitaniya, K., Causes for Non-Performing Assets in Public Sector, Dhruva College of Management, Hyderabad, *www.Indianmba.com*

Chaudhari, Datta Tamal (2005), Resolution Strategies for Maximizing Value of Non–Performing Assets (NPAs), Industrial Investment Bank of India (IIBI), Kolkota.

Chen, J. (2004), Non–Performing Loan Securitization in the People's Republic of China, Department of Economics, Stanford University

Dhanuskodi, R. (2006), A Study on Non–Performing Assets (NPAs)– With Special Reference to Commercial Banks of Ethiopia (CBE),A Research Report Submitted in the Fourth International Conference on Ethiopian Economy, June, 2006, Deptt. of Accounting, Faculty of Business & Economics, Jimma University, Jimma, Ethiopia.

Fadnis, M. (2005), Prudential Norms-Recent RBI Changes, The Chartered Accountant, *The Journal of ICAI*, Vol .53, No. 10, April.

Gordan and Natarajan (2005), Banking Theory, Law and Practice, Himalaya Publishing House, Mumbai.

Mor, N. and Sharma, Bhavna (2003), Rooting out Non-Performing Assets, ICICI Research Center.org

Ranjan, Rajiv and Sarat, D. C. (2005), Non Performing Loans and Terms of Credit of Public Sector Banks in India: An Empirical Assessment, Reserve Bank of India Occasional Papers, Vol. 24, No. 3, Winter, 003.

Reddy, K. P. (2002), A Comparative Study of Non-Performing Assets in India in the Global Context–Similarities and Dissimilarities, Remedial Measures, IIM Ahmedabad, India.

Sreekantaradhya, B.S. (2005), Banking and Finance, Perspectives on Reform, Deep & Deep Publications, New Delhi.

Venkatesan, S. (2007), Banking Industry Vision 2010, The Indian Banker, *The Journal of Indian Banks' Association*, Vol. II, No. 1, January, pp. 33-37.

Xu, Min (2005), Resolution of Non-Performing Loans in China, The Leonard N. Stern School of Business, Glucksman Institute for Research in Securities Markets.

20

Reduction of Non-Performing Assets (NPAs)-Emerging Challenges of Banking Sector

Parmanand Lal

Banking is the key sector of any economy. Its energy and vitality indicate the health and prosperity of any nation. In the liberalising economy, banking and financial sector reforms assume high priority. The new economic reforms have given a new thrust to the banking sector as a whole and private sector in particular. But still 85% of commercial banking at present belong to the public sector banks.

Economic reforms initiated in 1991 by the then Finance Minister Dr. Manmohan Singh would have remained incomplete without the overhaul of the Indian banking sector. The process, which began on the basis of recommendations of the Narasimhamam Committee Report (first report) is still continuing, though many of the sick banks have been able to come out of the red after repeat doses of fund infusion. A few of the them, however, as still in the red but the efforts are on to resuscitate them. However, the bigger challenge at the moment is to deal with the worsening financial health of the financial institutions. The other important financial institution IDBI is also not in the pink of health and needs government support for revitalising itself.

The other aspect of the banking sector reforms relates to liberalization of norms and guidelines for making the whole sector vibrant and competitive.

The most important dimension of the banking sector reforms was reduction of the non-performing assets (NAPs). In fact the whole effort to reform the banking sector would collapse if the banks are not able to contain and reduce their NPAs. It would be impossible for a bank with high NPAs to be either vibrant or competitive. What are these NPAs? These are the assets that do not yield any return. It is like owning a vast field where nothing grows, though the field was purchased at high rates.

Technically, NPAs consist of three categories of assets–sub-standard, doubtful and loss. As per the new norms for recognition, identification and classification of assets (changed with effect from March 31, 2001), assets classified as NPAs for a period up to two years belong to sub-standard category, while doubtful assets are those that remain NPAs for a period beyond two years. Loss assets are those which are identified as such either by banks themselves or internal/external auditors or RBI but not written off.

According to the Economic Survey (2002-03) gross NPAs of the public sector banks were of the order of Rs. 56,507 crore at the end of 2001-02. Private sector banks had gross NPAs of Rs. 11,672 and foreign banks Rs. 2,726 crore. Total gross NPAs of the banking sector amounted to Rs. 70,905 crore.

This was 10.4 per cent of gross advances of the banking sector. This means that banking sector does not earn any return on an investment of Rs. 70,905 crore. The strategy of the successive finance ministers have been to fight this menace of growing NPAs. These efforts are yielding fruits. Gross NPAs as percentage of gross advances were 12.7 per cent in 1999-2000. It came down to 11.4 per cent in 2000-01 and 10.4 per cent in 2001-02. similarly, net NPAs as percentage of net advances for the banking sector came down from 6.8 per cent in 1999-2000 to 6.2 per cent in 2000-01 and 5.5 per cent in 2001-02. The banking sector reforms are on the right track, though not many are happy with the pace of reduction of NPAs.

Weak and Strong Banks

The Narsimhamam Committee suggested recpitalisation of a host of public sector banks. These banks were expected to follow prudential norms with regard to asset classification. The Narsimhamam Committee-II revisited the banking sector reforms to carry forward the unfinished agenda. It defined a weak bank as one whose accumulated losses and net NPAs exceed its net worth or whose operating profits less income on recapitalisation bonds was negative for three consecutive years. Then came the working group on restructuring weak public sector banks headed by former State Bank of India chairman M. S. Verma. The group identified seven parameters for identification of weak banks–CAR and coverage Ratio under solvency; return on assets and net interest margin under earning capacity; and three ratios under profitability which include operating profit to average working funds, costs to income and staff cost to net interest income plus all other income. By and large the exercise, spread over a decade, achieved its objective to a large extent with many public sector banks being able to show results. At the end of March 2002, according to the Economic Survey 2002-03, 25 out of 27 public sector banks had CAR above the prescribed minimum level of 9 per cent. Of these, as many as 23 banks had CRAR exceeding 10 per cent. The two banks which failed to fulfill the minimum capital adequacy norms were Indian Bank and Dena Bank. Of the 30 private sector banks, Centurion Bank and Nedungadi bank could not attain the minimum CRAR level. Out of the 40 foreign banks operating in the country, only Slam Commercial Bank had a negative CRAR of 13.3 per cent. The CRAR of the commercial banks as a whole increased from 11.2 per cent at the end of March 2001 to 11.8 per cent at the end of March 2002.

NPA Recovery

The future of the Indian banking rests on the ability of bankers to recover its money, especially from those who are willful defaulters. This will ease pressure on interest rates and genuine borrowers would find it easier to obtain funds from banking channels at competitive rates. In a bid to help the banks and also financial institutions to recover funds, the government enacted the Securitisation, Reconstruction of Financial Assets and Enforcement of Security Interest Act 2002. The Act allowed creditors to take possession of secured assets; take over the management of secured assets; and to appoint a person to manage them, in case of the failure of the borrower to discharge the liabilities in the stipulated time.

Though the borrower have been allowed to appeal with the Debts Recovery Tribunals, they can do so only after depositing 75% of the amount claimed by the secured creditor. Borrowers aggrieved by the oder to of the Debts Recovery Tribunal have been permitted to appeal to an Appellate Authority within 30 days from the date of receipt of the order of the tribunal.

The Act, which has become operational, is currently being scrutinized by the Supreme Court. The industry feels that many of the provisions are draconian and the whole act needs to be redrafted. The bankers, on the other hand, are opposed to redrafting of the Act but agreeable to certain procedural changes. The apex court, however, will take a view after listening to the arguments of both sides. Hopefully, the prolem would be resolved amicably for the benefit of the both–banks as well as industry–paving the way for easy availability of cheaper credit.

The problem of non-performing assets (NAPs) is more in public sector banks (PSBs) as compared to private sector banks and foreign banks. NPAs have a direct impact on a banks profitability, liquidity and equity. The NPAs of Indian PSBs are considered relatively high by international standards. The biggest ever challenge that the banking industry now faces is management of NPAs.

The PSBs adopting many measures to reduce the NPAs by following the guidelines of RBI and the recommendations of various committees with the objective of reducing the average level of net NPAs for all banks. The PSBs can take several measures for improving loan recovery and reducing thereby NPAs like,

- Proper selection of the borrowal accounts,
- Financing viable schemes,
- Extending need-based financing
- Ensuring proper end use, proper post sanction follow up,
- Regular contact with borrowers and regular monitoring of the accounts,
- Holding recovery camps
- Seminar and conferences of defaulters, etc.

Several initiatives were taken to reduce the level of NPAs in the banking system and to manage them better. Some of the initiatives are: a special one time settlement (O.T.S.) scheme for small and marginal borrowers in all sectors. The Unions Budget for 2002-03 announced the establishment of Pilot Asset Reconstruction Companies (ARCs) to take over the NAPs. RBI has introduced corporate debt restructuring (CDR) scheme in Jan. 2002 Narasimhamam Committee suggested setting up of special debt recovery tribunals (DRTs). Recently, the Union Government outlined a five point strategy on recovering NAPs.

The Indian banking sector especially the PSBs have been facing the big challenge of NPAs is an important parameter in the analysis of financial performance of banks. Reduction of NPAs is necessary to improve profitability of the banks and comply with capital adequacy norms. To solve the problem of existing NPAs quality of appraisal, supervision and follow-up should be improved.

"Successful management pre-supposes that the right type and right amount of credit is given to the right type of client." The NPAs of Indian PSBs are considered relatively high by international standards. The judicial system needs to be revamped to facilitate quicker recovery of dues from defaulters. It is essential to enforce the securitization Act with more stringent provisions to reliase the securities and personal assets of the defaulters. Pre credit and post credit appraisals are to be done by banks more objectively. The banking secrecy Act must be amended to enable the publication of the defaulters names as willful default must be treated as a criminal offence and hence dealt with seriously.

Preventive Aspects

Prevention is better than cure. But recently, it was observed that there is unprecedented rise in fresh NPAs in some banks. During 1999-2000, recovery from NPAs in some public sector banks was to the tune of Rs. 3,000 crore but the amount involved in fresh NPAs was more than Rs. 6,000 crore. Consequently, the recovery efforts of these banks were nullified. Hence, preventive system should be strengthened. For this purpose, each bank has set up credit monitoring department cell at the corporate office and zonal office. Suitable reporting formats have been devised for branches to provide information on NPA borrowers. This inturn helps at the corporate office/zonal offices to carry out the migration analysis. This also helps in preventing slippage from standard assets to sub-standard assets. But this exercise is done quarterly. Hence, much needs to be done on an on-going basis at branch level. Traditional follow-up system consisting of stock inspection, study of ledger transactions, factory inspection, study of quarterly information system (QIS data), review of borrowal accounts, etc. should be strengthened in order to obtain signals of any account becoming an NPA at the earliest and initiate preventive action. During the post-VRS scenario the follow-up function is being given a low priority. In this regard, information technology should be used extensively to monitor each borrowal account. Credit Monitoring Officers (CMOs) should be identified to fix their accountability. Incentives should be provided for those branches which prevent slippage in standard assets considerably. In any case, preventive function deserves full appreciation in today's context.

Conclusion

In any financial institution, NPAs are inevitable in the loan portfolio. But efforts should be made to maintain a reasonable level NAPs. Keeping in mind the RBI plan to introduce the concept of 'one-quarter' for identification of NAPs by 2004, it is high time to go in for recovery drive on a war-footing. While doing so, prevention of NPAs should not be forgotten. These are the major challenges before banks which have gone in for VRS. But sincerity and hard-working alongwith professional approach on the part of bank this end, banks have to go a long way.

References

A. Q. Siddique (1999), "Some Aspects and Issues relating to NPAs in Commercial Banks", *RBI Bulletin*, July.

Master Circular-Prudential Norms on Income Recognition, Asset Classification and Provisioning Pertaining to the Advances Portfolio, Reserve Bank of India, September 1, 2001.

RBI Panel Defines Funds Diversion as willful Default", *Economic Times*, November 27, 2001.

RBI, Report on Trend and Progress 2001-02, Reserve Bank of India. Budget 2001-02.

S. R. Chaudhury, "Consider NPA Crisis, RBI Warns VRS Driven Banks", Financial Express, January 12, 2001.

V. S. Kaveri (2001), "Loan Default at Profitability of Banks", *IBA Bulletin*, January.

V. S. Kavery (2001), "Prevention of NPAs: Suggested Strategies" *IBA Bulletin*, August.

21

Outsourcing–An Avenue of Profitability

P. Dubey

Due to fast developments in information technology, the Indian banking sector is outsourcing a good portion of their routine activities. Fully automated banking transactions are the outcome of the outsourcing initiatives in banking. In the run for more profits and productivity, banks try to reduce cost through outsourcing. Of the available models of outsourcing, like joint venture, off-shore, on-shore, near-shore etc., banks will have to choose one according to their convenience. Based on the nature of need, banks can choose a method out of the available ones like package implementation method, problem solution method, traditional method or innovation method.

Outsourcing is not restricted to just a few divisions like canteen, HR placements. It encompasses almost all the function/divisions of a unit. This article proposes ways to outsource strategic activities of a bank, including a Branch of the Bank.

What is Outsourcing?

Outsourcing is, entering into a contract with another Organization/Agency to operate and manage one or more if its business processes.

In other words, outsourcing deals with the people and processes in & around a business.

Business process outsouring is not a new or novel concept. Management Guru C.K. Prahalad's slogan of "Focus on Core Competency" of the early 90's is the origin of today BPO Model.

The outsourcing concept has been there in the industrial sector (B2B) from ages. No manufacturer produces all the parts required for the finished goods that he manufacture. He gets lot of things manufactured from others as per his specifications. For example an Industry manufacturing Car gets lot of components, which are specific to its requirements from various other manufacturing units. Some of them may be ancillary units. Be it an ancillary unit or other wise, the concept of outsourcing is very much there. Here, we may add that certain large industries outsource their entire operations and do only assembling and branding of the finished product (E.g., Dell Computers).

Outsourcing bank back-officer processes also helps mitigate risk. And many banks choose BPO to gain access to intellectual capital and skill sets.

Off-Shore Outsourcing: When a BPO agency is outside a company's own country, it is called off-shore outsourcing

On-Shore Outsourcing: When a BPO agency is within a company's own county, it is called on-shore outsourcing.

Near-Shore Outsourcing: When A BPO agency is in a neighbouring country of the company outsourcing, it is termed near-shore outsourcing.

What are the Activities that a Bank Normally Outsources?

- Opening and closing of accounts, issue of chequebooks, statement of accounts.
- Processing of cheques.
- Customer query management (Call Centres)
- Selection, recruitment and training of personnel
- Administration of pay-roll and TDS.
- Marketing of bank's products
- Maintenance of computers and other electronic gadgets
- Cross selling of bank's products (Insurance & Mutual Fund)

- Credit card/debit card services
- Maintenance of ATMs

What "Strategic Activities" can the Hank Outsource?

- The entire Branch per-se
- Business loan/Letters of credit Processing
- Collection and discounting of bills
- Consumer loan (Retail) administration in toto i.e., I) sourcing of customers, processing of the request, documentation, maintenance of accounts, monitoring and recovery.

What are Strategic Benefits of Outsourcing?

- Improved customer Service
- Need for lesser capital investment
- Helps Bank to focus on its core competency activitieswhich improves its bottom line
- Helps bank to concentrate on brand building
- To gain a competitive advantage
- Helps in effective recycling of funds
- Redeploy resources to planning for the future

General Principles for Outsourcing

- Think outsourcing as a strategy
- Take up outsourcing as a part of change managementor a business process re-engineering initiative
- Be clear in what you expect from the services being outsourced
- Enter into a clear "Service Contract" with the BPO agency (outsourced). Note to include the following in the contract:
    - Inputs and the outputs
    - Processes
    - Service standards
    - Cost of service

  - Time deadlines
  - Confidentiality clause
- Inform all stockholders, including employees about the outsourcing and the need for it
- Have regular meetings with the BPO agency to know whether everything is on the right track

Outsourcee-Relationship Management (ORM)

- (In order to enable flow of thoughts, we have coined a new word "outsourcee" which would mean the suppliers/s who provide the outsourced services)

What are the Concerns of Outsourcing?

- *The concerns are:* Design of system, qualifying, suitable outsourcees, negotiation, buy-in and collaboration with outsourcee.
- *Design collaboration:* The objective is to match capability of the proposed system with the capability of the outsourcee. Good collaboration at this stage can create huge value. About 90% of the efficiency and productivity of a system is determined at the design stage. Suitable good software in this area can facilitate such collaboration. This would lead to effective on-line and continuous monitoring
- *Qualification of Outsourcee:* The qualification process involves source selection, source qualification, source evaluation and contract management. Sources are evaluated using several key criteria. These include reliability, quality and price.
- *Negotiation:* Negotiation with outsourcee involves many steps. The objective of this process is to ensure an effective contract. An effective contract should specify all the parameters including responsibilities of the outsourcee. To ensure compliance sureties and bank guarantees should be provided.
- *Buy-in:* The buy-in process executes the actual outsourcing of the activity by the bank to the outsourcee. This includes

the creation, management and approval of the contact. In the case of banks continuous on-line monitoring of key-parameters is mandatory to ensure full and continuous compliance. This is very important as more and more processes get outsourced.

- *Outsourcee collaboration:* The supply chain performance can be enhanced by collaborating on forecasts, activity norms, productivity levels, customer relationship management, etc. Good and innovative software in this area should facilitate collaborative forecasting and planning the supply chain.

Conclusion

Reserve bank of India Issued guidelines for merger/ amalgamation in the sector. According to the guidelines, the Reserve Bank of India will consider proposals for merger and amalgamation in the urban banks sector. The author firmly believes that banks should think of strategic outsourcing on the line suggested above. The bank cannot outsource Treasury activities. The innovative concept of "Banker's ATM" should be adopted. Strategic outsourcing would give the banks the competitive advantage. This would also ensure increased business volume better customer relationship and improved bottom-line for a effective based on the above discussions, it is a foregone conclusion that may activities of banks including its strategic activities should be outsourced to make unviable branches into viable ones.

In general banks activities can be divided into three segments:

- Liability Products (depositor oriented)
- Asset Products (loans and advances oriented)
- Treasury oriented (funds management).

References

Laxminarashimha A., ICFAU Business School, Bangalore.

Murali S., ING Vysya Bank Staff Training College, Bangalore.

IBA Bulleting, May, 2005.

Indian Bankers, Jan. 2006.

22

Outsourcing of Banking Services

D. M. Khandare & Mohan S. Rode

In Today's era of 21st century a drastic changes has to be faced due to process of globalization and liberalization and has virtually transformed the way the business is being conducted across the globe. Due to information & technology globe has come very near to each other. The technological innovation followed by revolutionary improvements in communication network is responsible for marked change in way banks re-engineer their business models to offer cutting-edge serviced to their customers. Competition in the market intensified and profit margins started declining rapidly. Banks started looking at new business models to reduce their operational costs and at the same time maintain their service levels to their customers. More and more back office operations hitherto conducted in-house are gradually becoming potential scope for outsourcing.

Outsourcing has emerged as a separate rapidly growing industry. Due to fast developments in information technology, the Indian banking sector is outsourcing a good portion of their routine activities. Fully automated banking transactions are the out come of the outsourcing initiatives in banking. In the run for more profits and productivity, banks try to reduce cost through outsourcing. Right from mobilizing deposits to the disbursal of loans, banks engage outsourcing agencies in different degrees. Of the available models of outsourcing, bank will have to choose like joint venture, off-shore, on-shore, near-shore etc.

The factors that influence banks to out source are primarily the cost savings, access to cutting-edge technology infrastructure and skilled, efficient labour resources.

What is Outsourcing?

Out sourcing means "an investment strategy of delegation some of the business processes to an outsider, without doing it in-house". It aims to reduce staff & to cut-off expenses on unwanted work and to focus on productive business/earnings. It is thus, shifting of some responsibilities to a service provider, who performs the services for the outsourcer. This responsibility makes take the form of manufacturing, accounting, compiling, marketing, advertising technical know-how, inspection, audit etc. Eventually, the concept spread to the territory sector like information technology, telecom, banking, insurance, management and consultancy etc.

Outsourcing is entering into contract with another organization/Agency to operate and manage one or more of its business processes.

Concept Emerged

The concept of outsourcing emerged from the economic theory of "division of labour and specialization", which professed economies of scale, innovation and more productivity, which form the basic objectives of outsourcing. In today's global platform, running a business is more complex than yester years. To refrain from stress or strain, outsourcing is adopted for sharing their burden. The rationale underlying outsourcing is, "one should do only what one can do in the best way, otherwise leave others to another to do in better ways."

Why Outsourcing?

The major trigger for outsourcing is identified as cost reduction by various surveys. Besides, cost reduction, access to new technology, focus on core competency, scale of economies emerge as valid motives for outsourcing decisions by banks across the world.

In other words we can say, by strategic outsourcing the bank will be in a position to improve customer service, reduce costs, improve the bottom line and on the top of it have a competitive advantage.

Types of Outsourcing

Off-shore: When a outsourcing agency is outside a company's own country it is called off- shore outsourcing.

On-shore: When a outsourcing agency is within a company's own country, it is called on-shore outsourcing.

Near-shore: When a outsourcing agency is in a neighbouring country of the company outsourcing, it is termed near- shore outsourcing.

Areas for Outsourcing of Banking Services

- Automation of banking activities.
- Distribution of of loans Products.
- Processing of loan application.
- Loan documentation.
- Cross-selling of para-banking products
- Innovation of new deposit & loan products.
- Management of plastic money.
- Maintenance of ATM's
- Risk Management.
- Process of cheque books
- Customer query management (Call Centres)
- Selection, Recruitment and training of personnel.

Advantages of Outsourcing of Banking Services

The primary driving force behind the spurt in outsourcing activities is the cost saving involved. Outsourcing to third parties can result in cost savings of up to 30-40 per cent as compared doing the same work in-house. " Saving through IT outsourcing is more of a long-term perspective. Over a period of five years the costly savings vis-a-vis-in-house work can be as high as 50 per cent."

The is also another inherent advantage for banks apart from cost saving and greater expertise. There is no liability for the bank in terms of the business process being outsourced. "If at any point of time the bank wants to quite a particular area like credit cards, there is no exit barrier involved."

Reasons for Outsourcing of Banking Service

1. Cost Reduction
2. Strategic Focus
3. Risk Reduction
4. Improved Quality
5. Faster Reaction to change

Benefits of Outsourcing of Banking Service

1. Improved customer service
2. Ample time for focusing on Core functions
3. Lesser Capital requirements
4. Helps banks to concentrate on brand building
5. To gain a competitive advantage
6. Helps in effective recycling funds
7. Saving of resources-Profitability increase.

Outsourcing is a two-edged sword, through, it harbours particular risks. Firms mainly hesitate to outsource because they fear to lose direct control. Moreover, there is the fact that confidential information is processed outside the firm as well as the risk and cost related to the migration process.

Reasons against Outsourcing of Banking Service

1. Migration cost
2. Migration risk
3. Confidential information processed externally
4. Loss of direct control

Risk in Outsourcing of Banking Service

Banks around the globe have been outsourcing certain functions which enable them to economize their cost of operation. But in doing so, they are exposed to several risks that may include strategic, reputation, compliance, operational, exit-strategy, counterpart, country, contractual, access, concentration and systemic risk. The failure of a service provider in providing a specified service, a breach in security/confidentially, or noncompliance with legal and regulatory requirements by either the service provider or the outsourcing bank, could lead to substantial financial losses to the bank concerned. Hence, there is a need for adoption of sound and responsive risk management practices for effective oversight, due diligence and management of risks arising out of the outsourced activities.

Principal of Outsourcing of Banking Service

1. Take the outsourcing as a strategic issue.
2. Take it as a part of change management
3. The concept should be cleared
4. Take all the stake holders into confidence.
5. Enter into a clear service contract with the outsource agency and have a regular follow-up, supervision and control.

Conclusion

Banks now have a platform to stand on and outsource. The banks world over have learnt how to reduce costs, utilize the best tech-skills and to offer superior products to prosper. To achieve this end, they should outsource to an agency of world class standard and maintain the high level quality and precision. But the success of outsourcing decision primarily rests on the edifice of three pillars, viz. the proper identification of activities to be outsourced, selection and monitoring of a service provider to ensure that there is no disruption in the timely delivery of quality service as per the agreed terms and most importantly structuring a service level agreement that is flexible enough to make amendments, review at regular intervals in the event of any unforeseen situation. It is to be well ingrained in the minds of people who are party to the bank's outsourcing decision that changes in banking are taking place with rapid speed and are unpresidented many times. Unless these aspects are factored into the process of outsourcing decision mere delegating of activities for cost implications alone does not bring desired efficiency or effectiveness for the growth of the organization. It is very important to note that the outsourcing arrangement is of long tenure and absence of proper exit clause in the service level Agreement may drive the bank to either pay more than warranted or satisfy with the poor service level standards of the provider. It is therefore essential that the top management spare valuable time and resources for all the processes of an outsourcing decision. Handled properly with a bent of professionalism, outsourcing proves an excellent business opportunity to reduce costs and increase efficiency/ productivity, which are the primarily concerns of well managed banks.Hence, bank should be wise to choose right.

References

Srinivasan H.S. & V.S. Murthy (2005), Outsourcing in Banks as a Business Model–ATM, Credit Cards, *IBA Bulletin,* Volume XXVII, No. 10 October.

P. Suresh Kumar (2006), Outsourcing in the Banking Sector–An Analysis, *IBA Bulletin,* Volume 1, No. 4 April.

S. Murali and A. Lakshminarasimha (2005), Strategic Outsourcing-The New Mantra to Improve the Bank's Productivity, *IBA Bulletin,* Vol. XXVII, No. 5, May.

Dr. Ch. Ibohal Meitei (2005), Managing Business Process Outsourcing–Opportunities and Challenges, *Indian Journal of Marketing,* Vol. XXXV, No. 12 December.

Dr. S. Jagadees Pandi (2006), Outsourcing and IT Enabled Service Sector in the Globalised Scenario: Emerging Challenges, *Indian Journal of Marketing,* Vol. XXXVI, No. 4 April.

Srinivas R. Kandula (2004), Human Resource Management in Practice with 300 Models, Techniques and Tools, Prentice-Hall of India Private Limited, New Delhi.

Dr. D.S. Sangwan (2007), Outsourcing An Avenue of Profitability, *The Indian Banker* Vol. II, No. 1, Janunary.

23

Outsourcing in the Banking Sector– A New Business Mantra

Sasanka Sekhar Bhaumik

The concept of outsourcing emerged from the economic theory of "Division of Labour and specialization", which professed economies of scale, innovation and more productivity, which form the basic objectives of outsourcing. On today's global platform, running a business is more complex than yester years. To refrain from stress or strain, outsourcing is adopted for sharing their burden. The rationale underlying outsourcing is "One should do only what one can do in the best way, otherwise leave others to do in better ways."

Outsourcing, being one of the oldest practice of last 80 years, is an important management concept to face the challenge of competition. Outsourcing is explained as the strategy of identifying the core competence of the organization, pointing the focus on it and simultaneously transferring the execution and delivery of non-core activities to a service provider. As per Shreveport, Consultancy, it is defined as the transfer to third party of the continuous management responsibility for the provision of a service governed by a service level agreement. It has moved its way up the value chain to the point where it holds strategic importance. Outsourcing is considered as a transition to reshape the organisational structure to move from past vertical structure to more flexible, focused organization. This helps undoubtedly in increasing the core capabilities and in creating bond relationship with the customers. Flexible organisational structure is considered as one of the key factor for survival in the present globalised market.

Emergence of Outsourcing

Outsourcing, as an organized profession, first made its appearance in United States in the early 1990's. Companies resorted to outsourcing activities comprising of bill processing, security facilities management, payroll processing, housekeeping etc. Since the last two years, the range of outsourcing possibilities multiplied and even critical activities, like manufacturing, distribution logistics, finance, human resources etc. came under its ambit. The outsourcing market in the world in 2001 was $ 300 billion and the same is expected to reach $ 1 trillion by 2007. Today, world over, distribution logistics take the largest share (29 per cent), followed by human resources (24 per cent) and payment service (16 per cent) in the outsourcing Industry.

Reasons for Outsourcing

In this changing scenario, Banks are feeling that many of the functions may be outsourced more gainfully without affecting the quality of service. Organizations are opting for outsourcing of various services for the reasons mentioned below:

(a) Outsourcing of services helps in cutting the costs, which ultimately leads to profit maximization. Some of the major players in the financial outsourcing sector state that their clients enjoy the benefit of cost saving between 35 and 40 per cent. Though saving through IT outsourcing is a long-term perspective, over a period of years the cost saving *vis-a-vis* in-house work can be high. Assumption regarding the cutting of costs is from the experience of the banks that have already outsourced their business process.

Secondly, when a bank resorts to outsourcing of its services, its own manpower, which will now be available, can be deployed for increasing banks business. This will contribute by way of increase in profit.

(b) Improved efficiency reduced operating and capital costs and increased concentration on strategic Banking initiatives are the main reasons of opting for outsourcing.

(c) Outsourcing helps to develop process improvement if in house staff has more time to handle the other issues, they will have the time to identify the best way to accomplish their task.

(d) It helps to hedge against technology obsolescence, in cases where outsourcing of Information Technology Enabled Services (ITES) is done. Access to best of breed software, freedom from specific IT operational responsibilities and a rapid IT deployment time frame are the additional advantages. This allows banks to focus on its core business area of Banking. The technology risk is passed on to the service provider.

(e) Efficient, dependable and uninterrupted services are available.

(f) There are no exit barriers involved for the Banks. At any point of time Banks can decide to quit a particular area that is outsourced.

(g) Banks are not required to maintain a huge strength of IT staff as manpower expertise and adequate skill sets are readily available through outsourcing.

Desired Areas

Having emerged as a separate rapidly growing industry the business process outsourcing in the Banking sector, is of course, inevitable and desired in some specific areas of banking activity. Here, an attempt has been made to briefly highlight the areas where it can be more effective and instrumental in the promotion of Banks businesses.

The main areas of outsourcing in Banking are:

Automation of Banking Activities

Technological advancement has transformed the banking sector into a high-tech park for financial services. One chooses a bank for his financial needs, based on the level of automation and availabiity of the latest techno-products. Here in comes the role of the outsourcee, who converts manual Banking to paperless Banking.

Distribution of Loan Products

The outsourcee popularizes the schemes of Bank's loan portfolio and canvasses customers. According to the needs of the customer, they offer suitable products. This channel helps the Banks to boost up the retail segment of advances. They act as intermediary between the prospective customer and the Banker.

Processing of Loan Applications

The application forms for loans are supplied by the vendor and who helps the customer to fill them up. The relevant documents are also collected and after scrutiny, forward them to the bank for finalizing the decision of financing or not to finance.

Loan Docmentation

After the bank shows the green signal for sanctioning the loan, vendor submits the loan documents to the customer for execution. The loan documents, as prescribed by the bank will be obtained by the outsourcee and handed over to the bank for custody and the loan is disbursed accordingly.

Cross-selling of Para-banking Products

The banker's foray into the insurance and mutual funds sectors has given much scope for outsourcing. The vendors cross sell the mutual fund and insurance products along with the deposit products.

Innovation of New Deposit and Loan Products

In any competitive field, introduction of new products and methods marks an impact in the market. For retaining the market lead, banks intend to spend more for innovations of new deposit and loan products. The service providers help to develop new competitive products evolved through detailed study of the products already available in the market.

Management of Plastic Money

The management of credit cards and debit cards is undertaken by vendors who have a well-knit information system. In this case, updated technology is a must, which the banks may not be at ease to acquire because of its exorbitant cost. More over, it requires skilled man-power to man the operations.

Maintenance of ATMs

The is another area, where the banks have better advantage if the work is outsourced. The technical know-how for maintaining ATMs, which is highly technological and costly, is supplied by IT perfessionals and the IT companies on contract basis.

Risk Management

Some of the managerial functions are also now outsourced by many banks. The preparation of risk profiles, risk measurement and its mitigation process are framed by the outsourcee.

Other Functions

The other functions, like maintenance of pay rolls, tax collections and its payment to the government etc are also outsourced by banks, sometimes. Outsourcing is certainly not passing on one's headache to another. It is the actual starting of a travel with a new partner to improve efficiency. Banks are able to reap lot of benefits through outsourcing, like the following:

- Outsourcing will relieve some of its human resources, which can be better utilized in other fields of more importance.

- Outsourcing increases net income through reduction of costs. The cost of outsourcing is normally less than the cost of processing in-house.
- Outsourcing helps the corporate management to focus more on core activities.
- Cost of maintaining a large labour force gets reduced. Downsizing of work-force is considered rightsizing.
- The evils of strikes and labour-unrest among the employees get minimized. When a good portion of the activity is outsourced and when work force is reduced, the strength of labour for unjustifiable demands gets weaker.
- Outsourcing enables to provide better tools, practices and policies, since they are specialized in their area of operation.
- Better scope for innovation of new and better products or methods is another advantage of outsourcing Specialisation leads to innovations.

Advantage of Outsourcing

Outsourcing as the term implies, delegation of back office functions that are essential for running a business, but are not the part of core functions, has some inherent points of strength contained in it. It will be not out of order to present have the advantages of this age old practice of banking operations.

The advantages of outsourcing are phenomenal. A study of ASSOCHAM reveals the following benefits:

- Achieving cost reduction and control on cash outflow.
- Access to advanced technology state of the Art.
- Access to expertise and specialist area.
- Improving Service Quality.
- Focus on core Competency areas resulting to more productivity.

  Shreve ports Survey discovered the leverage benefits as well:

- Acting as a catalyst for change by focusing on improvement elsewhere.
- Aiding and improving other initiatives like IT, credit and reengineering of the respective process.
- Stimulating critical credit analysis.

Disadvantages of Outsourcing

- From security point of view, as banking operations are a sensitive area there are risks involved in outsourcing of services viz. Personnel of service providers gaining intimate knowledge of bank's systems and misusing the same.
- There is a possibility that banks may lose control over the work process that has been outsourced. So, it is very important for banks to remember that they have to outsource the delivery of its plan and not the plan itself.
- Once the outsourcer gains the customer information, its bargaining power increases.
- The relationship enjoyed by the vendor and the bank starts with a well-defined contract, but sometimes at a later stage, management of this relationship becomes difficult due to difference of opinion on certain issues. Service agreement disputes are very common in such cases.
- Outsourcings of business processes bring along with them the operational as well as legal risks.
- In case where customer support has been outsourced, the attitude of the employees of the service provider has an impact on reputation of the bank. Here the banks are always facing the reputation risk.
- The required modifications in systems and procedures of the banks after outsourcing of certain business processes if not properly planned; there is a possibility that banks may lose control over the processes outsourced.
- The possibility of disruption in service and defective services is also there. In case the service provider fails to perform its duties properly, operational problems may crop up, leading to disruption in business.

- Outsourcing agency takes care of execution of processes and functions but is not accountable to the customers.

Latest Developments

Now, very recently, the Reserve Bank of India has advised banks to maintain a strict control over the service providers. The guidelines prescribed by the Reserve Bank of India are furnished below:

- Bank have to construct a managerial structure for monitoring and regulating outsourcing, since the sharing of the facilities operated by service providers could compromise the bank's data.
- The outsourcing functions should adhere to the regulatory and supervisory requirements, prescribed by the Reserve Bank of India.
- Banks cannot outsource their work in countries where they have no branches.
- For off-shore outsourcing by banks, RBI's prior permission is required.
- To undertake 'door-step banking' permission from RBI is required.
- Banks should frame and put in place a comprehensive outsourcing policy, approved by its board of directors.
- Banks cannot outsource core management functions, like; corporate planning, organization, management and control and decision-making functions, compliance functions etc.
- Outsourcing contracts should include the contingency plans to ensure disaster recovery and business continutity.
- The outsourcees' work should be audited either by internal auditors or by another outside agency.
- The policy should provide for a clause for inspection of the service provider and their books of accounts by RBI.

- The service provider should not harass or ill-treat any customer.
- A time limit of 60 days should be given to the customers for perferring a complaint.
- Bank should constitute a Grievances Redressal Machinery, which should resolve the problems faced by the customers.
- Access to the customers' information should be limited for the service provider.
- Banks cannot outsource the management of investment portfolio.
- Banks should not engage in outsourcing activites that may weaken the internal control or compromise their business conduct or reputation.
- Banks should notify RBI in case any overseas authority seeks access to customer information.

Conclusion

The risks and disadvantages associated with outsourcing need not be held against its implementation. These are not more than the normal risks attached with any business. Also there will never be dearth of nay sayers from either within the management or from the unions. Such minor irritants are not uncommon while implementing any new idea or concept. They should not be allowed to come in the way of larger benefits that the banks would derive by going in for outsourcing in these days of intense competition.

All said and done, the benefits accruing from outsourcing cannot be undermined as it will reduce the investment in infrastructure to a large extent and will result in a higher ROI. Even the apprehensions about breach of trust by the service providers may also prove unfounded once the terms and conditions of the agreements are clearly spelt out with suitable penalty clauses included. Therefore, the utility of outsourcing should be viewed with an open mind and given go ahead.

References

Contemporary Banking and Finance-Different Issues. Insider Outsourcing, C.L. Goy & T. Essinger.

Insider Strategies for Outsourcing information System, K. M. Ripin & L. R. Sayles.

The Indian Baker, April, 2006.

Bank Net India-Report on BPO in Financial Sector.

Kulkarni, V. N. "*The Indian Banker*", October, 2006, p. No. 48-49.

24

Outsourcing in the Banking Sector– A New Lookout

Ashis Kumar Nandi

Outsourcing has emerged as a seperate rapidly growing industry. Due to fast developments in information technology, the Indian banking sector is outsourcing a good portion of their routine activities. Fully automated banking transactions are the outcome of the outsourcing initiatives in banking. In the run for more profits and productivity, banks try to reduce cost through outsourcing. Right from mobilizing deposits to the disbursal of loans, banks engage outsourcing agencies in different degrees. Of the available models of outsourcing, like joint venture, off-shore, on-shore, near-shore etc, banks will have to choose one according to their convenience. Based on the nature of need, banks can choose a method out of the available ones like package implementation method, problem solution method, traditional method or innovation method. For an effective outsourcing arrangement, banks must follow certain principles like, adoption of a policy, identification of areas for outsourcing, prioritization of them, linking the outsourced processes and integration of the system etc. Very recently, RBI has come out with a set of norms for banks' outsourcing, to have regulatory control. It stipulates the prohibited areas and the principles to be followed by the banks.

Therefore, banks will have to adhere to them for maintaining discipline.

Definition of Outsourcing

Outsourcing may be defined as a bank's use of a third party (either an affiliated entity within a corporate group or an entity that is external to the corporate group) to perform activities on a continuing basis that would normally be undertaken by the bank itself, now or in the future. Joint Forum of Bank for International Settlement further explains that Outsourcing can be the initial transfer of an activity or a part of that activity from a regulated entity to a third party or the further transfer of an activity or a part there of from one third party service provider to another some times referred to as "subcontracting". In some jurisdictions, the initial outsourcing is also referred as subcontracting.

National Bank of Slovakia issued the methodological instructions relating to outsourcing and defined it as "Outsourcing means the long term ensuring of the services support for conduct of banking activities for a bank by another person i.e. service provider on a contractual basis with the aim of achieving higher effectiveness of the conduct of the banking activities".

According to the regulation in Holland outsourcing is defined as "causing of the supply of services, goods or facilities that form a part of the banking or auxiliary business processes on a structural basis by other group entities or by independent third parties except in so far as this relates to purchasing". The Czech National Bank defines outsourcing as the "supplying of banking activities or activities supporting banking activities by another entity for the bank on a contractual basis".

In brief, outsourcing is defined as the "act of transferring bank's activities to another firm or organisations, an activity that was formerly conducted in house and by extension, the resulting state of not conducting that activity in house any more".

Classifications of Outsourcising

Financial Services companies have developed a wide variety of outosurcising phenomena over the course of recent years.

To conceptualise these phenomena to the extent that they can be specified in descriptive dimensions, thus making it possible to differentiate between different scenarios. This classification will form the basis for the subsequent development of scenario specific methods. Only them will it be possible for the companies in the financial services sector to depart from their previous approach to outsourcing which up to now has largely been individual if not initiative in many cases.

Outsourcing can be broadly into two classified principal categories:

- *Traditional Outsourcing* where the routine jobs or tasks are identified and the service provider hire staff for this job.
- *Green field outsourcing* without hiring the service provider the organisation can directly hire an imminent company, which can execute their business, which was not done in the organization internally.

Common Types of Outsourcing are:

Business Process Outsourcing: Denotes the outsourcing of an entire business process or a complete enterprise function to an external service provider. The service provider takes on the full IT systems, which support the business process. The activities of the service provider include both operation and maintenance of the IT systems and management and execution of the business process. Employees of the organisation cease to perform the same jobs and the service provider normally hires employees. For e.g. call centres, payroll, finance functions and activities, e-publishing, book keeping services, accounting, and human services.

IT Outsourcing: Denotes that the service provider takes on the operation and maintenance of the service customer IT systems. The service provider is responsible for the customer's computer and communication systems as well as their data centres. In most cases the service provider also takes on the company's internal IT personnel. shared hosting, application service providing and application hosting to customize standard software is also made available to a specific customer (one to one approach) and operated by service provider in a central data centre. Specialised tasks are entirely done by service providers. Website, software development, network backbone service and IT remote support are few examples. E outsourcing is buying information technology products and services that could be furnished in-house from one or a variety of sources on the Internet.

The other various ways of Outsourcinsing are:

Off shore Outsourcing: is the practice of hiring an external organization to perform some or all business functions in a country other than the one where the product or service will be sold or consumed. It can be contrast with off shoring, in which the functions are performed in a foreign country, whether by the foreign subsidiary of the same company or a third party. The general criteria for job to be offshore are that the job does no require customer interaction and there is a significant wage difference between the original and offshore countries. The work has a high information content, can be transmitted over the Internet, easy to set up and is of repeatable nature. Off shore outstanding is also known as near shore outsourcing. Geographic proximity means that travel and communications are easier and less expensive. There are likely to be at least some commonalities between the cultures, and people are more likely to speak the same language.

On Shore outsourcng: Onshore outsourcing (also called domestic outsourcing) is the obtaining of services from someone outside a company but within the same country.The process of engaging another company within your own country for BPO or ITO services. For the US, it means hiring a US based company to provide services.

Reasons for Outsourcing

In this changing scenario banks are feeling that many of the functions may be outsourced more gainfully without affecting the quality of service.Organisations are opting for outsourcing of various services for the reasons mentioned below:

(a) Outsourcing of services helps in cutting the costs, which ultimately leads to profit maximization. Some of the major players in the financial BPO sector state that their clients enjoy the benefit of cost saving between 35 and 40 per cent. Though saving through IT outsourcing is a long-term perspective, over a period of years the cost savings *vis-a-vis* in-house work can be high.

Assumption regarding the cutting of costs is from the experience of the banks that have already outsourced their business processes. Secondly, when a bank resorts to outsourcing of its services, its own manpower, which will now be available, can be deployed for increasing banks business. This will contribute by way of increase in profit.

(b) Improved efficiency reduced operating and capital cost and increased concentration on strategic banking initiatives are the main reasons of opting for outsourcing.

(c) Outsourcing helps to develop process improvement - If in house staff has more time to handle the other issues, they will have the time to identify the best way to accomplish their task.

(d) It helps to hedge against technology obsolescence, in cases where outsourcing of Information Technology Enabled Services (ITES) is done. Access to best of breed software, freedom from specific IT operational responsibilities and a rapid IT deployment time frame are the additional advantages. This allows banks to focus on its core business area of banking. The technology risk is passed on to the service provider.

(e) Efficient, dependable and uninterrupted services are available.

(f) There are no exit barriers involved for the banks. At any point of time banks can decide to quit a particular area that is outsourced.

(g) Banks are not required to maintain a huge strength of IT staff as manpower expertise and adequate skill sets are readily available through outsourcing.

Benefits of Outsourcing

- Ability to increase product quality and lower costs.
- Ability to purchase intellectual capital i.e. ability to utilize the technical know-how of other organization to find the specific requirement they need to implement their target objectives.
- Ability to focus on core competencies.
- Ability to better anticipate future costs.
- Ability to make more efficient use of worldwide labour, capital, technology and resources.

According to Price Water HouseCoopers, some of the value propositions for banks from an outsourcing model include hedging against technology obsolescence, access to best of breed software, freedom from specific IT operational responsibilities and a rapid IT deployment time frame. This in turn reduces the total cost of ownership (TCO) and enables the bank to focus on its core business area of banking. Another advantage apart from cost savings, greater expertise, no liability for banks in terms of the business process being outsourced is the ready availability of adequate skills sets and manpower expertise.

Risks in Outsourcing

There are various risks associated with outsourcing and one of the dominant ones is the "fear of unknown" as many mangers feel there is a certain feeling of lack of information in engagements. The only way to mitigate this risk, apart from top management commitment is to involve the customer at every stage in the delivery process. In the January 2001 Basel II consultative package, operational risk was defined as "The risk of direct or indirect loss resulting from inadequate or failed internal processes, people and systems or from external events, This focus on operational risk, which has been generally welcome by the banking and financial services community.

The key risks in outsourcing needs to be evaluated by the banks are:

(a) *Strategic Risks:* is the risk arising from adverse business decisions, improper implementation of decisions or lack of responsiveness to industry changes. This risk is a function of the compatibility of an organization's strategic goals, the business strategies developed to achieve those goals, the resources deployed against these goals and the quality of implementation. The service provider may conduct business on its own behalf, which is inconsistent with overall strategic goals of the banks.

(b) *Reputation Risk:* is the risk arising from negative public opinion. The risk may expose the institution to litigation, financial loss or a decline in customer base. poor service from the service provider and its customer interaction with not being consistent with the overall standards of the bank.

(c) *Compliance Risk:* is the risk of legal or regulatory sanctions, financial loss or reputation loss that a bank may suffer as a result of its failure to comply with any or all the applicable laws. Regulations, Codes of conduct and standards of good practice. It is also called integrity risk since a bank's reputation is closely linked to its adherence to principles of integrity and fair dealing.

(d) *Operational Risk:* includes both compliance risk and transaction risk and arises due to technology failure, fraud, error, inadequate financial capacity to fulfil obligation and/or provide remedies.

(e) *Legal Risk:* is not limited to exposure to fines, penalties or punitive damanges, resulting from supervisory actions as well as private settlements due to omissions and commissions of the service provider.

(f) *Exit Strategy Risk:* could arise from over reliance on one firm, the loss of relevant skills in the bank itself preventing it from bringing the activity back in house and contracts entered into wherein speedy exits would be prohibitively expensive.

(g) *Counter Party Risk:* Due to inappropriate underwriting or credit assessments.

(h) *Contratual Risk:* arising from whether or not the bank has the ability to enforce the contract.

(i) *Country Risk:* due to political, social or legal climate creating added risk.

(j) *Concentration and Systematic Risk:* Due to lack of control of individual banks over a service provider, more so often when overall banking industry has considerable exposure to one service provider.

The most significant issue facing banks in relation to Basel II is aligning and upgrading data and existing IT systems infrastructure for completeness, consistency and integrity across the organization. The systems to comply with Basel II requirements under the advanced approach for market, credit and operational risk must be compatible with the existing IT architecture and provide suitable reporting facilities and analytics. The second driver is Corporate Governance and complete buy-in. The role and responsibilities of each managing individual, department and vendor have to be clearly defined to avoid confusion, especially with regard to operational risk. The third is a clear risk awareness culture - a feeling of risk avoidance unless necessary for business. Outsourcing of IT functions can free up several divisions inside the IT divisions and management for risk measurement and mitigation measures.

RBI Guidelines on Managing Risks and Code of Conduct in Outsourcing of Financial Services by Banks

In view of the extensive use of outsourcing by banks, RBI had issued draft guidelines on 6th December 2005 for laying down a framework for managing the attendant risks in outsourcing and on the basis of the suggestions received from all concerned, the draft fuidelines have been suitably modified on 3rd November, 2006.

These guidelines are concerned with managing risks in outsourcing of financial services:

1. Are not applicable to technology-related issues and activities not related to banking services like usage of courier, catering of staff, housekeeping and janitorial services, security of the premises, movement and archiving of records etc.
2. Are intended to provide direction and guidance to banks which choose to outsource financial services to adopt sound and responsive risk management practices for effective oversight, due diligence and management of risks arising from such outsourcing activities.
3. Are applicable to outsourcing arrangements entered into by a bank with a service provider located in India or elsewhere. The service provider may either be a member of the group/conglomerate to which the bank belongs, or an unrelated party.

The underlying principles behing these guidelines are that the regulated entity should ensure that outsourcing arrangements neither diminishes its ability to fulfill its obligations to customers and RBI, nor impede effective supervision by RBI. Banks, therefore, have to take steps to ensure that the service provider employs the same high standard of care in performing the services as would be employed by the banks, if the activities were conducted within the banks and not outsourced. Accordingly banks should not engage in outsourcing that would result in their internal control, business conduct or reputation being compromised or weakened.

Banks which desire to outsource financial services would not require prior approval from RBI whether the service provider is located in India or outside India.

The major highlights of these guidelines are as listed below:

Activities that should not be Outsourced

Banks which choose to outsource financial services should however not outsource core management functions including Internal Audit, Compliance function and decision-making functions like determining compliance with KYC norms for opening deposit accounts, according sanction for loans (including retail loans) and management of investment portfolio.

Material Outsourcing

During Annual Financial Inspections, RBI will review the implementation of these guidelines to assess the quality of related risk management systems particularly in respect of material outsourcing. Material outsourcing arrangements are those, which if disrupted, have the potential to significantly impact the business operations, reputation or profitability. Materiality of outsourcing would be based on:

- The level of importance to the bank of the activity being outsourced
- The potential impact of the outsourcing on the bank on various parameters such as earnings, solvency, liquidity, funding capital and risk profile;
- The likely impact on the bank's reputation and brand value, and ability to achieve its business objectives, strategy and plans, should the service provider fail to perform the service;
- The cost of the outsourcing as a proportion of total operating costs of the bank;
- The aggregate exposure to that particular service provider, in cases where the bank out sources various functions to the same service provider.

Bank's Role-Regulatory and Supervisory Requirements

The outsourcing of any activity by bank does not diminish its obligations, and those of its Board and senior management, who have the ultimate responsibility for the outsourced activity. Banks would therefore be responsible for the actions of their service provider including Direct Sales Agents/Direct Marketing Agents and recovery agents and the confidentiality of information pertaining to the customers that is avilable with the service provider. Banks should retain ultimate control of the outsourced activity.

It is imperative for the bank, when performing its due diligence in relation to outsourcing, to condider all relevant laws, regulations, guidelines and conditions of approval, licensing or registration. Outsourcing arrangements should not affect the rights of a customer against the bank, including the ability of the customer to obtain redress as applicable under relevant laws. Since the customers are required to deal with the service providers in the process of dealing with the bank, banks should incorporate a clause in the product literature/ brochures etc., stating that they may use the services of agents in sales/marketing etc of the products. The role or agents may be indicated in broad terms.

Outsourcing, whether the service provider is located in India or abroad should not impede or interfere with the ability of the bank to effectively oversee and manage its activities nor should it impede the RBI in carrying out its supervisory functions and objectives.

Banks need to have a robust grievance redressal mechanism, which in no way should be compromised on account of outsourcing.

The service provider if is not a subsidiary of the bank should not be owned or controlled by any director or officer/ employee of the bank or their relatives having the same meaning as assigned under Section 6 of the Companies Act, 1956.

Conclusion

Outsourcing allows better alignment between cost structure and revenues, greater flexibility to introduce new products, more innovative investment structures, access to new technology, rapid integration of the same into the company's systems and greater ability to keep pace with changing regulations and markets. The core activities presently being outsourced by Indian Banks includes hardware and software maintenance, hosting, management of data centers, outsourcing of data center operations, application support, disaster recovery facilities management, comprising network management and monitoring, maintenance of websites and maintenance and management of ATM's While these are the more popular activities, some of the emerging opportunities exist in areas of e-banking initiatives, e commerce outsourcing, complete outsourcing of the IT function and outsourcing the entire ATM set up and operation to a third party.

Outsourcing can take place at individual, process and functional levels. But its important to note that if managed properly, outsourcing can be an efficient risk mitigation tool. Outsourcing in Banks and financial services may finally be coming of the age. Financial services organizations continue to struggle with capital adequacy, operational costs and need to improve shareholder return and to meet all these challenges by continuing focus on their main business and organisation's vision-Outsourcing is one such solution.

References

Kumar P. Suresh (2006), Outsourcing in the Banking Sector-An Analysis, *The Indian Banker,* April, Volume I, No. 4.

Bhasin Narinder Kumar (2007), Outsourcing: A Strategic Management Option, *The Indian Banker,* March, Volume II, No. 3.

Roy P. K. (2003), Outsourcing & IT Outsourcing-A New Look, BECON.

Sangwan, D. S. (2007), Outsourcing An Avenue of Profitability, *The Indian Banker,* Vol. II, No. 1, January.

25

Indian Banking: Pivotal Role of Technology

Sanjay Kumar Gupta

There has been a paradigm shift in the Indian banking industry in the way they operate and manage their diversified banking portfolio especially during the last one decade. More and more new products and services are now being handled by bank is on technology platform. Technology is acting as a catalyst and an enabler for bringing in speed, efficiency and accuracy in handling the complex banking functions and ever-changing needs of the customers.

With the major initiatives undertaken by the Reserve Bank of India (RBI) and the Institute for Development and Research in Banking Technology (IDRBT), banks have achieved considerable level of infusion of contemporary technology in their operations.

Investments in Information Technology (IT)

The banking industry has made major investments in the induction of technology during the past few years and it was expected that after incubation/gestation period of three to four years, investments made by banks in IT shall start giving commensurate returns. Now, over a period of time, the technology across various banks has matured and the staff handling the IT based banking services are fully trained and groomed to derive optimal benefits from deployment of technology. However, it is felt that the Return on Technology Investment (ROTI) is still not forthcoming in line with the expectations. On the top of that, additional expenses on annual maintenance contracts (AMC), depreciation, upgradation of systems and prevention are required to be made to thwart cyber crimes and hacking threats in view of increased use of network and technology in the banking sector.

The investments in the IT security are further expected to go up as the fragmented security technologies currently deployed by the banking sector namely, firewalls, intrusion detection systems (IDS) and intrusion prevention systems (IPS) shall have to be replaced by unified technology based security solutions which cover the entire gamut of security and anti-virus related IT gadgets into one single box.

With the net interest margins of various banks continuing to shrink, the cost of operations must come down with cptimal use and leveraging of technology. The major challenges which are faced by the banks in terms of leveraging the technology for the business benefits are summarised herein below:

(i) Major investments have been made by banks in implementation of the CBS, Wide Area Network (WAN), ATM network, etc with heavy capital expenses and ongoing recurring expenses in terms of AMC, telecom rentals, maintenance and upgradation of hardware and IT infrastructure deployed by them.

(ii) Very little or no Business Process Reengineering (BPR) has been implemented to commensurate with the induction of technology, with the result that there is a major mismatch between technology and the age-old business processes existing in the banks. Hence, benefits of the technology are not reaching the customers.

(iii) It is becoming difficult for the banks to recruit and retain highly skilled technical staff to maintain and upgrade the complex IT infrastructure created. This has resulted in increased dependency on the third-party vendors. In the process, banks have to invest huge sums for any upgrades and/or maintenance of the IT infrastructure.

(iv) In spite of heavy investments made by banks in the electronic delivery channels, a large number of transactions are continued to be handled at the branch level resulting into cost per transaction going up instead of getting reduced.

(v) Average hits per ATM are considerably low and it requires consistent and sustained efforts by all concerned to augment the card base and transaction hit levels even to reach the breakeven point.

(vi) There have been major gaps in recruitment of skilled manpower in the banking industry. The average age of the employees in Public Sector Banks (PSBs) is not favourable which is creating a major stumbling block in meeting the present day challenges and competition posed by the new generation peer group banks.

(vii) Fast, efficient and accurate newer inter-bank remittance facilities such as Real Time Gross Settlement (RTGS), National Electronic Funds Transfer (NEET) are not getting popularised and the traditional modes of making such payments continue. In general, the PSBs are not able to route even 5 per cent of their total transactions through RTGS and NEFT. As a result, the operational costs involved in the traditional mode of inter-bank remittance continue to remain at the same higher level and the investments made by the banks in setting up IT infrastructure to support RTGS, NEFT remain highly underutilised.

Better late than never. The time is now ripe when all-out efforts on addressing above constraints need to be initiated and completed on a war footing. The investments made in the IT during the past few years by the banks shall have to be converted into tangible returns and benefits thereby strengthening the bottom-line of the banks instead of adding to their overheads.

Age-old business processes must be revisited and fine-tuned in line with the state-of-the-art banking softwares which have been put in place, to reduce the customer reaction time, thereby improving customer service. All back-office operations such as printing and dispatch of statement of account, issuance of chequebooks, clearing operations, account opening process, etc should be taken away from the branches and shifted to back-office. The frontend branches should have lean and thin structure primarily focusing towards the customer needs.

Pivotal Role of Information Technology

The most visible impact of technology in banking has been in distribution and customer access channels. Growing customer demand for better products and higher service level expectations, as well as the pressure on banks to improve operating efficiency and manage costs of delivery, have been the prime drivers for Indian banks to embrace information technology. From the staid over-the-counter delivery mode to ATMs, phone banking, net banking, and now mobile banking- the number of deliery channels deployed by banks has increased by leaps and bounds.

Traditionally, banking players relied extensively on their physical reach as a key competitive strength.This led new banks to develop strategies that could help them reach out to end-customers in a cost effective manner. The solution came in the form of a delivery channel-ATMs. This turned out to be one of the biggest growth drivers for private sector banks in India. Offering multiple channels to access the bank is now seen as a customer service quality standard. Customer expectation from banks in terms of an account's accessibility has risen. Central to introduction of alternative channels is a change in the mindset within the bank. The level of change could be as drastic as re-engineering the business process. This led to a re-examination of the role and utility of a bank branch.

A challenge every bank faces is to redefine the concept of a branch. In the past the branch was almost a standalone bank-taking deposits, making loans, servicing, transacting and processing. The new paradigm views the branch as one of several possible channels-and an expensive channel, that needs to be deployed judiciously. As large-scale branch rationalisation is not seen possible, as there is a general apprehension that it could adversely affect under-banked areas, or be time-consuming, branch reinvention has largely been focused on enhancing the productivity of existing branches and limiting new branches. An example of these productivity initiatives is extended banking hours and holiday banking. This enables banks to more fully utilise the existing physical infrastructure. This also helps in distributing the peak load on the branch at any given time.

While customers see gains of unhindered access, banks are waking up to the cost benefits of offering better customer service through these channels. Every transaction shifted to a lower cost channel leads to a reduction in operating costs for the bank. Further, this also avoids "transaction clogging" and "customer crowding" at the branch level, and the related service issues. Now with the recent trend of sharing ATM networks among banks, ATM is turning out to be even more cost-effective and efficient delivery channel, as banks are able to achieve lower transaction costs with a lower level of capital expenditure. The other important delivery channels, such as internet banking and call centres, have even lower transaction costs than those of ATMs.

However, it is not enough merely to adopt new technologies and set up these alternative delivery channels. The key to success in this initiative is migration of customers to the new, cheaper channels for carrying out transactions. Banks need to analyse customer behaviour, explain the benefits of these channels to customers and actually incentivise customers to transact through these new channels. Only by achieving high utilization levels at these channels can the bank meet its goal of reducting transaction costs on an overall basis, or supporting business growth with lower capital and operating expenditure.

In addition to customer-induced transaction, banks have also moved towards shifting back-office processing to centralised hubs rather than undertaking this activity at the branch. These two initiatives-shifting customer transactions to other channels and back-office to centralised hubsenable the branch to be used as a value-added channel for higher end activities like cross selling to the customers, rather than repetitive transactions.

One more important factor to consider in the evolution of delivery channels is the requirement of a multi-channel architecture which should support all future delivery channels, while also seamlessly integrating with existing delivery channels. Among all the delivery channels used by banks today, ATMs remain the most successful (more so because of the recent trend of sharing ATM networks among banks), followed by telephone banking and Internet banking. But the biggest potential could lie in mobile banking. With cellphone tariffs falling and increased bandwidth, the potential for banking player to tap this channel is enormous.

As mentioned earlier, consumer banking has emerged as the new growth area for the banking system. The growing retail business poses greater operational risks risks because it is a high-volume and operations-intensive business. Tight processes are needed to check fraud as lapses could set in if the system gets overwhelmed by the sheer magnitude of operations. Retail risk management will have to be based on statistical methodologies. This mandates an improvement in managment information systems (MIS). Technology assumes a vital role in value-added monitoring of retail accounts.

Indian banks have realized that it no longer pays to have a 'transaction-based' operating model. This has led to the development of a relationship oriented model of operations focusing on customer-centric services. While banks have to ensure product superiority and operational excellence, the biggest challenge today is to establish customer intimacy without which the other two are meaningless. In the financial world, product superiority does not last long as it is relatively easy to copy products. So the real strength comes from operational excellence and understanding the customer and developing rapport with him. In this context, it is very important that banks identify and understand customer needs. This will help banks in tailoring their products according to customer needs.

The cost of getting new customers is much higher as compared to the cost of cross selling to existing customers. Ultimately, in consumer banking, profitability will come not from transaction banking (which is only one of the many financial requirements) but from servicing the entire balance sheet of the customer. So cross-selling must be a core aspect of a bank's strategy. The cross-sell must happen at customer touch points (delivery channels) like branches, ATM centers, call centers or the website. Techniques employed for cross selling will vary according to the channel. Of course, this will also require technology support, which might be complex in nature. Customer relation management solutions, if implemented and integrated correctly, can help significantly in improving customer satisfaction levels. Data warehousing can help in providing better transaction experiences for customers over different transaction channels. This is make possible because data warehousing intergrates systematically data all the transactions coming from different channels. Data mining helps banks analyze and measure customer transaction patterns and behavior. This can help in improving service levels and finding new business opportunities.

Centralized operations and process automation using core banking applications and internet protocol-based networks improve efficiency and productivity levels tremendously. Core banking applications help a bank to shift away from 'branch banking'. This basically means that a customer will be treated as a bank's customer than just the customer of a particular branch which was the case earlier. Risk assessment is another area where technology can play a major role. The increasing complexity and sophistication of financial services means that banks' operations are more volatile, and more exposed to risk in various forms. Technological solutions are critical to measure, monitor and manage these risks. Technology also helps banks to manage organisational knowledge. Internal webs (in the form of Intranets) have helped banks bridge their currently separate pools of IT deployment and leverage their internal data resources for competitive decision making.

If there is one factor that distinguishes banks from one another, it is the value created through service levels of the respective banks. Channels, products and even segmentation strategies can be duplicated. However the ability to leverage these to provide seamless delivery to the customer is what differentiates a bank in the market place. However, creating value in service is no easy task. Banks need to evaluated the process flow and optimise it while simultaneously keeping costs under control. Banks must assess and measure every aspect of the branch operations, ranging from giving and receiving cash to high-end activities like cross seling.

Road Ahead

Information technology is central to banking and its criticality will only increase. It is one of the major drivers of survival and success in an increasingly competitive space. Successful banks have been able to leverage on low-cost channels such as ATMs and net banking, achieving a more efficient business model. The increasing sophistication of financial services also enhances the importance of technology as a risk management tool. Technology will be the major differentiator among 21st century financial organisations.

References

Kaptan, S. S. and Choubey, N. S. (2003), Indian Banking in Electronic Era, New Delhi, Sarup and Sons.

Karkal, Gopal (1997), Perspectives in Indian Banking, Bombay: Popular Prakashan.

"RBI Introduces Electronic Clearing Service", Anil Balan, Express Computer, 17 August 1998, India.

"Any Time Any Where Banking", Ivorsoan, Express Computers 2 June 1997, India.

"Banking in the E-business Era", M. Ganesh, Express Computers, 21 September 1998, India.

26

Information Technology in Indian Banking Sector

Anand Kumar & Raj Bihari Lal Srivastava

Information Technology is a term that encompasses all forms of technology utilized to create, capture, manipulate, communicate, exchange, present and use information in its various forms (business data, voice conversations, still images, motion pictures, multimedia presentations, and other forms, including those not yet conceived.

In other words we can say Information technology means the use of hardware, software, services and supporting infrastructure to manage and deliver information using voice, data and video whereas wikipedia, the free encyclopedia on net defines information technology as the technology required for information processing.

Information Technology and Banking

Technology in banking can lower transaction costs, allow banks to cross-market new and existing products to customers and generate a high rate of innovation in improved and new financial products. From an accounting point of view, technology can speed up the financial reporting process and the timeliness with which banks can make public disclosures via regulatory reports. Finally the use of technology can improve and enhance systems for administrative control such an enabling better management of risk. Hence technology can be the key to differentiation, competitive edge and institutional survival.

A challenge for it in banking is that some institutions are having difficulty quantifying the benefits of investing in information technology. These banks have viewed technology in terms of obtaining a competitive advantage over their competitors. However the direct measurement of a competitive advantage is difficult (violino, 1997) But this dilemma is still mot coming on the way of their moving forward with it investments due to the compulsions of high competitive intensity and ever changing customer requirements and expectations. Information technology has basically been used under two different avenues in banking. One is communication and connectivity, and the other is business process reengineering. It enables sophisticated product development, better market infrastructure, and implementation of reliable techniques fir control of risks and helps the financial intermediaries to reach geographically distant and diversified markets. In view of this, technology has changed the contours of three major functions performed by banks, i.e. access to liquidity, transformation of assets and monitoring of risks. Further it and the communication networking systems have a crucial bearing on the efficiency of money, capital and foreign exchange markets.

Information Technology and Indian Banking

Indian banking industry, today is in the midst of an IT revolution. A combination of regulatory mechanism and competitive intensity are leading to the increasing importance of banking automation. The impact of IT in banking can be gauged from an excerpt from the speech of Mr. Vepa Kamesam, Chairman IDRBT at the centenary celebration of a bank at Hyderabad on March 21, 2004:

"The two letters that has changed the way businesses operate has been IT as an acronym for Information Technology. No other facilitating service has resulted in such large-scale benefits as Information Technology. IT has become such an essential ingredient of one's way of life in today's world that it is difficult to imagine a world without it. And no other sector has benefited to such a large extent as the financial sector, with the Banking sector in particular, from the inroads made by IT."

The Indian banking industry has been operating successfully in meeting socio-economic needs and aspirations since the last two centuries. In 50s Government of India embarked on the policy of using the banking system as an instrument of economic development and social change. The first step was the nationalization of the then Imperial Bank of India and its renaming as State Bank of India (SBI). This entity was given the mandate of a massive branch expansion programme particularly in rural areas which resulted into an explosion in the volumes of transactions. The inter-branch reconciliation became a serious management problem that defied manual handling. Volumes of transactions started increasing multifold leading to tremendous pressures on customer service resulting in somewhat dissatisfaction at certain levels. Coupled with increased trade unionism, it slowly became apparent that unless computerization of customer accounts and other banking services like remittances, allocations and re-allocations etc. were achieved, the situation further deteriorates.

At this juncture RBL got into the act and set up two committees in quick succession to hasten the process of mechanization of banking operations. In the early 80^s, a high level committee was constituted under the chairmanship of Dr. C Rangarajan, then Governor of the Reserve Bank of India with a mandate to draw up a phased plan for computerization and mechanization in the banking industry over a five year time frame of 1985-89.The focus by this time was on customer service and two models of branch automation were developed and implemented.

- Front office mechanization where front desk operations were computerized while back office work was done manually.

- Back office automation covering mechanization of general ledger and back office operations while the front office work was done manually.

Both the models were designed to provide the customer with error free accounting and making available regular statement of accounts but despite these being major steps towards computerization the pace of their implementation was tediously slow and also faced a stiff resistance from employee unions.

With this experience in hindsight the second Rangarajan committee constituted in 1988 drew up a detailed plan for computerization in bank and for extension of automation to other areas like funds transfer, electronic mail, BANKNET, SWIFT, ATMs, etc. The Committee also made studied recommendations on the 'single window concept', 'all bank credit cards', credit clearing, office automation etc.

In the evolution of it in Indian banking industry, role of unions too played an important part as post-independence, PSB unions began to play an increasingly important role in bank decision making and started voicing strong opposition to the adoption of technology in bank branches. However the situation changed rapidly in the 1990s as the liberalization of the banking sector brought in competition in the form of new private banks and new foreign banks. Bank unions were put under tremendous pressure to permit the adoption technology within banks.

Narasimhan Committee (1991) that had led the financial sector reforms liberalizing the Indian banking industry and had opened it to competition from within and outside, had not only chastised the unions for their resistance to technology adoption, it also documented that bank managers initially resisted the implementation of new technology because of the lack of flexibility in restructuring employment in the face of automation. Narasimhan Committee submitted two reports, in 1992and 1998 that laid significant thrust on enhancing the efficiency and viability of the banking sector.

The journey of IT in Indian banking industry can be described in terms of three waves of changes. The first wave in banking technology began with the use of Advanced Ledger Posting Machines (ALPMs) in the 1980s. The RBL advised all the banks to go in for massive computerization at the branch level. Out of the two options of automating the front office or back office, many banks opted for automating the front office using ALPMs in the first phase. With the second wave of development in 1990s came the concept of Total Branch Automation. This automated both the front end and back end operations within the same branch. TBA comprised of total automation of a particular branch with its own database. The third wave characterized the entry of new private sector banks that opted for a single centralized database thus launching the popularity of core banking solutions. Similarly the evolution of ATM delivery channel led to the first stage of empowerment of the customer to handle his own transactions. The newer delivery channels being set up and experimented included Internet banking and mobile banking. The core focus of these channels became the number of customers they can service at a lower cost than traditional channels apart from providing the customer flexibility of choices.

The RBI's role in the promotion of IT initiatives in Indian banking industry too deserve special mention. The text in the report dealing with Technology in banking mentions the following IT initiatives of RBI:

Electronic Funds Transfer (EFT), Real Time Gross Settlement System (RTGS), Centralized Funds Management Systems (CFMS), Structured Financial Messaging Solution, Imaging of Instruments, Electronic Clearing Services, Indian Financial Network (INFINET) and MICT based Cheque Clearing.

Apart from these initiatives, on the recommendations of Committee on Financial Sector Reforms (also known as second Narasimhan Committee) a committee on Technology Up gradation was set up by the RBI for the Banking sector in 1994.

The Committee realized the urgent need for training, research and development activities in the Banking Technology area. Banks and Financial institutions started setting up Technology based training centers and colleges. However a need was felt for an apex level Institute that could act like a Think-tank and brain trust for banking technology. As recommended by the Committee, IDRBT was established by RBI in 1996 as an autonomous center for Development and Research in Banking Technology at Hyderabad.

Another push to computerization in Indian banking industry came from Central Vigilance Commission. It issued a directive that 70 per cent of the banking business in public sector banks need to be computerized before January 1, 2001 that perforce increased the speed of deployment of IT at a massive scale in Indian banks.

The issues that need to be tackled by bank managements are changing with changes in the environment and technology. The banker's mindset towards various aspects of banking technology should change radically for survival of banks in the future constant leveraging of latest technology and introducing innovative financial products/services that yield competitive advantages will be the guiding factors for survival of any financial institution in the 21st century.

The potential competitive advantage of banks lies in leveraging their knowledge of customers and the peculiar circumstances in which they work. But very few banks use their IT infrastructure to aggregate industry data, plot demand trends, identify best practices among their clients etc. generally the banks in India are at one or mix of the various levels of automation as depicted in the following.

All the banks are at one of these levels of automation Indian Banks Transition Process.

Conclusion

Information Technology that encompasses all forms of technology innovations that influence at its various levels and needs has evolved from a mere efficiency tool to become one of the most critical port of the strategy of a banking organization in its day to day operation and internal and external linkages. Its role in banking in general and Indian banking in particular has become more pronounced and today no banker can think of organizational survival let alone success without it acting as one of the most critical strategic component playing its appropriate promotional service and strategic role.

A major organization transformation for Indian banking is in the process reaches its maturity stage the gains will be multifold and for all the constituents and stakeholders since banking is the key-sector for socio-economic transformation and upliftment indication and absorption of it has to be a key initiative constantly being evaluated as part of overall strategy judicious application of it in banking is going to help Indian achieve a notable role in the WTO operated efficient of globalization. It will make possible for banks to offer efficient 24 hour banking, financial, foreign exchange and capital market operations in the form of dealings in economic value-additions, futures, options, derivatives etc. making the whole process paperless and almost location independent.

References

Gulati, V. P., Sivakumaran, M.V., C. "It Framework for the Indian Banking Sector", *ASCI Journal of Management*, Vol. 31, Nos. 1&2. Mohan R. (2004), "Indian Banking and E-security". Reserve Bank of India Bulletin, November.

Rishi, M. and Saxena S. C. (2004), "Technological Innovations in the Indian Banking Industry: The Late Bloomer, *Accounting, Business & Financial History*, Vol. 14, No. 3, pp. 339-353.

Sarkar, J. India: A Financial Sector for the Twenty-first Century, New Delhi, Oxford University Press.

Sisodia, R. S., "Marketing Information and Decision Support Systems for Services", *The Journal of Services Marketing*, Winter.

Business Today (April,2005), "Information Technology and Corporate Governance".

Reserve Bank of India (Annual Report 2005-06), New Trend in Indian Banking.

Patrick, R. A. (2005), "Tech Update: Technology in Banking, The Tech Factor in Banking". *Networkmagazineindia.com, 20.3.2005*

Vartak, U. "Impact of Information Technology Act of Banking Sector", *http://www.asianlaws.org/projects/banking_impact.htm*

27

Technology and Core Banking Solution: A Boon for Banking Sector

Gopal Kumar Singh & Ashutosh Kumar

Technology is traditionally defined as 'the technical means which people use to improve their surroundings'. It is the knowledge of using tools and machines to do tasks efficiently; to make lives easier; and to communicate in a better way. It is a wide term that includes both, simple tools such as a wooden spoon, and complex tools such as the space station or the written sets of procedures and maintenance manuals for it.

Technology is 'the current state of knowledge' of how to combine resurces to produce desired products, to solve problems, to fulfil needs, or to satisfy wants. Technology in this sense includes technical methods, skill, processes, techniques, tools and raw materials. The cultural force of technology is the driving force that sets us apart from the rest of the flora and fauna of earth. This article looks at banking technology within the Indian context. Besides describing the history of technology and its rationale, it reviews the present of banking technology; describes the enablers for technology and has a look at the future of banking technology.

History of Information Technology (IT)

Reasearchers have estimated the past time frame of various technologies. Fire was invented 800000 years ago while clothing and stone tools are 100000 years old. Copper is rather recent, at 8000 years B.C.; while the well and writing systems are from around 3500 to 4000 B.C. Chariots came much later by 2500 B.C.

Information technology is a broad subject concerned with all aspects of managing and processing information, especially within a large organization or company. IT deals with the use of electronic computers and computer software to convert, store, protect, process, transmit and retrieve information. Since computers are central to information management, computer departments within organisations are often called IT departments. Some companies refer to this department as IS (Information Services) or MIS (Management Information Services).

IT sector includes more than 40 categories of products and services from information itself to the communication networks; the hardware used to send, transmit, receive information; the software that manages it; the technical support for it and the services associated with it. This sector also refers to as 'the Information and Communication Technology (ICT) sector.

Computers were invented in 1940s and in 1950s. IT was introduced in the banking sector in USA and England, which produced jobs like data entry operators/console operators/programmers/system analysts/EDP managers, etc. It was used for less complex and heavy 'data volumes' processing applications'. As such, IT was far away from the customers. In 1960s and early 1970s, minis were used and OLTP (On-Line Transaction Processing) at branches are introduced, bringing IT a little closer to the customer. During the late 1970s and 1980s, PCs (Personal Computers) and networking helped in the innovation of new products & services, thus, bringing IT only a degree away from the customers. In the 1990s, with advent of Internet, it was made available for the comforts at home and office, i.e.; at zero degrees away from customers.

These developments impacted positively the use of IT by customers and began the era of global electronic one-step financial integration'. It was from 1990s onwards, that the globalization trends became more visible.

During the last decade, no face of banking or financial sector has remained untouched by IT. In fact, IT became the driver of all business plans for expansion and diversification. Bank planners now build plans around the technology power rather than taking IT as an input while planning for business in a traditional way.

Rationale for IT

Globalization measures of the early 90s encouraged entry of private and foreign players in the Indian financial market. The competitive environment for the setor became more challenging as the new entrants had no legacy-baggage of bad loans. These banks, which had fully computerized operations, which was a pre-condition for their establishment, demonstrated visible positive benefits of technology. They could attract the new generation customers as also, young and highly qualified talent as employees. The average age of employees in public sector banks (PSBs) would be anywhere above 45. Realising that they could not face the new competitors with their inadequate technology support, PSBs that covered 85% of banking business, went on to acquire technology.

The intended benefits were:

- Establishing and acquire huge capacity to address prevalent and planned business.
- Imroving yield on investments and reducing expenses.
- Facilitating new product development.
- Lending support for risk management, CRM (Customer Relationship Management), porfolio management.
- Costing/pricing of products by using data warehousing, data mining, and data marts.
- Improving customer service/satisfaction through user/customer friendly processes.
- Facilitating multi-channel operations.

- Attaining operational efficiency in areas like granting of loans, transfer of funds, deposit transactions, etc.
- Networking of branches and other channel partners for products marketing with thin and lean overheads.

The Status

The IT packages and services available in India can be broadly classified into the following six types :

1. Stand-alone branch-level packages
2. Multi-branch solutions
3. Foreign packages
4. Packages for specialized niche areas
5. Service branch/high-volume transaction processing packages
6. IT services

PSBs, the mainstay of the Indian banking system, were in the process of shedding their flab in terms of excessive manpower, excessive Non Performing Assets (NPAs) and excessive Governmental equity. On the other hand, private sector banks were consolidating themselves through mergers and acquisitions (M&As). Reserve Bank of India's Reports on Trend and Progress of Banking in India, (2004-2005) and 2005-06 provide the following information about technology initiatives:

Table 1

(In %)

Computerisation of Banks	*31/03/06*	*31/03/05*
Branches already Fully Computerized #	48.5	60.0
Branches Under Core Banking Solution	28.9	11.0
Fully Computerized Branches (i+ii)	77.5	71.0
Partially Computerized Branches	18.2	21.8

 # Other than branches under Core Banking Solution.

Between Septemper 1999 and March 2006, PSBs incurred an expenditure of Rs. 10.676 crores on computerization and development of communication networks. While new private sector banks, foreign banks and a few older private sector banks have already put in place 'core banking solutions' (CBS), PSBs are in the process of adopting similar systems. As on end-March 2006, 100% branches of PSBs were either fully or partially computerized. Out of 27 PSBs, 10 had 100 per cent computerized branches, while only 05 had less than 50% computerized branches. Now, banks could concentrate on their core competencies of banking and deploy their staff to get into new roles of marketing. This helps in taking higher responsibilities through job enrichment and job enhancement using IT.

Banking and financial services (BFS) continues to be the domestic IT market's best-loved vertical accounting for over 20 per cent of the total business. The initial cycle of automation was likely to be fianlly be over for the banking industry in 2-3 years, with the exception of a few laggards. The early starters have recognized the significance of analytics, risk management, business process management (BPM)', shared ATM network services and outsourcing in the form of remote infrastructure management.

Convenience Banking, by means of different delivery channels, has become the buzzword, with new channels, like; mobile and internet banking coming to the fore. With the progress achieved in telecommunication sector, the delivery channels are multiplying. Minimizing the service delivery cost is the key in these efforts.With proliferation of plastic money, Indian banks have increased ATM installation.

The increase in the number of 'On-site' and 'off site' ATMs installed by the nationlized banks, State Bank group, old private sector banks, new private sector banks and foreign banks during the one year period of March 2005 to March 2006 have been shown in Table 2.

India still has to catch up a lot, considering that China has 65,000 ATMs, UK 100,000 and USA 300,000. A number of other functionalities like utility payments and routine transfers are likely to be included under the purview of ATMs.

Enablers for IT Growth in Indian Banks

There are competitive forces that exhort the banks for technology offensive. It is not merely to manage high volume/low complexity

Table 2

	Number of ATMs 31/03/06			Number of ATMs 31/03/05		
Bank Group	*On-site*	*Off-site*	*Total*	*On-site*	*Off-site*	*Total*
Nationalized Banks	4,812	2,353	7,165	3,205	1,567	4,772
State Bank Group	1,775	3,668	5,443	1,548	3,672	5,220
Old Private Sector Banks	1,054	493	1,547	800	441	1,241
New Private Sector Banks	2,255	3,857	6,112	1,883	3,729	5,612
Foreign Banks	232	648	880	218	579	797
Total	10,128	11,019	21,147	7,654	9,988	17,642

transactions. It can be put to even better uses, for which, some basic understanding needs to be developed, as follows:

- IT must be thought of as a strategic tool; not as an automation tools and effective use of IT must be made to construct business models. IT can be leveraged to improve performance through decision support systems.
- It facilitates M&As as integration of business is easier with enterprise-wide deployment
- IT infrastructure requires optimization and possibility of sharing resources among banks (even competing ones)
- IT systems of a bank require taking a holistic view of the entire technology issues.
- IT calls for having a mechanism to assess the impact of IT systems at every stage of growth

As identified by IDC reasearch, IT in any industry can be successful when the following enablers are addressed:

- An educated and willing workforce
- Academic centres of excellence (universities and reasearch labs)
- A stable business climate
- Strong and flexible communications infastructure
- Good climate for investment for start-up activities

In banking technology terms, what is needed, is totally reliable hardware (H/W), software, communication network and electricity supply. Identification of information needs across the bank in clearer terms also needs to be looked into relevant fallback (redundancy provisions) such as H/W, UPS, generator set, data centre, security & safety policy, authorization procedure, 'disaster recovery plans' and infrastructural availability are other aspects of preparedness.

India and Abroad

India's IT expenditure totalled $19 billion and represented 3.9% of its GDP, but more importantly IT products and services constituted 20.4% of India's total exports, thus making it the primary source of foreign exchange. India has a 2.8% share of the global IT market. Technology has served as a modernizing force for developing countries. IDC data estimates that almost 55 countries today qualify as 'information societies'. IT sectors being one of the facilitators, only those nations that make the IT industry a priority, will have the capacity to complete and thrive in the digital world.

What Indian IT has done globally, is being done by the same companies in India and that too in banks. At present, the Indian banks, particularly PSBs, may seem lagging behind a bit, put it would be running successfully in the world-wide race for technological excellence.

Computerisation

Technology has played a significant role in improving efficiency of the financial system in recent years. Information Technology (IT) has enabled sophisticated product development, better market infrastructure, implementation of reliable techniques for control of risks and access to geographically distant & diversified markets.

The arrival of foreign and private banks with their superior, state-of-the art technology-based services, pushed Indian banks also to follow; so as to meet the threat of competition and retain their customer base.

Table 3
Computerization in PSBs (As on March 31,2006)

Branches already Fully Computerized #	48.5%
Branches Under Core Banking Solutions	28.9%
Fully Computerized Branches (i+ii)	77.5%
Partially Computerized Branches	18.2%
Non Computerized Branches	4.3%

: Other than branches under Core Banking Solutions.
Source: Reserve Bank of India.

The number of branches providing Core Banking Solutions (CBS) in India has increased significantly in recent years. CBS provides as host of benefits such as, anywhere banking, anywhere access and quick fund movement at optimal costs in an efficient manner. While new private sector banks, foreign banks and a few old private sector banks have already put CBS in place, public sector banks (PSBs) are catching up. The total number of branches providing CBS increased from 11.0 per cent as on March 31, 2005 to 28.9 per cent as on March 31, 2006.

More than 95 per cent of the PSB branches were fully or partially computerized at end-March 2006. Out of the 27 PSBs, the branches of as many as 10 were 100 per cent computerized, while those of another 12 were more than 50 per cent computerized.

Core Banking

In layman terms Core Banking Solution (CBS) is a platform where communication technology and information technology are merged to suit core needs of banking. Here, an application-software is developed to perform core operations of banking from a centralised location. The front-end application is installed at different branches of a bank and then interconnected by means of communication lines to a Central Server Situated at a physical location known as the Data Centre. The convenience of this technology to the customer is that he/she can access or operate any of his/her accounts from anywhere.

Centralised Online Realtime Environment Banking (COREB) or Core Banking enables Anywhere Banking. Bank's customers can operate their accounts from any branch of the bank. The customer no longer remains tied down to a particular branch, where he/she maintains his/her account. He/she becomes a customer of the bank. This is achieved through centralised processing of transactions. All the transactions put through in the branches are processed at a central site called central data centre (CDC)', where all the data relating to all the core banking enabled branches reside. Therefore, the first step in implementation of core banking is connecting the branches with the CDC. Declining cost of technology components, in general, and networking in particular have enabled even small banks to implement core banking. In any case the advantages of implementing core banking far outweigh the costs. Moreover, if a bank has to stay in competition, there is no other way, but to introduce technology in its operations. However, implementation of core banking involves huge change management issues. Processes have to be aligned with the new technology to derive optimum advantages. Employees have to be trained and their mindset has to be oriented towards the paradigm shift that core banking has been doing in its wake.

What Core Banking Offers: Core Banking offers great advantages to all-customer, employees, management and the shareholders.

Advantages to Customers: Apart from the advantage of 'Anywhere Banking' the customer is empowered for 'Anytime Banking' and 'Self Service Banking' through integration with alternate channels, like 'ATMs and internet banking. Most basic banking transactions can be executed by the customers from any remote location through internet banking. This saves the time, money and efforts a customer had to incur in going to the branch for transacting his/her business. Remittances from one branch to another can be made instantaneously. Corporates can pay the salaries to their geographically dispersed employees with just a click of the mouse. There are many more functions being enabled progressively. The advantages of 'Online Realtime environment used innovatively in combination with alternate channels have thrown open unlimited possibilities for enhancing customer experience.

Advantages to Employee: Core Banking offers all the advantages that were available in a fully automated standalone branch. Branch staff does not have to bother about the arithmetical accuracy of transactions. They do not have to go through the drudgery of balancing their 'books of account. Interest rates and other charges are inbuilt into the system. In addition, core banking has virtually eliminated inter branch reconciliation. Branches have been relieved of annual/half yearly/quarterly closing exercise. CDC takes care of all back office functions like preparing periodical accounting statements, regulatory and MIS reports and reports required by internal and external auditors. This relieves the branch staff from performing repetitive and time consuming tasks and gives them more time for performing sales and service functions at the branch.

Advantages to Management: Core banking enables capture of operational information, which can be analysed electronically in a very innovative way which can be analysed electronically in a very short time. Thus, the management has access to almost real time information required for decision making. 'Asset liability management' and 'treasury management' become more efficient. The checks inbuilt into the system mitigate risks and service charges, etc. applied automatically through the system help in stopping income leakage. Since all the data is available centrally, it can be made available for audit purpose at any convenient site. The auditors can carry out almost all the audit functions of any branch from the convenience of their. In a core banking environment, new products can be rolled out in a very short time and regulatory issues, like; Anti Money Laundering (AML) measures and Basel-II compliance can be addressed with greater ease.

Advantages to Shareholders: The advantages accruing to customers, employees and management ultimately translate into advantages accruing to the shareholders as they provide cost cutting enhancing customer service and improving competitiveness. All this makes the environment conducive to the growth of business and profits with lesser degree of risks.

Core Banking Implementation in India & Extent: Due to the inherent competitive advantages of core banking, almost all categories of banks in India have either already invested or are in the process of investing in core banking solution (CBS). The new private sector banks and foreign banks along-with some old private sector banks, have had the advantage of adopting core banking early on. Public sector banks are also catching up fast. The number of core banking branches is rapidly increasing. The total number of branches under core banking in India increased from 11 per cent ason March 2005 to 30 per cent as on March 2006. Encouraged by the experience of banks who have implemented core banking in a big way, even co-operative banks are now showing keen interest for implementing core banking. [Although networking costs have become affordable with the introduction of new telecommunication technologies, and the presence of multiple service providers in the market, there is still the challenge of connecting far flung rural branches, where no service provider is presently able to provide economical, secure and technically feasible connectivity. For this reason, banks having remotely situated rural branches (mainly public sector banks), have yet to migrate all their branches to core banking, while new generation private sector banks, which have their branch networks mainly in metros and tier-I centres, started their operations with all their branches on core banking.

References

Naidu, V. N. and Nair, M. S. (2002), Technical Efficiency of Scheduled Commercial Bank Groups (July-September).

Srivastava , R. (2000), Computerization in Indian Banks, Banking Finanance (February).

Sankara Rao (2002), The Dynamics of Customer Service, *IBA Bulletins* (March).

Ambashta, M. K. (2000), Customer Oriented-A Pre-Requisite for Banks Success, *The Journal of Indian Institute of Bankers.*

Roy, D. C. (2001), Customer Loyalty Management; Branch Level Perspective, Vinimaya XXI, (2).

Reinartz, W. and Kumar, V. (2002), The Mismanagement of Customer Loyalty, Harvard Business Review, (July).

Diwan, P. (1997), Prpductivity and Technology Management. A Pentagan Press Publication, Hari Nagar, New Delhi.

28

E-Banking Scenario in India

Surya Prakash & Sarika Sharma

Explosion in the field of information technology, security system and encryption (coding) models have brought in significant changes in modern banking services in India. The trend of Non-branch-service Delivery in banking started with the growing popularity of electronic payment services which enable banking services to be delivered to the customer's door step. It started with Electronic Fund Transfers (EFT), Credit cards, ATMs and smart cards were next in evaluation banking history. Gradually with the advancement of technology, telephone banking and Computer Technology Integration (CTI) has become a more powerful medium of delivering banking services. The newest product is E-banking, where the technology and other issues are still under evolution. All possible banking transactions can be made through the ATM (Automation Transaction Machine) without ever going to the bank.

The E-banking has changed the face of banking industry and enables a customer to do banking transactions through the website of the bank on Internet. E-banking is also known as virtual banking, net banking, cyber banking or web banking. E-banking involves in the use of Internet for delivery of banking products and services. In other words successful E-banking solution offers:

- exceptional rates of savings, CDs.
- checking with no monthly fee, free bill payment.
- credit cards with slow rates.
- easy online application for all accounts like personal loans and mortages.
- 24 hours account access
- quality customer service
- remove geographical barriers

Evolution of Banking in India

India got independence in 1947 and declared as secular, socialist and democratic republic. Reserve Bank of India (RBI) was set up in 1935 and banking regulation act was passed in 1949. The highlight of the act was to bring the RBI under government control. Another major development happened in banking sector in the year 1955 when RBI acquired control on Imperical Bank of India and renamed it as state Bank of India (SBI). SBI, then over control of eight private bank managed by princely states and made its 100% subsidiary. Through mergers and acquisitions number of banks were reduced to 566 in 1951 to 85 in 1960.

The Narasimhan Committee report suggested wide ranging reforms for the banking sector in the year 1992 to introduce internationally accepted banking practices. The major participants in the financial institution, non-banking financial companies (NBFCs) and other market intermediaries such as stock brokers and moneylenders. Further commercial banks are divided into public sector banks like HDFC, ICICI and co-operative banks.

Financial Sector Reforms: It is useful to very briefly recall the nature of the India banking sector at the time of initiation of financial sector reforms in India in the early 1990s. The government appointed Narasimham committee under the chairmanship of M. Nariasimhan in the year 1991, to address the problem and suggest remedial measures. Focus on the reforms of the banking sector, section-I deals with a brief description of the Indian banking scenario in the pre-reform period. Section-II deals with a brief description of the Indian banking scenario in the pre-reform in India. Section-III is concerned with the critical examination of the two phases of the banking sector reforms.

Government has taken bold steps since 1991 to give banking a whole new shape. Reserve Bank of India (RBI) has set up a working group on Internet Banking to examines different aspects of Internet banking. The group had focussed on three majors areas of E-banking, (i) technology and security issues (ii) legal issues and (iii) regulatory and supervisory issues.

Electronic Banking in India

Banking has established an Internet presence with various objects. Most of them are using the Internet as a new distribution channel. Financial services, with the use of Internet may be offered in an equivalent quantity with cover cost to the potential customers. Through internet contacts to each and every corner of the world at any time is become possible and easy, it means banks may enlarge their market without opening new branches. At present banks are using the web to reach opportunities in three different categories: to market information, to deliver banking products and services, and to improve customer relationship. New technological capabilities reduce banking relationship and transaction cost. Though e-banking in India is still in the evolutionary stage, it is much clear that it is having a significant impact on traditional banking activities.

In modern era Internet has penetrated Banking a Finance more than any other sector. Information and Communication Technologies (ICT's) has brought the fundamental revolution in banking sector, online banks are totally different to traditional banks. Traditional banks with the internet presence is eminent not only in India but also anywhere in the world. Most of the Indian banks are still public sector banks and private sector banks like ICICI, HDFC, UTI. These banks are fast becoming choice of citizen in urban and rural areas where technology, penetration is high reach. After five years, majority of the transactional services will be provided by the way of Internet, New based banking comes at only 10% of the operating cost of conventional banking practices and services.

As per the recent survey, traditional banks spend 60% of the revenue generated to run a branch, whereas, the cost of providing. Some services Internet comes out to be only 15%. This is huge saving for banks and consumers. Which can be easy to understand by this chart.

Fig. Cost of Internet banking over other mode of banking (*Source:* Access from Internet).

Chart shows that the cost of internet banking per transaction is much lower than Branch telephone and PC Banking. Definitely the consumers are the principle beneficiary of the e-banking. They will be access the same services with more efficiency at low cost as well as they can see their time for making transition with various banks, through electronic banking.

Factors Affecting the Growth of E-banking

At present the banking industries stand at a crossroads. Recent bank consolidation and the entrance of numerous non-bank organisations into financial services have increased level of competition. But, the same time, technology has forced banks to reconsider the traditional methods of marketing and delivery of products. The following factors influenced the growth of e-banking.

- Facilitation accessibility to customers.
- Improving customer loyalty
- Attracting new customers.
- Reduce customer friction
- Rapid growth of the Internet
- Limited time resource
- Fierce competition
- Facilitates the offering of more services.

Services Offered by E-banking

The E-banking services can be classified in to two areas:

(A) Basic level services under this services bank's website disseminates information about different products and services to customers, by this bank receive and reply to customers queries through e-mail.

- Simple transactional web sites.
- Fully transactional websites

Following are the comprehensive account services which are available with E-banking:

(a) Transaction histing
(b) Bills payment
(c) Funds transfer

(B) Periodical Payment under this section customer can get the list of periodical payments and allow him to maintain them. He can change the due date, amount or frequency of any of his periodical payments. He can even delete one that he wishes to discontinue. They are:

- Statements download
- Credit card payment
- Change customer profile
- New fixed request
- Fixed deposit inquiry
- Demand Draft/Bankers cheque request
- ITs Inquiry
- Stop payment request
- Cheque status inquiry
- Cheque bank request
- Customer support
- Demat on the NET
- Direct pay etc.

Advantages of E-banking

At present E-banking is part & parcel of banking activities involves numbers of advantages. They are:

- It confers the advantages of lower cost of handling a transaction.
- It reduces staff cost and enhances efficiency.
- Approach new markets.
- In most of the cases the customer need not visit in the bank for getting banking services.
- Any time and anywhere banking service leads to customer satisfaction and convenience.
- Ability to introduce new products and services quicklyand successfully.
- Ability to understand its customer need.
- Greater customer loyalty.

Emerging Challenges

In spite of several benefits of Internet in the banking industry, it may prove to be a double edged sword. Bank may gain revenue advantages on the retail side by charging for services such as EBPP (Electronic Bill Presentment and Payment) and may improve cross selling of products . But on the other hand, the effect of the internet on the commercial side of the bank is negative. Cash managers are worried about potential revenue decreases as the processing of paper bills declines and third parties attract customers to competing services. There are some basic challenges before E-banking, there are as:

- One of the challenges before the banks, which is trying to become e-enabled is that the data is scattered across the countries. Integration of this data is necessary if the banks have to succeed on the net.
- The second challenge is related to the move towards expanding the basket of financial product being offered by financial services providers.
- Demand side pressure due to increasing access to low cost electronic services.
- Emergence of open standards for banking functionality.
- Growing customer awareness and need of transparency.
- Global players in the fray.

Moreover, the Internet poses a range of risks some of them are:

- Security risk that may arise due to the unauthorised access to a bank's key information like accounting system, risk management and portfolio management system.
- Operational risks that may arise due to inaccurate processing of transactions, nonenforceability of contracts, comprises in data integrity, data privacy and confidentiality, unauthorised access to bank's systems and transactions etc.
- Bank face the risk of wrong choice of technology, improper system design and inadequate control processes.
- Legal risk arises when violation of lower, rules and regulations or prescribed practices taken place, or when the legal rights and obligations of parties to a transaction are not well established.
- Cross border risk involves legal and regulatory risks as there may be uncertainty about legal requirement in some countries and jurisdiction ambiguities with respect to the responsibilities of different national authority.

Present Indian Scenario of E-banking

Indian banks have established an Internet presence. Financial services, with the use of Internet, may be offered in a equivalent quantity with lower costs to the more potential customers. The banks in India are using the web to reach opportunities in three different categories: to market information, to deliver banking products and services, and to improve customer relationship. At present approximately two per cent of high and middle income group banking customers connected banking on the internet. A Reserve Bank of India survey revealed that more than 20 major banks were either offering e-banking services at various levels or planned to do so in the near future. The banks have begun to collaborate with various utility companies to enable the customers to perform various functions online.

Multinational and local banks have been very successful in setting up E-banking services. Most multi-national banks already have efficient E-banking infrastructures running all over the world. This may be emulated in India. On the local scene, ICICI Banks kicked off online banking way back in 1996 and a host of other banks such as Citi bank, Indus Bank, HDFC Bank and Times Bank (now part of HDFC) were the early ones to bite the technology bullet in the year 1999.

Unfortunately Nationalised Banks have been unable to evolve as fast as most of the private sector and Multinational banks. As a result, in many nationalised banking organisation there may be mix of automated system and manual system with both systems running parallel. This often creates a chaotic scenario. There are however, very few nationalised banks like State Bank of India, Bank of Baroda, Allahabad Bank, Syndicate Bank and Bank of India etc. that offer Internet Banking Services (IBSs).

Conclusions

Modern India is exploiting all the benefits of technological advancements. There are radical reforms in banking field. Customer require relating services and they feel splendid life. India as a nation, is having 24 hours entertainment programmes, transport, internet facilities and so on. Emergency of the E-banking is changing the banking industry and is having major effects on the bank-customer relationship. However, there are few challenges, which can be overcome with good planning and phased implementation. Those banks that are planning to build their online businesses will have to understand several strategic issues like do they have the right business model for e-banking. At present Consumer to Business (C_2B), Business to Consumer (B_2C), Government to Business (G_2B) & Government to Consumer (G_2C) communications transaction are possible in easy way, through E-banking. Now a days IT is a essential part of Individual life and modern society. Banking sectors are also enjoying the benefits of IT.

Through IT, they provide 24 hours Automated Teller Machine (ATM) services, to their customers.

References

Banking Finance, September 2004, p. 13-18.

Indian Management, November 2000, p. 77-85.

Southern Economist, October 15, 2005, p. 27-30.

Yojana, October 2003, p. 15-19.

Business of E-commerce: Paul May.

E Business or out of Business, Mark J. Barrenechea

Core Banking Solution, Relevance for Banks, IBA Bulletin, September 2002 by N. Sreenivasan.

29

E-Banking in India: Major Issues

B. B. Mansuri & Badruzzama Siddiqui

Rapid Technological Development witnessed by the corporate sector during the nineties have changed the way business needs to be conducted. I.T. has introduced new business paradigms and is increasingly playing a significant role in improving the services in the banking industry. E-banking is becoming more and more popular today, as is banking via digital television.

E-banking refers to the deployment of Information Technology (IT) by banks using the infrastructure of the digital age to enable a dramatic lowering of transaction costs and create new types of banking opportunities that address the barriers of time and distance. Banking opportunities are local, global and immediate in E-banking. The current web-based variant of electronic banking is the latest of several generations of systems: *Automated Teller Machines* (ATMs) were the first well-known machines to provide electronic access to customers of retail banks.

Electronic banking has been around for quite some time in the form of Automated Teller Machine (ATM) and telephone transactions. In more recent times, it has been transformed by the internet a new delivery channel that has facilitated banking transactions for both customers and banks. For customers, the internet offers faster access is more convenient and available around the clock irrespective of the customer's location.

The Indian Experience

India is still in the early stages of E-banking growth and development. Competition and changes in technology and lifestyle in the last five years have changed the face of banking. The changes that have taken place impose on banks tough standards of competition and compliance. The issue here is– 'Where does India stand in the scheme of e-banking.' E-banking is likely to bring a host of opportunities as well as unprecedented risks to the fundamental nature of banking in India. The impact of E- Banking in India is not yet apparent. Many global research companies believe that e-banking adoption in India in the near future would be slow compared to other major Asian countries (E-business, June, 2002). Nair (1999) observes that Indian E-banking is still nascent, although it is fast becoming a strategic necessity for most commercial banks, as competition increases from private banks and non banking financial institutions.

To cope with the pressure of growing competition, Indian Commercial Banks have adopted several initiatives and e-banking is one of them. The completion has been especially tough for the Public Sector Banks (PSBs), as the new established private sector and foreign banks have already sharpened their competitive edge. Some of the pro-active public sector banks have been striving hard to make their structures flexible enough to accommodate technological changes.

Adoption of Technology has facilated alternative channels for delivery with the public sector banks and in turn put pressure on them to restrict or limit the branch network and employ a better skilled workforce. E-banking facilitated by the technological revolution, has strongly impacted strategic business considerations for Indian banks by cutting down costs of delivery and transaction massively.

In India, there are two types of customers one who is a multi-channel user and the other who still relies on the branch as the anchor channel. The primary challenge for banks is to provide consistent service to customers irrespective of the kind

Table 1
PSBs Investment Plans in IT Development.

Bank	*Investment (Rs. crore)*	*Period (years)*
Bank of Baroda	400	5
Bank of India	100	2003-04
Bank of Maharashtra	150	3
Canara Bank	100	2003-04
Indian Bank	120	2003-04
Oriental Bank of Commerce	280	5
Punjab National Bank	300	2003
State Bank of India	500	2003-04
Uco Bank	200	NA
United Bank of India	150	2

Source: The Financial Express, October 17, 2003.

of channel they use. The channels broadly cover the primary channels of branch (i.e. teller, platform, ATM) phone (i.e. Call Centre interactive voice response unit) and internet channel (i.e., personal computer, browser, wireless) banking. Banks in India have been working towards a vision that includes transformed branches, enhanced telephone services and leading-edge internet banking functions that provide a consistently positive multi-channel experience for customers. Even for public sector banks, the ongoing and future investment in technology are massive. At present, the cumulative amounts earmarked by 10 major public sector banks add upto a hefty Rs.2200 crores plus (Table 1). It is expected that the provision of financial services through a versatile technology, platform will enable these banks to acquire more customers cut costs and improve service delivery. Though may positive signs are already visible in India, including a higher acceptance of technology by banks and customers. It is a reality that most projects have not yet been deployed on a large scale.

E-banking Regulation in India

At present there are three major statutes or guidelines governing e-finance operations notably, The Information Technology–2000; The Information Technology (Certifying Authorities) Rules 2000; and Central Bank (RBI) guidelines on Internet Banking in India. The Reserve Bank guidelines have

300 New Dimensions of Indian Banking

defined the operational framework on Internet banking with a focus on security issues. However, the guidelines details the organizational, operational and supervisory structure that banks will have to implement while offering internet banking. The Information Technology–2000 and the IT rules for certifying authorities lay down the framework for appointment of digital certifying authorities, acceptance of digital signature etc. we should enable the orderly development of cyber business.

The Major Issues in E-banking

Although it is evident that the electronic revolution has commenced in India, widespread electronic banking may still be several years away. In India (where poverty ratio is still adverse at 26.1 per cent of total population), it is likely that wealthier people will rapidly migrated to e-banking platforms leave the poor to bear the cost of the physical infrastructure of branches in the form of transaction fees or non-competitive interest rates on their deposits.

A handful of foreign banks operating in our country first offered e-banking services to their customers such as Automated Teller Machines (ATMs), computerized monthly statements, secure online operations etc. The new generation of private sector banks (who did have developmental obligations, similar to their counterparts in the public sector) did not possess a legacy of manual practices and hence, were able to adopt easily modern banking facilities with state of art operations. However, challenges before the public sector banks are plenty and a different kind. While they have to handle volumes which are mind boggling, there are also issues of legacy, old habits and political pressures. For public sector banks the major problems are in the form of security risk network bound time, scarcity of trend personnel, expensive system upgrades and recurring cost given the massive scale of their current operations.

A research study by D'souza (2002) on the comparative performance of public and private sector banks indicates of the 1990s shows that though the turnover/employee ratio rose in PSBs, the turnover per employee in private and foreign

E-Banking in India: Major Issues 301

banks doubled relative to the ratio of PSBs. Also this is not due to the presence of a large rural and semi-urban concentration of bank branches among PSBs but rather due to technological up gradation in private and foreign banks. Private and foreign banks have changed the structure of their employment towards a higher skilled workforce by increasing the recruitment of officers and reducing clerical and sub-ordinate staff. The combination of higher technology and higher skills had posted a higher turnover for these banks as they have been able to provide better customers support and have managed their assets well.

E-banking has created many new challenges for banks management and regulatory and supervisory authorities. They originate net just from increase potential for cross border transactions but also for domestic transactions based on technology applications which raise many security related issues. The Basel Committee on Banking supervisions Electronic Banking Group (EBG, 2001) has defined risk management principles for electronic banking. They primarily focus on how to extend, adopt and teller the existing risk management framework to the electronic banking setting. It is necessary to know whether the efforts undertaken by RBI are sufficient to ensure a reasonable level of security.

Conclusion

Although it is evident that electronic revolution has commenced in India, widespread electronic banking may still be several years away. The e-banking revolution has changed the business of banking by scaling borders and bringing about new opportunities. In India also, it has strongly impacted the strategic business considerations for banks by significantly cutting down cost of delivery and transactions. One of the main factors which would be essential for the success of electronic banking is setting up of the appropriate infrastructure. Once the infrastructure is in place then the commercial bank can start to push customers to accept the new delivery channels by ensuring that the necessary security measures are in place.

References

Basel Committee on Banking Supervision (2001), Risk Management, Principles for Electronic Banking, paper 82, May, (*www.bis.org*).

D'souza, Errol (2002), How Well Have Public Sector Banks Done? A Note: *Economic and Political Weekly*, Vol. XXXVII, No.9, pp. 867-70.

David Carse (1999), The Regulatory Framework of E-banking Available (online) *http;//www.e-banking.*

Denny, Stephanie (2000), The Electronic Commerce Challenge, *Journal of Internet Banking and Commerce,* November, Vol. 3, No. 3, E-business, June.

Economist (2003), Banking on Technology Cycle. The Economist's Technology Quarterly, September 6. pp. 12-16.

Kohli, S. S. (2003), Indian Banking Sector: Challenges and Opportunities, *Vikalpa,* Vol. 28, No. 3, pp. 85-89.

Kumar, S. (2001), E-finance in a Developing Country Like India ICICI Bank.

Nitsure, R. R. (2003), E-banking: Challenges and Opportunities, *Economic and Political Weekly*, pp. 5377–5380.

30

E-Banking: Emerging Challenges

Ratna Shanker Mishra & Amit Verma

E-banking is the banking of the new era. Making banking products and services available to whole sale and retail consumers, through an electronic distribution channel is called e-banking. E-banking is the outcome of the technological innovations and competition. Banks have been using electronic and telecommunication networks for delivering a wide range of value added products and services. The devices have been telephone, personal computers including Automated Teller Machine (ATM). The delivery channels have been direct dial up connections, private and public networks. Newer editions of e-banking are being added:

- Internet banking
- Mobile banking

The use of ATM's lead to the concept of 'anywhere' and 'anytime' banking. Through the use of ATM cards, one can operate his bank account to withdraw money from any of the bank's ATM installed or available at the nearest site.

Definition of E-banking

E-banking is defined as the automated delivery of new and traditional banking products and services directly to customers through electronic, interactive communication channels. E-banking includes the systems that enable financial institution customers, individuals or businesses, to access accounts, transact business, or obtain information on financial products and services through a public or private network, including the Internet. Customers access e-banking services using an intelligent electronic device, such as a personal computer (PC), personal digital assistant (PDA), automated teller machine (ATM) and touch Tone telephone. The two primary types of Internet websites:

- Informational and
- Transactional.

Informational Websites

Informational websites provide customers access to general information about the financial institution and its products or services. Risk issues examiners should consider when reviewing informational websites include:

- Potential liability and consumer violations for inaccurate or incomplete information about products, services and pricing presented on the website;
- Potential access to confidential financial institution or customer information if the website is not properly isolated from the financial institution's internal network;
- Potential liability for spreading viruses and other malicious code to computers communicating with the institution's website; and
- Negative public perception if the institution's on-line services are disrupted or if its website is defaced or otherwise presents inappropriate or offensive material.

Transactional Websites

Transactional websites provide customers with the ability to conduct transactions through the financial institution's website by initiating banking transactions or buying products and services. Banking transactions can range from something as basic as a retail account balance inquiry to a large business-to-business funds transfer. E-banking services, like those delivered through other delivery channels, are typically classified based on the type of customer they support. The following table lists some of the common retail and wholesale e-banking services offered by financial institutions.

Retail Services	*Wholesale Services*
Account management	Account management
Bill payment and presentment	Cash management
New account opening	Small business loan applications, approvals, or advances
Consumer wire transfers	Commercial wire transfers
Investment/Brokerage services	Business-to-business payments
Loan application and approval	Employee benefits/pension
Account aggregation administration	

Since transactional websites typically enable the electronic exchange of confidential customer information and the transfer of funds, services provided through these websites expose a financial institution to higher risk than basic informational websites. Wholesale e-banking systems typically expose financial institutions to the highest risk per transaction, since commercial transactions usually involve larger dollar amounts. In addition to the risk issues associated with informational websites, examiners reviewing transactional e-banking services should consider the following issues:

- Security controls for safeguarding customer information;
- Authentication processes necessary to initially verify the identity of new customers and authenticate existing customers who access e-banking services;
- Liability for unauthorized transactions;
- Losses from fraud if the institution fails to verify the identity of individuals or businesses applying for new accounts or credit on-line;
- Possible violations of laws or regulations pertaining to consumer privacy, anti-money laundering, anti-terrorism, or the content, timing, or delivery of required consumer disclosures;

- Negative public perception, customer dissatisfaction, and potential liability resulting from failure to process third-party payments as directed or within specified time frames, lack of availability of on-line services, or unauthorized access to confidential customer information during transmission or storage.

Level of Services

The earlier from of e-banking services like telebanking were used to give information regarding previous transactions, or receiving instructions regarding insurance of cheques and other instruments. Similarly, the electronic clearance of remittances between the branches was introduced. The newer versions of software are adding new services. Primarily the services offered through Internet can be put into three categories:

Level-I

The basic level services are the bank website, which disseminates information on different products and services to customers. This is generally combined with e-mail to receive and answer queries;

Level-II

In this level simple transactional web sites are used. In this type of e-banking customers are allowed to submit their instructions or applications or queries on their bank balances or status of certain transactions etc. However, fund based transactions relating to the accounts of customers are not allowed.

Level-III

This is the highest level of internet banking services. In this case banking services are offered through Fully Transactional web sites. This permits customer to operate their accounts through Internet. They can transfer funds, pay bills, subscribe to other products or purchase or sell other securities etc. through the medium of internet.

E-banking Components

E-banking systems can vary significantly in their configuration depending on a number of factors. Financial institutions should choose their e-banking system configuration, including outsourcing relationships, based on four factors:

- Strategic objectives for e-banking;
- Scope, scale, and complexity of equipment, systems, and activities;
- Technology expertise; and
- Security and internal control requirements.

Financial institutions may choose to support their e-banking services internally. Alternatively, financial institutions can outsource any aspect of their e-banking systems to third parties. The following entities could provide or host (i.e., allow applications to reside on their servers) e-banking-related services for financial institutions:

- Another financial institution,
- Internet service provider,
- Internet banking software vendor or processor,
- Core banking vendor or processor,
- Managed security service provider,
- Bill payment provider,
- Credit bureau, and
- Credit scoring company.

E-banking systems rely on a number of common components or processes. The following list includes many of the potential components and processes seen in a typical institution:

- Website design and hosting,
- Firewall configuration and management,
- Intrusion detection system or IDS (network and host-based),
- Network administration,
- Security management,

308 New Dimensions of Indian Banking

- Internet banking server,
- E-commerce applications (e.g., bill payment, lending, brokerage),
- Internal network servers,
- Core processing system,
- Programming support, and
- Automated decision support systems.

These components work together to deliver e-banking services. Each component represents a control point to consider. Through a combination of internal and outsourced solutions, management has many alternatives when determining the overall system configuration for the various components of an e-banking system. First, one or more technology service providers can host the e-banking application and numerous network components as illustrated in the following diagram. In this configuration, the institution's service provider hosts the institution's website, Internet banking server, firewall, and intrusion detection system. While the institution does not have to manage the daily administration of these component systems, its management and board remain responsible for the content, performance, and security of the e-banking system. Second, the institution can host all or a large portion of its e-banking systems internally. A typical configuration for in-house hosted, e-banking services is illustrated below. In this case, a provider is not between the Internet access and the financial institution's core processing system. Thus, the institution has day-to-day responsibility for system administration.

- Internet banking customer sends an e-banking transaction through their Internet Service Provider (ISP) via a phone, wireless, or broadband connection;
- The customer's ISP routes the transaction through the Internet and sends it to the e-banking service provider's ISP, which routes it to the provider;
- The transaction enters the provider's network through a router, which directs the e-banking transaction through a firewall to the application running on the Internet banking server;

E-Banking: Emerging Challenges 309

- The website server and Internet banking server may have host-based intrusion detection system (IDS) software monitoring the server and its files to provide alerts of potential unauthorized modifications.
- Network IDS software may reside at different points within the network to analyze the message for potential attack characteristics that suggest an intrusion attempt.
- The Internet banking application processes the transaction against account balance data through a real time connection to the core banking system or a database of account balance data, which is updated periodically from the core banking system.
- The Internet banking server has a firewall filtering Internet traffic from its internal network.
- Internet banking customer sends an e-banking transaction through their Internet Service Provider (ISP) via a phone, wireless, or broadband connection.
- The customer's ISP routes the transaction through the Internet and sends it to the e-banking service bank's ISP, which routes it the provider.
- The transaction enters the bank's network through a router, which directs the Internet-banking transaction through a firewall to the application running on the Internet banking server.
- The bank typically has several Internet application servers that could include a website server, e-mail server, proxy server, and domain name server (DNS) in addition to the Internet banking application server.
- The router will typically send the transaction around the other application servers directly to the Internet banking server unless it is a non-banking transaction.
- The website server and Internet banking server may have host-based intrusion detection system (IDS) software monitoring the server and its files to provide alerts of potential unauthorized modifications.

- Network IDS software may reside at different points within the network to analyze the message for potential attack characteristics that suggest an unauthorized intrusion attempt.
- The Internet banking application processes the transaction against account balance data through a real time connection to the core banking system or a database of account balance data, which is updated periodically from the core banking system.
- The Internet banking server has a firewall filtering Internet traffic from the bank's internal network.

What is Required to Make Online Banking Successful?

To make online banking successful, the banks should pass on some benefits of the cost-effectiveness to the customers. The bank should offer:

- Higher rate on deposits;
- 24 hour access;
- Free bill payment and rebate on ATM surcharges;
- Credit card with low interest rates;
- Innovative products and high quality of services

Factor Promoting I-banking

Following factors will help I-banking:

- Low cost electronics services;
- Increased access;
- Improved awareness;
- Entry of global banks;
- Growth of e-commerce;
- Open standards in the banking industry;
- Convenience;
- Emergence of payment gateway and online shopping.

The Indian Scene

Internet banking has gained wide acceptance internationally. In India also the things are changing fast. India is on the threshold of a major banking revolution with the introduction of "Net-banking". In the year 2002, only a dozen or so banks are providing services at different levels. However, almost double those numbers are ready to make entry. Others may be compelled to follow.

Services Offered

Indian banks are at different stages of web-enabled banking business. These stages are generally of the following type:

- First stage type banks are those, which do not have web site. However, allow its customers to communicate through e-mail. These services are only at limited branches and for limited customers.
- Second stage is where banks have put up their own web sites. These provide general information about products and services and allow communication through e-mail. This is more of advertising method.
- Third stage is where banks allow customers to transact with them electronically. They can open accounts, request for cheques books, print statement of accounts, request for opening of letter of credit etc., and at the most transfer of funds from one account to another with the same bank.
- In fourth stage they go a step further by allowing transfer of funds by the accounts holder to another account holder of the bank.
- In fifth stage, the banks offer the facility of receipt, review and payments of bills online. These banks have tied up with utility companies.

Future Scene in India

The Indian banks lag far behind the international banks in providing online banking. The experience of ICICI Bank Ltd. and HDFC Bank Ltd. shows that the number of transactions carried out on the Net are very limited. Some of the reasons and problems being faced are as follows:

- Although security options in e-banking are available, there is no certifications of the appropriates Certification Authority;
- The available communication bandwidth available is not enough to meet requirement;
- Most of the banks lack uninterrupted power supply, which is essential for such services;
- The interact details for such services are one-sided, with banks enjoying supremacy. This does not give confidence to the customers (ATM & telebanking get preference);
- In Internet geographical boundaries are eliminated.
- Cyber crimes are difficult to control. There is urgent need to have appropriate cyber laws.

However, despite these hindrances, it is becoming popular and certain steps are being undertaken to promise I-banking.

- Department of telecommunication is making additional bandwidth available;
- Steps have been initiated to appoint Certification Authority.
- The RBI has put the real-time funds transfer through the Real Time Gross Settlements (RTGS) system in place. The access will be through only one specified gateway. This will ensure rigorous access control.
- Various levels of security are being accessed by RBI;
- Dematerialization of share has made significant progress, this will help I-banking;
- The payment gateway being created by ICICI bank and HDFC bank will give boost to I-banking.

References

Apel, K. O. (1996), "Transformation der Philosophie," Volume 2, Das Apriri der Kommunikationsgemeinschaft, Frankfurt, 1976.

Blickle, G. and S. Hauck, "Assertion and Consensus Motives in Argumentation," Paper presented at the European Business Ethics Network's 9th Annual Conference: Working Across Cultures, Frankfurt, 18-20 September.

E-Banking: Emerging Challenges 313

Brenkert, G. (2000), "Social Products Liability: The Case of the Firearms Manufacturers," *Business Ethics Quarterly* 10 (1), pp. 21-32.

Bush, V., B. Venable and A. Bush (2000), "Ethics and Marketing on the Internet: Practitioners' Perceptions of Societal, Industry and Company Concerns," *Journal of Business Ethics* 23(3), pp. 237-248.

Castells, M. (2000), "Information Technology and Global Capitalism", in Giddens, A. and Hutton, W. (Eds) On the Edge: Living with Global Capitalism, Vintage, London, pp. 52-74.

Chown, J. F. (1994), "A History of Money from AD 800," Routledge, London.

Cooper, D. E. (1996), "World Philosophies: An Historical Introduction," Blackwell, Oxford.

French, W. and B. Muhlfriedel, "Discourse Instead of Recourse: Is it Worth using a Guided Approach to Negotiation when Working Across Cultures?" in Lange, H., Löhr, A. and Steinmann, H. (Eds), Working across Cultures.

31

Retail Banking: Gearing UP for Growth

Ajay Kumar

The boom in retail banking has encouraged banks like Deutsche Bank to open its first Asian retail branch in India last year, and enter into the credit card segment this year. Bank of Baroda opened 650 automated teller machines (ATMs) and 114 retail loan boutiques called "Moneyplex". The boom has changed the complexion of banking in India–right from the traditional corporate working capital financing to customized retail services like home loans, credit cards, education loans etc. It has enabled banks to avail of multilevel opportunities like Internet, Tele-Banking and Mobile Banking to increase their retail loan assets.

In the year 2007, Indians bought 80 million mobile phones, 15 million television sets, 8 million personal computers and over a million new cars, A consumer boom of this kind has not been seen in India ever before. But all that happened last year. This year is expected to be still better, though not many are willing to hazard a guess on what these numbers will be. The growth is not restricted to just products. It is being driven by big infrastructure projects. The rising incomes in India have seen people investing in new flats and cars. All this has resulted in a sharp increase in demand for basic items. There is tremendous demand for availing bank loans and acquiring retail assets. Predominantly, the middle class is taking advantage of this retail boom. Banks like HDFC Bank and ICICI Bank have witnessed 70% growth in their retail loan assets. According to McKinsey, the global consultancy firm, the retail banking sector in India will grow from the present level of US$ 6 billion to US$ 16 billion by 2010. However, this amount of US$ 6 billion is only 8% of our GDP at present, as compared to Korea's 55%, and Taiwan's 41%. Hence, there is vast potential growth for in this sector in India.

Loans: Buy Our Dreams

Not only have they fuelled the desires of the common man, loans have also made it possible that those desires are fulfilled without us having to shell out cash immediately from our pocket. All we have do is fill a form, part with a few personal details and voila! We have ready cash in tour hand. We can choose to pay back the money (of course with interest!) in equated monthly installments (EMIs) spread over a period of time, say two, three or five years! Combine this with not having to produce any guarantors or collateral security and, you have a real good deal in your hands. Whether it is for your personal requirement, or for the dream car or house 'A wanted to buy, there are loan for everyone, to suit individual needs and occasion.

All this is first-hand information, coming from yours truly who just availed a small personal loan from a reputed bank. And trust me, the experience has been good. We could also get a lower rate of interest or a special rate of interest if, our company has a tie-up with the bank. Yup! Loans are getting bigger and better by the day. And why not, for who does not want to live their dreams in one life-time? The buy now-pay later credit culture that loans endorse has fuelled the growing need in people to spend beyond their means and acquire things they have always secretly dreamt of obtaining for themselves and their families.

Now, we would say that is all for the ones with a clean record as far as their credit history are concerned. What about those who have fallen into the bad credit gap. Though personal loans for bad credit are hard to find, in countries like the UK, personal loans for bad credit are also getting approved. Sooner than later, we could find them on the home turf as well. However, the things inseparable from personal loans with bad credit is higher interest rates or additional security (down payment). Most likely, one of these would be attached with the personal loan offered to us if, we have a bad credit history: Interest rates for personal loans for bad credit are usually dependent on credit history, presence of collateral, personal income, loan amount etc.

Loans of course are a one-stop shop for all our requirements today. Starting out with minimum advantages for the person, loans have come a long way. In terms of categories, Personal, Housing and Auto loans are the most commonly availed and these three categories have evolved with the years to provide increased benefits to customers.

Take for instance personal loans and we are likely to find a plethora of easy payment options and easy availability with each bank offering something better than the other. After all, this is the era of competitiveness, attracting more consumers and addressing their needs while getting good returns. For instance, in the personal loans section, HSBC Bank offers us smooth personal loan repayment with low interest rates. They give us the option of making an affordable repayment on our personal loan in the first year, after which year we can pay a higher EMI. Moreover, they make it further easier by charging interest on utilized personal loan amount only. Just estimate the maximum personal loan amount we need. Interest will be charged only on the amount we withdraw! All this coupled with facilities like last EMI waiver, flexibility in choosing the EMI dates etc. are helping those garners good response. (*Source*: HSBC Bank Online)

ICICI Bank offers some really good options apart from providing loans for both salaried & self-employed individuals. Loans are available from Rs.20000 to Rs. 15 lakhs with repayment tenures from 12-60 months. We are required to pay no security-collateral or guarantors. The loans can be used for any purpose with no questions asked regarding the end use of the loan. A balance transfer facility is available for those who want to retire any higher debt. All loan repayments can be done via equated monthly installments (EMI). (*Source:* ICICI Bank Online).

HDFC Bank, a pioneer in personal loans offers similar easy payment option for its customers. In the Home Loan arena, this bank is really doing well by providing loans to meet all our requirements for us to make that house a home. 'Imagine, we can get a loan for anything pertaining to a house- Home Loans, Home Improvement Loans, Home Extension Loans, Loans to professionals for office or clinic, Home Equity Loans (Loan against Property), Loan against Rent receivables, Short Term Bridging Loan. The icing on the cake is that these loans are available on Adjustable Rate, Fixed Rate with money market condition and Fixed Rate without money market Conditions. (*Source:* HDFC Bank Online). Not just this, now have loans available for almost everything ranging from farm and office machinery to construction and medical equipments. It is a whole new world out there where life is rocking and wishes can be realised by using money that is not ours.

In the auto loans section or car loans section, ICICI Bank is the number 1 financier for car loans in the country with a network of more than 1800 channel partners in over 1000 locations and tie-ups with all leading automobile manufacturers to ensure the best deals. All the big banks like HDFC, ICICI, SBI and others offer flexible schemes & quick processing and hassle-free application process on the click of a mouse. Nationalised banks like SBI offer interest rate of as low as 13% on personal loans, however they may give us a maximum of three years time to pay back through EMIs.

Most of the banks today have tie-up with the major companies and that is not just for opening salary accounts alone! we could avail an interest rate lower than the prevalent rate of interest in the market if we happen to work with one of these companies (which is likely in any case). There could be a difference of a good 2% between the market and the special rate of interest offered to us. In some cases we do not even need an employers' certificate or a bonafide certificate! The last three salary slips would suffice and you should be in service with the company for no less than a period of one year. Sounds easy, is not it?

But then, if there are advantages, the disadvantages too come our way. Having a loan on our head to pay every month means we cannot (a) quit our job if we are salaried (the fear of having to pay it is enough to make us stick to our sloppy office!) (b) make sure we have enough dough if we are self employed, in case our business takes a plunge downwards (c) depending on our income and how much loan we have taken we cannot escape its vicious cycle and yes, you have to make those small personal sacrifices (in terms of spending on yourself and holidays) for that Honda Civic you booked! These may not work as deterrents though as the advantages are many. Gone are the days when it was thought that a loan is a headache, a trouble that weighs on our heart all the time. With changing times, the conservative Indian consumer has embraced the credit culture and is enjoying the charms of living beyond their incomes–for a short period, at least! (G. Dutt, 2006).

Boom in Retail Banking

In the credit card segment, co-branding has enhanced customers' spending patterns. Many private banks have arranged for tie-ups such as ICICI Bank with Big Bazaar, HSBC Bank with Star India Bazaar, and Citibank with Shoppers Stop. According to RBI statistics, medium and large industries have played a major role in the growth of retail credit. During the year 2007-08, the housing loans grew by nearly 50%, taking advantage of the lower interest rates offered by the banks.

Innovative products offered by private sector banks have forced the public sector banks to follow suit. With the boom in housing loans, the Reserve Bank of India has naturally been worried about the bubble. The success of tomorrow's leading retail bank will come from changes that are happening to customers, from the impact of changing technology that is already available to service customers more efficiently than ever before and cheaper than before, and from competitors who also change with responding times and circumstances.

The greatest challenge for large retail banks will be the need to provide 'Anytime, Anywhere, Anyhow banking' for all their customers. This is to be combined with other ingredients like financial and brand strength.

Time is more precious. Customers are demanding more flexible and conveniently situated distribution channels available that suits them—and not the banks. Consumers are increasingly knowledgeable. They are also becoming more cost conscious and less tolerant of mistakes. So getting it right first time is the new mantra for banks and consumers want trust in the form of responsible and ethical behavior from banks. This is a basic and minimum requirement.

Technology works for the benefit of both customers and the banks. Transactions can now take place with minimal paper work. IT enabled services allow flexible remote banking channels to be developed. This spells cut in costs, and speedier disposal of information for the customer. (Chatterjee, 2008).

Banking products have to be branded as a process of product differentiation. Other sectors start with an entry advantage and lower cost base, e.g. retail industries, etc. However, it is different in banking where a combination of electronic banking will be required to deliver the retail products, and, more so, to be price competitive to increase customer base. How to become a leading retail banker? The head of strategic planning of New Zealand Bank observed that they needed to ensure that they were in a position where they could satisfy any customer's needs any time. 24 hours a day, seven days a week. Price Waterhouse Coopers has worked out a blueprint which advocates Triple-A banking—Anywhere, Anytime, Anyhow banking for all customers. The price and the service will determine the brand equity and the value for money.

Managing the Transformation

Bank have to be proactive to the changes in the market place to meet the challenges critical strategic decisions like turning historical information into knowledge, taking the best technology bet, encouraging change in customer channel usage, and managing new risks.

The distribution channels for Triple-banking will have the remote delivery and face-to-face delivery systems. The remote delivery systems will be screen-based like ATMs, kiosks, and PCs, as well as telephone systems like phone banking, interactive voice communication, etc. The face-to-face distribution channel includes traveling bankers, express bankers, mobile banking, and wealth management banking. These distribution channels will have to find out the customer needs and how they behave with different channels. Accordingly, a realignment of distribution channels will have to be made to meet customer needs and profit targets. Banks will have to investigate outsourcing and franchising for distribution networks to improve the variable and fixed cost ratios.

Current Situation

Human resources are a vital part to retail banking. Changing the skill sets will involve re-training new recruitment, and voluntary retirement schemes. For a successful HR management, banks will have to study the current environment and define their operating vision. They will also implement radical changes successfully while at the same time maintaining competitive advantage. The staff values are likely to be aligned with customer propositions by introducing flex-time and extended working hours. Triple–Banking will be customized to match employees' and customers' needs. Understanding current situations will help to find out the gap the gap with reference to world class performance. This can be done on a scale of 0 to 10 by considering factors like market focus, resources, structure, processes, and brand and culture.

Credit Cards

The penetration of retail banking is fast in credit card usage. The rapid growth in the new card membership has already crossed the 10 million mark. It is growing at a compounded annual growth rate (CAGR) of 80%. There is an increase in both new card holders and spending per card. Followed by this credit card boom, is a plastic explosion environment. The internet revolution has not left the credit card industry unaffected.

The new start-up organizations have the state-of-the-art technology, while the old issuers had established their brand names and customer relationships in credit card business. At present, they have economies of scale to their advantage. However, they have to make their presence felt in the virtual world to survive. (Chatterjee, 2008).

Other Products

The retail banking also includes other loans like home loans, auto loans, consumer durable loans, personal loans, and educational loans. Apart from this, ATMs, tale-banking, and internet banking have been added to the retail banking products. The Automated Teller machines is changing the behavior of the consumer, from a cash economy to a plastic card economy. Current account holders and savings bank account holders with a minimum balance in their accounts are issued with ATM cards. There are a lot of advantages of an ATM as they are working round-the-clock, and make cash available when necessary. It also eliminates the need for traveling to the branch where the customer is maintaining his account.

However, instantaneous accounting is possible and offers a cost-effective solution to the banks. By maintaining the PIN diligently, a customer can avoid frauds, misappropriation and robberies. Phone banking is an exclusive facility wherein the 'customer is given access to his account query. Internet banking is a strategic product and a new distribution channel. Complex products can be offered at low cost and contracts can be entered from any place at any point of time. This helps the banks to enlarge their market areas without brick and mortar. Offering special information to close user groups results in customer bonding as well as customer commitment.

Internet banking involves using the internet to offer interaction between the banks and customers, such as, e-mail queries, feedback forms, and product information. However, security is of prime concern.

Home Loans: A variety of home loans are available from the banks now to the retail customers. There is a loan for purchase of a new home, repairs and renovations of the existing house, expansion of the existing house, second loan to repay the first loan and top-ups to acquire extra funds, etc. There. are also loans for purchasing plot of land to build independent houses. Bridge loans are given to persons who want to sell their existing homes and purchase another. This loan helps to finance the purchase of a new home until the old one is sold. Re-finance loans are also eligible to repay the debts incurred from relatives and friends, etc, which were taken to purchase the house. Stamp duty loans help the customers to meet the stamp duty expenses on the purchase of a home. Loans are also earmarked to NRIs as it earns foreign exchange.

Eligibility for Home Loans: The repayment capacity to meet the EMI is reckoned by the banks by taking into consideration factors like income, age, qualifications, number of dependents, assets, liabilities, and savings history. At the pre-approval, stage, the following documents are commonly asked for: proof of income; copy of bank account statements for the last 6 months; copy of the latest credit card statement; passport size photo, and proof of residence.

At the post-approval stage, the following documents are required: allotment letter; photocopies of title deeds; sale agreement; non-encumbrance certificate, and approved plans. The repayment of the loan ranges from 5 to 15 years. The NRIs are eligible for a maximum of 7 years. The EMI are met through post-dated cheques covering both the principal and the interest. There are collateral securities in the form of guarantees in the form of LIC policies, and shares. These collateral securities are in addition to the mortgage of the property being purchased.

New features like floating rate of interest have come into operation which is linked to the market lending rate. There are some charges which some banks levy, namely, processing charge, prepayment penalties, commitment fees, and documentation charges. However, in view of the tax exemption and free availability of home loans, this sector has been booming in the recent years. The RBI is concerned with the overheating of the economy through home loans, as stated earlier.

Auto loans: Auto loans have been equally attractive for the past decade. These loans are in the form of new car loan, used car loan, and auto refinance. The eligibility for auto loans is normally for borrowers between the ages of 21 to 58 years. The size of the loan amount depends on the cost of the vehicle, and the type of the car. While new cars can get up to 90% of the financing, the old cars get lower amount of financing. The documents required are salary certificate, and TDS certificate of the borrower, copy of bank statements of last 6 months, copy of latest credit card statement, passport size photo, and proof of residence.

At the post-approval stage, the borrower submits registration certificate, insurance policy, road tax, etc. Normally, the loan is repaid within 7 years. However, some banks give a lower EMI in the first few years and higher EMI at a later stage. The registration certificate is endorsed to the bank as hypothecation of the vehicle to the bank. The interest rate is charged upfront, on a reducing balance basis which could be daily, monthly, quarterly or annually. There are processing fees, stamp charges, and insurance before the transaction is completed. Two-wheeler loans are also given for purchase of mopeds, scooters and motor cycles on similar lines.

Consumer Durable Loans: Consumer durable loans are also usually given for smaller amounts depending on the nature of durable goods. However, the loans are repayable between 12 to 36 months. There are no collateral securities called for in respect of consumer durable loans. The interest rates are varied depending on the seasonality and there is also a flat processing fee. These loans help customers to buy consumer durables like fridges, TVs, microwave-ovens, etc.

Personal Loans: Personal loans are eligible for people in the age group of 21 to 58 years, depending on their current income. The bank calculates the EMI which does not exceed 40% of the net take-home pay. The maximum amount of loan sanctioned is 11 times the net take-home pay, which is arrived at by deducting normal household expenses and EMI on other loans. Most of the banks give loans ranging from Rs.15 to Rs.10 lakhs towards personal loans. The documents required are bank account statements, proof of residence, and transfer of shares, etc. Personal loans are usually repayable within 3 years. However, the interest currently ranges from 15% to 30%.

Educational Loans: Educational loans have become very attractive in India in view of the large number of students taking up professional courses in India and abroad. Banks give loans up to Rs. 12 lakhs for studies in India and up to Rs. 15 lakhs for studies abroad. No margin money is required by the banks for loans up to Rs 4 lakhs. However, the parents' income is considered by most of the banks apart from a confirmed admission letter from the educational institution. The loans are allowed to be repaid 6 months after the completion of the course or commencement of the job, whichever is earlier, In view of the income tax benefit available in respect of the interest on loan taken for educational purposes; these educational loans have become popular among students pursuing higher education. (Chatterjee, 2008).

Opportunities and Challenges

Focus shifts to retail banking with spreads shrinking, Indian banks are following their global counterparts and focusing on increasing the share of their fee-based income. The ratio of non-interest income to total funds has already increased for some banks and the results of the past years affirm this fact.

Conclusion

The growth in the economy has been sluggish and banks can no longer afford to rely on big corporate customers. There is a shift in focus towards retail banking. Most banks are targeting the middle class and lower middle class segment. Huge non-performing assets (NPAs) are plaguing old private sector banks. The asset quality of banks is largely dependent on economic growth and makes it difficult for them to recover loans till the economy revives.

Flexible financing with lower interest rates has resulted in brisk activity in the sector. SBI and other banks have launched voluntary retirement scheme (VRS), an effort to bring down operating cost. There is an increased focus towards auto loans, car loans, funding for infrastructure, and other fee-based services such as guarantees and commissions on drafts, gold banking, derivatives and the like.

Overall, HDFC Bank, ICICI Bank and SBI have shown good performance and appeared to be geared to take on the challenges. These banks are changing their strategy and shifting focus from big corporates to mid-corporates and also retail banking and housing finance. The Indian banking system is in the midst of a technological revolution with banks offering anywhere banking, 24x7, and also attempting to become a one-stop financial shop offering all financial solutions.

References

Chatterjee, Shreedharan and Koriri (2008), Retail Banking: Opportunities and Challenges, *Southern Economist*, Bangalore, Vol. 46, No. 19, February 1.

Cho, Y. J. (1989), *Finance and Development: the Korean Approach*, Oxford *Review of Economic Policy*, Vol. 5, No. 4

Dutt, G. (2006), Loans: Buy Your Dreams, Now., *Business Standard*, Kolkata, July 13.

Garbis, V. (1977), Financial Intermediation and Economic Growth in Less Developed Countries: A Theoretical Approach, *Journal of Development Studies*, Vol. 13.

Ghosh, D. N. (1979), *Banking Policy in India*, Bombay.

———(2008), *Report on Currency and Finance*, 2006-08, Reserve Bank of India, Mumbai.

———(2008), *Economic Survey*, 2007-08, Government of India, New Delhi.

Palat, R. (2006), *Retail Banking*, Cortland Rand Consultancy Pvt. Ltd., Bangalore.

Raja J. Chelliah (1993), Finance and Fiscal Sector Reforms in Asian Countries, *Asian Development Review*, Vol. II, No. 2.

Shekhar, R. (2008), Negotiating the Best Value for Money, *The Business Line*, April 7-12.

32

Branch Banking and Retail Banking: Its Future in India

P. S. Tripathi & Shweta Dikshit

This paper entitled "Branch Banking and Retail Banking. Its future in India", is divided into five sections. The first section deals with the introduction which highlights the importance of banking sector in our country, with respect to branch as well as retail banking. The second section discusses the objectives of the paper. The third section deals with the expansion of the branch banking, section four with the future of retail banking and the last section brings out the conclusion and suggestions so as to improve the services related to the branch and retail banking in India.

I

The advent of liberalisation, coupled with deregulation and competition has completely transformed the banking system - on both the delivery system and the range of products offered. Indian banking industry has transformed from social banking to technology based customer-centric and profit-seeking competitive banking. The advent of global competition and technologies are altering the business methods and raising new and complex issues like low costs, new products, asset-management and so on. In this background, we shall be focussing on the changing face of bank lending on the retail sector and the importance of bank branches in the modern distribution network.

Banking industry is going through a process of transformation, as clearly evident from the financial markets, institutions, products and modes of delivery. In the wake of ever increasing expectations of the people, who are aware regarding banking and banking products offered to them are very demanding, leading to transformation of markets from being bank - centric market to customer centric market. In other words, markets have made rapid advancement from being a seller's market (bank-centric) to buyer's market (customer-centric market). Foreign banks with their superior technology and new private sector banks with their aggressive marketing strategies have enhanced the competition. These have forced public sector banks (PSBs) not only to offer broader range of products at low costs but simultaneously change modes of delivery process and operation so as to remain competitive in the market. The implementation of the Narsimham Committee (I and II) recommendations which the basis of financial sector reforms, has completely changed not only on the credit disbursement front but also on the distribution end.

II

Objective

The objective of this paper is to study, how with the advent of globalisation and competition, modern distribution network with reference to branch network and retail lending becoming synonymous with mainstream banking. It also foccuses on the future prospects of branch banking and retail banking in the country.

III

Branch Banking

The speed and efficiency offered by technology on one hand and the pressure on the banks to reduce transaction and operational cost on the other is raising questions about the relevance of vast branch network of banks (especially of the public sector banks) across the country while it is indisputable that we need to rationalise and restructure the branch network, yet there are certain facts to be borne in mind.

To study the growth of branch network in India, we have divided the growth period in four phases-pre-nationalisation period stretching from independence to nationalisation or phase I (1947-68); post nationalisation period or phase II (1969-92); phase III from 1992-2000 and phase IV from 2000 onwards.

Phase I (1947-68): During this phase, banking was of private character. It was_mainly of urban orientation centred around big trade centres and fulfilling needs of the rich. Banking was for elite class. There was a close association between banks and industry. Many industrialists were on the board of the banks and utilized funds for their benefits. There was complete neglect of the rural economy, and, hence there was hardly any branch in the rural areas.

Phase II (1969-1992): This phase started with the nationalisation of the fourteen banks with the objective of providing banking facilities in unbanked and underbanked regions in rural and semi-urban areas coupled with extensive branch network in urban areas to earn profit. In order to give further impetus to the branch expansion programme, Lead-Bank Scheme (1969) and Service Area Approach (1989) were started by Reserve Bank of India. All these measures helped in phenomenal growth of bank branches (refer to Table 1) bringing down the average population covered per branch from 64,000 in 1969 to around 16,000 by 2004-05.

Table 1
Branch Expansion by Commercial Banks
(in Thousands)

Year	*Rural Branches*	*Semi-urban Branches*	*Urban Branches*	*Metropolitan Branches*
19691	860	3,322	1,447	1,661
1991	33,990	11,356	8,279	5,666
1995	36,800	–	–	–
2002	32,423	14,688	10,540	8,625
2005	19,645	12,504	10,546	8,725

*Source:*RBI; Report on Trend and Progress of Banking in India, Various Issues.

Two following observations can be made from Table 1.

(1) Bank have come a long way; from less than 2000 rural branches in 1969 to more than 36,000 in 1995; serving more and more rural people;

(2) With large scale use of technology from 2000 onwards raw consequent decline in physical branches through conversion into satellite branches, consolidation and mergers thereby restructuring the branch network.

After 1995, or during phase III, stretching through the decade of 90's was a transitory phase. Branch expansion and social banking was showing effect on the balance sheet of the banks in the form of high operational and transaction cost and poor profitability. Liberalization, along with the deregulation of the financial sector, marked end of isolation from rest of the world. Competition forced public sector banks, especially, to change their ways. It pushed banks to be more systematic in their geographical spread. Specialized branches catering to the specific requirements of the customers were introduced. For eg; in the business centres, those kind of branches were opened which provided speedy services to the businessmen, like fast cheque clearing, demand draft etc., required by them instead of general banking services. The population coverage criterion, for opening a branch was removed and banks were free to open their branches on pure economic considerations. During this period, technical upgradation was in its early stages as per the recommendations of the Narsimham Committee (I and II). In order to restructure the branch network voluntary retirement scheme (VRS) was introduced in order to reduce the pressure of excess staff. This measure greatly helped in restructuring the bank branches and cost reductions. The opening of financial sector led to establishment of new private sector banks like ICICI, HDFC etc., further intensifying the competition. Thus branch banking passed through many phases before becoming technology driven.

Phase IV (Since 2000 onwards): This phase saw technology making in-roads into the banking operation on a very large scale. The banking system has been increasingly searching means for technology based delivery channels and progressive reduction in the physical branches. There have been a series of closures and conversion of branches into satellite branches in order to achieve the target. This trend has been visible more markebly in the rural branch network. Real Time Gross Settlement (RTGs) system, core Banking Solution (CBS), telebanking, mobile-banking, remote access, automated teller machine (ATM) network, electronic fund transfer (EFT), Electronic Clearing Service (ECS) and so on are all examples of now technology is being used to provide good service in quicker time, from anywhere and anytime without having to make a bank visit. These developments have really forced us to think the relevance of such a vast branch network.

But this is one sided picture restructuring and nationalization of branch network involves certain issues which need to be kept in mind.

1. Human confidence on which banks are built. Moving from traditional banking to the technology based banking should essentially maintain this element;
2. Cross-country evidence-how that many established banks have to reestablish "Brick and mortar" branches along with electronic delivery channels. Hence, the concept of "Click and mortar" branches is increasingly becoming popular.
3. In a country like India, where illiteracy is quiet high and technology has still not reached the remote villages, bank branches cannot be substituted by anything.

The Narsimham Committee II (1998) has set the tone for consolidation within the industry, "there is clearly a need for consolidation of structure and this could be brought about essentially through a process of negotiated rather than imposed mergers on profitability consideration and also for the reason of business strategy." (Lelladhar, V.; March 2003). The branch infrastructure in Indian situation is fairly spread out and the scope for strengthening branch banking through a structured process of consolidation and restructuring. In a globally competitive scenario, where technology based delivery channels are being evolved, it is of great importance that branches should increase in just members but should be so expanded that they fulfill the requirement of the people and also serve the economic preposition.

IV

Retail Banking

Retail banking or lending refers to the dealing of commercial banks with individual customers. The typical products offered in the retail banking segment are housing loans, loans for consumer durables, educational loans, personal loans and many more. These loans are marketed under different names to differentiate products offered by different banks. As far as its prevalence in India is concerned, it is not a new phenomenon. After nationalisation banks did start financing individuals for consumer durables but the amount sanctioned was limited and mostly given to bank's own employees. Credit goes to the foreign banks who started financing this segment in 1980's in a large way to the general public. For the last few years, it has become synonymous with the mainstream banking for many banks.

Growth in retail banking, has been consequence of many factors which are:

(a) Emergence of Indian middle-class with high household income and purchasing power coupled with liberal attitude towards taking loans has given filling to the consumer boom;

(b) Great variety offered in the consumer durables ; and increased usage of plastic money (Credit card, debit cards etc.).

(c) High demand for housing loans due to various tax incentives;

(d) India has second largest population in the world with nearly 70 per cent of the population below 35 years of age. Younger population wields its purchasing power more freely than then previous generation. Their migration to different cities in search for better jobs is also contributing to this trend indication of vast growth potential in changing consumer demographies,

(e) Technology has played a very crucial role, convenient banking in the form of mobile banking, on-line transaction, ATMs, etc. have galvanised a new set of customers lending to high demand for retail credit.

RBI has also taken initiatives to promote retail banking. Retail loans not only provide additional income but defaults are very low in it thus making a good business prospect It helps to diversify banks' sources of income with low level of non productive assets (NPAs). Today, in a highly competitive markets, all financial service providers, including commercial banks are forced to increase their profits with low level of defaults and good customer service Retail banking is the most "in thing" in the banking sector. It is estimated to constitute about one fifth of the total bank credit by March 2005, which is expected to rise further as the economy expands and grows. bank loan as a ratio of country's gross domestic product (GDP) grew at a rate of 6.2 per cent between 2003-05.

Table 2
Variation's in the Segment of Retail Credit

(in Per cent)

	Year Ending				
Particulars	*March 2001*	*March 2002*	*March 2003*	*March 2004*	*March 2005*
Non-Food Gross Bank Credit	14.31	12.5	12.5	28.4	27.9
Retail Credit	12.9	23.0	22.0	34.4	40.8
Housing	14.5	38.43	55.1	50.0	44.6
Consumer Durables Against Shares and Debentures Bonds	44.4	26.03	1.6	19.8	4.6
Loans to Individuals Fixed Deposits	-20.9	-10.43	15.9	14.6	18.3
Advances Against	5.7	6.5	6.9	16.1	11.3
Other Personal Loans*	17.1	29.6	11.5	34.8	67.3

* Include personal loan, credit cards, debit cards, smart cards education loans etc.

Source: RBI, Report on Trend and Progress of Banking in India, Various Issues.

Following observations have been made from the above Table:

- According to the sectoral deployment of the credit data, credit flow to the retail sectors has accelerated from 12.9 per cent in March 2002 to 40.8 per cent in March 2005.
- The biggest share in this sector is of housing loans which has grown by 44.6 per cent between 2004-05. The other big contributors are credit cards, debit cards automated teller machine (ATM) card and smart cards, and personal loans.
- It is clear that retail segment has been growing on a continuous basis though variations in the composition exist. For eg; while in March 2001, housing credit was 14.5 per cent of the total retail credit, it increased to 44.5 per cent in 2005. Loans for consumer durables also changed considerably during the period. However, it is to be noted that loans to individuals against shares and debentures have picked up remarkably after being in negative figures other personal loans which include "Inter-alia", education loans, credit cards etc. have registered a high growth. As a result of this boom, in the retail lending, the share of bank advance to the household sector in gross domestic product (GDP) has increased from 1.02 per cent in 1999-2000 to 3.52 in 2004.05. A close inspection reveals two characteristics of today's retail banking.
- First, it points out to the fact that banks are no longer locking their funds in Government securities and in lending to the corporate sector. They are showing desire to land shown by the performance of their balance sheets.
- Second, it shows that things have completely changed from what they were twenty years ago. The single biggest change is in the attitude of the customers. They are ready to buy services from those providers who offer them the best deal. They are ready to purchase services even from entirely new providers and

establish retail companies with no record of financial services. This has contributed significantly to the growth of the new private sector banks, foreign banks and non banking finance companies (NBFCs).

Infact, new private sector bank like ICICI, UTI etc. have created a niche in this regard. Anywhere and anytime delivery, on line marketing, internet banking, mobile banking and phone banking and less amount of paper work, all have boosted the growth. It shows that new banks do not refrain from lending but on the other hand, they are trying to convince customers to do business with them. Traditional service provides, especially public sector banks have realized that if they have to survive this tough competition, they have to provide what people want. In other words and as has been said that markets have transformed from being a sellers market to buyers market, and it is the consumer who decides their action. The biggest advantage in the growth of the retail credit is the fact that banking is touching lives of common man directly. For eg. housing loans are fulfilling dreams of millions of Indian to own a house. Personal loans leave helped people to raise standard of living and live a better life instead of not consuming until they saved enough for it Rising culture of the plastic money has helped in not only easier and faster transaction but has also given inputes to the "Consumer and mall" culture. Establishment of new shopping centres have led to growth in employment opportunities. Retail banking is not just about lending in urban areas but has a huge potential in rural and semi-urban areas where the "real India", lives. Kissan Credit Cards and micro-finance are two most innovative products of rural retail lending. Government and banks should aim at building more innovative products, like these. Retail banking does not only mean retail lending but equally important is the role played by the retail depositors like small savers, retail traders etc. In the area of rural retail lending and deposit, public sector banks enjoy definite advantage of vast branch network over their private and foreign counterparts. In view of huge potential in the rural areas, it is their asset. While the scene is somewhat opposite in the urban areas, where new private sector banks and foreign banks with their aggressive marketing and superiors customers service have an edge.

Technology in Retail Banking

Implementation of the technology is very crucial in attaining success in the retail banking segment. New Private sector banks have used e-banking and "at your doorsteps" service to build customer value. Some products are suited more to e-commerce for eg. general insurance or car insurance, which has proved suitability to e-commerce and has become intensely competetive product. The new delivery channel and ease with which consumers can switch between banks and other financial product providers have forced banks to concentrate on customers service. One such area, where competition is fierce is of credit card segment. With increasing usage of these cards as a medium of transaction, every service provider is trying to attract customers, and technology is crucial in this segment.

Retail loans, which are considered self liquidating, is often not the case. Current procedure of recovery is time consuming and cumbersome. Daily publishing of the list of the defaulters and various harsh means for recovery bears testimony to the fact. At times the wilful defaulters welcome legal action to get a passage in repayment and relief from interest charges. All those issues are needed to be addressed. A proper legal mechanism should be devised, for recovery of dues without harassing them. This will not only help in the reduction of non-productive assets but will also help to build a better relationship between the customers and the banks. Bank should also keep changing their schemes according to the changed requirement of the customers.

Innovating constantly is a pre-requisite in retail banking. For better tomorrow, a paradigm shift in bank financial through innovative products and mechanism involving constant upgradation of banks internal system has be restructured. Bank now need to use of retail as growth trigger and for this they have to develop new products, less paper work, easy repayment, reassessment of business procedures on banks' side, prudent pricing, micro planning, marketing, customization and most importantly technical upgradation. Indian banks should always keep in mind the fact that they cannot be just profit seekers but also play a significant part in the development of the country.

CONLUSION

Following conclusions have emerged from the study of branch & retail banking in India.

(1) Indian banking has transferred from social banking to commercial banking in true sense. Concept of ensuring presence in every corner without having consideration for economic potentialies has changed;

(2) Large scale lending to corporate clients and only being saving galvanisers from the general public has been replaced;

(3) The speed and efficiency offered by technology banking on one hand and the pressure on banks to reduce transaction cost on the other, has led to a firm view that branch banking is a luxury which cannot be sustained in the present form.

With the changing priorities and pressures of cost reductions, it is a fact that banks have to deal with the psychology of Indian customers.

(4) Branch banking cannot be done away with for the reason that still if one has to take loan he/she would like to make a personal visit to the bank. Survey by Nonametric with Cap Gemini Ernst & Young revealed that still even 76 per cent of the Europeans considered branch proximity as an ideal sort of relationship with banks.

(5) In a country like India, where literacy late is low and the level of computer knowledge still lower, branch banking is a necessity. If there is a problem, people like to meet the concern authorities personally instead of just on-line complaining, especially in rural areas.

(6) Retail banking is growth trigger in the banking sector because of the fact that India has one of the fast growing economy of the world, after China and more than 70 per cent of its population is less than 35 years of age. With the multinationals expanding their operations in the country, job opportunities are also rising. This has led to rise in income and purchasing power.

(7) As the level of defaults is low; they are a profitable avenue.

On the basis of above conclusions it can be suggested that retail banking can be boosted further with branch banking in the following ways.

(1) Branch infrastructure in Indian situation is fairly well spread and offers excellent scope for strengthening branch banking through conversions, closures and mergers for restructuring.

(2) Retail banking is the most buzzing word of current times and bank could encash upon the opportunity by consumer friendly loan offers through various branches;

(3) Technology in branch network and retail banking is a very powerful means to achieve greater level of customer satisfaction.

(4) Less complex products like car insurance or non-life insurance, are very much suited for e-banking. More products like this could be developed.

Technology based banking is a peaceful mode of attracting customers and earning profit. In such a scenario, branch banking could be a boon for promoting the growth of retail segment. As people will demand more, business would expand leading to development of the country. Hence, in such a scenario, it could be said that both branch banking and retail banking have ample scope for improvement and innovation. In this regard, training, acquiring new skills, delivering results are very crucial.

References

Arora, Kalpana (2003), "Indian Banking: Managing Transformation Through Information and Technology", *IBA Special Bulletin*, March.

Jhingan, M. L. (1999), "Monetary Economics", Vrinda Publication's New Delhi.

Leeladhar, V. (2003), "Branch Banking-Its Future in India", *IBA Special Bulletin*, March.

Roy Mahua (2005), "A Review of Bank Lending to Priority and Retail Sector", *Economic and Political Weekly*, March.

Ruddar Datt & Sundaram, K.P.M. (1997), Indian Economy, S. Chand and Company Ltd., New Delhi.

Sharma, Dinesh. K., Alade, Julius A., Sharma, Hari. P. (2002), "The Role of Information Technology in the Banking Industry", *International Journal of Developmental Banking*, Vol. 18, No. 1 January.

33

Retail Banking: Opportunities and Challenges

K. C. Jha & P. C. Badalia

Liberalization and de-regulation process started in 1991-92, has made a sea change in the Indian banking system. From totally regulated environment, banks moved into a market driven competitive environment. The traditional banking approach to depend upon 'walk in customer' has given way to super market where all financial needs of the customers are satisfied under one roof.

After introduction of financial sector reforms in 1992, banks are facing numerous challenges, like increasing competition from private and foreign banks, low productivity, high operational costs, pressure on spreads and focus on 'NPA management' due to tightening of prudential norms. But they are awash with liquidity. This has forced the banks to look for new avenues for growth and survival by repositioning themselves in new business segments of the economy, where opportunities are more and risk is less. Retail customers who represents huge untapped market for credit has suddenly become a new credit mantra for banks.

Across the globe, retail lending has been a spectacular innovation in the commercial banking sector in recent years. The growth of retail lending, especially, in emerging economies, is attributable to the rapid advances in information technology, the evolving macroeconomic environment, financial market reform and several micro-level demand and supply side factors.

India too experienced a surge in retail banking. There are various pointers towards this. Retail loan is estimated to have accounted for nearly one-fifth of all bank credit, housing sector was experiencing a boom in its credit, the retail loan market had decisively got transformed from a sellers' market to a buyers's market. Gone are the days where getting a retail loan was a cumbersome task. All these emphasise the momentum that retail banking is experiencing in the Indian economy in recent years.

Retail banking in India is not a new phenomenon. It has always been prevalent in India in various forms. Retail banking is probably as old as banking itself for it is nothing but providing banking products and services to individuals.

Retail banking (retail lending to be more specific) as applicable to modern times, may be defined as providing credit to individuals for non-entrepreneurial activities. This is because, usually retail loans are used towards consumption and the loan has to be repaid by the borrower out of his/her own resources and not from the income-stream generated by deployment of the loan. Retail loans do not form the income-generating assets. There are exceptions, such as housing loans which may generate rental income; but if the house is being used by individuals for self-occupation, the loan has to be repaid from the individual's own repayment capacity (for e.g. his/her income) and not from the income-stream generated by the deployment of the housing loan. This is different from a situation where the individual is given a loan to set up a small shops, wherein the loan itself would create its own servicing ability.

Retail Banking: Changing Face

Retail banking has always been important in India, where banks were nationalised with the objectives of reaching the masses across the country. But the growth in retail banking, in terms of volumes and types of products, has been quite pronounced in the recent years. Some of the basic reasons attributed for this spurt are India's economic prosperity and consequent increase in purchasing power; changing consumer demographics with one of the highest sections of the population below the age of 35 years; technological innovations, such as ATMs, credit cards, etc.; decline in treasury income causing retail banking to be the focus of profit maximization and decline in interest in recent years (Gopinath, 2005).

There has also been an expansion in the nature and products offered under retail banking. Retail banking used to be synonymous with savings account and fixed deposits with cheque based/deposit slip based transactions. Retail loans were usually restricted to housing loans. This has changed considerably in the last decade or so, especially in India. There had been a revolution in the range of products and the way these are serviced. For e.g., previously one had to physically visit a bank's branch in order to open an account, whereas today the bank often 'visits' a customer who shows or may show an inclination to open an account with it. Earlier, one was a customer of a particular branch of the bank, today one is a customer of the bank, thanks to 'core banking'. 'Universal banking' has also enabled customers to get an assortment of products at a bank whereas previously one might have had to be a customer of various other institutions (insurance companies, mutual funds, housing finance companies, etc.) to avail of various products. These changes indicate that retail banking has witnessed revolution of sorts, especially in India.

Retail Loan-Statistics

Welcome to a new India, where living off debt is a well-accepted norm of life. If recent statistics (see Table 1) on consumer finance are any indication, last few years have been trend setting. The conservative, cautious, thrifty and debt-averse middle class of past seems to have given way to a new middle class (population about 32 million) that is free from all inhibitions regarding conspicuous consumption.

Table 1
Retail Loan-Statistics

Type	*March 1996*	*March 2004*
Housing	6303	51981
Consumer	1476	8274
Shares bonds etc.	1933	2020
Real estate	1173	5577
Fixed deposits	12000	26346
Personal loan	12559	35165
Total	35454	129363

Amount in Rs. crores.
RBI report on trend and progress of banking.

It has no stigma of borrowing for consumer spending. Indian Corporate has been dreaming for a long time to tap this huge market of middle class that is hungry for consumer durables but short of cash. The cheap retail loan has made their dream come true.

Retail Lending as Now New Darling of Banks

The retail loan market crossed Rs. 100,000 crores mark during financial year ending 2004 and reached Rs. 134,000 crores by end March 2005 according to industry estimates. Home loan market constituted 47% (Rs. 60,000.00) in 2004-05 followed by car loan 22.3% and personal loan 8.1% (Economic times 07.05.2005). Present penetration level of retail loans in only 6.5% or our GDP, compared with 10.2% in Thailand, 49.3% in Malaysia and 68.4% in South Korea. (The Assian Banker) Thus untapped potential of retail loan in our country is very big. The over all demand for car loans and two wheelers has seen a 25-30% growth since January 04. Consumer durable loans have grown consistently more than 20-25% since 2000 while two wheeler loans have grown 30%. Car finance too has grown 30% Seeing big opportunity banks have become very aggressive in retail loan with the result, market volume is building up by leaps and bounds. The feisty private sector banks like HDFC banks and ICICI bank have already occupied much of the retail space. Public Sector banks are carving out space for themselves through (a) Wider reach (branch network), (b) Large customer base (c) Strong brand presence (d) Large product portfolio (e) Multiple delivery channels and (f) Leveraging technology (to handle large volumes).

Retail Loan-Going Rural as New Market Mantra

India's smaller cities and towns are beginning to assert themseleves in the credit market place as among the top 100 cities. The share of non-metros in total bank credit increased to 28% in 2003-04 from 15% in 2001-02. Further per capita income in rural India is Rs. 9481 where as in urban India it is Rs. 19,407 but in rural place no body pays for drinking water, primary health care or home rent. So disposable income in rural India is really high. As per NCEAR survey over a third of our middle class (annual household income of Rs. 2 lakhs to Rs. 10 lakhs) live in rural areas and another sixth reside in small towns of population less than 5 lakh. Consumer growth is taking place at fast pace in 17113 villages with population of more than 5000. Of these 9989 villages are in 7 states, namely Andhra Pradesh, Bihar, Kerala, Maharashtra, Tamilnadu, Uttar Pradesh and West Bengal. All this data indicates the amount of buying power of great rural India. It also indicates existence of enormous business opportunities particularly for retail loans. With more than 40000 rural and semi urban branches having powerful bonding with the customers and their implicit faith, banks are uniquely positioned to exploit this opportunity. Some of the major challenges of the rural marketing are- (a) scattered nature of population, (b) diversity, (numerous languages and dialects, caste, culture and religion) (c) poor connectivity leading to high distribution cost and (d) communication problem problem (low literacy and limited reach of mass media). Going rural is the new market mantra for public sector banks.

Modern Trends in Retail Banking

Capturing the trend and progress of retail banking in India would require dividing retail banking by products, services and technology at the very least. Even this classification would be quite simplistic, as the broad categories mentioned, could get further subdivided. For instance, speaking about the services rendered to a customer of retail banking, 'customer relationship management' (CRM) would be one of the areas of study. However, CRM is not a monolith, but has several nuances. It Includes but may not be limited to exception based banking wealth mangement, KYC-compliance and AML, internet and mobile banking, product life-cycle management, customer data integration and relationship banking among others (Dutt, 2006). Furthermore, being qualitative in nature, it is not possible to easily delineate the trends in customer services in terms of measurable quantities unless one conducts a survey of customers using the various bank services.

Products

There are two ways to look at bank products that are offered to customers. The traditional products (and the new ways in which they are offered) and new products. The website of any of the banks in India, would typically show the following products in the retail banking segment:

(a) Deposits
(b) Loans (housing, personal, educational, etc.)
(c) Investments
(d) Cards
(e) Insurance
(f) Demat services
(g) Online services.

It may be noted that deposits are parts of the liabilities of the banks, whereas all other products mentioned are either its assets or a part of its fee-based services. Therefore, only for deposits, banks have to 'pay' its customers, i.e. have an obligation towards them; whereas in case of the other products, the customers have to 'pay' the banks, i.e; customers have an obligation to the bank (other than online services, perhaps). While the above are provided to Indian residents, Non Resident Indians (NRIs) are provided remittance services and property solutions in addition to some of the products/services offered to resident Indians.

Services

Services means the ways in which bank customers are served. It may be divided into services provided through the branch, the internet and through mobile phones. Branch banking, also referred to as the brick and mortar banking, is the traditional way in which banking was/is conducted all over the world. The customer is a customer of the branch and gets all his/her banking services at the branch - be it depositing or withdrawing money, applying for a loan, getting an update on the passbook, etc. The advantage of 'branch banking is that it brings the bank and the customer face-to-face with each other. This face-to-face banking has a new variant these days, i.e; 'doorstep banking'-where there is still a direct interface with the customer but now it is the bank which visits the customer rather than the other way around. Despite various new ways in which customers are being served, branch banking still remains relevant all over the world. Even in a developed country like UK, studies have shown that over half of UK's bank customers visit the banks branch at least once a month even for mundane tasks like deposting cheques or withdrawing cash (Calder, 2006).

Technology

Retail banking would not have traversed the path it has in the recent times, if technology had not kept pace or shown the direction. Technological development has been hugely responsible for such rapid growth and spread of retail banking and products. In some instances like the Automated Teller Machines (ATMs), technology solutions have been a few steps ahead of customer problems (Global Finance, 2000). However, though technology has provided customers with solutions for their problems, it has also been accused of taking the customer away from the bank and making banking a non-intimate activity. That is why, banks the world over are not completely neglecting the 'brick and mortar' banking even while making rapid strides in clicks banking. Here, it will not be out of order to describe the factors responsible for expansion of retail banking, which can be termed as 'the drivers of economic growth also.

The Driver of Economic Growth

The spurt of retail credit in sectors like consumer finance, automobiles, two-wheelers, financial services, home loans, education and credit card indirectly helps the economy by pushing up the sales of the products and services involved. Government has increasingly pushing lending to this segment, because it has multiplier effect on the growth of the economy. The following factors have contributed to the explosion of retail banking world-over in the recent times:

First, economic prosperity and the consequent increase in puchasing power have given a fillip to a consumer boom. Note that during the 10 years after 1992, India's economy grew at an average rate of 6.8 per cent and continued to grow at almost the same rate which is not matchable in many countries of the world.

Second, changing consumer demographics indicate vast potential for growth in consumption, both qualitatively and quantitatively. India is one of the countries having highest production (70%) of the population below 35 years of age (young population). The BRIC report of the Goldman-Sachs, which predicted a bright future for Brazil, Russia, India and China, mentioned Indian demographic advantage as an important positive factor for India.

Third, technological factors played a major role. Technological innovations relating to increasing use of credit/debit cards, ATMs, direct debits and internet and phone banking have contributed to the growth of retail banking in India.

Fourth, the Treasury income of the banks, which had strengthened the bottom lines of banks for the past few years, has been on the decline during the last three years. In such a scenario, retail business provides a good vehicle of profit maximisation. Considering the fact that retail's share in impaired assets is far lower than the overall bank loans and advances, retail loans have put comparatively less provisioning burden on banks apart from diversifying their income streams.

Fifth, decline in interest rates has also contributed to the growth of retail credit by generating the demand for such credit.

Retail Banking in India: A Profile

The clients of the banks can be divided into three sectors: business, households and Government. In India, agriculture would be another sector.. Globally, growth in retail banking has received a shot in the arm in recent times due to reduced dependence of the business sector on bank credit. Traditionally, corporates have been the biggest clients of the banks. In India, during the slowdown in the recent times, banks had resorted to excess investment in Government securities (reflected in the excess SLR investment as compared to requirements).

With the economy having turned around and corporates resorting to borrowing from other sources, such as; equity issuances and external debt borrowings, households have started gaining importance in the bank's lending business.

Economic growth, which is cited as one of the important propellers of the growth of retail banking in India, is reflected in the income of the households. Income can be mainly divided into consumption and savings. Both provide fuel to the engine of retail banking. Let us examine the savings pattern in India as it directly affects deposit of lending. A notable feature of domestic savings in India is the upturn in the trend of public savings (Table 2).

Table 2
Domestic Savings in India (% of GDP at Current Market Prices)

	1999-2000	*2000-2001*	*2001-2002*	*2002-2003*	*2003-2004*	*2004-2005*
Gross Domestic Savings	24.9	21.2	23.6	26.5	28.9	29.1
(a) Public savings	-0.9	1.8	-2	-0.7	1	22
(b Private savings	25.7	25.3	25.6	27.2	27.9	26.8
Household	21.3	23.5	22	23.1	23.5	22
Financial	10.5	10.2	10.8	10.3	11.5	10.3
Physical	10.7	11	11.2	12.7	12	11.7

Source: Economic Survey 2005-06, Government of India.

It has turned from 2003-04. There is not much change in the share of private savings and household savings in India. It has remained more or less steady except in 2004-05, when domestic private savings reported a lower share than in the previous year, as did household savings. Since this has coincided with the fall in public savings it might beg the question of public savings 'crowd in' private savings in India. It may be noted that household savings in financial assets have always been lower than those in physical assets indicating perhaps to the inadequate reach of financial products in the country. Thus, there is nothing in the household savings data that would suggest an explosion in retail banking.

Let us explore this idea further. We examine the data for the latest three years for two reasons: One, the rate or growth of bank credit, which had touched a low of 1.4 per cent in 2002-03, accelerated to more than 30 per cent in 2004-05, and this was maintained in 2005-06. The turnaround has thus happened from 2003-04 onwards. Two, within bank credit, retail loans have been the prime drivers only in 2004-05 and 2005-06 (RBI, 2006). It may be desirable to have a brief look at the trends in deposits and bank credit in the latest years-since 2003-04.

Table 3

Commercial Bank Survey (% Age Variations)

	2003-04	*2004-05*	*2005-06*
Aggregate Deposits of residents	20.3	15.0	19.9
Demand Deposits	32.1	10.2	27.5
Time Deposits of Residents	18.3	14.3	18.4
Shor term Deposits	18.3	14.3	18.4
Certificates of Deposits	-	-	186.6
Long-term Deposits	18.3	14.3	18.4
Bank Credit	15.3	20.9	30.8
Non-food Credit	18.4	31.6	31.8

Source: RBI's Trend and Progress of Banking in India (2004-05, 2005-06).

From the above table it could be seen that growth in aggregate deposits of the residents had taken a dip in 2004-05 and had then substantially recovered in 2005-06. Within the deposits, the growth in demand deposits was most affected in 2004-05 and the recovery had been the highest in this category as well. It may be noted that short-term and long-term deposits had identical growth rates in all the three years viz., 2003-04, 2004-05 and 2005-06. It may be safely assumed that a good portion of these categories of deposits would belong to the retail depositors. Thus, one finds that there is no significant change in the growth variation of deposits between 2003-04 and 2005-06. Therefore, there is additional reason to believe that the rise in retail financing in 2005-06 was not driven by growth in retail deposits.

It is interesting to note that among the various types of deposits, there was a substantial growth in certificates of deposits or CDs (high value instruments of deposits of not less than rupees one lakh denomination) in 2005-06. However, since the variation is based on low/negligible base in the previous years, the percentage variation in 2005-06 could be seen too steep.

Table 4
Deployment of Retail Loans by Banks in India (variation)

(amount in Rs. crore)

	2003-04	*2004-05*	*2005-06*
Gross bank credit	94849	193229	404928
Non-food gross bank credit	108367	188069	405358
Housing	15394 (14.2)	23192 (12.3)	57701 (14.2)
Consumer durables	1055 (0.97)	108 (0.06)	300 (0.07)
Advances against Fixed Deposits	3638 (3.36)	3259 (1.73)	5047 (1.25)
Credit Card Outstandings		N.A.	3417 (0.84)
Loans to individuals against shares/Bonds, etc.	19 (0.02)	366 (0.2)	972 (0.24)
Education		N.A.	4938 (1.22)
Other non-priority sector Personal loans	7260 (6.7)	24876 (13.2)	36922 (9.1)

Source: RBI's Report on Trend and Progress of Banking in India (2004-05, 2005-06).

\# Figures in brackets are percentage share of each of the components in the total non-food gross bank credit

Yet, the contribution of CDs cannot be ignored. It may have contributed to the growth in retail loan products of the banks. It may also be noted that bank credit hasdseen substantial variation in 2004-05 over 2003-04 and in 2005-06 over 2004-05. In 2004-05, this was despite the dip in the growth rate of the various deposits and negligible growth in CDs. It is needed to examine the trends within bank credit, especially non-food credit.

It may be mentioned that RBI's latest Report Trend and Progress of Banking in India (2005-06) states that the data for 2005-06 may not be strictly comparable in absolute numbers to the previous years because of re-classification of sectors and also because the data for 2005-06 had been based on 52 banks as compared to 47 banks in the previous years (at least 2004-05). Therefore, we may restrict ourselves to comparing the shares of the various sectors in the gross bank credit extended that year over the the last couple of years. It would at least provide a clue on whether or not banks had drastically reshuffled their retail loan portfolio in the last couple of years. Some observations from the above Table (4) could be mentioned as follows:

- The share of housing loan in non-food credit had not changed dramatically in the last couple of years. In fact, at 14.2 per cent in 2005-06, the share of housing loans to non-food gross bank credit of the banks was the same as in 2003-04.
- The share of loans for financing consumer durables had actually been lower in 2004-05 and 2005-06 than in 2003-04.
- Share of advances against Fixed Deposit products (which include FCNR (B) and NRNR Deposits) had declined in 2004-05 as well as in 2005-06.
- Share of loans against shares/bonds, etc. had remained steady at 0.2% in the last three years.
- The share of non-priority sector personal loans had more than doubled in 2004-05 as compared to 2003-04, but had declined in 2005-06.

The retail banking activities are on the radar of the RBI, prompting it to take several steps in the recent past viz., increasing the risk weight assigned for a bank's exposure to real estate loans, capping the exposure of bank's lending to individuals for investing in 'Initial Public Offerings (IPOs)' of companies and so on. The gap in the growth rate of deposits and loans has also prompted the RBI to advise banks on the needs to re-balance their portfolio to ensure that they do enough to mobilise deposits while expanding their retail lending portfolio. Offering 'no-frills' deposit accounts to those in the lower income strata of the society is a major step taken by the banks to mobilise deposits and it is being actively supported by the RBI and the Government of India.

Sustainability is an issue that is being increasingly questioned with respect to the growth in retail banking in South Asia including India. Some of the factors that are prompting such questions are: excessive concentration on top-line without taking into the quality of growth of the top-line, increasing market share by increasing risk appetite and entering markets, where a bank may not have a competitive advantage (herd behaviour), among others (Pitman, 2006). While most Indian banks maintain the prescribed capital adequacy ratio, unsustainable growth could squeeze the banks bottom-lines especially when there is a cyclical downturn. Despite significant contribution and desirability of retail banking in India to promote the 'lower income strats of the country, there are some reflexive opportunities and refraincing challenges before its working and performances.

Opportunities and Challenges of Retail Banking

Retail banking has immense opportunities in a growing economy like india. As the growth story gets unfolded in India, retail banking is going to emerge as a major driver. The rise of the Indian middle class is an important contributory factor in this regard. The percentage of middle to high income Indian households is expected to continue rising. The younger population not only wields increased purchasing power, but as far as acquiring personal debt is concerned, they are perhaps more comfortable than previous generations. Improving consumer purchasing power, coupled with more liberal attitudes towards personal debt, is contributing to India's retail banking segment.

The combination of the above factors promises substantial growth in the retail sector, which at present is in the nascent stage. Due to bundling of services and delivery channels, the areas of potential conflicts of interest tend to increase in universal banks and financial conglomerates. Some of the key policy issues relevant to the retail banking sector are: financial inclusion responsible lending, access to finance, long-term savings, financial capability, consumer protection, regulation and financial crime prevention.

While the banks in India might be looking to rebalance of the portfolio, there are other facets of retail banking which they are also actively considering . One such facet is finding the competitive advantage in retail banking that would help each bank to reach out and retain the customer. Product homogeneity has become the norm. Therefore, product differentiation will provide a bank with an edge over competition and help it gain market share. Products have to be differentiated by user category as well. For instance, banks often classify their retail customers into 'branch loyalists', 'branch depositors', 'multi-channelers' and 'fully automated' (Pitman, 2006), or they may classify them as 'simplifiers', 'self directed', 'advice seekers' and 'fickle' (Sambamurthy, 2006). What each system of the classification norms reveals is that, the focus will increasingly have to be on the customer and products may have to be designed accordingly.

Following are the challenges to the industry and its stakeholders:

First, retention of customers is going to be a major challenge. According to a research by Reichheld and Sasser in the Harvard Business Review, 5 per cent increase in customer retention can increase profitability by 35 per cent in banking business, 50 per cent in insurance and brokerage, and 125 per cent in the consumer credit card market. Thus, banks need to emphasise retaining customers and increasing market share.

Second, rising indebtedness could turn out to be a cause for concern in the future. India's position, of couse, is not comparable to that of the developed world where household debt as a proportion of disposable income is much hiher. Such a scenario creates high uncertainty. Expressing concerns about the high growth witnessed in the consumer credit segments, the Reserve Bank has as a temporary measure, put in place risk containment measures and increased the risk weight from 100 per cent to 125 per cent in the case of consumer credit including personal loans and credit cards, (*Mid-term Review of Annual Policy, 2004-05*).

Third, information technology posses both opportunities and challenges. Even with ATM machines and Internet Banking, many consumers still prefer the personal touch of their neighbourhood branch bank. Technology has made it possible to deliver services throughout the branch bank network, providing instant updates to checking accounts and rapid movement of money for stock transfers. However, this dependency on the network has brought IT departments additional responsibilities and challenges in managing, maintaining and optimizing the performance of retail banking networks. Illustratively, ensuring that all bank products and services are available at all times and across the entire organization, is essential for today's retails banks to generate revenues and remain competitive. Besides, there are network management challenges, whereby keeping these complex, distributed networks and applications operating properly in support of business objectives becomes essential. Specific challenges include ensuring that account transaction application run efficiently between the branch offices and data centres.

Fourth, KYC issues and money laundering risks in retail banking are also important. Retail lending is often regarded as a low risk area for money laundering because of the perception of the sums involved. However, competition for clients may also lead to KYC procedures being waived in the bid for new business, Banks must also consider seriously the type of identification documents they will accept and other processes to be completed. The Reserve Bank of India has issued detailed guidelines on application of KYC norms in November 2004.

Future of Retail Banking

Discussions on the future of retail banking invariably draw comparisons to other retail businesses such as food chains, grocery stores, garment stores and even the airline industry. There is talk of emulating the best practices of each of these industries in retail banking. some experiments are already underway such as, making retail banking products available at outlets other than banks e.g, post offices. Banks have been increasingly looking at post offices as partners in reaching the rural masses. The RBI has recently asked the Indian Banks Association to explore the possibility of banks tying up with post offices to provide rural credit. This scheme is initially being experimented within Maharashtra and will be implemented in other states, if it turns out successful (IIBF, 2006). While the channels of delivery may multiply, the banks will have to work with two caveats: one, banking products (loan products) get derived either from money for which they are acting as custodians (deposits). Two, unlike with other retail businesses where footfalls in their premises are sales opportunities, footfalls in bank premises add to the operational cost of the banks. The rising costs of servicing customer at the branches had spawned off-location ATM centres and online/telephone banking. But though ATMs have led to a decline in cost per transaction, they have increased the cost per customer (Sambamurthy, 2006). Call centres too are viewed more as cost centres than as a source for generating revenues. Though there is some trend worldwide for converting service calls into sales calls in retail banking, the pace has been rather slow (Eichfeld et. al, 2006). Branch is where the action is likely to happen in the coming days in banking. The attestation of making efforts to find out some of the attributes leading to the emergence and desirability of 'retail banking' of course, does deserve attention there.Following are the major attributes of the shape of things to come in this sector

First, customer service should be 'the be-all' and' end all' of retail banking. The a document released by the British Bankers Association, entitled "UK Retail Bankers Manifesto": Addressing the Challenges that Lie Ahead for the Industry and its Stakeholders (September 29,2000), analyzed the key polilcy sector and highlighted the role of financial inclusion, responsible lending, access to finance, and consumer protection. It is in this context, that one is reminded of the needs to develop the standards and codes for banking. The contribution of the Committee on Procedure and Performance Audit on Public Services (CPPAPS) (Chairman: Shri S.S. Tarapore), has been invaluable and has provided great insight. Based on the recommendation of the CPPAPS, the Annual Policy Statement for 2005-06 announced the decision to set up an independent Banking Codes and Standards Board of India on the Model of the Mechanism in the Uk in order to ensure that comprehensive code of conduct of fair treatment of customer is evolved and adhered to. The codes and standards, together with the institutional mechanism to monitor them, are expected to enhance the quality of customer services to the individual customer in particular. The codes will bring about greater transparency in the system and also tackle the issue of information asymmetry. The Board would function as an industrywide watchdog of the banking codes and ensure that the banks comply with the banking codes. The codes would establish the banking industry's key commitments and obligations to customers on standards of practice, disclosure and principles of conduct for their banking services. The Board will monitor compliance with the codes by the affiliated banks.

Second, sharing of information about the credit history of households is extremely important as far retail banking is concerned. Perhaps due to the confidential nature of banker-customer, banks have a traditional resistance to share credit information on the client, not only with one another, but also across sectors. Globally, Credit Information Bureaus have, therefore, been set up to function as a repository of credit information, both current and historical data on existing and potential borrowers. The database maintained by these institutions can be accessed by the lending institutions. Credit Bureaus have been established not only in countries with developed financial systems, but also in countries with relatively less developed financial markets, such as Sri Lanka,

Mexico, Bangladesh and the Philippines. In Indian case, the Credit Information Bureau India Limited (CIBIL), incorporated in 2000, aims at fulfilling the needs of credit granting institutions for comprehensive credit information by collecting, collating and disseminating credit information pertaining to both commercial and consumer borrowers. At the same time banks must exercise due diligence before declaring a borrower as defaulter.

Third, outsourcing has become an important issue in the recent past. With the increasing market orientation of the financial system and to cope up with the competition as also to benefit from the technological innovations such as, e-banking, the banks are making increasing use of "outsourcing" as a means of both reducing costs and achieving better efficiency. While outsourcing does have various cost advantages, it has the potential to transfer risk, management and compliance to third parties who may not be regulated. A recent BIS Report on "Outsourcing in Financial Services" developed some high-level principles. A basic requirement in this context is, that a regulated entity seeking to outsource activities should have in place a comprehensive policy on outsourcing including a 'comprehensive outsourcing risk mangement programme' to address the outsourced activies and the relationship with 'the services provider. Application of these principles in the Indian context is under consideration.

Finally, retail banking does not refer to lending only. In the whole story of retailing, one should not forget the role played by retail depositors. The homemaker, the retail shop keeper, the pensioners, self-employed and those employed in unorganised sector-all need to get a place in the banks. It is in this backdrop that 'the Annual Policy for 2005-06' pointed out issues relating to financial exclusion and had announced that the RBI would implement policies to encourage banks which provide extensive services, while disincentivising those which are not responsive to the banking needs of the community, including the underprivileged. Furthermore, the nature, scope and cost of services need to be monitored to assess whether there is any denial, implicit or explicit of basic banking services to the common persons and banks have been urged to review their existing practices to align them with the objectives of financial inclusion.

From the above discussion it is evident that retail banking seems to have come to a full circle. It started with 'branch banking and after going through a phase of 'non-intimate banking, it has once again come back to 'branch banking'. And, it seems that branch is a reality that is here to stay. The value of branch banking is viewed as arising from the benefits of face-to-face interaction, shared tactile experience and establishing an informal bond between the customers and the bank (DiVanna, 2004). Branches are also graduating from being plain 'vanilla teller-driven' places for execution of transactions to being 'state-of-the-art' places which aim to improve the total customer experience.

Conclusion

'Excelling and managing customer relationships are the future of any business, or everybody's business being Customer focusing is not to be viewed just as a business strategy but should become a corporate mission. Unless this mission percolates through out the organisation at all levels, the chances are that the attempts to address customer issues, will receive only lip sympathy. Building value for customers should be seen as equal to building shareholder value. The challenge for banks will be in the area of people (changing their beliefs and attitudes), technology and competition.

The financial sector reforms emphasised the commercial character of the banking system and helped banks to compete with others. Banks, both in private sector, as-well-as, in public sector have to gear up their speed to adopt the fast changing technology. Organisational structures have to be changed to suit the customer needs. Banks should realise that the customer is the "focus point" to improve the business. Banks have to evolve plans and strategies to cater better services and enhance satisfaction levels and try to create a brand image.

Skills of personnel working in front office, as-well-as support services should be enhanced through continuous and updated training programmes. Service culture is to be developed among the staff. HRD standards should be maintained in recruitment and selection of personnel at all levels. Customer service should be the main motto for improvement of business.

Technology implementation should be speeded up, such as computerisation, electronic banking through e-mail, tele-banking, mobile phone banking and wide net of ATMs through channel migration process.

All these factors will help to increase customer service. Ultimately banks should prove that they are providing essential services as already branded for development of the economy. The banking industry is vibrant and active in India due to technological revolution. Banks will have to utilise this opportunity to become more and more strong organisations providing essential services.

The changing portfolio of retail banking in India has many dimensions. While there is a discernible change in the number and nature of products being tossed up along-with the way, in which banking services are being offered, there is also a concern (especially in the mind of the regulator) that growth in retail banking is skewed in favour of assets and is not balanced equally with growth in liabilities (retail deposits). An added concern is that banks are not reaching out to the lower income segments of the population. However, banks in India have already started taking steps to include those so far excluded from formal banking services. To foster the growth in retail banking, banks have started sharing up their services through various channels keeping the main focus on the bank branch. It is going to be challenging for banks to maintain costs at a level such that their profitability is not affected; a concern that soon may become a top priority for them in the near future.There is a need of constant innovation in retail banking. In bracing for tomorrow, a paradigm shift in bank financing through innovative products and mechanisms involving constant upgradation and revalidation of the banks' internal systems,and processes is called for. Banks now need to use retail as a growth trigger. This requires product development and differentiation, innovation and business process like re-engineering, micro-plannig, marketing, prudent pricing, customisation, technological upgradation, home/electronic/mobile banking, cost reduction and cross-selling.

While retail banking offers phenomenal opportunities for growth, the challenges are equally daunting. How far the retail banking is able to lead growth of the banking industry in future, would depend upon the capacity building of the banks to meet the challenges and make use of the opportunities profitably. However, the kind of technology used and the efficiency of operations would provide the much needed competitive edge for success in retail banking business. Furthermore, in all these, customers' interest is of paramount importance.

References

Gopinath, Shyamala (2005), ' Retail Banking Opportunities and Challenges', *Reserve Bank of India Bulletin,* June 2005 *http://en.wikipedia.org/wiki/Bank accessed on 4th Aughust, 2006.*

Global Finance (2000), 'Retail Banks Under Siege', *http://www.allbusiness.com/technology/internet technology/. 8828501. html accessed on 1st Nov. 2006.*

Pitman, Brian (2006), 'Building a Sustainable and Profitable Retail Banking Franchise', Address at the *Retail Bankers Academy South Asia, 2006* Organised by the Asiab Banker and IIBF held on 16-17 November, 2006 at Mumbai.

Sambamurthy, B. (2006), 'Re-engineering the Branch', Presentaion at the *Retail Bankers Academy South Asia, 2006* Organised by the Asian Banker and IIBF held on 16-17 November, 2006 at Mumbai.

Divanna, Joseph A. (2004), 'The Future of Retail Banking', Palgrave Macmillan New York.

www.google.com.

Online edition of *Economic Times.*

Online edition of *The Hindu Business lines.*

34

Bancassurance: Issues and Scope for the Banks

Manju Kumari

Bancassurance has started taking strong roots in our country and there are expectations that average collection through banking channel will rise to 50% in next five years. This product offers vast cross selling opportunity to banks by bundling with their own financial products besides building fee-based income. There are several reasons why banks should consider bancassurance: for one, it can increase return on assets because banks can increase their fee income through sale of insurance products. Banks which effectively cross-sell financial products can leverage their distribution and processing capabilities for profitable operating expense ratio. Banks with their wide branch network spread over the country (with more than 70,000 branches) have a very good opportunity to enter the insurance business since; the network has 33,000 rural branches and 14,000 semi-urban branches, where insurance penetration remains largely untapped. More than 8.5 lakh manpower of these banks can help in effective distribution of insurance products. In today's competitive environment, offering more and more services under one roof would also help banks to improve their market share. This will result in easy access to claims settlement, cost savings and improved financial products. Customers will be able to obtain financial consultancy services from trained staff of the banks.

The success of bancassurance in France has been mainly due to the convenience factor. Banks have significant brand awareness within their geographical region, which facilitates the marketing of insurance products at lower per head cost. The banks large customer data base containing the names, profiles and contact numbers, etc. becomes very useful to the insurance companies. The expected higher conversion ratio (using bank database) into sales means higher productivity than other agencies. Moreover, they also have access to multiple communication channels such as direct mail, ATMs, telemarketing, internet banking, etc.

This new venture would also help banks in better asset liability management. Banks convert liquid short-term liabilities into long-term assets. It exposes them to default rate risk, liquidity risk and interest rate risk. By owning an insurance activity, banks can accumulate huge and stable liabilities by collecting premium and can decrease its vulnerability to different types of risks. In order to capture these long-term liabilities, banks have to develop their long-term liabilities, banks have to develop their long-term savings product portfolio to include many of the structured products used by insurance industry.

Challenges before Banks in Entering into Insurance

The insurance business faces a number of risks like underwriting risk, timing risk and investment risk. As a part of proactive management, these risks call for maintenance of adequate capital at all times. With huge level of NPAs for which banks have to maintain large provisions without earning anything on them, it becomes even more difficult to meet capital adequacy level standards. The banks in the country are already saddled with high level of NPAs that are eating away into their profitability. It also puts to an end to the recycling of funds mobilized, on which cost is being incurred. Presently, five PSBs have a capital lower than 10% of risk weighted assets. With the tightening of capital adequacy norms, banks need more capital for normal banking operations. Experience shows that fresh issues of capital are also not taken enthusiastically. Insurance business requires large capital in the beginning and further, even more for the purpose of growth.

Moreover, the forces of change that are sweeping through the banking system worldwide have further increased the volume and the potential impact of risks facing the bank. In fact, the speed, volume, value and complexity of international transactions have established new linkages and interdependency between markets and institutions which have the potential to transmit problems and disruptions from one place/institution to another, at breakneck speed. Risks that banks face can be broadly divided into two groups: balance sheet risks and off balance sheet risks. Balance sheet risks include leverage risk, capital inadequacy, asset management risk (liquidity and credit risk), liability management risk, etc. Other key risk elements include the technological risk, regulatory risk, operating risk, exchange rate risk and customer risk. Moreover, banks are facillitators of payments. They deal in short term funds, both on the deposits and on the advances front. There is a doubt about their capability to venture into a business such as insurance which involves dealing in long term funds and requires a high degree of expertise in risk assessment and forecasting. Risk assessment in insurance is complex and involves a detailed actuarial exercise. In life insurance, the risk is measured in terms of obligations assumed by way of policies outstanding for the remaining tenure and in terms of yield levels guaranteed on the policies over their tenure.

Contributing Factors for Potential Growth of Bancassurance in India

Traditionally, banks transform short-term liabilities into long-term assets. This generate credit risk on the asset side and liquidity risk on the liabilities side. The maturity mismatch between assets and liabilities makes the banks vulnerable to interest rate risk. The bank can address this specific issue by entering into the insurance business. An insurance activity accumulates substantial amount as premium receipts. With long-term funds banks can decrease the possibility of liquidity and solvency problems.

Even if banking and insurance are carried out through separate entities, through a holding arrangement, an insurance outfit can offer a potential source of liquidity for the parent.

All over the world, governments are known to intervene in the insurance business through regulations. Keeping in view its long term asset management cycle; the Indian Government has also issued detailed guidelines regarding the same. IRDA has made it mandatory for every insurer who starts business after the commencement of IRDA Act, 1999 to ensure the prescribed levels of business from rural and social sectors. The guidelines mention that a life insurer must cover a minimum business of 5% in the first financial year; 7% in the second financial year, 10% in the third financial year; 12% in the fourth financial year and 15% in the fifth year of total policies written during that year for the rural areas. In respect of a general insurer, the prescribed limit is -2% in the first financial year; 3% in the second financial year and 5% thereafter of total gross premium income of that year for rural areas. In respect of the social sector, all insurers are supposed to cover 5000 lives in the first financial year, 7500 lives in the second financial year; 10,000 lives in the third financial year; 15,000 lives in the fourth financial year and 20,000 lives in the fifth financial year. These rural and socially disadvantaged sectors are very difficult to service.

They are scattered geographically in small indigenous social groups and it is very difficult to identify their needs and design the products that are viable as well as acceptable to them. In fact, the real issue is cost effectiveness but the marriage of banks and insurance can provide substantial synergy here. Massive infrastructure and the fact that the spread of banks possess a vast array of market intelligence (including for the rural and disadvantaged sections) can be leveraged to design appropriate products for the specific requirements of the target population. Collaboration between banks and insurance can be of great benefit to service this target group in a cost effective and financially viable manner. Generally, insurance companies suffer from substantial losses in the initial years of their operation, especially due to a social obligation mandated by the Government. International experience shows that even in relatively developed countries, it takes a long time to reach out to less privileged regions and segments of the population. Obviously, in India the problem is much larger and complex and bancassurance is an appropriate strategy in this connection. In fact, if banks enter into a fast growing sector like insurance, the problem of excess staff can be overcome easily. Of course, banking personnel needs rigorous training to adapt to insurance business. But given the opportunity and requisite training, they can also become successful in the insurance sector.

Current Scenario of Bancassurance in India

With the insurance industry being opened up for banks, a number of the PSBs, newly established private banks and foreign banks are seeking opportunities in this market. Bancassurance is emerging as an important distribution channel for insurance in India. Some insurance companies like SBI life are heavily devoting their resources to implementing bancassurance successfully. There are several insurance companies and their individual banking partners with which they have bancassurance arrangements (Table 1). Several features can be observed from this list of partnerships : the first feature is the 'natural partnerships'. Specifically, HDFC Standard Life is linked to HDFC Bank, ICICI Prudential Life with ICICI Bank, and so on. The second striking feature is the proliferation of banks partnering with single insurance companies. Given that there are only two dozen insurance companies and hundreds of banks, this outcome was anticipated. The third feature is best illustrated by an example. Allianz Bajaj does not have the same banking partners in the life sector as in the non - life sector. The same is true for several other companies. Coupled with concerns over privacy of customer data, it is known that the regulators prefer banks to have exclusive corporate agency relationship with only one insurer. As can be seen from Table 1, insurance companies can have tie-up with a number of banks.

Table 1
Existing Relationships between Insurance Companies and Banks

Life insurance Company	*Banking Partner*
HDFC	Standard Union Banks of India, Indian Bank, HDFC Bank
ICICI Prudential	Federal Bank, ICICI Bank, Bank of India Punjab & Maharashtra co-operative Bank, Allahabad Bank, South Indian Bank, Citibank, Lord Krishna Bank, Goa State Co-operative Bank, Indore Paraspar Sahakari Bank, Manipal State Co-operative Bank and, Manipal State Co-operative Bank and Jalgaon People's Co-operative Bank, Shamrao Vithal Co-operative Bank.
Birla SunLife	Citibank, Deutsche Bank, IDBI Bank, Development Credit Bank, Bank of Rajasthan, Bank Muscat, Catholic Syrian Bank Ltd., Andhra Bank, Karpur Vysya Bank Ltd.
Tata AIG	HSBC, Citibank, IDBI Bank, Union Bank of India
Old Mutual KM	None
SBI Life	SBI, BNP Paribas
ING Vysya	Vysya Bank, Bharat Overseas Bank
Allianz Bajaj	Standard Chartered Bank, Syndicate Bank
MetLife	Dhanalakshmi Bank, J & K Bank, Karnataka Bank
AMP Sanmar	Manjeri Co-operative, Perunthalmanna Bank, Nilambur Bank (all Kerala Based).
Aviva	ABN Amro, American Express, Canara Bank, Lakshmi Vilas Bank.
LIC	Corporation Bank, Oriental Bank of Commerce, recently signed MoU with Nedungadi Bank, Central Bank of India, Indian Overseas Bank, and Bank of Punjab, Vijaya Bank, Centurion Bank, The City Union Bank Ltd. Repco Bank.
Bajaj Allianz	Bank of Punjab, Bank of Rajasthan, Jammu & Kashmir Bank, Karur Vysya Bank, Lord Krishna Bank, Punjab & Sind Bank, Shamrao Vithal Co-operative Bank, Karnataka Bank.

Contd...

Life insurance Company	*Banking Partner*
Royal Sun Alliance	Citibank, ABN Amro, Standard Chartered, American Express, Repco Bank, SBI-GE, Karur-based Lakshmi Vilas Bank.
Tata AIG	HSBC, IDBI, Development Credit Bank, Union Bank of India.
IFFCO Tokio	Not formally tied up with any bank as yet.
ICICI Lombard	ICICI Bank and others in the pipeline.
Reliance	Not formally tied up with any bank as yet.
United India	Punjab National Bank, Andhra Bank, Dhanalakshmi Bank, Indian Bank, South India Bank, Federal Bank.
New India	Union Bank of India, SBI, Corporation Bank, and United Western Bank.
Oriental	Department of Posts, Oriental Bank of Commerce, State Bank of Saurashtra.

Source: Swiss Re Sigma, No. 7/2002.

Bancassurance has been growing very rapidly in India. Within two years till 2004, the share of insurance business distributed through bancassurance has gone from 0% to 20% of new business in the private sector.

Table 2
Bancassurance Business Conducted by Companies

Company	*% of Policies*
ICICI Prudential	15% in 2002, 30% in 2004
SBI Life	15% in 2002, 50% in 2004
Birla Sun Life	25% in 2002, 40% in 2004
ING Vyasa Life	10% in 2002
Aviva Life	50% in 2002, 70% in 2004
Allianz Bajaj Life	25% in 2003
Royal Sundaram Allianz	40% in 2002
HDFC Standard life	10% in 2002, 40% in 2004
Met Life	25% in 2002

Source: Swiss Re Sigma, No. 7/2002.

Some experts predict that within a decade, it can rise to 35% to 40%. Policies sold through bancassurance add more value. The average size of policy for the agency is Rs. 19,500 whereas for the bancassurance channel, it is Rs. 39,000 per policy (Asia Insurance Post, July 2003). In the General Insurance segment gross premium underwritten went up by 16% during 2005-06 to Rs. 20,378 crore. It was contributed by the four state-owned and 10 private insurance companies. Six out of the ten private companies have made strategic alliances with 28 financial institutions and the state-owned insurers have made strategic alliance with 31 banks. SBI has established a joint venture called SBI-Life Insurance with Cardiff SA of France, whereas ICICI, the largest private sector bank in India, has established its joint venture with Prudential. The company has recruited about 2000 agents to sell policies. It is expected to get Rs. 160 millions in the new insurance premium business. HSBC is the first foreign bank in India to establish its wholly owned insurance subsidiary after acquiring a corporate agency license from the regulators. In spite of all these developments Life Insurance Corporation (LIC) continues to dominate the life insurance business. LIC has also repositioned itself by acquiring a 33.1% stake in Corporation Bank and has increased its share in Oriental Bank of Commerce to 11%.

Yet, despite bancassurance being a very new feature for the Indian insurance market, it is becoming a key channel for the distribution of insurance products. The flexibility demonstrated by IRDA in prescribing the relevant regulatory framework has proven to be a major catalyst in this regard.

Conclusion

We conclude that, by leveraging their strength and findings ways to overcome their weaknesses, banks can change the face of distribution of insurance products. Issues critical to making bancassurance successful are: business model suitability, functional compatibility and attitudinal flexibility. As on 'date, no major insurance company has moved away from bancassurance and the future seems to be bright. The only matter of concern is how the existing players will adjust to the changing scenario of increased competition which is expected to further increase due to entry of big players, both from the banking and insurance sector, to capture the huge untapped market.

References

Sinha Tapen (2003), 'Insurance Industry: Challenges and Prospects', Swiss Reinsurance Company Economic Research and Consulting Working Paper.

Swiss Re Sigma (2002), 'Bancassurance Developments in Asia-Shifting into High Gear' Swiss Reinsurrance Company Economic Research and Consulting Working Paper No. 7/2002.

Sinha Tapen (2005), Bancassurance in India: Who is Tying the Knot and Why?', Working Paper Series, *www.ssrn.com.*

'Bancassurance: Will it Work', *ww.msnindia.com.*

Reserve Bank of India (2003), ' Insurance: The India Experience', RBI Occasional Paper, June.

Reserve Bank of India (2000), 'Insurance and Banking Issues of Overlap', Report on Trend and Progress of Banking in India, Reserve Bank of India, Mumbai.

Krishnamurthy, R. (2000), 'Bancassurance in India: The Emerging Regulatory Issues', *Prajnan*, Vol. XXIX, No. 1, April-June.

Malik, Debasis (2001), 'Insurance Sector: Towards an Assured Future', *Chartered Financial Analyst,* Vol. VI, Issue-X, June.

Gupta, Ashish (2001), 'Today, Behemoths; Tomorrows Universal Banks', *Business Today*, September 2.

Dutta, Sonali (2001), 'SBI Life Insurance Company', *Indian Infrastructure*, Vol. 3, No. 12, July.

Bala Krishra, P. (2001), 'Banks Get Into Insurance', *Indian Infrastructure,* Vol. 3, No. 8, March.

Dorfman, Marks S. (1994), 'Risk Management and Insurance', Prentice Hall, New Jersey.

35

Bancassurance Emerging Trend in India

Avnish Kr. Shukla, Amit Verma &
Pramod Kr. Verma

Bancassurance is a combination of banking and insurance. The concept behind bancassurance is that doing the banking within the marketing of insurance services.

According to Christon De Juniac of Boston consulting group "bancassurance is selling insurance through banking outlets."

According to H. Narayanan "bancassurance is channel for the cost effective distribution of insurance and pension product by penetrating divers market."

The bancassurance term has origin insurance France. This concept came in to existence in mid 1985, when simple interest bearing annuity by the Brand name "sorosaving" under written by L.I.C. Groupama, was distribution through the branches of credit aqricode of France bank. Due to the earlier initiative by Germany in utilizing this bancassurance products are also known as "allfinanz." The main aim of bancassurance is the distribution of insurance product through bank's distribution channels.

Significance there are no. of reasons, why bancassurance is become "hot cake" for the banker, insurer, and customers. For banks it is means of product diversification and source additional fee income. Fee income (non interest income) can cover more of the operating expenses of banks and by product diversification banks can create a great no. of customers also.

Marketing of insurance product, at a time when the interest rates are falling, will help them to recover the loss of insurance on fee based transactions.

Insurance companies see bancassurance as a tool for increasing there market penetration and premium turnover. Insurance companies can take the advantages of bank's Brand, skill full employees, large network of branches and service quality etc. and insurance company can promote their products easily, because the customer visit regularly in bank and take the interest several scheme offer by bank.

From the customer's point of view bancassurance is a bonanza in the term of reduce price, high quality product and delivery door steps. The relationship between a customer and bank is based on loyalty and honesty. Degree of loyalty and honesty is very high in this relationship by which a customer believes easily on banks, offering insurance product as compare to an agent.

Bank and insurance companies complementary to each other on one hand bank can provide lone to customer on the basis of their credit and asset security and on other hand insurance companies assure that there is no loss of security, so all parties are benefited.

Strategy of Bancassurance

Factors are to be considered in formulating bancassurance strategy Brand equity: Brand equity is the positive differential effect that knowing the brand name as on customer response to product or service. The strategy should leverage the bank's brand equity with the customers rationalized bancassurance strategy will built on superior Brand equity of bank by integrating insurance into bank product portfolio and distribution infrastructure.

Distribution System

Distribution system is a process of flowing the product or service to the ultimate consumer through marketing channel as soon as possible. One of the key economic advantages of bancassurance is the saving achieved through efficient utilization of the bank's existing distribution channels.

Technology

Bancassurance should plan a technological infrastructure that will exploit customer information found in the bank's database to uncover sales opportunities and produced transactional simplicity for insurance customers.

Distribution strategy in market: to succeed in emerging market bank marketers will have to develop unique strategy for local customer expectation and bank distribution capability.

A success full bancassurance strategy focused on middle and lower middle income segment of the bank of market place requires insurers to rethink assumptions to fully exploit the potential of the mass market banking channel insurer need new types of distribution, underwriting, administration, policies issue and delivery, premium collection procedure, customer service strategy and sales approaches.

Bancassurance in Indian Scenario

In India no any company can do the business of banking and insurance together, as well as no one insurance company can do the life insurance and general insurance business together, because of guide line given by IRDA that both business should be operate separately. So the Indian banks are not getting as facilities as in European countries.

So in India, bancassurance is a result of alliance, venture, franchisee and as corporate agent. Bank can market both life and general insurance products as a corporate agent. As per banking regulation act 1949, Sec. 6 (1) (0), a bank which is acting as corporate agent for the distribution of insurance product, is permitted to distribute the product of life insurance and non insurance companies.

RBI approval is also required for setting up insurance joint venture with equity participation or for investing in insurance companies for the purpose of providing infrastructure and service support.

For joint venture, RBI has given following guidelines:

- At list net asset of 500 crore
- Non performing asset should be kept at sufficient level
- Net profit of past 3 years
- Well performing records of its subsidiary companies
- Risk bearing ratio should 10% with the capital of banks
- The shares of bank should not be more than 50% of the insurance company, RBI can consider in exceptional cases
- FDI, if any up to 49% of capital.

As for as India is concern the nationalized bank have very wide network of branches. All banks- nationalized banks , private banks, foreign banks, urban banks, rural co-operative banks and regional rural banks together have network of more than 70,000 branches, 50% of the branches work in rural areas, and the banking density is 75 branches per million.

The first Indian international bancassurance conference was held in November 2001. SBI life is confident that in the next 5 year it will generate substantial income through this avenue. ICICI launched its first bancassurance in India in July 2002. Initially the product was offer to ICICI bank's clients. The first product was a term assurance produced under the Brand name "easy life" with accident death cover as rider. An other interesting product that followed was "treasure plus" by AVIVA LIFE insurance company in association with ABN Amro bank life insurance cover a part, that has built in accident and permanent disability benefits.

Future of Bancassurance in India

In the Asian region, countries like Malaysia, Thailand and Singapore are moving towards tapping the potential of the banks to the market insurance product even though in many of these countries, the regulation on Bancassurance are yet to be formalized.

As far as Asian countries are concerned, Bancassurance is the new channel of distribution. As experience indicates, this channel is bound to succeed in the Asian region. India apart, the channel that was launched in Korea during the year 2003 is progressing impressively. Since its introduction in mid 2003 the channel has accounted for sales exceeding $1.25 billion.

The market expectation is that in India too, the concept of Bancassurance should succeed. In India, there are more than 66,000 branches of banks with 50% of them in rural area and 18 cr. regular and loyal customer that banks kept. We can compare banks with insurance branches and see the essential for the development of any bancassurance project. There are a lot of opportunities to provide insurance product to banks visitor and customer through banks branches- sky is limit for the insurance products.

References

Narayan H. (2007), India Insurance: A Profile Marketing, Channels, Jaico Publisher, p. 492-93.

Insurance Institute of India, Life Insurance 2006, p. 249.

Philip Kotlar and Armstrong, Principle of Marketing, Brand, p. 292

Motihar, M. (2007), Insurance: Principle and Practices, Sharda Pustak Bhawan, Allahabad, p. 176-177.

Visit on website: *www.iciciprulife.com*

IRDA act 2002, Licensing to Corporate Agent, Sec. 42 and 42(c)

Statistical abstract 2006.

36

Bancassurance: A Vital Channel for the Banks

Amit Kumar

The liberalization and deregulation of the financial sector, the greater use of financial engineering techniques and models, significant advances in information technology and telecommunications, and growing consumer demands have resulted in greater competition and finer pricing.

As a consequence banks find it more difficult to meet the expectations of shareholders based on net income alone and have to devise new strategies in order to generate more fee based income, and income from non traditional sources. The financial sector today is witnessing a convergence of Banking, insurance business, mutual fund and other financial products. This is evident from the fact that more and more banks/financial institutions are giving one stop services. Distribution of insurance products by Banks through their own network of branches has come to known as Bancassurance.

Bancassurance known as Allfinanz constitutes a package of financial services that can fulfil both banking and insurance needs at the same time. Thus bancassurance is the arrangement whereby branches of a bank distribute insurance products by an insurance company owned wholly or partially by the bank, or the branches distribute products developed by other insurance companies with which the bank has entered into selling arrangement.

Bancassurance-A Win-Win Solution

Bank	*Insurance Company*
• An additional product to be made available to help improve retention ratio of existing customers	• Revenue and channel diversification.
• Satisfaction of more financial needs under the same roof	• Quality Customer access
• Revenue Diversification - Increase in return on assets through fee income.	• Quicker geographical reach
• More profitable resource utilization	• Creation of brand equity
• Enriched work environment	• Leverage service synergies with Bank
• Establish sales oriented culture	• Establish a low cost acquisition channel and increased premium

Bancassurance has grown at different pace and taken shapes and forms in different countries depending upon the demography, economic and legislative prescription in that country. During the last two decades, bancassurance has taken deep roots in various countries, especially in Europe. In UK about a third of policies are sold through banks. In France, banks distribute more than 50 per cent of the total life policies sold in the country. It is relatively new concept in Australia and Asia.

Bancassurance in India

Bancassurance has started picking up after the Insurance Regulatory and Development Authority, IRDA notified Corporate Agency Regulations in October 2002. Since then, a large number of private and public sector insurance companies have tied with banks both in private and public sector for selling insurance products. To name a few LIC with Corporation Bank & Oriental Bank of Commerce, The New India Assurance Co. Ltd. with Punjab National Bank, HDFC

Standard Life with HDFC Bank, Union Bank and Indian Bank, ICICI Prudential with bank of India etc. Allahabad Bank has also proposed to launch a low cost insurance scheme for its depositors. This is gaining more and more popularity due to shrinkage in interest margins. IT is expected that bancassurance will become a major channel of sale of Insurance products in the country as well.

Banks are interested in selling insurance products as they have captive insurance business. They require that their borrowers should get the assets purchased with bank's finance insured and are generating huge business for the insurance companies. Banks have tremendous business opportunities, which can be converted into sales by convincing clients to buy cover from insurance company they have, tie up.

Banks have an established distribution network of more than 65000 branches spread throughout the country. Insurance companies are eager to enhance their geographical reach without any additional cost by utilizing this existing network.

Banks can leverage their brand equity and recognition particularly in rural and urban areas where branch managers enjoy the faith of local people. Banks particularly public sector banks which have gone in big way for computerization and networking, are saddled with surplus staff that needs to be utilized optimally.

The central government has constituted a nine-member study group to examine the issues related to bancassurance. The study group, headed by SBI Life Managing Director and Chief Executive officer R. Krishnamurthy, studied all the issues pertaining to bancassurance.

Entry of Banks in Insurance Business

Banks are now not required to obtain prior approval of RBI to undertake insurance agency business or referral arrangement without any risk participation. This is subject to compliance with IRDA regulations and certain other conditions. However, banks intending to set up insurance joint ventures with equity contribution on risk participation basis or making investments in the insrance companies for providing infrastructure and service support, would continue to obtain the prior approval of RBI. The risks, if any, involved in insurance agency/referral arrangement should not get transferred to the business of the bank.

Public sector banks, newly established private banks and foreign banks, among others, are seeking opportunities in this market. The banks plan to go in for a cross-sell exercise for its existing customers through direct mailers of regular insurance products. Off-the-shelf products would be sold through the customer service executives in the branch lobby; bundled offerings along with auto loans and cards would be sold through the sales force; while complex life products would be sold to high networth customers through relationship managers and investment advisors. Banks are particularly hopeful about insurance products which have synergies with their mainline loan products. Similarly, a housing loan could be entwined with a life insurance policy.

Bancassurance Strategy-Key Steps

Analyse and Select Target Segment

Analyse existing customer profile & market potential. Assess the assumptions about various segments.

Focus on Customer requirements

Provide easy to understand solutions with convenience Meet the needs of each segment-design the product accordingly.

Product Innovation

Design simple and easy to understand Customer need centric

Product Delivery/Distribution

Branch network be utilized for selling insurance products. Delivery channels like Interest/ATMs etc.

Marketing and Distribution Channels

Distribution is the key issue in bancassurance linked to the regulatory climate of the country. Over the years, regulatory barriers between banking and insurance have diminished and has created a cordial climate for bancassurance. Gramm-Leach Billey Act of 1999 in US and IRDA Bill in India in 2000 have stimulated the growth of bancassurance by allowing use of multiple distribution channels by banks and insurance companies.

Insurance products have been promoted and sold principally through agency systems in most countries. With new developments e.g. consumer behaviors, evolution of technology and deregulation, new distribution channels have been developed successfully and rapidly. Bancassurance make use of different distribution channels such as career agents, special advisors, salaried agents, bank employees/platform banking, corporate agencies and brokerage firms, Direct Response and Internet.

Integration of Various Distribution Channels

It seems very difficult for a single distribution channel to successfully reach the bancassurer's goals and specific target markets. Many bancassurers are using multiple distribution channels. This way they are not confined to one channel and they can offer services to a greater number of target markets. Multiple distribution channels provide another valuable feature.

A customer may chosse to query or transact products of an insurance company through various available distribution channels. Customer should get the same information/experience across all the channels. Bank branches need to work in tandem with other channels like Internet and should be a part of an overall unified customer relationship and management strategy.

Bank's Vision

Success of Bancassurance requires that its strategies are consistent with bank's vision. Banks have defined sales process for introducing insurance service and offers simple yet complete products for sale.

Challenges

The common issues in implementing the bancassurance for insurers and banks are commitment of top management, training of staff, accessing database expertise, marketing orientation, framework for incentives, proper manpower management, level of commitment at grass root level, product promotions, integrating market plans, sales channel linkage and resistance to change.

Training of the Bank Staff

Extensive and specialized training must be imparted to banks staff for selling of the insurance products. IRDA also prescribes some minimum training for bank staff before they can start marketing insurance products.

As the insurance market grows, more complex products are introduced; customer becomes more convergent. The bank staff has to compete with the specialist insurers. The banks have to have in place a continuous process for upgrading the skills of the staff.

Technology Focus

The challenge for the banks will be to match the expectations of insurance companies at the distribution points. In developed market, where bancassurance is successfully practiced, the sale of insurance is completed and the customer is serviced almost online. Banks in India have to gear up for substantial IT orientation to undertake insurance distribution.

This in turn would require for several changes in internal systems at most banks. Certain systems are to be installed for effective coordination of sales by bank branches. Further such systems would need to be coordinated with rest of the system at the branch.

Performance Recognition

Bancassurance can be a successful exercise where good selling efforts is recognized and rewarded. For public sector banks, it would be a major challenge to install an arrangement to motivate employees to take higher levels of selling specific products on behalf of outside insurance companies. There is an urgent need to modify the system so as to make employees take stock of their specific contribution in terms of enhancing fee-based income of the branch.

Mining Database

Banks have huge database of the clients. Banks must have relevant and flexible database systems. Bank staff have to learn the art of mining the database to be the leader.

Work Culture

Success of a bancassurance venture requires change in approach, thinking and work culture on part of every body involved. But there is a definite threat of resistance to any change that bancassurance may bring in. Any relocation to a new company or subsidiary or diversion will be resented.

Obstacles/Success Factors

The most common obstacles to success of bancassurance are insufficient product promotion, failure to integrate marketing plans, marginal database expertise, poor sales channel linkages, inadequate incentives, resistance to change, negative attitude towards insurance.

Conversely, the Key Factors for Success of Bancassurance Ventures are

- Significantly lower cost of distribution - due to higher sales productivity
- Bank/Customer relationship.
- The trust and esteem in which customer hold banks.
- The existing bank branch network/infrastructure.
- Bank Customers mostly middle income.
- Life insurance products based on insurers desires (sales driven) rather than consumer's needs (market oriented).

Dual Regulation

The convergence between banking and insurance poses the difficulty of dual regulation. While RBI will regulate the banking arm, the IRDA will look into the insurance operations. Such duality will lead to conflict of interests as well as other related issues.

Cultural Issues in Distribution

The managers of banks and of the insurance companies can come from quite different cultures. There may be differences in the way of thinking and business approaches of bankers and managers of insurance companies. These differences cerate a communication and implementation problem in bancassurance operations. Banks are traditionally demand driven organizations with a reactive selling philosophy. Life insurance organizations are usually need-driven and have an aggressive selling philosophy.

Product Differentiation

Although theoretically public sector banks can achieve cross selling through the large branch network and vast customer base, in practice, realizing such synergies would be far from easy. This is because of the fundamental differences in the product groups viz., banking and insurance as well as the organization culture. An insurance product is "purchased" while a banking product is driven, while in case of an insurance product, the demand is created through hard selling. The organization culture as exists in the banks, which has been shapped over by the demand-driven product structure would pose significant difficulties in cross selling.

Bank and Life Insurance Companies have Different Regulations, Culture and Images

	Bank	*Life Insurer*
Products	Demand Driven (Bought)	Sold (Requires Proactive Sales)
	Process Driven (Forms & Paperwork)	Personality & Relationship Driven
	Short Term	Long Term
	Simple	Complex
People	Does not require Motivation & ego	Require large doses of motivation & ego
	Management Style-Directive	Management Style Relationship
	Conservative	Aggressive

- *Incentive:* The different nature of compensation for bank employees and insurance specialist representatives and agents is a source of conflict. Insurance Companies provide commission to agents commensurate with the efforts made for selling the insurance products. Public sector banks may experience some difficulties in motivating their staff for selling the insurance products. Some incentive mechanism to increase the productivity in marketing insurance products have to be employed.
- While the facility of "one-stop-ship" may be welcomed by bank customers, they may still have preferences to deal with different institutions for varied financial needs. In that case bancassurance strategy may not succeed.
- Banks may alienate their customers in their enthusiasm to cross sell.
- Any intra-group exposures in the banking and insurance arms of the financial conglomerate could get reflected in the consolidated accounts and affect the solvency and liquidity, leading to the financial distress of the bank itself.
- The banks are more involved in life insurance rather than non-life insurance as the banks are generally hesitant to get into non life insurance product distribution because of the perfeived fear of the disputes over the non-life insurance claims leading to the banks losing their banking relationship with the clients as well.
- There are also limits to diversification. Beyond a certain point diversification would add to complexities in managing the organization which could prove counter productive. A relationship between diversification and profitability of industrial conglomerates shows that profits increase up to a point and tapers off thereafter.
- The quick sales process in a banking hall by the bank's staff *vis-a-vis* the home visit of an insurance agent may raise questions as to whether the customer has had

sufficient opportunity to consider the purchase carefully, especially taking into account the long term commitment associated with insurance products. And whether in the limited time available sufficient information was elicited from the customer to sell based on the customer's needs rather than merely pushing a product.

- Evidence suggests that in countries where local banks have been powerful players in the economy and play important role in local communities, they have proved to be efficient channels of distribution of insurance products (e.g. Spain Italy etc.). However, in countries where financial consumer is well-informed and where private pensions are well developed, bancassurance has met with limited success.

Conclusion

Bancassurance operations has a material impact on the financial services industry at large Banks, insurance companies and traditional funds management houses are converging towards a model of global retail financial institution offering a wide variety of products. It leads to the creation of 'one-stop shop' where a customer can apply for mortgages, pensions, savings and insurance products.

Despite issues, Bancassurance can be expected to develop into an important distribution channel for insurance products. Ultimately, it is a question of customer choice and Bancassurance gives the customer another choice. To conclude Bancassurance can be a success if the top management of the Banks is fully committed, necessary infrastructure for the selling of the insurance products is made available, staff is properly trained and motivated.

References

Marketing and Distribution Channels in Bancassurance by Sh. Manoj Kumar.

DBOD. No. FSC. BC. 27/24.01.018/2003-2004-Entry of Banks into Insurance Business.

Bancassurance: A New Opportunity for Banks in India by Sh. R. Krishnamurthy.

Distribution Channels: Vital Link in economics of Insurance by Sh. R. Krishnamurthy.

Bancassurance with Special Reference to the Indian Market by Manoj Kumar.

Bancassurance: Business Standard Annual Year Book 2002.

Bancassurance by Shri K. Cherian Verghese.

Bancassurance by Allen J. Pathmarajah.

Bancassurance-New Avenues for Banks.

Bancassurance-A Suitable Model for India by Stuart Purdy.

Sekhar, Y. Chandra and Kumar, K. B. S. (2001), 'Bancassurance: Big Forces Together', *Chartered Financial Analyst,* Vol. VII, Issue 1, October.

Reserve Bank of India (2000), 'Monetary and Credit Policy for the Year 2000-2001', *Reserve Bank of India,* Mumbai.

Boyle, Charles E. (2000), 'Bancassurance Model is Business as Usual in European Countries', *Insurance Journal,* June 12, West Issue.

Ranada A. and R. Ahuja (1999), 'Insurance in India Development Report: 1999-2000', Indira Gandhi Institute of Development Research, Mumbai.

Murty, G. R. K. (2001), 'Banks Foray into Insurance: Adaptation Challenges', *Chartered Financial Analyst,* Vol. VI, Issue-X, June.

37

Bancassurance: Opportunities and Challenges

Sanjay Singh

Bancassurance is a word coined in the western world, When Banks began to get involved in the marketing of insurance business. In some countries, the same institution would offer both banking and insurance products, separately or together as the customers may need, managing both the businesses themselves. This was possible when the institution is allowed to transact both insurance and banking businesses. This was permitted in certain countries. The product or service offered to the customer was the product of the bank and had in it some elements of insurances. In practice, however, there are variations.

- Some banks have now set up joint venture insurance companies with the objective of developing and marketing their own insurance products in addition to the traditional banking activities.
- Some other banks, instead of setting up their own insurance company, have taken up a corporate agency for distribution of insurance products of an insurance company.
- The reverse has also happened in some countries, Some insurance companies have acquired banks or have taken an agency to market banking products.

- Such a clubbed activity of banking and insurance has been termed as 'Bancassurance'.

Concept of Bancassurance

- The concept of Bancassurance is based on the availability of natural synergy between bank and insurance companies.
- Banks and the Life insurance companies target the same segments of population for mobilizing the people's savings.
- Both banks and insurance companies have a huge customer network and the supporting infrastructure, Which can be used crossselling each other's products.
- Both Life and Non-life insurance product can be marketed through Banks.
- A Bank-insurer is an organisation that, in addition to providing money transactions and lending services, sells insurance products.

Incentives to Banks

Bancassurance means a major gain for the banks. While it is a source of additional income for them, it also helps them in enhancing employee productivity with additional business. Distribution of insurance products through banking channels helps them to add more customers while providing additional services to the existing ones. For a common man, his banker is still the best financial consultant and this trust provides a unique advantage to the banks in distribution of insurance products as well as other investment instruments such as mutual funds or even unit-linked insurance plans as a combination of insurance and mutual funds products. A bank providing a whole range of financial services definitely stands a better chance to attract more customers and increase revenue. Cost reduction as a corollary to the rise in the number of policies sold per employee is an obvious benefit that the banks derive from enhanced customer access fostered by the bancassurance.

Incentives to Insurance Companies

For insurers, the biggest benefit is the huge and trusted banking network without any administrative hassles for maintaining such network. Insurance not being an off-the-shelf product requires personal counseling and persuasion. Hence, distribution poses a major challenge for the insurance companies. Further, the vast untapped insurable interests spread all over the country makes the traditional channels of the insurable interests spread all over the country makes the traditional channels of the insurance distribution uneconomical. The increasing competition has made it impossible for the insurers to enjoy the flexibility of incurring heavy distribution expenses and passing them to the customer in the form of high premiums. As such, the far and wide reach of the banking network provides the most obvious and economical distribution alternative. In addition, insurers also get the benefit of customer database like customers' financial standing, spending habits, investment and purchasing capability, which can be used to customize products and sell accordingly. Since the banks already have an established relationship with their customers, conversion ratio of leads to sales is also likely to be high. Further, service aspect can also be tackled easily.

Advantages to Customers

Bancassurance benefits the customers by providing comprehensive financial advisory services under one roof, i.e., insurance services along with other financial services such as banking, personal loans, mutual funds, etc. So, when banks turn into financial super-malls, customers stand to benefit the most. Enhanced convenience to the customers in paying premiums and getting other facilities at his familiar and friendly place is of course an added advantage.

Bancassurance Models

There are various models, used independently or in combination, through which bancassurance operates internationally:

- *Strategic Alliance Model:* It involves a simple 'marketing tie-up' between a bank and the insurance company where the banker assists the insurer in the distribution of insurance products for some commission. Except for marketing the products, no other insurance products for some commission. Except for marketing the products, no other insurance functions are carried out by the bank.

- *Integrative Model:* Under the integrative model, branch bankers themselves directly sell insurance products. Banks may also enter into joint ventures with insurance companies to offer bancassurance products. This requires the bank staff to have a thorough knowledge of all the insurance products.
- *Specialist Model:* In this model, specialized personnel who are generally employees or representatives of the insurance company itself, distribute the products. Bankers utilize their database to identity prospects who are then contacted by the insurance professional.
- *Full Integration Model*: This arrangement entails a full integration of banking and insurance services. The bank sells insurance products under the its brand, acts as a provider of financial solutions as per the customer's needs. The bank controls sales and the insurance providers, including claims settlement. Under such an arrangement, the bank has an additional core activity almost similar to that of an insurance company.
- *Financial Planning Model:* This offers every customer a complete financial planning package that attends to his or her entire financial concerns. This process is considered beneficial to the customer, the bank as well as the insurer. This generally considered as an extremely useful way to reach a large number of customers.

Conflicts in Bancassurance

Bancassurance, though beneficial to the bankers, insurers and customers, yet, entails certain potential areas of conflict which must be carefully monitored and addressed suitably.

Competing Products

In India, insurance is perceived more as a 'savings product' rather than as a risk management product'. This makes an insurer's products to compete directly with the deposit products of banks. In such a situation, bankers may not find it in their interest to hard-sell insurance products.

Conflicting Interest

Another potential source of conflict arises in a situation where an insurance company is promoted by an international bank which may also have a non-insurance business interest in India. This may cause strategic withholding of customer information by the domestic banking partner of the bancassurance.

Staff Reluctance

For banks, especially the public sector banks, it is very important to manage any staff unrest due to additional work on account of bancassurance. Lack of knowledge about the nitty-gritty of an insurance product could also be another deterrent.

Identity Predicament

Developing and promoting brand equity of bancassurance while retaining the unique identity of the bank is also a matter of conflict. After all, for a banker, bancassurance is primarily a source of additional income an obviously, it cannot become a substitute of the regular business of the bank. Maintaining an 'arms length relation' between a bank's regular and insurance business is another difficult issue.

Functional Incongruities

Although banking and insurance are both financial services, yet they are quite different in terms of systems, procedures, culture and business ethos.

Such difficulties in the convergence of banking and insurance may be resolved by a high degree of functional co-ordination with suitable institutional mechanism and business models. Developing appropriate human resource policies to groom the staff to undertake the addition responsibility is equally important to make the venture successful.

Regulatory Framework for Bancassurance in India

In order to reap the benefits of synergy between banks and insurance companies, banks' entry in the insurance business was permitted by a notification of the Government of India in August 2000, specifying insurance as a permissible form of business under section 6 (1) (0) of the Banking Regulations Act, 1949. The guidelines issued by the Reserve Bank in August 2000, permitting banks to enter the insurance market lays down some terms and conditions: (i) banks' minimum net worth should be Rs. 500 crore; (ii) capital adequacy ratio should be 10 per cent; (iii) reasonable level of non-performing assets (NPAs) which should be at least one per cent below the industry level; (iv) earning net profit for three consecutive years in the immediate past; (v) good track record in case of subsidiaries; (vi) entry should be through a joint venture; and (vii) minimum capital requirement of Rs. 100 crore.

As per the guidelines, the commercial banks, if they satisfy the specified eligibility criteria can take any of three routes: (i) undertake distribution of insurance products as agents of insurance companies on fee basis; (ii) make investments in an insurance company for providing infrastructure and services support; or (iii) set up a joint venture company for undertaking insurance business with risk participation. In the 2001 'Report on Currency and Finance', The RBI put forth its views on bancassurance in more concrete terms. "The Reserve Bank, in recognition of the symbiotic relationship between banking and the insurance industries, has identified three routes of banks' participation in the insurance business, viz., (i) providing fee-based insurance services without risk participation, (ii) investing in an insurance company for providing infrastructure and services support, and (iii) setting-up of a separate joint venture insurance company with risk participation. The third route, due to its risk aspects, involves compliance to stringent entry norms. Further, the bank has to maintain an 'arms length' relationship between its banking business and its insurance outfit. For banks entering into insurance business with risk participation, the prescribed entity (viz., separate joint-venture company) also enables avoiding possible regulatory overlaps between the Reserve bank and the Government/IRDA. The joint venture insurance company would be subjected entirely to the IRDA/ Government regulations."

The guidelines have made the corporate agency form of bancassurance very attractive for banks. By becoming a corporate agent, a bank does not share risk in the insurance business and hence, it is a good source of revenue without much regulatory hurdles. Though profit-sharing is not permitted, yet banks can sufficiently supplement their income with the commission. It also provides an avenue to the banks to get a feel of the insurance market which may come handly while entering the insurance sector on a comparatively larger scale through a joint venture.

Scope in Indian Context

Bancassurance has enormous scope in our country where people are either not insured or they are under insured. It will be interesting to have a critical look on the following data:

- Less than 25 per cent of the insurable population in India has been insured.
- India is the second largest populated country in the world but its share is only 0.5% of the total insurance in the world.
- Insurance premium constitutes just about 5% of the total GDP. It is expected to go up to 18% in the next 10 years.
- Per capita life insurance premium in a year in our country works out to 5 US Dollars as against the world figure of 225 US Dollars.
- All these figures show that there is a vast scope of insurance in our country.
- Banks are well spread out in our country even in remote rural areas. Banking concept and practice have grown well even in rural areas and people often visit the branches to do transactions.

Even in urban areas and in metros, notwithstanding the proliferation of ATMs & e-banking etc., a sizeable number of customers do call on the banks personally for their transactions. Personal interface with the bank staff members who sell insurance is a critical factor in bancassurane and that is possible in our banks.

- Following statistics are very relevent to the scope of banker's activities in the field of insurance:
- There are as many as 64,000 bank branches in our country and each branch caters to about 15000 people.
- State Bank of India alone has over 9000 branches.
- 60 per cent of the bank branches are said to be in the rural and semi urban areas.
- Although it may not be possible to sell insurance through all the bank branches, yet the scope is enormous. While quite a few banks, such as SBI, HDFC, ICICI and Vysya Bank, have set up their own joint venture insurance companies, almost all the new insurance companies have entered into MoUs with some banks.
- Even LIC has entered into a MoU with corporation Bank.

Conclusion

With a huge untapped market, the insurance sector is witnessing a lot of activity in India in the form of product innovation or distribution channel mix. Bancassurance, the emerging distribution channel for the insurers, is making a large impact on the Indian financial services industry. Traditional modes of distributing financial service are being challenged and innovative, customized products are emerging. Banks are using their customer database, leveraging their reputation and making use of the personal contacts with their clients. These are very crucial for the success in the insurance business, which a new entrant cannot manage. This is an added advantage to the bancassurance. In the customers' point of view, today a plethora of products are available to him. More customized insurance product, at multiple distribution levels are bound to come into existence. Bancassurance is not just selling insurance but it is also about changing the mindset of doing a plain vanilla banking. The time has come for banks to move beyond their traditional businesses to turn into a financial super-mail; of course, with necessary safeguards and after a meticulous due diligence process. In addition to acting as insurance distributors as corporate agents, several banks having recognized the potential of insurance market in India, have gone ahead and forged joint venture with insurance companies to reap the maximum benefits of bancassurance.

Globally, wherever the legislation has allowed, bancassurance has mostly been phenomenal success and although slow in gaining momentum, it is now taking off in India. The factors and conditions making it a success elsewhere also exist in India and their is no doubt that banks are all set to become significant distributors of insurance-related products and services. Finally, success of the bancassurance will primarily depend on the customers' response, ability of insurers and banks to understand each other's businesses; iron out differences and seize the emerging opportunities.

References

Bhatt, A. (2000), "Bancassurance: Issues in Marketing", in Padwal S.M. and Parchure R. K. (ed.), Bancassurance in India".

Mankidy, Jacob, "Competency Building: A Critical Dimension in Managing Bancassurance Effectively", in Padwal S. M. and Parchure R. K. (ed), "Bancassurance in India".

Munich Re Group (2001), " Bancassurance in Practice".

Bancassurance: Business Standard Annual Year Book 2002.

Allenj. Pathmarajah: Bancassurance.

38

Mutual Funds: Opportunities and Issues for Banks

Lucy Kumari

The mutual fund industry in India in 1963 with the formation of Unit Trust of India (UTI), at initiative of the Government of India and The Reserve Bank of India (RBI). The history of mutual funds in India can be broadly divided into four distinct phases.

Unit Trust of India (UTI) was established on 1963 by an Act of Parliament. It was set up by the Reserve Bank of India and functioned under the Regulatory and administrative control of the Reserve bank of India. In 1978, UTI was de-linked from the RBI and the Industrial Development Bank of India (IDBI) took over the regulatory and administrative control in place of RBI. The first scheme launched after the takeover was US-64.

1987 marked the entry of non-UTI, public sector mutual funds set up by public sector banks, Life Insurance Corporation of India (LIC) and General Insurance Corporation of India (GIC). SBI Mutual Fund was the first non-UTI Mutual Fund established in June 1987 followed by Canbank Mutual Fund (Dec, 1987), Punjab National Bank Mutual Fund (Aug, 1989), Indian Bank Mutual fund (Nov, 1989), Bank of India (Jun, 1990), Bank of Baroda Mutual Fund (Oct, 1992). LIC established it mutual fund in June 1989, while GIC had set up its mutual fund in December 1990.

At the end of 1993, the mutual fund industry had assets under management of Rs. 47,004 crores. With the entry of private sector funds in 1993, a new era began in the Indian mutual fund industry, giving the Indian investors a wider choice of fund families. Also, 1993 was the year in which the first Mutual Fund Regulations came into being, under which all mutual funds, except UTI were to be registered and governed. The erstwhile Kothari Pioneer (now merged with Franklin Templeton) was the first private sector mutual fund registered in July, 1993.

The 1993 SEBI (Mutual Fund) Regulations were substituted by a more comprehensive and revised Mutual Fund Regulations in 1996. The industry now functions under the supervision of SEBI (Mutual Fund) Regulations 1996.

The number of mutual fund houses went on increasing, with many foreign mutual funds planting their feet in India, following which the industry has also witnessed several mergers and acquisitions. As on the end of January, 2003, there were 33 mutual funds with total assets of Rs. 1,21,805 crores. The Unit Trust of India with Rs. 44,541 crores of assets under management was leading the other mutual funds.

In February 2003, following the repeal of the Unit Trust of India Act 1963, UTI was bifurcated into two separate entities. One was the Specified Undertaking of the Unit Trust of India with assets under management of Rs. 29,835 crores as on end January 2003, representing broadly, the assets of US 64 scheme, assured return and certain other schemes. The Specified Undertaking of Unit Trust of India, functioning under an administrator and under the rules framed by Government of India, does not come under the purview of the Mutual Fund Regulations.

The second was the UTI Mutual Fund Ltd, sponsored by SBI, PNB, BOB and LIC. It is registered with SEBI and functions under the Mutual Fund Regulations. With the bifurcation of the erstwhile UTI, which in March 2000 had more than

Rs. 76,000 crores of assets under management and with the setting up of a UTI Mutual Fund conforming to the SEBI Mutual Fund Regulations, and with recent mergers taking place among different private sector funds, the mutual fund industry has entered its current phase of consolidation and growth. As on the end of September 2004. There were 29 funds, managing assets worth Rs. 1531108 crores under 421 schemes.

Concept of a Mutual Fund

A Mutual Fund is a trust that pools the savings of a number of investors who share a common financial goal. The money thus collected is invested in capital market instruments such as shares, debentures and other securities. The income earned through these investments and the capital appreciation thus realized, are shared by its unit holders in proportion to the number of units owned by them, Thus, a mutual fund is the most suitable investment for the common person as it offers an opportunity to invest in a diversified, professionally-managed basket of securities at a relatively low cost.

Advantages of Mutual Funds

The advantages of investing in a Mutual Fund are:

- Professional Management
- Diversification
- Convenient Administration
- Return Potential
- Low Costs
- Liquidity
- Transparency
- Flexibility
- Choice of Schemes
- Tax benefits
- Well regulated

Banks as Channel Agents For Distribution of Products

The aggregate deposits mobilized by commercial banks amounted to Rs. 28.64 lakhs while the combined AUM of the mutual funds industry, which is akin to bank deposit mobilization, is just Rs. 4.81 lakhs.

Bank deposits, particularly current and savings, are an important source of funding the credit growth for the banks. However, individuals who understand investment climate changes-like, in China, are preferring to invest these almost-idle funds in higher yielding and riskier assets like equities. Mutual funds offer the best possible and hassle free entry to riskier asset classes like equities and banks offer ready clients of theirs to the mutual funds. Banks have enormous geographic reach and a varied customer base with different resource profiles. Bankers cannot stop their customers from investing anywhere but it is ideal to know where their money is going to be invested. With synergic tie-ups with mutual fund houses and by playing an active advisory role, the banks should guide their clients for investing sensibly. The investors' investments outside the bank books may be treated as remote assets. Knowing the client investments, the banks can even take care of the customers' credit requirements in times of need using their investments as collaterals.

Despite many players, the mutual funds today have neither gathered a large investor base nor garnered huge AUMs. The same urban investor is tapped again and again. The industry AUM is getting rotated in the same limited geographical boundary created by them. Whether it is a big insurance player like LIC or the banking industry, the customer base and per customer mobilizations have improved mostly on the basis of reach. However, it costs a lot to create a reach. Mutual funds operate with a thin margin and the margin itself is contracting as the demand for returns keeps increasing.

Today the banking industry needs a well diversified revenue model. It is no longer a 'get deposits and lend the money' game. The banks have increasingly realized that they must build a strong fee income from various operations. The banks increasingly need to look like financial malls and they need to sell every conceivable financial product designed and managed by others on a fee basis. They can potentially become huge retail intermediaries in an institutional garb.

It makes sense for the mutual funds to sell through banks which meet the primary banking needs of the people of all hues. The banks should act more as an advisor and a service provider with strategic and operational support from the fund houses.

From the customer point of view, it has become apparent that, rather than commit to any one channel in particular, many customers are choosing to make use of the full range of channels available to service their accounts, be it to perform basic transactions or research and buy new products.

The bank branch remains the most important channel in terms of revenue generation, with customers preferring to make high-value/complex product purchases face-to-face. E-banking is becoming an increasingly important channel for commodity product sales. Customers are using call centres and channels for basic transactions and to service their accounts.

Mutual Banking-the Clear Solution

Fee based income by selling or cross-selling from within is a risk-less operational model which should help banks achieve the much needed retail banking growth of the order of 30 per cent and above. With equity markets growing like never before due to robust economic growth, mutual funds alone can play a greater role. Mutual fund distribution is set to be very lucrative since mutual fund distribution by banks is emerging very fast. Alliances between banks and mutual funds have come into existence in a big way. Initially, the private sector players were shy of alliances with PSU banks but the reality of the PSUs' reach opened their eyes. SBI is a very active MF distributor selling all MF products though they have their own fund house.

A new concept-mutual banking-has emerged offering new products and service innovations for the customers who avail of mutual fund products through banks like co-branded debit cards for withdrawals of units.

MF distribution offers good scope for augmenting the banks' fee-based income. Upfront Commission, Trail (loyalty) Commission, Mobilization incentives, Special Incentives, Collection Charges are the income triggers for New Fund Offers. For a Single application, there are multiple revenue streams.

The existing customer base serves as a captive prospective investor universe. The stage and the setting are already there. Only, the players have to play.

Banks as a distribution channel have a huge potential to build and improve the retail side of the investors' universe of MFs, which is skewed towards the institutional side now. There is no other distribution channel for MFs that can offer such a lucrative retail base on a platter by a tie-up.

Trained frontline staff of the bank will serve as ready-made marketers for distribution. For the bank, a strike rate of even 10 per cent of the targeted customers will translate into huge volumes for the MFs to encash. In addition, the database can be used effectively for "Experience Marketing" of future products and "Product Co Creation" based on segments.

The opportunity for customers to avail of non-banking financial products with multiple return matrixes from their banking services providers without the strain of shopping in the market, are many. Based on their risk-appetite, customers are offered a buffet of MF products with different themes and return expectations through the bank. They are also offered counselling support from the bank and the MF personnel.

Developing a PROPAGATE (Product, Risk, Opportunities (Returns), People, Appetite, Geography (Place), Attributes, Training & Education) matrix for MF distribution is the key for the success of the distribution strategy. Right structuring of the matrix will synergize the efforts of the banks and the MFs. Since banks are selling the MF products to and through their customer base, any deficiencies in the matrix directly create an imbalance in their desired objectives and customer satisfaction levels.

Following are important ingredients of the matrix:

Product: Banks with multiple tie-ups should decide on products of different MFs based on their customer segment and time preferences. New Fund Offers are there for all but in the case of existing schemes, a careful selection of MF products is a precursor for customer-oriented selling.

Risk: Unlike fixed deposits of banks, MF schemes carry capital risk and return risk. MFs should ideally, not guarantee returns for their investments and investments are subject to market vagaries. Banks should have an in-house research team in place to identify schemes based on the risk profile of their customers. Selection of products with performance above the level of their benchmark indices will minimize risk in a big way.

Opportunities: Investments in MFs are opportunities for customers to create wealth. In case of growth schemes, buoyant capital market creates better opportunities for capital appreciation and returns, and the expertise of professional fund managers enhances the opportunities and delivers better returns.

Products which offer better returns over a period over the benchmark indices will increase the return expectations and should be factored in, while structuring the matrix.

People: People i.e. both, the internal and external customers, are the driving force. Internal customers comprise line staffs who actually market the schemes and external customers are target customers to whom the schemes are marketed to by the internal customers. Selecting a marketing staff with the right aptitude and attitude will make sure that schemes reach the external customers and trigger the purchase intentions that are translated into sales.

A careful selection of internal sales staff (who is going to sell) and right targeting of the external customers (to whom it is going to be sold) will make the distribution model more effective.

Appetite: The penchant for risk taking varies with customers across segments. The risk appetite of a rural affluent customer will be comparatively less than his/her urban counterpart.

Product-offering across segments should match the risk appetite of the respective segments.

Geography: Geography of the bank is the foremost advantage for the banks and MFs in the distribution model. In a single tie-up model, the idea is to simply sell across geography.

With multiple tie-ups, borders have to be clear. Banks should draw the distribution design based on the brand equity of the MF in specific or across geographic boundaries for better distribution efficacy. Banks should first zero-in on the branches through which they are going to distribute MF products.

The awareness level about MF in general and schemes in particular, varies across geographies (rural, semi-urban, urban and metro) and also customer segments. A properly graded geographical strategy will propel a smooth, seamless customer penetration and sales volumes.

Attributes: Attributes of products are borne out of product structuring and investment objectives. Growth Schemes, Income Schemes, Balanced Schemes, Index Schemes etc., are some of the product attributes and Monthly Income Plan (MIP) and Systematic Investment Plan (SIP) are return and investment attributes. Attributes and their impacts should be effectively communicated to the investing customers. Otherwise, it will result in customer dissatisfaction at a later stage.

Training: Training is the axle on which the entire mutual fund distribution revolves. Teaching the nuances of mutual funds to the sales staff is the starting point of implementation. Training and Certification Programme by the Association of Mutual Funds in India (AMFI) for distributing mutual fund products is essential for successful implementation of the distribution strategy.

The content and communication of the trained staff will translate to better counselling to the target investors and better satisfaction levels. Banks should aim to achieve the training objectives for distribution objectives.

Education: Educating the external customer about the MFs first and the nuances of MF investments next will be the ultimate determinant for distribution success. Customers will always look for direct assistance by the staff whose responsibility is to educate and guide them into making investments based on their risk return appetite, life cycle and wealth cycle. The education exercise is to be on a continuous basis. Developing and implementing a robust PROPAGATE matrix will definitely give a good direction to MF distribution. The staff involved in the banks should be convinced about the distribution as a potential profit generation model for the bank. There may be apprehensions among staff in selling an alien product and about its impact on the liability base of banks. But history has it that any investment is recycled over a period of time and outflows are almost always matched by inflows and there is benefit in the form of income from outflows also.

Moreover, if banks give customers other financial products as well, customer satisfaction increases and brand loyalty improves.

Ultimately that is what matters. So, banks, race now with a PROPAGATE matrix and reap the benefits of fee-based income by MF distribution. Selling Financial products such as mutual funds is lucrative business worth over Rs. 1 lakh crore every year. A surfeit of mutual funds is constantly wooing distributors such as banks to sell their products. Organizing training sessions at a central location for distributors or sales is a common and cost-efficient practice. There couldn't be a better and more cost effective way of educating intermediaries. The fund houses and banks coming together can do a better job in this area.

In fact, in large global banks there is a clear distinction where mutual funds and other such financial product companies interact only with the bank's product team that decides which products the bank will market. This is one area which the fund houses and the banks have to sort out. The banks which just sell a product are not to keen to know the performance standards of the products of the fund houses concerned but the ones which sell the products as part of a wealth advisory model are keen to weed out substandard performers from the product shelf. As the banks evolve, the wealth advisory role would dominate and fund houses too would strive to keep their products in the best shape, as far as performance is concerned. It is a win-win situation for all banks, fund houses, and the customers. However, a vast majority of small and medium intermediaries are simply indulging in selling and their advisory role is questionable.

As the banks emerge as true financial malls of India, fund houses need not launch so many so-called NFOs (New Fund Offers) and instead can sell the existing schemes for the good of all and reduce the cost across the board. Small intermediaries may work for the banks as sub-agents. The regulator, SEBI, precisely desires that highly disciplined and investor oriented intermediaries play the game for cost reduction and better reach.

Almost 50 per cent of the staff in private banks comprises relationship managers (RMs) whose main job is to sell mutual funds or insurance products. Both contribute equally to the pie of fee based income for banks. Relationship managers, who sell mutual fund products to investors, are worried that removal of entry load will end their incentive-based careers. HSBC is one of the biggest distributors of mutual funds.

Since 2001, banks have sold mutual funds aggressively to investors in a bull market first in the debt market and then in the equity market it was not a difficult job. Initially, they started by selling debt funds, as interest rates were down and bond prices were moving up. The equity market was not very attractive. Banks slowly realized the importance of this fee-based income, which started to account for almost 50 per cent of their total income over the next six years. As the equity market took wing, banks started aggressively selling equity-related funds where the commission is the highest. "In a bull market, banks have made money and so have RMs. But if SEBI's proposal becomes a reality then an RM's job will come under tremendous pressure".

Banks have also realized that their fortunes will always be linked to assets under management (AUM) of mutual funds.

The AUM for mutual funds may not keep doubling every year, but banks want to double their fee-based income. Thus, over a period of time many banks may start to churn their investor portfolios to get higher fees. Investors may be ill-advised to move into different schemes to maximize commission income for banks.

References

Fein, M. L. (1993), Mutual Funds Activities of Banks, Aspen Law.

Friend, Irwin, M. Blume and J. Crockett (1970), Mutual Funds and Other Institutional Investors, McGraw-Hill, New York.

Horowitz, Ira (1965), 'A Model for Mutual Funds Evaluation', *Industrial Management Review*, Vol. 6, No. 3, (Spring).

Iyer, Anantharaman T. N. (1991), The Indian Money Market-Recent Developments, Discount and Finance House of India, Bombay.

Kale, Sumita and S. Uma (1995), A Study on the Evaluation of the Performance of Mutual Funds in India, National Insurance Academy, Pune.

Kaufman, J. (1988), Mutual Funds, Chelsea House, New York.

Kaufman, K. (1986), Interest Rates, Markets and New Financial Instruments, *Times Book*, New York.

Laderman, J. M. and G. Smith (1993), 'The Power of Mutual Funds', *Business Week*, 10 January.

Laderman, Jeffrey M. (1994), Business Week's Guide to Mutual Funds (4th edition), McGraw-Hill, New York.

Mutual Funds Education Alliance (1996), The Investors' Guide to Law Cost Mutual Funds, (20th edition), Kansas City.

Powely, M. (1991), UK Financial Institutions and Market, Macmillan, UK.

Rugg, Donald D. (1988), New Strategies for Mutual Funds Investing, Irwin Professional Publishing, Burr Ridge.

Sadhak, H. (1992), 'Money Market Mutual Funds-Scope and Implications in Indian Context', *Journal of Discount and Finance House of India*, Bombay.

Simonson, Donald G. (1972), "The Speculative Behaviour of Mutual Funds', *Journal of Finance*, Vol. 27, No. 2.

Verma, J. C. (1992), Mutual Funds and Investment Portfolio, Bharat Law House Pvt. Ltd., New Delhi.

Whitford, David (1997), "The Mutual Fund Revolution: Is it Good for You,' *Fortune*, Vol. 2.

H. Sadhak (2007), Mutual Funds in India Marketing Strategies and Investment Practices, Response Books, New Delhi.

Singh Daryab (2003), Mutual Funds India, Rajat Publications, New Delhi.

39

Are "Mergers and Acquisitions" Necessary in Indian Banking?

Jaishanker Prasad Singh

Mergers and takeovers on a larger scale could be viewed as the next step in Indian banking sector evolution. World over, increasing competition in the banking field has generated a rece to consolidate the industry and achieve a grater scale as a necessary prerequisite for improving efficiency. The implicit hypothesis behind this strategic movement is that a greater market share is always equivalent to greater profitability. History shows that the top managements of many banks have felt that the best way of increasing size by a relatively quick route is merging with another bank. In the banking industry internal growth is a rather slow process and, therefore, the easiest path is often mergers or takeovers.

Mergers and acquisition (M&As) have become an integral part of the corporates finance world. We find innumerable M&A transactions bringing together separate companies and turning them into large ones or splitting of companies through spin-offs, carve-outs or tracking stocks.

Institutions decide to merge because they perceive that they can together create greater shareholder value than what they could when they were separate.

Global Experience

M&As are a global phenomenon, with an estimated 4000 deals taking place every year. They are also not a recent development. They have happened at various times in history and in different countries. The current merger wave, started in early 1990s, was exceptional from the angle of value and volume of transactions. In the United States, because of M&As the number of banking organizations declined between 1980 and 1997 from 12,333 to 7,122. Europe has also experienced M&A; examples include-Unicredito/Credito Italiano and Generale Bank/Fortis in 1998, UBS/SBS, ING/BBL, Credit Suisse/Winterthur Group and Vereinsbank/Hypobank in 1997 and so on. Between 1980 and 1995 the number of banking establishments in Europe fell, particularly in Denmark (57%) and France (43%).

Indian Experience

The early history of mergers in the Indian banking industry reveals that it had occurred at the instance of the central bank of the country, viz., the Reserve Bank of India (RBI). India had 566 commercial banks (of which 474 were non-scheduled) by the end of 1951. This number came down to 292 (with 210 non-scheduled banks) by the end of 1961. In the next five years, the number further declined to 100 (27 non-scheduled). In 1969, when the Government embarked upon nationalization of 14 major banks, there were only 85 (14 non-scheduled) banks. Simultaneously, the number of bank branches increased from 4151 in 1951 to 9005 in 1969. The RBI took measures to weed out unviable banks following the failure of two major banks in 1960. The world over, M&As generally involved banks in the private sector. Therefor, there is no ready reference for public sector banks mergers. In the early 1990s, when the then New Bank of India was merged with the Punjab National Bank, problems of personnel intergration had cropped up.

There have been no mergers within the public sector category. However, a few private sector banks opted for mergers in late 1990, for gaining financial strength, increasing their retail portfolio and attaining geographical expansion. For e.g., Bank of Madura was merged with ICICI Bank, Times Bank was merged with HDFC bank.

A few private sector banks were merged with public sector banks, for e.g., Benaras State Bank was merged with Bank of Baroda, Nedungadi Bank was merged with Punjab National Bank and recently, Global Trust Bank with Oriental Bank of Commerce.

Reasons for Indian Banks to Opt for M&A

In the present context of global financial market integration, Indian banks also find M&A a convenient way to make an international presence by exploiting the economies of scale and if possible, of scope.

The main reasons for bank mergers are "to reduce costs, extend the range of products and services, increase the market share, participate in the process of privatization (in transition economies). Diversify risks, geographical diversification, improvement in solvency, transfer of know-how, etc".

Demonstrating that M&As improve efficiency is thus, central to making a case for mergers and in assessing their potential impact on consumers. If mergers improve efficiency, then larger, combined firms may be expected to pass some savings on to consumers through lower prices or improved service.

The questions arising at this juncture are:

- Can Indian banks achieve the size to complete with global banks in the international markets?
- Is efficiency proportionate to size?
- Does it lead to increase in profitability?
- Is cost an inhibiting factor in the area of product development?
- In a country like India, where 30% of the population lives below the poverty line and more than 75% of them do not have access to financial services even under the present competitive conditions, can the laws of the land protect these vulnerable sections from denial of financial services when mergers take place and mega banks are formed?

The Ability to Face Global Competition Argument

The total assets of the public sector banks (PSBs) in India is only 40% of the 10th largest bank globally as may be seen from the following Table 1.

Private sector banks are too small to be even mentioned.

It is in this regard that Prof. T.T. Ram Mohan has concluded in his article on the subject in Economic and Political Weekly dated 11 December, 2004 that India's PSBs cannot acquire the critical mass to take on the global major banks. The State Bank of India, the largest PSB in India is not even one tenth of the ninth bank in the list of global bank arranged according to size of assets. Implementation of Basel II norms would raise the entry bar further, preventing our PSBs from becoming global players. He argues that:

- Literature on the subject points to an inverted u-shape relationship between size and efficiency,
- Mergers are a response to faltering earnings-growth. Earnings-growth is not under threat in India. On the contrary, the spread has been improving in the recent past, as may be seen form the following:

Table 1

Name	*Assets Size (USS billions)*
Mizuho Financial Group	1285
Citi Group	1234
UBS	1121
Credit Agricole Group	1105
HSBC holdings	1034
Deutsche Bank	1015
BNP Paribas	989
Mitshubishi Tokyo Financial Group	975
Sumito Mitsui Fin Group	950
Royal Bank of Scotland	806
PSBs of India	327

Source: Banker, CMIE, RBI Report on Trend and Progress of Banking (2003-2004).

Table 2

Year	*Spread (%)*
2001-02	2.57
2002-03	2.77
2003-04	2.856

Source: RBI Report on Trend and Progress of Banking (2003-04).

If we scan the performance of Indian PSBs, it can be observed that size did not have any correlation with profitability. Return on assets, for most of the smaller banks, was more than 1.5% whereas the largest bank in the country had less than 1% as Return on Assets (ROA), as may be seen from the Following:

Unlike in the USA and Europe, where pressure on bank spreads provided the motivation for mergers, spreads in the banking system in India have been consistent even after liberalization and deregulation. The spread of 2.97% in PSBs in 2003-04 is higher than the average spread of 2.72% in the initial years of deregulation (1992-95).

There is still no official view on the optimal size or number of banks in a country. The Banking Commission in India had recommended, as early as 1972, that national banks be reorganized into two or three all-India banks and six other entities, each specializing in developing services in a broad region. Though this was not implemented, there is need for intense research on the issue, before one takes a judgmental view about the number of Indian banks that can have international presence and can compete for international banking business.

Can the PSBs, if merged, attract more capital from the market? Perhaps, no. In today's policy environment, Government is on record that the shareholding of the Government will not be allowed to go below 51% of the equity capital. Many of the PSBs are on the threshold of 51% and therefore, even if merged, they will not be able to tap the market. At the most, they can go for subordinated capital. Even there, a restriction exists that the same should not exceed 50% of the Tier I capital; it is not clear whether this restriction will apply only to capital adequacy regulations and whether banks will have the freedom to mobilize such resources for their own business purposes.

Table 3

Name of the Bank	*Operating Profit/ Working (%)*	*Return on Assets (%)*
Corporation Bank	3.53	1.96
Vijaya Bank	3.96	1.91
State Bank of Indore	4.34	11.73
Andhra Bank	3.69	1.72
Oriental Bank of Commerce	4.10	1.70
Syndicate Bank	2.51	1.67
State Bank of Patiala	4.28	1.60
State Bank of Bikaner & Jaipur	3.70	1.49
State Bank of Saurashtra	4.16	1.38
Allahabad Bank	2.73	1.34
Canara Bank	3.23	1.34
State Bank of Mysore	3.19	1.28
Bank of India	2.78	1.25
United Bank of India	2.49	1.25
State Bank of Hyderabad	3.55	1.25
Union Bank of India	2.77	1.22
Indian Bank	2.39	1.21
Bank of Baroda	3.00	1.20
UCO Bank	2.47	1.13
Dena Bank	3.41	1.11
Indian Overseas Bank	2.93	1.08
Punjab National Bank	3.28	1.08
State Bank of Travancore	3.29	1.02
Central Bank of India	2.70	0.98
Bank of Maharashtra	2.48	0.95
State Bank of India	2.50	0.94
Punjab & Sind Bank	0.97	0.06

Source: RBI Report on Trend & Progress of Banking 2003-04.

The proposition that banks would be 'too large to fail' has been proved wrong in the wake of the 1990s financial crises. Banks have to be of optimum size. But who decides what is the optimum size? The question about the optimal number of banks in a country and the associated issues of their capital adequacy and their capacity to help globalization of banking, are matters yet to be settled in India.

Table 4

Name of the Bank	*% of Govt. Share Holding*	*Capital Adequacy*		
		Tier 1	*Tier 2*	*Total (%)*
Allahabad Bank	55.2	6.5	6.1	12.50
Central Bank of India	100	–	–	12.84
Andhra Bank	62.6	8.0	4.1	12.10
Bank of Baroda	66.8	8.2	4.4	12.60
Bank of India	69.5	7.1	4.5	11.50
Bank of Maharashtra	76.8	7.1	6.6	12.70
Canara Bank	73.2	7.3	5.5	12.80
Corporation Bank	57.2	13.6	2.7	16.20
Dena Bank	51.2	6.6	5.3	11.90
IDBI	58.5	14.9	3.4	18.70
Indian Bank	100	–	–	12.82
Indian Overseas Bank	61.2	7.1	7.1	14.20
Oriental Bank of Commerce	51.1	5.4	3.8	9.20
Punjab National Bank	57.8	8.9	5.9	14.80
Punjab & Sind Bank	100	–	–	11.06
State Bank of India	59.7	8.3	5.2	13.50
Syndicate Bank	73.5	6.1	4.6	10.70
UCO Bank	75.0	5.8	5.5	11.30
Union Bank	60.9	6.1	6.0	12.10
United Bank	100	–	–	17.40
Vijaya Bank	53.9	7.6	5.3	12.90

Source: RBI Report on Trend & Progress of Banking India & Balance Sheets of Individual Banks.

The position of private sector banks is not similar to that of public sector ones. All old private sector banks do not satisfy even the minimum capital requirement of Rs. 300 crore leave alone acquiring the optimal size (which is not yet settled). Hence, there is a strong case for merger or acquisition in the private sector.

Many of the banks do not have the net worth of Rs. 300 crore.

Although size mattrers, there is also no unanimity on the optimal size required for a bank to remain competitive. Optimal size is decided by the following factors:

- Size of the economy
- Diversity of the economy
- Level of financial intermediation
- Stage of market development & competition.

Therefore, the macro policy makers also have a role to play and it cannot be left entirely to the market forces.

Table 5

Name of the Bank	*Capital (Rs. crore)*	*Net worth (Rs. crore)*
Bank of Punjab	105.00	243.70
Bank of Rajasthan	107.60*	350.70*
Bharat Overseas Bank	15.80*	198.40*
Catholic Syrtan Bank	10.60*	194.00
Centurion Bank	101.30*	103.00
City Union Bank	24.00	202.90
Development Credit Bank	39.40	286.40
Dhanalakshmi Bank	32.10	134.10
Federal Bank	21.80	648.80
ING Vysya Bank	22.70*	747.30
J&K Bank	48.60*	1593.70
Karnataka Bank	40.40	696.20
Karur Vysya Bank	18.00*	712.00
Lakshmi Vilas Bank	11.00	226.60
Lord Krishna Bank	66.70	139.20
Sangli Bank	22.30	86.20
South Indian Bank	47.70*	394.90
Tamilnadu Mercantile Bank	0.30	476.80
United Western Bank	29.90	304.00

Data Relates to 2004-05 in other cases for 2003-04

Source: Balance Sheets of Banks

Effects of Mergers

While there are many unanswered questions about the benefits of mergers, we cannot lose sight of the following effects:

Employment: Some fear that M&As will lead to chasing size and create ugly super banks. Sectoral consolidation and reduction in competition suggest no immediate benefits for customers or staff who find themselves in the front line of rationalization and have to bear the brunt of its costs. "Such mergers, however, can be worthwhile if they lead to rationalization of the work force and branch network; otherwise the mergers of PSBs would tie down the management with operational issues and distract attention from the real issue. It would be necessary to evolve policies aimed at "rightsizing" and redeployment of the surplus staff, either by way of retraining them and giving them appropriate alternate employment or by introducing a VRS with appropriate incentives", states Indian Banks' Association's paper on bank mergers in India.

Consistent with the findings of many others, a study by the Bank for International Settlements (BIS) reports the experience of the majority of mergers as "disappointing", with organizational problems almost inevitable underestimated and most acquisitions overpriced. The super banks' sheer size and unwieldiness can encourage complacency and offer no more protection against failure.

On the other hand, consolidation leads to greater cost efficiency, competitive intensity and consequent tighter pricing. Protected historically from competition by regulation, the banks were enjoying a price umbrellas. In the early days of deregulation and consolidation, removal of these price umbrellas allowed the low-cost, high productivity players to earn huge profits. Price competition takes over and margins get severely squeezed, driving out the inefficient players and opening the door to further consolidation by the productivity leaders. Definitely these developments would benefit customers.

Consumers: Mega mergers of banks in the USA are alleged to have stifled competition and affected the quality of service that the banking industry provided. Mergers could lead to charging of higher fees for the services rendered, especially if there is no 'effective' competition or if smaller banks exhibit 'herd behaviour' in imitating the bigger entities. "Big is bad for consumers" is the complaint. Are consumers harmed or helped by mergers and the creation of huge companies? Particularly in financial services, we hear much about the dangers of big firms, while, the potential benefits for consumers, the possible efficiencies of scale and scope that mergers can bring, are often downplayed or overlooked entirely.

The bank mergers that took place in USA in the 80s and 90s were market extension mergers that combined banks that operated in different geographical markets. Therefore, there was an increase in the deposits and business. The Indian situation is different. All the geographical regions are well covered by PSBs as a group. Mergers may help individual banks to grab market shares from others if they provide better service to the customers. But, whether they could generate new business is doubtful. How then are the customers going to be benefited?

Small business: Small and medium business enterprises are not in a position to tap capital markets or bond markets for finance. Banks continue to be the source of funds for them. It is generally experienced world over, that whenever banks increase in size, the proportion of funds allocated to the Small and Medium Enterprises (SME) sector declines. Certainly there will be other lenders like Non Banking Finance Companies (NBFCs) in developed countries to fill in the gap. But in India, non banking financial institutions are yet to stabilize. Hence, in the transitional period after mergers, if at all it happens, SMEs would suffer for want of finance unless alternative mechanisms are in place. One such measure could be to strengthen NBFCs and Urban Cooperative Banks (UCBs) in our country. Recent research in USA indicates that the bank merger wave has not reduced the amount of credit available to small businesses. Not surprisingly, this research finds that mergers among small banks do not reduce lending to small businesses. The more interesting finding is that, acquisitions of small banks by large banks can reduce small business loans especially if the acquiring bank did not make many small business loans prior to the merger, but that due to this merger-induced reductionism, small business loans tend to be offset by increased lending by other banks operating in the local market.

Given the importance of credit access by small businesses to employment creation, it is essential to recall the findings of a report on the impact of bank M&As on small business lending. The report stresses that the weight of evidence points to a more negative than a positive effect of banking industry. Consolidation on small business lending. Small firms can expect some difficulties in obtaining bank credit as, the banking industry undergoes structural change and resultant adjustments in competitive market conditions. Whether the negative effects were short-run or long-run was impossible to discern from the data reviewed and the report recommends further research on the effects of consolidation on small business credit.

Agriculture: The availability of credit to agriculture may be affected by increasing bank consolidations and acquisitions. Analysis on the effects of bank consolidations in the USA indicates a decline in the agricultural lending activities. It is often argued that larger organizations, which usually have an urban base, neglect the credit needs of their rural constituents. It is all the more true in Indian conditions. Even under the Government stipulations, banks have not been keen on lending to agriculture. For many years, the achievement had fallen short of the set goal of 18% of bank credit. Even within the agricultural sector, only people in the upper income brackets were able to access bank credit. A recent survey in Uttar Pradesh and Andhra Pradesh indicated that nearly 70% of the rural poor had no access to any kind of financial services. This situation could worsn. As Ralph Nader, noted consumer activist of USA said in a Congressional testimony. "The mergers and the move to giant conglomerates only serves to remove basic bank services and needs, further from the mainstream consumer. Is the intent to build a financial system for the affluent, leaving the rest of the population to the crumbs of ATMs and impersonal 1-800 numbers connected to some distant corporate voice?"

"Unless there are clear consumer safeguards, strong means to ensure that all consumers have a share in the benefits of possible efficiencies and detailed commitments to meet local and regional community reinvestment needs, these mergers are likely to be harmful to consumers," consumer unions have stated.

This being the state of affairs and learned views in America, we are justified in being wary of M&As in India.

Post-Merger Challenges

Change management: M&As require that organizational changes be made in one or both firms for strategic benefits to be realized. Ultimately, the quality of the changes conceived and the extent to which they are effectively implemented will determine the financial success of M&As. The change process requires decisions concerning the depth, location and nature of changes, the speed of the change process and interventions for facilitating the change process.

Post merger cultural adjustment: Given the nature of corporate culture, any meaningful acquisition of knowledge is difficult. The concept 'culture' is subject to a wide variety of definitions, and therefore difficult to classify. And there is also no unanimity among scholars and researchers, about the best way to identify and qualify culture. Each bank has its own culture, its own way of doing business. Reconciliation of different cultures is a problem.

Technological compatibility: Technology is another determining factor in the success of a merger. Some mergers lose out in the end because of technological incompatibility. The faster the merged company can integrate the technologies of the two banks, the more successful the merger will be. Unification of technology platforms and data integration are the critical functions of merger activity. While banks first look at the business and financial drivers in any potential merger situation, they have also to consider the integration of technology, processes and support functions so that the merger objectives are achieved. Technology typically. Plays a secondary role driven by the particulars of the banks involved. For example, if a target bank is hard pressed to implement a new branch automation system, this factor has to be incorporated into the initial proposal itself. Whether or not banks actually realize the expected IT benefits is debatable. Most merged banks continue to struggle with rising maintenance costs and system integration issues.

Communication: Effective and transparent internal communication helps to build and sustain a new organizational culture but there have been a number of instances where the CEOs/top management failed in this regard and so have the mergers. The experience of other industries emphasises that successful responses to the challenges of regulation and corporate social responsibility rely on behaviour rather than rule observance and HR may take on a broader role as "corporate conscience". To get the most out of a merger or acquisition, buiders need to know how to:

- Assess the available talent prior to and during the deal
- Manage the integration process
- Handle any post-merger challenges.

Also, home builders should recognize that a merger or acquisition provides them with the unique opportunity to rethink their organizational structure and realign their talent.

When Pulte merged with Del Webb, the company adopted a unique approach to help new employees acclimatize to the organization. Over a three-week period, all Del Webb managers were brought to Colorado for a series of informal discussions and fireside chats regarding Pulte's culture. According to Dugas, it was imperative that the company spend a lot of time sharing its vision with the new employees and talking about its culture.

Conclusion

In short, we could conclude that there are definitely certain advantages emanating from synergy on merger, as size is important upto a stage. However, size alone cannot be the reason for merger. Further, merger, before putting in place appropriate internal control measures and risk management systems, will complicate the situation and cause irreparable damage to the financial viability of the banks. Recently, Citi bank had to pay or put aside nearly US $10 billion towards settlements in the cases of WorldCom and Enron where investors are suing banks for their role in the collapse of these companies. The compliance failures were a direct result of a series of mergers. Though the group has commenced divesting some of these units, still the problem remains.

The lesson which the Indian banks have to learn from the experience of world over, before embarking upon unbridled mergers are:

- tighten risk management
- improve human resources
- design rewards and punishments intelligently
- put proper internal control mechanism in place
- introduce transparency practices.

References

The Economist 'Successful Mergers' Getting the People Issues Right by Marion Devin, 2003.

Harvard Business Review (2000), Alex Mandl, Chief Executive of Teligent, an American Provider of Voice, Data and Internet Services to Small to Medium Sized Businesses.

Extract from a Speech given by Steve Case, Chairman, AOL, Time Warner to the Investors during the AOL Time Warner Investors 'Day' 30 January, 2001.

A. N. Berger *et al* (1999), *Journal of Banking and Finance,* Vol. 23, (Elsevier, Netherlands), pp. 135-194.

The Impact of Mergers and Acquisitions on the Efficiency of the U. S. Banking Industry.

Bank Mergers: Boon or Bane for Consumers? (Cover Story) Consumers' Research Magazine; 8/1/1998; Smith, Frances B.

Mergers and Acquisitions in the Spanish Banking Industry: Some Empirical Evidence by Ignacio Fuentes and Teresa Sastre Banco de Espana.

The impact of bank mergers and acquisitions on small business lending, a conference report prepared by the Office of Economic Research of the United states Small Business Administration's Office of Advocacy (Washington, DC), Oct. 1997.

The People Side of M&A, H. R. Strategies, John Mumm and David Beuerlein 12/01/2004.

European Central Bank (2000), 'Mergers and Acquisitions Involving the EU Banking Industry-Facts and Implications', Report Prepared by the Banking Supervision Committee (BSC).

Harle, Philipp (2005), 'Negotiating Better Cross-border Banking Mergers in Europe', *The McKinsey* Quarterly, December.

IBA (2005), 'Performance Highlights, Public Sector Banks-2004-05', Indian Banks' Association (IBA).

40

Consolidation of Banks: Mergers and Acquisitions

Naveen Kumar Mishra

Consolidation in Indian banking is a contemporary issue being debated in various circles, today. The need for consolidation in Indian banking was identified as early as in 1998 by the Narasimham Committee II, which recommended an urgent need for 3-4 large international banks among Indian banks, a few national banks and the balance regional level banks. It is recognized that Indian banking is fragmented and Indian banks are very small in size by international scale. Our biggest bank ranks only 82nd among the global banks and that is the only Indian entry in the 'Top 100' banks in the world. Not to talk of Europe or USA, even in our neighbourhood the biggest bank in China is 8 times bigger than the biggest Indian bank. World over consolidation of banks has further added to this size difference. Globally, the main drivers of consolidation process have been:

- The constant need to upgrade technology requiring huge investments.
- Rapid commoditisation of banking products, which puts pressure on the spreads. Thus, it becomes necessary to attain a particular size and scale to remain profitable.

- For the banks to be profitable and also to retain customer patronage they have to develop the full suite of financial products and capabilities. The larger the number of products from a bank being used by a customer, the greater is the profitability. The customer's bonds with the banks also become stronger. Multi product capabilities require the banks to have a minimum size.
- The recapitalisation requirements particularly for Basel II would require the banks to raise capital from the market since internal accruals may not be sufficient. Banks with larger size and more dominant position may command better 'price-earning ratios' and find it easier and more viable to raise equity from the market than smaller banks. In the present stage of globalisation, the banks may also require to approach the foreign market for rasing capital where the size is important. Higher 'price-earning ratios' and size would also act as a check on predatory moves.

Narasimham Committee II while advocating the need for mergers, stated that mergers need to be based on synergies and locational and business specific complementarities and should make commercial sense. Mergers should be worthwhile only if they lead to rationalization of staff and branch network. Mergers should lead to the whole being greater than the sum of the parts.

Remaining almost dormant for a few years, the matter has recently gained some priority. In fact, the three important challenges for Indian banking as enumerated by the Finance Minister include consolidation, competition and convergence. Perhaps the geo-political and global realities of the emerging economic landscape with increasing free movement of capital and services across the countries and shrinking of the world into a global village, has made it urgent for the Indian banks also to scale up. The road map for expansion of the role of foreign banks in India set out by RBI would substantially open up the Indian banking space to foreign players after 2009. The time allowed upto 2009 is in fact meant for Indian banks to make themselves stronger and grow in size so that they can ward off predatory moves, have multi product protfolio and capabilities, and develop comparable technological capabilities to give competitive service and achieve cost efficiency in transactions.

Indian banking, with dominant players being public sector banks, has had two major ills-one, limited range of products and two, high transaction costs. Added to that is the lack of capability to provide multiple delivery points, and poor MIS and data management hampering good risk management practices. This was due to the fact that till about a decade ago, Indian banking was mostly manual. The initial I.T. forays were mainly stand alone or 'branch transactions' modules. The real networking, particularly with centralized data base is of recent origin. The I.T. capabilities further need to be scaled up to meet customer demands as also for sophisticated risk management systems. Data warehousing, data mining, CRM, HRM and other decision support systems would continue to involve substantially more investments in I.T. going forward. To derive value out of such heavy investment, the banks would need to scale up. 'M&As' in the banking sector is, therefore, almost an imperative need of the times.

The last twenty-five years have witnessed a spate of mergers and acquisitions (M&A) in the banking industry in the developed countries such as USA, U.K., Germany, France, Switzerland, Netherlands, Italy, Japan , etc. There were also many cross border mergers within and outside Europe. The average size of a bank has significantly gone up in these countries and giants have been created in the banking industry through this M&A process. While the jury is still out on the long term effects of these M&A in banking, in the short and medium run there does not appear to be a revolutionary improvement in scale and cost efficiency and only a moderate improvement in scope and profit efficiency while the gains from diversification were quite big (Berger, A. (1998), Berger, Demsetz, and Strahan (1999).

Despite the not so impressive record of the merged banks abroad, their ability to produce financial services seamlessly across products, geographies and clients have attracted attention in developing countries like India. In a number of recent speeches, the Finance Minister of India noted that one of the basic driving forces in Indian banking in the future is going to be consolidation and suggested that the Indian public sector banks (PSBs) should pay attention to the M&A trends abroad and the potential in the domestic market. He also noted that Indian banks did not feature in the top 20 or 50 global banks and indicated that a major consolidation drive is required to make Indian banks world class in terms of size and quality. In this context, it should be noted that the consolidation of PSBs was first recommended by the Narasimham Committee on Financial Systems (1991) and working group was constituted by the government on bank mergers which has submitted it recommendation in October 2004.

It is not clear whether we are going to see a significant number of mergers between Indian PSBs in the near and distant future. It is not at all clear whether such a merger wave will take place automatically without regulatory intervention to induce PSBs to merge with each other can be challenged. Clearly, the Indian context is different and unique enough to warrant a selective policy framework for bank mergers. A tendency to import trends and policies across the board would be likely to backfire. For example, in USA, the deregulation in terms of relaxation of interstate barriers to bank branching has been catalytic in the M&A process. Further, the banking industry was based on small unit banks rather than branch based banking. As a result there was significant potential for M&As. Such conditions do not hold in Indian context where banks are based on significant branching and where there are no barriers to interstate branching. Perhaps one can justify M&A in the Indian context given the technological revolution in banking which has been acknowledged globally to be one of the major causes of M&A wave in banking. However, before one does so, one should pay attention to the labour intensive character of Indian PSBs. Lakshminarayanan (2005) points out that in terms of cost of funds and capital base, Indian banks are at a disadvantage. While his argument certainly has merit, one could argue that India could import cheaper capital from abroad through better banking practices and through capital convertibility. As far as size of the balance sheet is concerned, one has to clearly establish the need for it and the ability of the Indian banks to manage such a huge increase in the capital base in the short run. In Japan and Germany, banking consolidation increased the intensity of the relationship between banks and firms 'within' business groups and 'between' groups of borrowers and banks. Risk sharing motives that have generated these mergers are not necessarily present in the Indian context. Market power can surely be increased through bank mergers as in U.K. and some European countries. However, the need for enhancing market power is not readily apparent for our banks since managerial slack or x-inefficiency in banking typically moves proportionately with market power. Dymski, A. (2002) suggests that historically, most of the bank M&As in the developing countries have taken place in terms of distressed restructuring in response to macroeconomic shocks or consolidation of undiversified small local banks prone to high risks and overexposure of portfolio in certain industries and geographies. To make a proper assessment of the need for consolidation among the Indian PSBs (as well PSB takeovers of small private banks), one has to have a clear idea about the interplay of dynamic factors in shaping the structure and performance of the banking industry.

Envisioning the Future

The future presents both threats and opportunities for the PSBs. The banking industry structure will undergo some basic changes in respect of overall growth capability, risk management potential and competitive pressures. These changes, taken together, will imply an enhanced complexity in the banking industry structure and performance.

In the last few years the Indian GDP has been growing at a rate of 7-8%. Demand for industrial and agricultural credit have accordingly grown faster than that in the 1990s and the demand for credit by the retail sector, export sector and the infrastructure sector have been growing at significantly higher rates. In the short run the Indian economy is poised to overtake many economies in terms of GDP, and there lies significant potential in small scale trade and retail credit in the semi-urban areas and in micro credit in the rural areas. In the medium and long run the Indian economy is expected to become a global player with significant presence in world markets and lucrative rural markets. This provides an opportunity as well as a threat for the PSBs. Growth will create flexibility in asset structure, higher capital base and market share and therefore enable PSBs to generate adaptation efficiency. On the other hand, without efficient adaptation to the growth process, the PSBs cannot sustain their competitive edge and asset leverage and therefore will not be able to exploit the opportunities afforded by the domestic and the international market.

A new cohort of risk management professionals and new systems of risk management built into banking software offers tremendous advantages to all banks. The impact of these professionals and systems are bigger with respect to these professionals and systems are bigger with respect to the PSBs in particulars, in upgrading their relatively backward risk management processes. However, the new systems and people come at cost of adaptation to older systems and the costs will be highest for the PSBs for obvious reasons. A bank with a better risk management systems, process and people will be able to generate better performance than others. Such a bank can also think in terms of buying out other banks and replicating the superior risk management process on the assets bought out.

Competition for deposits, loans and other products offered by banks will be in terms of service quality, product differentiation and interest rates. Increased competition will create finer market segments through specialization and differentiation. Across these market segments, competition will be limited due to product differentiation and specialization. Within market segments the competition in terms of quality and interest rates will accentuate the difference between the winners and losers by providing the winners with the cream customers at the retail and wholesale levels while pushing the losers to the residual market. Thus, the competitive forces will provide significant gains for those banks which are able and willing to develop niche areas and improve market share in those areas. It seems probable that the winners will have an incentive to acquire the assets of the losers since they can generate greater value from those assets by combing them with the winning strategies. In banks with farsighted management, we should expect that the hunt for assets to be already on in terms of information acquisition and processing. Also, the more the PSBs become well capitalized in the stock market and the greater the sensitivity of the stocks to performance, the greater will be the incentive for one PSB to monitor and acquire the other PSBs.

Growth will be accompanied by increased risks which have to be managed in terms of efficient portfolio diversification, better operational risk management and innovations of risk transfer mechanisms. Competitive forces will continuously expose banks to new types of on balance sheet and off balance sheet risks. Growth, risk management enhancement and competition taken together will undoubtedly create complexity in the banking landscape by restructuring risk, return and liquidity of financial assets. Banks will be forced to choose between the following very different growth strategies:

- Focus on comparative advantage and grow on that basis while covering risks through off balance sheet instruments
- Focus on niche areas and be small and efficient
- Develop into an universal bank with several wholesale and retail services and products growing under one roof
- Carry on business as before

Optimal Strategy

The optimal strategy will depend on the special historical conditions in the operations of each bank and the orientation towards future growth, competition and risk. For moderate sized PSBs that have succeeded in some special areas of their protfolios, the strategy that should be adopted will be that of high growth based on comparative advantages and specialization. For bigger PSBs, market power should be leveraged together with special areas of expertise to grow into a full fledged universal bank. For the remaining PSBs, the choice should be between that of carrying on business as before (diversified but not too high or profitable) and that of focusing on being small and efficient in niche areas.

The fundamental dilemma in the choice of growth strategy is whether a PSB should try to grow organically or grow through mergers and acquisitions. Organic growth tends to be slow and is dependent on the clients and regions served by a bank, but preserves the corporate ethos and culture of a bank better. On the other hand, consolidation with another bank may lead to expertise and synergy gains and enables the merged bank to grow faster. This creates a higher value in banking in a relatively short time. While some PSBs have unique culture and are decidely regional in nature and highly dependent on specific corporate ethos for their functioning, there are those which are national level players that can absorb other banks better in the process of growth. For the latter group, a consolidation policy is required. For the former group, organic growth is the more suitable strategy though this will imply overxposure in terms of regions and industries. However, appropriate off balance sheet activities can counter those risks.

Mergers are strategic decisions justified by some intrinsic advantages that they confer through increased market power, economies of scale and scope and diversification benefits. Any bank would like to capture market power benefit of a merger, however the cost of acquiring a market power is potential governance problems of a bigger and more complex organization (diseconomies of scale and scope). Economies of scale gains may turn out to be quite small (as in USA and some countries in Europe) and have to be appraised well enough during the merger negotiations process. Many times, the realized economies of scale depend on the post merger restructuring of assets and reationalization of the work force. In the case of Indian PSBs this clearly turns out to be a difficulty. Economies of scope or 'synergy' is a more distinct possibility in the sense that a product launched by a PSB in one region may be more easily distibuted in another region after marger. Many times, a PSB may have overexposure to assets in one region or industry, in that case it maybe sensible to find a partner which has a portfolio of assets that varies inversely with it such that a lower risk can be achieved for the same mean rate of return. Of couse, if off balance sheet asset markets like bank interst swaps are well developed, then a better hedging strategy does not necessarily require a bank merger (Mallick 2004).

For a regulator, it is not necessarily easy to find which bank should be merged and with whom. In such circumstances it is best to let the capital market decide. But the capital market will not function in the present environment where only minority private investors drive the value creation process. Since all the PSBs by definition are owned by the government, there will be no effective change of ownership in mergers between PSBs. With protected ownership, there will be less internal and external monitoring of a PSB and more inefficiency (especially x-inefficiency). If PSBs tap the capital market and get privatized so that the majority of a bank's stocks are listed and traded regularly with a high volume, it will be relatively easy to pick winners, losers and 'synergies' through informationally efficient asset pricing. The real challenge then would be to have antitrust authorities in banking to evaluate merger bids in terms of total value creation in terms of shareholders and other important stakeholders. For example, if merger creates significant market power then the potential beneficiary banks will have an incentive to engage in M&A, but such mergers can increase the concentration index in the industry and lead to lower social surplus (high interest rate spread and low quality of services) created by the banking system. Such mergers should be blocked by the regulator for the sake of efficiency and equity. However, if such mergers increase the stability of the banking system by creating safer banks, or generate economies of scale and scope that enhances the efficiency of the banking industry, then the regulator should welcome them. It may be the case that the management of a PSB does not feel ready to go for M&A despite obvious gains, under such circumstances the regulator should step in through creating the necessary change in management and incentive structures. However, before intervening, the regulator has to clearly establish the potential gains through M&A.

Implementation

The merger strategy can be implemented through organizational, contractual and management restructuring. For those PSBs whose optimal growth strategies are through mergers and acquisitions, the organizational challenge is that of decentralization and delegation through a multidivisional structure. As emphasized by Chandler (1962) and Milgrom and Roberts (1992), under such a structure the divisional units have to be given considerable autonomy and incentives while the group offices and the corporate headquarters have to take the responsibility of coordination among divisions and framing the overall policy direction. To apply this organization design principle in banking., several issues should be borne in mind. One is that some divisions or departments like the rural credit and small scale credit divisions are usually subsidized by other activities, and as a result there arises a moral hazard problem of under-effort and low monitoring in such units. To cope with this moral hazard problem in such units, they should be organized as profits centres with the division heads and other employees receiving a bonus for generating profit. Keeping in mind the problem of loan recovery in such priority sector lending areas, the transfer price of funds should be set lower than for other divisions or departments. The second issue has to do with the fact that some divisions or departments have overlapping zones of activity that need to be coordinated by grouping the units under a group executive. For example, the credit risk management department of a bank will need to coordinate with the statistical and planning division for appropriate data transfer and processing and will need feedbacks from the credit recovery unit regarding information about the latest pattern in recovery. The retail credit division will need better coordination with the personnel and marketing division to create financial products and services which are of high quality and that create customer satisfaction and loyalty. The grouping of divisions has to be structured to optimise with respect to such coordination issues. The third issue is that of assigning costs and benefits of transactions to the different divisional units to maximize corporate profits. The major allocation problems are with respect to the cost of funds and that of the overheads. When a division like merchant banking raises its own funds the problem is not so severe. However, when a division like corporate or retail credit gets the funding from resources raised at branches and cash managed at the treasury, then the issue of allocation of the cost of funds become appropriate. Units should be given incentives to economize on funds through sufficiently high transfer prices while at the same time ensuring that it does not lead to too high lending rates that will cause adverse selection and moral hazard. With Basel II, operational risks have entered into the formal category of risks and provisioning, management and control of such risks have accordingly become important.

Conclusion

Indian PSBs have long been burdened with the responsibility of development banking through mobilizing deposits at the countryside and providing finance to agriculture and small scale industries at subsidized rates. It is time to marry the social responsibility of these banks with proper commercial orientation so that they can survive and prosper in an environment of high growth, competition and risks. For some PSBs today, this implies the need for mergers. For a bank that has the capacity to grow in terms of its intrinsic comparative advantage but is constrained due to the problems of inter-regional penetration, merger with a similar bank (in terms of comparative advantage and portfolio) will provide an avenue to grow optimally. Similarly, a bank of the size and experience of SBI can aspire to become a universal bank by acquiring smaller banks with lucrative retail and wholesale protfolio and through strategic alliances with investment banks, insurance companies and asset management firms. For others, there are other strategic configurations that are optimal. Given the current distribution of assets and protfolio performance of the PSBs, most of them belong to the residual category.

The process of M&A will be socially beneficial and value adding if PSBs are privatised before placing merger bids. Since bank privatisation is not immediately on the anvil, one may have to resort to relatively more distortionary means like partial privatisation and restructuring the incentives of the bank management.

References

Rhoades S. A. (1998), The Efficiency Effects of Bank Mergers; An Overview of Case Studies of Nine, *Journal of Banking and Finance* (Elsevier, Netherlands), Vol. 22, pp. 273-291.

Banking Consolidation Must be Synergy Driven by Manoranjan Sharma in *Hindu Business Line.*

KPMG: Unlocking Shareholder Value: The Keys to Success (London, 1999).

Financial Services and Convergence: Advancing to the End Game. *Business Economice;* 10/1/1998; Wilson, Greg.

Berger, A. (1998), "The Efficiency Effects of Bank Mergers and Acquisition: A Preliminary Look at the 1990s Data" in Bank Mergers & Acquisitions, edited by Y. Amihud and G. Miller. Boston, MA. Kluwer Academic: 79-111.

Berger A, R. S. Demsetz and P. E. Strahan (1999), "The Consolidation of the Financial Service Industry: Causes, Consequences and Implications for the Future", *Journal of Banking and Finance,* 23,135-90.

Chandler, Jr A. D, (1962), Strategy and Structure. (Cambridge, MA, MIT Press).

Dymski, A. (2002), "The Global Bank Merger Wave: Implications for Developing Countries", *The Developing Economies,* XL, 4:435-66.

Lakshminarayanan, P. (2005), "Consolidation in the Banking Industry through Mergers and Acquisitions", *IBA Bulletin,* 92-99.

Mallick, I. (2004), "Comparative Advantage in Banking and Stratefic Specialization in Cournot Games", in Trade, Finance and Development, edited by B. Chatterjee and A. Raychaudhuri, Deep & Deep Publications Pvt. Limited.

P. Milgrom and J. Roberts (1992), Economics, Organization and Management. (Prentice Hall, Englewood Cliffs, New Jersey 07632).

Huizinga H. P., J.H.M. Nelissen and R. Vander Vennet (2001), 'Efficiency Effects of Bank Mergers and Acquisitions in Europe', Tinbergen Institutie Discussion Paper # 2001-88/3.

41

Mergers and Acquisitions in Banks: An Analysis

Prabhat Kumar

Mergers and Acquisitions (M&As) are a part of corporate finance strategy and is often used by firms inter alia to increase their asset size, gain market share and diversify. There could be three types of mergers between firms: horizontal, vertical and diversification (The Economist). In horizontal integration, two similar firms come together; vertical integration happens when firms at different stages in the supply chain tie the knot; when two firms with different business come together such a merger is referred to as diversification. Though one has been hearing about it more frequently in India in recent times, 'mergers and acquisitions' in banks in particular is not a new phenomenon either in India or in the world. One of the earliest known mergers between banks dates back to 1930 when Chase National Bank (in the USA) acquired Equitable Trust (also in the USa(Rhoades, 1996). In India the earliest recorded merger between banks occurred in 1969 when Bank of Bihar Ltd. was merged with State Bank of India (RBI, 2005). Europe and Japan too have witnessed several mergers and acquisitions between banks. It may be noted that M&A of banks have not been confined marely to the contours of a country or even a continent. In fact, M&As have often been cross-border (especially in

Europe) and even cross-continent (US and Japanese banks, for instance).

Rationale for M&A

In recent times, M&A has often been seen as a way out of a crisis that has hit the banking sector. This is especially true of Japan (Madzharova and Kolev, 2005), Europe (Robinson, 2002) and even the USA (FRB, 1998). In Japan, in the nineties, post the real estate and stock market bubble burst, the government prescribed deregulatory measures known as the 'Big Bang' (1996) to help the banking industry come out of the crisis. In the crisis their non-performing assets or NPAs burgeoned beyond manageable limits. As a part of this , the Japanese government encouraged the merging and acquiring of weak banks by strong banks. Thus, the Long Term Credit bank of Japan was taken over by the U.S. investment firm Ripplewood Holdings; Fuji Bank, Dai-ichi-Kangyo Bank (DKB) and the Industrial Bank of Japan (IBJ) merged in 2000. In the USA, high levels of merger activity were seen since 1980 coinciding with large number of bank failures in that period. Back home in India, the merger of Global Trust Bank with Oriental Bank of Commerce, was in response to the financial mess that GTB had got into.

While it seems that world over M&As have been used as a medicine to cure ailing banks, there are other motives for M&As that have been chronicled in literature. Some of these are:

- *Economies of scale:* Theses arise form the fact that the combined entity can often reduce departments or operations, lowering the costs of the company relative (at least in theory) to the same revenue stream, thereby increasing profitability.
- *Increased market share:* This is the natural outcome of a takeover and can help the company increase its presence in the market and be the price maker.
- *Cross-selling:* This is particularly true of M&As in the financial sector. For instance; a bank taking over a

mutual fund can use its customer base to sell products of the mutual fund.

- *Synergy:* If two entities have strengths in different areas, a merger can help them synergise their respective strengths and can become more efficient in its delivery. For example if a bank that has good geographical reach mergers with one that has developed a lot of hybrid products, then the two strengths can be used effectively to their combined advantage.
- *Taxes:* A profitable firm can buy a loss-making unit to use the latter's tax write-offs.
- *Diversification:* Geographical or product diversification is often the motive behind mergers. This motive is further driven by the desire to smooth earnings and avoid cyclicality in profits/revenue streams.

Mergers and Acquisitions in Banking: Some International Experience

If the proof of the pudding lies in its eating then the gains from M&As can be best understood by studying some of the pre and post experiences of some of the banks from all over the world. In the USA, M&As in banking has led to a decline in the number of banks and banking organizations but interestingly, an increase in the number of bank offices. Between 1980 and 1997, a spate of mergers in banks in the USa led to the number of banks coming down from 14,407 to 9,064. However, the number of banking offices (banks as well as their branches) increased from 52,710 to 71,080 (FRB,1998). Thus, fewer banking organizations has not meant, at least in the case of the USA, fewer bank offices serving the public. The other notable effect of M&As in the US banking industry has been the increase in the share of the total banking assets controlled by the largest banks. However, there has not been much change reported in the percentage of bank deposits accounted for by the largest three banks. One interesting experience of M&As in the banking industry in the USA has been the response of 'other' banks to mergers announced between two given banks. For instance, mergers have not affected lending to small businesses because in markets where mergers have taken place, other banks have increased their supply of loans to small businesses. Similarly, other banks have also opened offices in areas where mergers have led to closing down of bank branches. In a way, the behavior of 'other' banks has often offset the possible negative effects (for customers) of bank mergers. Efficiency gains too have been reported by mergers and acquisitions in the US banking industry. With respect to profitability, it was found that banks in relatively more concentrated markets (less competition) exhibit higher profits compared to those that operate in relatively less concentrated markets (more competition). Studies have also shown that banks in relatively more concentrated markets tend to charge higher rates for certain types of loans than do banks in less concentrated markets (FRB, 1998).

In contrast to the US, experience in Europe has been mixed. While the experience with domestic mergers has been satisfactory, cross border deals have been largely disappointing (Harle, 2005). With respect to domestic mergers substantial productivity gains were recorded by banks in Italy and Germany in the 1990s. This was largely because of unexploited scale economies that became available on mergers (Huizinga, *et al*, 2001). Improved cost efficiency was reported in consolidating banks in case of both large and small banks. On the issue of profitability, it was found that profit efficiency rose for small banks and reduced for large banks. In EU, it was found that merged banks offered higher deposit rates to its customers in a bid to increase their share of deposit market. clearly not a priority for banks in the USA. Cross border deals in the EU have generally not been happy marriages mainly because of the actions of the regulatory authorities, unions and incumbent management (Harle, 2005). In ten such troubled mergers it was found that in order to maintain peace with the stakeholders, the management in the acquiring bank often entered into complex negotiations that almost guaranteed a status quo in the acquired bank. This had impeded the acquirers' ability to integrate the acquired bank with itself in a manner that would enhance its efficiency.

Like any other strategy, M&As have their inherent risks which often cause M&As to fail. In a study conducted by the European Central Bank (2000) on M&As in the banking industry, it was found that mergers took place either because small banks wanted to achieve economies of scale or large banks wanted to strategically reposition themselves. Often the process of consolidation led to the formation of financial conglomerates. Like with everything else, M&As are not without their share of difficulties/problems. The ECB in its report identified the following risks that M&As in the banking industry entailed:

- *Operational risk:* Owing to the difficulties faced in integrating different risk management systems as well as different accounting and control procedures.
- *Culture blending risk:* This arises from the difficulty faced in reconciling different cultures (for instance, working culture or certain practices) among the staff and business units of the two different business units and this could often lead to a loss of key employees.
- *Failure to achieve gains:* There is always the risk that the purpose of M&A is not achieved either because of labour market rigidities or the complexity arising out of operating a merged entity.

The risks were clearly articulated in the case of failed M&As in the EU. Despite the fact that more often than not M&As have destroyed value for the acquirer's shareholders, world over corporations have not given up on M&A as a corporate strategy. This is because it is equally true that M&As have the potential of creating value for shareholders. In fact it is seen that some of the world's top-performing companies are unusually acquisitive (Mathieu and Brown, 2002). What distinguishes these companies from the rest is that in these companies, M&As are a means to implementing a strategy and not a strategy by itself. In addition, each acquisition was value-creating as part of the strategy it sought to implement. The few success stories have meant that M&As as a strategy has not yet been given up.

M&As in the Indian Banking Industry

During the last few years, there has speculation in the market about the likely merger of Union Bank of India with Bank of India. There were also murmurs of a merger between Bank of Baroda and Dena bank. The Ministry of Finance as well as the Reserve Bank of India (RBI) have been vocal in their favour of mergers and acquisitions in the Indian banking industry. In fact, the RBI came out with guidelines on mergers and amalgamations between banking entities as well as between a Non Bank Financial Company (NBFC) and a banking entity (RBI, 2005). While the guidelines pertain to the private sector banks, the RBI has specified that these principles underlying the guidelines would apply to public sector banks as well. Consolidation is one of the important philosophies that drives thinking on the banking industry at both the Ministry as well as the RBI. The genesis for this philosophy is often credited to the Narasimham Committee Report on banking reforms (1998). The Report had recommended consolidation among banks while at the same time retaining the competitive structure of the Indian banking industry (Narasimham, 1998). Consolidation has been suggested by the Committee as a means to reaping benefits such as stronger balance sheets permitting larger exposures, economies of scale, avoiding duplication of Information Technology (IT) investments, branch rationalization, among others. The Committee suggests that there should be 8-10 national level banks with large network of branches and 3 to 4 banks with international presence. The Committee categorically states that the decision to merge should emanate from the managements of the banks and the government's role should be of supporting nature only.

Since the release of the Narasimham Committee Report, there have been several mergers and acquisitions in the Indian banking industry. These have been of different 'types'. The merger of Times Bank Ltd. With HDFC Bank Ltd. (2000), of Bank of Madura with ICICI Bank Ltd. (2001) were initiated at the instance of the banks' management and were in keeping with the spirit of the Narasimham Committee recommendations. The merger (or takeover, to be more precise) of Global Trust

Bank with Oriental Bank of Commerce (2004) or that of Nedungadi bank Ltd. With Punjab National Bank (2003) or the proposed merger of Ganesh Bank of Kurundwad with Federal bank Ltd. (2006) are at the behest of the RBI and have been recommended in the hope of turning around the weak banks that have been taken over. While the nature of merger (voluntary or regulator led) may or may not make a difference to the success of the merger, what would matter is the basic strategy behind the merger. As mentioned above, success of M&As depends on the underlying strategy as 'M&As depends on the underlying strategy as 'M&As' is a means to a greater end and not an end in itself.

M&As Between PSBs in India: A Poser

Given that M&As can succeed only if it is a part of a larger strategy of banks, we attempt a clinical examination of the touted merger between Union Bank of India and Bank of India and between Bank of Baroda and Dena Bank by examining their balance sheets, profile, etc. to try to see what the future will hold if these banks were indeed to be merged. Though one is not aware of the underlying strategy that is dictating these mergers, between similar banks can serve mainly one purpose: create a large banking entity which is able to compete globally. Currently, the SBI, India's largest bank (asset size of US $127 billion) is ranked 83rd among the World's banks in terms of asset size. Merger of any two public sector banks will still not leapfrog us into the World's top banks in terms of asset size. For instance, the merger of Bank of India with the Union Bank of India will make the combined asset size of the merged entity Rs. 1,67,391 crore. In comparison, the asset size of SBI is Rs. 4,59,882 crore.

If the merger is between two dissimilar banks (in terms of business, branch spread, etc.), the strategy behind merger could be to maximise synergies and diversify the banks' business both in terms of types of business and geographical spread. Therefore, an analysis of the balance sheets of the banks will give a clue as to whether it is going to be a merger of similar entities or dissimilar entities. That would further throw light on the underlying strategy of the banks for the proposed merger.

Bank of India (BoI) and Union Bank of India

The similarities between these two banks are striking. They are similar in the size and geographical spread of the branches (Table 1) with a strong presence in Western and Central India. BoI's 1,356 branches (50.8%) and Union Bank's 1,142 branches (53.4%) are located in western and central region of the country. Some of the branches of BoI and Union Bank in these regions are located in the same area/street. Bank of India (BOI) has more branches in the East than the Union Bank of India. whereas the latter has more presence in the North-East compared to the latter. Which means, that if merged, the East and the North-East are likely to be served more than in the past by merged entity, at least in terms of number of branches (i.e. if branch rationalisation does not lead to paring down of bank branches).

Table 1
Bank Branches (2004-05)

Name of the Bank/Regions	*Bank of India*	*Union Bank of India*	*Bank of Baroda*	*Dena Bank*
Northern Region	220	246	494	6
	(8.2)	(11.5)	(17.8)	(6.3)
North Eastern Region	11	45	25	2
	(0.4)	(2.1)	(0.9)	(0.2)
Eastern Region	734	233	260	42
	(27.5)	(10.9)	(9.4)	(3.9)
Central Region	503	(653	706	142
	(18.9)	(30.5)	(25.5)	(13.3)
Western Region	853	489	1018	736
	(32.0)	(22.9)	(36.7)	(69.0)
Southern Region	347	473	268	78
	(13.0)	(22.1)	(9.7)	(7.3)
All India Branches (2004-05)	2668	2139	2771	1067
	(100.0)	(100.0)	(100.0)	(100.0)

Source: RBI's Statistical Tables related to Banks in India, 2004-05.

Bank Branches (2004-05)

There are other similarities as well. The asset and liability structure are similar both in terms of structure and amount. Both of them report higher interst income than non-interest income; Union Bank of India reporting marginally higher interest income than Bank of Inida. A point to note is that. Return on Assets (ROA) of the Union Bank comes at a lower asset base than that of Bank of India (Table 3). As far as the liabilities are concerned, the borrowings of Bank of India are more than twice that of the Union Bank of India (Table 3). There is not much difference in the business garnered per employee but there is a difference in the profit/employee as well as the ratio of operating profit to working funds of the banks. Thus, if the two banks were to come together, assuming a mere merger of the balance sheets, we can expect the following characteristics in the merged entity:

- Higher asset and liability base
- Marginally higher interest income/working funds
- Lower ROA for post-merged Union Bank (higher for post-merged Bank of India)
- Lower profit/employee for post-merged Union Bank (higher for Bank of India)
- Lower operating profit/working funds for post merged Union Bank (higher for Bank of India).

Some issues that may require attention is the merger of the Information Technology (IT) systems in the banks. This may call for additional cost in the initial stages.

If these banks are indeed are indeed merged, this is what the new merged entity will look like:

- Asset size will be to the tune of Rs. 1,18,692 crore
- NPA ratio will rise as Dena Bank's NPA/net advances ratio is much higher than that of BOB (Table 2).
- Not much effect on financial parameters like interest income/working funds and no interest income/working funds or business/employee

Table 2
Select Financial Parameters of the Banks

Financial Parameters	*Bank of India*	*Union Bank of India*	*Bank of Baroda*	*Dena Bank*
CRAR	11.52	12.09	12.61	11.91
Net NPAs/net advances	2.77	2.64	1.45	5.23
Interest income working funds	6.71	7.96	6.86	7.48
Non-interest income/working funds	1.29	1.23	1.39	1.35
Operating profit/working funds	1.62	2.52	2.45	1.94
ROA	0.38	1.1	0.75	0.26
Business/employee (Rs. Lakh)	320	346.72	31037	313
Profit/employee (Rs. Lakh)	1.71	2.81	1.71	0.6

Source: RBI's Trend and Progress of Banking in India, 2004-05.

Table 3
Asset Composition of the Balances Sheet of the Banks
(Ratio of Total Assets, in %)

Assets	*Bank of India*	*Union Bank of India*	*Bank of Baroda*	*Dena Bank*
Cash and balance with RBI	4.11	5.04	2.87	6.20
Balances with bank and money at call	3.81	4.04	6.91	1.21
Investments	29.69	31.48	39.16	40.36
Advances	58.97	55.38	45.85	47.06
Total Assets (Rs. Crore)	94978	72413	94664	24028

Source: IBA's Performance Highlights of Public Sector Banks, 2004-05.

Table 4
Computerisation of the Banks (as on March 31, 2006)

(in %)

Name of the Bank	*Bank of India*	*Union Bank of India*	*Bank of Baroda*	*Dena Bank*
Branches # Fully Computerised	74.5	0.1	83.1	93.8
Branches under Core Banking Solution (CBS)	4.9	29.3	–	-
Fully Computerised Branches	79.5	29.4	83.1	93.8
Branches Partially Computerised	20.5	70.6	16.9	6.2
Expenditure incurred on computerisation & development of Communication networks (Up to end-March 2005) (Rs. Crore)	1,874	3,11	3.01	1,21

\# Other than those under CBS,

Source: RBI's Trend and Progress of Banking in India, 2004-05.

- Profit/employee will be lower for the merged entity than it was for BOB prior to the merger
- IT costs can be optimized as CBS implementation is pending in both the banks.

Essentially, what emerges from the above analysis is that the merger of the public sector banks mentioned will help creating larger entities but these will be much smaller than the existing size of the current State Bank of India. No apparent synergising of competencies is seen, however, it could give the merged entities greater strength to open new branches in areas where they currently don't have any presence. If branch rationalization does take place, then some of the staff manning the branches can be made available for jobs like deposit mobilization, marketing, conducting road shows, etc. Bank of Baroda as well as Bank of India are quite heavily staffed. This is apparent from the fact that their staff strength goes. Therefore, some of the staff can be made available for other jobs. Implicit in this is the assumption that the mergers will be smooth technologically as well as culturally. In conclusion, it appears that mere mergers of two public sector banks may not lead to significant benefit to the society/sector.

References

Ansoff, H. Igor (1965), Corporate Strategy, New York: McGraw-Hill.

Berkovitech, Elazar, and M.P. Narayanan (1993), "Motives for Takeovers: An Empirical Investigation", *Journal of Financial and Quantitative Analysis,* 28, September, pp. 347-362.

Bogue, Marcus C., III, and Elwood S. Buffa (1986), Corporate Strategic Analysis, New York: Free Press.

Boston Consuloting Group, The Strategy Development Process, Boston: Boston Consulting Group, 1985.

Brealey & Mayors (2002), Principles of Corporation Finance, 6th Edn.

Cuerard John and Vaught H. T. (1989), The Handbook of Financial Modlling, Probus Publishing Co., Chicago.

De-Pamphilis, Donald, Mergers (2001), Acquisitions and other Restruchuring Activities, Academic Press, San Dieago.

Eisenhardt, Kathleen M., and Donald N. Sull (2001), "Strategy as Simple Rules," *Harvard Business Review*, 79, January, pp. 106-116.

Gaughan, Patrick A., Mergers (1996), Acquisitions and Corporate Restructurings, John Wiley & Sons.

Reserve Bank of India (2005), Report on Trend and Progress of Banking in India, 2004-05.

Rhoades, Stephen A. (1996), 'Bank Mergers and Industrywide Structure, 1980-1994', Washington: Board of Governors of the Federal Reserve System, January 1996, Staff Study # 169.

Robinsor, Karina (2002), 'The Forces Driving Bank Mergers', The Banker, 2nd August.

Andrade, Gregor, and Erik Stafford (1999), "Investigating the Economic Role of Mergers", Working Paper, August.

Anslinger, Patricia L. and Thomas E. Copeland (1996), "Growth through Acquisitions: A Fresh Look," *Harvard Business Review*, 74, January-February, pp. 126-135.

Federal Reserve Bank (1998), 'Mergers and Acquisitions in Banking and other Financial Services', Testimony of Governor Laurence H. Meyer before the Committee on Banking and Financial Services, U.S. House of Representatives, April.

Harle, Philipp (2005), 'Negotiating Better Cross-border Banking Mergers in Europe', *The McKinsey Quarterly*, December, 2005.

IBA (2005), 'Performance Highlights, Public Sector banks-2004-05', Indian Banks' Association (IBA).

Madzharova P. and Ivo Kolev (2005), 'Mergers and Acquisitions in the Financial Sector: A Solution to Banking Crisis in Japan?' Research Proposal for Asian Studies Initiative.

Mathieu Bruno E. and Collin Brown III (2000), 'Making M&A Pay: Lessons from the Word's Most Successful Acquirers, Research Report by Marakon Associates.

Narasimham, M. (1998), 'The Banking Sector Reforms Report', Nabhi.

42

Bank Mergers and Acquisitions–A Panacea for Globalization

Dipak B. Bhamare

In todays globalized world, banks will have to be competitive in order to face to challenges and leverage the opportunities. The ultimate goal of a bank is to increase its market power, become more diversified, reduce the risk of entering a new business and real time the competitive edge through acquiring mergers and acquisitions a new stream of banking business. The issue of Mergers and Acquisitions of Indian banking has occupied an importance place among policy makers of Banking system in recent years. During the last few years the Indian Banking system the witnessed same very high profile mergers. The critical tool of Mergers and Acquisitions of business strategy is also now increasing in Banking Sector along with Indian economy. The Process of Mergers and Acquisitions have brought new life to the style of doing Banking business, hence it is necessary to study the concept of Mergers and Acquisitions

Concept of Merges and Acquisitions

Though mergers & acquisitions are used jointly but they have different meaning.

(i) *Merger:* According to RBI 'Merger may be defined as a combination of two or more companies in to the single to where one survies and another lose his existence.

(ii) *Merger/Amalgamation:* mean combining of two commercial company in to one and merging of 2 or more business concerns in to one respectively.

Acquisition

May be defined as an act of acquiring effective control by one corporate over the assets/mgt. of the other corporate without any combination of both of them.

In another words acquisitions in general is acquiring the ownership in the property. In short merger is essentially a partnership between equals where as acquisition is often made by stronger entity of a weaker one. In merger survivors acquire the assets as well as Liabilities for example. Sikkim Bank Ltd. were amalgamated with Union Bank of India.

History of Banks Merges and Acquisitions

Merges and acquisitions in banks in particular is not a new phenomenon in Indian and dates back from Imperial Bank of India which is as formed by the amalgamation of 3 presidency Bank i.e. Bank of Bengal, Bank of Bombay, Bank of Madras in 1921. There after few mergers have taken place mainly in PSU, to protect the interest of depositors of weak private banks. To make public and depositors confidence in banking system a new section 45 was inserted in Banking Company act in September 60. Consequently in 1961, 30 banks was merged compulsorily with the Bank.

The following table shows the number of Banks merged since 1960 to 1990.

Table 1
Banks Mergers Since 1960-1990

Year	*1960*	*61*	*62*	*64*	*65*	*69*	*70*	*85*	*86*	*89*	*90*	*Total*
No.of Banks mergered	03	30	02	09	04	03	01	03	01	01	04	34

Mergers and Acguisitions Since Nationalization

Since nationalization in 1969 Banks system. In India more significant progress in geographical spread and functional but at the same time due to poor competition, unremunrative for expansion political interference in decision, trade Union pressures and Mgt weakens create various problems before P.S. Banking, hence 2nd Banking Commission and various other Committee suggest merger. Along this Sarraiya Committee (72) N. Vaghul Report, Manubhai Shah Commission (76) Suggest the reduction in the number of existing bank.

Not only this Narasimham Committee Report 1991 had recommended board pattern of structure of Banking system. The committee was of the view that to move towards this revised system shall be market driven and based on profitability considerations & brought about through aprocess of M&A. The 2nd Narasimham Commission report in April 1998 say that merges of Public Sector Banks were expected to emanate from mgt of the banks with Govt. as Common Shareholders playing a supportive role.

This Report recommended consolidation among banks while at the same time retaining the competitive structure of the Indian banking industry (Narasimham, 1998) Consolidation has been suggested by the Committee as a means to reaping benefits such as stronger balance sheets permitting larger exposures, economies of scale, avoiding duplication of Information Technology (IT) investments, branch rationalization, among others. The Committee suggests that there should be 8-10 national level banks with large network of branches and 3 to 4 banks with international presence. The Committee Categorically state that the decision to merge should emanate from the managements of the banks and the government's role should be of supporting nature only.

Since the release of the Narasimham Committee Report, there have been several mergers and acquisitions in the indian banking industry. These have been of different 'types'. The merger of Times Bank Ltd., with HDFC Bank Ltd. (2000) of Bank of Madura with ICICI Bank Ltd. (2001) were initiated at the instance of the banks' management and were in keeping with the spirit of the Narasimham Committee recommendations. The merger (or takeover, to be more precise) of Global Trust Bank with Oriental Bank of Commerce (2004) or that of Nedungadi Bank Ltd. With Punjab National Bank (2003) or the proposed merger of Ganesh Bank of Kurundwad with Federal Bank Ltd., (2006) are at the behest of the RBI and have been recommended in the hope of turning around the weak banks that have been taken over.

Later on Joint Parliamentary Committee also recommended for such mergers and Acquisitions, before the merger sanction of RBI under section 44-A of Banking Regulation Act.1949 is necessary. The committee made 4 programmer for M & A Last but not least Finance Minister. Mr. P. Chidambaram in 2005 of Budget & his proposal above show autonomy of P.S. Banks and their M & A. All above steps discussion above boost the process of Mergers and Acquisitions in banking sector. Following table explain the detail information of mergers. During post liberalized period from (93-2004).

Table 2
List of Banks Merger during Post Liberalised Period

Name of Bank Merged	*With whom merged*	*Date of Merger*
Bank of India	Punjab National Bank	4-9-93
Bank of Karad Ltd.	Bank of India	1993-94
Kashinath Seth Bank Ltd.	Oriental Bank of Commerce Ltd.	1995-96
Punjab Co-op. Bank	Oriental Bank of Com. Ltd.	1996-97
Bari Doab Co-op. Bank	Oriental Bank of Com. Ltd.	1996-97
Times Bank Ltd.	HDFC Bank Ltd.	26.2.99
Baeilly Co-op. Bank. Ltd.	Bank of Baroda	03.6.99
Skkim Bank Ltd.	Union Bank of India	22.12.99
Benerso State Bank Ltd.	Bank of Baroda	20.7.02
Nedungadi Bank Ltd.	Punjab National Bank	01.2.03
Bank of Madura Ltd. Mar. 2001	ICICI Bank Ltd.	
Global Trust Bank Ltd.	Oriental Bank of Comm.	24.7.04
South Gujrath Local Area Bank	Bank of Baroda	2004
Ganesh Bank of Kurnwed	Federal Bank	June 2006
The Sangli Bank Ltd.	ICICI Bank (proposed)	Feb. 2007

Ref: IBA Bulletin Special Issue, Jan. 2005 page 98, *Bank Quest*, Vol. 77, Jan. Feb. 2006.

Objectives of Mergers and Acquisition of Banks

The objectives behind the merger and acquisition in the banking sector of India may be highlighted as under:

1. To receive a loss making bank as it may not be able to restore the NPA on its own.
2. To unlisted underutilized resources (i.e.H.R./physical/ or managerial skill)
3. To curve a niche for oneself as a strategic empire builder of a mass vast economic power.
4. To gain economics of scale and increase income in proportion to less amount of investment.
5. To achieve some sort of diversifications.
6. To Limit competition & prevent over crowding and mushrooming up of many banks.
7. To utilized market power in term of regional or geographical coverage in the best possible manner.
8. To over come the problems of slow peace of growth & profitability of winding up of Bank sector.

Why Indian Banking Accept M & A

At present Indian banking industry depicts highly skewed structure. It has 286 scheduled commercial banks (SCBs) with around 67000 branches all over the country. Around 23% of total branches (located in top 100 centre) account for at most 64% of aggregate deposits and 75.5 % of credit. This mean 75% bank branches account for less than 25% of Bank business. Further more 75% of the total business of SCBs accounted for by the group of 27 PSB whose share in the branch network is as high as 70% Thus India has at present a few big & too many small sized player with out a proper level playing field among them. Given this Narasimham Committee – II felt that 'Mergers alone can remedy isolated problems in small banks.

Along the above view the main motives behind the Mergers and Acquisitions of present banking are as follows:

(a) International competitiveness

(b) Systemic stability

(c) Strategic alliance

(d) Monopolistic ambitions

(e) Technology

(f) Motivation by Government and Reserve Bank of India

(g) Forcible mergers for survival.

In the present stage of globalization, banks are expected to have the expected products and presence to serve them anywhere. Even retail customers are expecting wider reach from their bankers, as the new generation is more mobile and convenience conscious. Banks do need a greater resource base and presence across and wide range of markets to satisfy their corporate customers and as such restrictions on Mergers and Acquisitions, including among major domestic financial institutions, should be relaxed to enable the development of institutions with the size and resource to compete globally.

For making banking system of world class Mergers and Acquisitions is must Global reach can be achieved not only by opening branches. Throughout the world, but also by entering into business arrangements with other banks and opening new delivery channels like ATMs and virtual banking channels like Internet Banking that expandssize interms of business. Similarly, globalization of capital markets opened doors to invite foreign investors also.

However, risk absorbing capacity and good governance practices are required to attract funds from international market for which size plays vital role. Coming to the world class service a bank needs wide range of products and world class technology as most part of the banking now-a-days is driven by technology. World class technology requires world class infrastructure, which again big size in terms of resources, network for optimum use of infrastructure and utility value is required. Thus size, technology and good governance are interrelated to each other and part and parcel of creating world class banks.

Mergers and Acquisitions and consolidation for size and increased efficiency is for many the chosen strategy to stay alive and remain competitive. As such, the reduction in cost need not necessarily result in improved operating efficiency. Mergers aim at this task for achieving cost reduction simultaneously, improving assets and revenues and appear to be successful in past. Not only improving efficiency parameters, mergers are beneficial in multiple ways.

Merger facilitates synergies between merged organizations, generate efficiency improvements and increase competitiveness. Mergers provide services at lower prices. It improves efficiency and achieve synergies.

Indeed merger, by increasing economics of scale and spreading costs over and larger customer base, enable financial operations to provide services at lower cost and prices. Merger is thus, central to making the case for the consumer benefits in assessing their potential impact on consumers.

If mergers improve efficiency, then larger, combined firms may be expected to pass savings on consumers through lower prices or improved services. Synergy is achieved by combining the forces of the two banks with complementary strengths.

The promerger argues that rather than size problems, banks have "excess capacity in their domestic markets, which derives up their costs, marking them uncompetitive both domestically and internationally" According to this argument, mergers enable rationalization of network and associated cost reductions. Considering the issue of stability, larger universal banks benefits from higher earnings-source diversification increased operating earnings stability and higher valuations".

A bank can, in principle, reduce its risk by expanding their activities into product lines whose returns are imperfectly correlated with those for the bank's existing products and services. The benefits from earnings diversification may increase bank value in several ways, since diversification may lower bank risk and reduce the possibility of failure.

Taking in to consideration the above facts merger & Acquisitions become an important tool for facing the challenges of globalization.

Advantages of Merger and Acquistions

Indian Banking sector accept the new trends of Mergers and Acquisitions because of following advantages.

(a) It will make the introduction of core banking solution at maximum number of branches due its being cost effective.

(b) The unhealthy competition will be stopped.

(c) Own system, software, lease lines etc. can be developed and own officials, buildings, residences can be created decorated will all new facilities, technique and comforts, similar to better than the world class banks.

(d) Increased number of product shall be available to customers.

(e) More employee welfare schemes can be introduced. More remunerations, better facilities may be provided to the employee/officers.

(f) It will be easier for the Government and the regulatory to make on-site and off-site surveillance for less number of banks. The guidelines and changes in the same can also be easily implemented.

(g) Banks can form their own Asset Reconstruction Companies as they will be transferring their large size NPA loans, economic for the company also.

(h) Floating provisions can be made on NPAs. More banks can write off entire NPA and can become NPA free due to availability of more net profits.

(i) It will increase the productivity of Banks. Thus business per employee will be increased.

(j) The human resource shall be managed in a proper way. It will provide more career opportunities to employees. Maximum output or productivity can be achieved by optimum capacity utilization as

(k) well as efficiency utilization of each individual putting right persons on right jobs.

Conclusion

In short we conclude that globalization has brought several opportunities, it has also brought some challenges for Indian Banking Sector i.e. challenge to reduce cost, extend the range of product and services, increase the market Share, participating in the process of privatization, diversity risks, geographical diversification, improvements in solvency, transfer of knowledge classifying NPA rules, computations from international banks. To over come these challenge both on the infernal front as well as an global. The best solution is to implement the policy of mergers and acquisitions as recommended by the Narasimham Committee According to this there should be 3 to 4 big banks having branches thought the country 8 to 10 banks at National level banks having the start of International banks.

In short the message of the panacea of Merger and Acquisition is "Merge to Emerge" and also from Large number of small banks to small number of large Banks.

Reference

Issues & Challenges of Mergers and Acquisitions by Dr. Mohan Shrivastava (Article published in Indian Banking & Financial Sector Reform Books Published by-Abhiject Published Delhi 2006.

Consolidation in Banking Industry: Merger & Acquisition by Dr. Anajali Prasad. (Article published in Indian Banking & Financial Sector Reform Books Published by-Abhiject Published Delhi 2006.

Financial Inclusion case for Mergers and Acquisitions by M. Balchandra. (Articles Published *Bank Quest* Vol. 77, January-March 2006).

Mergers and Acquisitions in Indian Banking by R. Bhaskar and T. Mqzonder. (Articles Published *Bank Quest*, Vol. 77, January-March 2006).

Mergers and Acquisitions Successes in Banking-by Unni Krishna and David. Published in The Hindu Business Line 6 October 2004.

Mergers moves don't go for Enough by P. Devragan. Published in *The Hindu Business Line* 13 May, 2005 (7)Indian Banking Under Globalization–by Dr. Ashutosh Raravikar. Paper published in 2 day National Seminar on Globalization and Challenges for Banking sector held on 9 to 10th February, 2007 as S.S.V.P.S. College, Dhule.

Website of R.B.I.

43

Consolidation in Banking Industry Through Mergers and Acquisitions

Jitendra Kumar

This era is the era of Globalisation, liberalisation, privatisation and competition. Consolidation in Banking industry through mergers is the most important method and process for the development of Indian Economy. All over the world Joint stock company or Business companies, Firms, Financial Institution, Technological Companies and Banking industries are taken super fast interest through marger, Amalgamation, Acquisition and take over for the purpose of improvement of down fall image of Banks. Merger is the weakness of small and unprofitable bank with large, strong and profitable Banks.

The Narasimhan Committed (1998) has made out a strong case for a stronger banking system in the country, especially in the context of capital account convertibility (CAC) which would involve large inflows and outflows of capital and consequent complications for exchange rate management and domestic liquidity. To handle such problems, India needs a strong and resiliet banking and financial system. For this purpose, the Narasimhan committee on Banking Sector Reforms (1998) has recommended the merger of strong banks which will have a "multiplier effect" on industry, The committed has, however, cautioned the merger of strong and weak banks, as this may have a negative impact on the asset quality of the stronger bank. The committee has also supported that two or three large Indian banks be given international or global character.

Consolidation in Bankig industry has further become important due to the following reasons:

- Unhealthy competition amongst banks;
- Expansion of branches, unviable branches;
- Clusters of branches of various banks at particular centers;
- Regional imblance/unequal VRS;
- Improper development of staff;
- Restrictions on transfer of clerical staff;
- Inter-zone transfer policy of officers up to specified scale in various banks;
- Uneven promotions;
- Computerisation/installation of ATMs/Networking/ core banking solution.

Objectives of Mergers and Acquisition

- End of unnecessary competition and increase the maximum/more possibilities of profit in banking business.
- Development of co-operation, toleration and mutual relation in Banks after merger and Acquisition.
- Reduction in the fixed expenses after the merger of two or more Banks.
- For the strong economic structure of Banks through the control on money inflation and deflation.
- Maximum work on minimum cost from centralisation of equility in policies and methods. inspection, control and managerial functions.
- To create more customers for their product.
- Proper management and use of humen resources.
- Increase sufficient capital of Bank and progress in investigation work.

- To face with effective technique for improper burden of workers association.
- Increase in participation in the determination of plitical effect, enterferance and eco nomic policies due to increase size of Bank.
- To get all advantages of busines combination.
- Development of organistional Banking.
- Increase in fixed existence value of shareholders.
- To get all the advantages of large size as latest information Technology, New Trends and services of Exports.

Advantages of Consolidation in Banking Industry

Internationally one of the largest causes of consolidation through mergers and acquisitions is that companies as well as individual users of banking services are increasingly demanding more sophisticated banking services, particularly in the fields of electronic banking and e-commerce. The advantages of consolidation of Indian Banking Industry are as below:

- Classing down branches which are located within a short radius of the merged entity thereby cutting expenditure and development of surplus staff in marketing of other fee based services or products.
- Reduction in number of controlling offices i.e. regional or zonal offices thereby reduction in administrative expenses.
- Increase in number of transactions at ATMs and more availability of ATM to the customers.
- Reduction in payment of annual maintenance charges for software as well as numer ous other items such as services, computers, machinary equipments etc.
- Reduction in other operative expenses to a great extent.
- The consolidation will make it convenient to introduce Core Banking Solution at maximum number at branches due to its being cost effective.

- After the consolidation there will be substantial reduction in take over of accounts.
- Increased number of products available to customers.
- It will be easier for the government and the regulatory to make on-site and off-site surveillance for less number of banks.
- The consolidation will increase the productivity of banks.
- More employee welfare schemes can be introduced.
- More remunatration and better facilities may be provided to the employees/officers.
- Floating provisions on NPA can be made.

Challenges for Consolidation

- The challenges of consolidation of Banking industry through mergers and acquisitions are as below:
- To provide better and proper management.
- To face strongly all the causes of monopoly.
- To complete the legal formalities regarding Banking companies.
- To reduce casts in management.
- Fear of over capitalisation.
- No possibility to change quick in policy of large size Banks.
- Increase in centralisation of Economic power.
- Fear of over-expansion
- To maintain the faith of depositors and investors.

The procedure of consolidation of banking industry through merger and Acquisition is provided strongness and reduced enough in the number of working banks.

After getting the right under Banking Regulation Act See. 44 (A), The reserve Bank of India executes the scheme of Amalgamation of Banks after getting the permission from the central Government. After this following banks are merged amalgamated/acquisited:

The List of Merger of Banks Acquisition in India

Name of Banks	*Merged / Amalgamated with*	*Year*
Mayur Bhanj State Bank	State Bank of India	1961
Bank of Baghelghand	State Bank of India	1961
Bank of Devash	State Bank of Indore	1962
Vor State Bank	State Bank of India	1962
State Bank of Jaipur	State Bank of Bikaner & Jaipur	1963
Ram Durg Bank	State Bank of Maisoor	1963
Vashuday Vilasham Bank	State Bank of Trawankor	1963
Devas Senior Bank	State Bank of Indore	1965
Himalay Bank	State Bank of Patiyala	1966
Bank of Bihar	State Bank of India	1969
National Bank of Lahore	State Bank of India	1970
Eaxtern Bank Limited	Chartered Bank	1971
Krishna Ram Balabh Bank	State Bank of India	1974
Belgam Bank	Union Bank of India	1976
Laxami Commercial Bank	Canera Bank	1985
Bank of Cochin	State Bank of India	1985
Miraj State Bank	State Bank of India	1985
Hindustan Commercial Bank	Punjab National Bank	1986
Traders Bank Limited	Bank of Baroda	1988
United Industrial Bank	Allahabad Bank	1988
Bank of Tamilnadu	Indian Overseas Bank	1988
Bank of Tanjavur	Indian Bank	1988
Purbanchal Bank	Central Bank of India	1988
Parur Central Bank	Bank of India	1988
New Bank of India	Punjab National Bank	1993
Bank of Credit & State commerce International	Bank of India	1993
Bank of Karad	Bank of India	1994
Kashinath Seth Bank	State Bank of India	1996
S C I C I	I C I C I	1996
I T C Classic	I C I C I	1997
Bari Doaab Bank	Oriental Bank of Commerce	1997
Punjab Co-operative Bank	Oriental Bank of Commerce	1997
Angagram Finance	I C I C I	1998
Barelli Corporation Bank	Bank of Baroda	1998
20th Century Finance	Century Bank	1999
British Bank of Middle East	H S B C	1999
Times Bank	H D F C Bank	1999

Contd...

Name of Banks	*Merged / Amalgamated with*	*Year*
Sikkim Bank Limited	Union Bank of India	1999
Bank of Madurai	I C I C I	2001
I C I C I Limited	I C I C I Bank	2002
Banaras State Bank	Bank of Baroda	2002
Nedungadi Bank	Punjab National Bank	2003
South Gujarat Local Area Bank	Bank of Baroda	2004
Global Trust Bank	Oriental Bank of Commerce	2004
Four R R B's (Bihar)	Madhya Bihar Gramin Bank	2006
seven R R B's (Bihar)	Uttar Bihar Gramin Bank	2006
other R R B's (Bihar)	Bihar Gramin Bank	2006

Human Resource Management Through Consolidation

All persons are not equal. Different persons have different qualities some are expert in marketing, some in table work where as some in field more, some others are expert in making policies, And some develop specific skills and efficiency which others do not have. Maximum output or productivity can be achieved by optimising capacity utilisation as well as efficiency utilisation as well as efficiency utilisation of each individual and by putting right person on the right job.

If a person is given a job of his choice or expertise, he starts loving his job profile. Then the job no more remains a job for him but becomes playing a game or singing a song. Thus there will be more oppertunities for the employees and they may be affered the different job of their choice and skill. Thus the human resources will be managed in a better and proper way after consolodation. It will also provide more career opportunities to employees.

Consolidation and Risk Management

Consolidation of Banks through merger and acquisition can result in a reduction in some dimensions of Risk, Which can motive the post merger banks to take more latitude to shift to a higher return, through perhaps higher risk, output mix. The source of diversification could be the range services, the portfolio mixes, or the regions served by the marging banks.

Risk is inherent in any commercial activity and banking is no exception to this rule. Rising Global competition, increasing deregulation, introduction of innovative products and delivery channels have pushed risk management to the forefront of today's financial landscape in the regulated banking environment, bank had to primarily deal with credit or default risk As we move into a perfect market economy, we have to deal with a whole range of market related risk like exchange risks, interest risk, etc. Oerational risk, which had always existed in the system, would become more pronounced in the coming days as we have technology as a new factor in doday's banking. Traditional risk management techniques become absolute with the growth of derivatives and off-balance sheet operations, coupled with diverfications. The expansion in E-banking will lead to continuous vigilance and revisions of regulations.

The consolidation of Banks are acting significance role from the point of view for making Indian banking strong and solid, a part from its growth and development to become sustainable. It is strongly felt in the Indian banking circles that a suitable consolidation process through mergers and acquisition is long due to address some of the structural problems that are being faced the banking industry in India. Sooner the process takes-off, greater the benefits to the economy as a whole.

It is the matter of great happiness that in Bihar State, four Regional Rural Banks Bhojpur-Rohtas, Magadh, patliputra and Nalanda are amalgamated in Punjab National Bank in the form of Madhaya Bihar Gramin Bank on 10th Feb, 2006, and Seven Regional Rural Banks Saran, Gopalganj, Siwan, Vaishali, Madhubani, Champaran and Darbhanga are amalgmated in central Bank o0f India in the form of Uttar Bihar Gramin Bank on 1st March, 2006. And the Regional Rural Banks of Bhagalpur, Saharsha, Purnia, Madhepura are amalgamated in the form of Bihar Gramin Bank in 2006.

Today, Mergers and Acquisitions of Banks are most important and latest need in the field of re-construction/ re-structure for Indian Banking institutions, But, Mergers and Acquisitions should be useful beneficial and meaningful. It will be possible, when before taking decision about mergers, valuation should be must done broadly regarding alternative should be selected. Thus, it is suggested that for the more powerful of Banking Industries, regular or continuous research and investigation should necessarily be done.

Refercences

Agarwal, A.N. (2003), *Indian Economy*, p. 509, Wishwa Prakashan.

Datt, Ruddra and Sundram, K. P. M. (2002), Indian Economy, p. 813, S. Chand & Company, Ltd.

IBA Bulletin, January (2005), Vol. xxvii, No. I.

Kulshareshtra, R. S. (2005), Financial Management, Sahitya Bhawan, p. No. 794.

Seth, M. L., Money & Banking, p. No. 480, Shiv Lal, Agrawal & Company, Agra.

Sharma, H. & Sharma, R. (2004), Money & Banking, Sahitya Bhawan, Agra.

Shukla, M. C., Grawal, T. S., Gupta S. C. (2001), Advanced Accounts, p. 21.01, S. Chand & Company Ltd.

44

Risk Management in Banks

Udita

Risk is defined as uncertainty, i.e., the deviation from an expected outcome and what one achieves from what one had planned. This unpredictability of the future is due to uncertainties associated with the steps that one undertakes in the process or various external factors that influence the processes that are necessary to achieve planned objective. Uncertainty can be differentiated into:

1. *General Uncertainty:* Complete ignorance about any potential outcome makes both rational decision-making and any quantification impossible.
2. *Specific Uncertainty:* Objective or at least subjective probabilities can be assigned to the potential outcomes and hence allow for quantification.

In financial parlance, risk is always associated with loss that is expected to be incurred due to the happening or non-happening of certain events or activities. To meet these emerging challenges, Reserve Bank of India has been preparing Indian Banking system for an integrated risk management framework since 1999.

Sources of Risk

There are many sources from which risk may emanate like (a) Globalization of business due to integration of Indian economy with the rest of the world, (b) Progressive liberalization of economic policies leading to surge in new products, (c) Vicious competitive business environment, (d) Promoters/ borrowers, (e) Technology and (e) Market dynamics.

Risk Management Process

With the generalized opening of trade and of capital movement across the world over the past decade and a half, risk management has become all-pervasive across the whole financial sector. Financial risks are uncertainties resulting in adverse variation of profitability or outright losses. Risk management begins with identification and quantification and may be further subdivided into following processes:

- Risk identification
- Risk measurement
- Risk pricing
- Risk monitoring and control

Risk Identification

Risk identification consists of identifying various risks associated with the risk-taking at the transaction level and examining its impact on the portfolio and capital requirement. All transactions would have one or more of the major risks i.e, liquidity risk, interest rate risk, market risk, default or credit risk and operational risk with their manifestations in different dimensions. Although all these risks are contracted at the transactional level, certain risks such as liquidity risk and interest rate risk are managed at the aggregate or portfolio level. Risk such as credit risk, operational risk and market risk are taken cognizance of at transaction level as well as at the portfolio level.

Risk Measurement

Risk measurement relies on quantitative measures of risk. It seeks to capture variations in earnings, market value, and losses due to default arising out of uncertainties associated with various risk elements. Quantitative measures of risks can be classified into three categories: Based on sensitivity, volatility and downside potential.

Risk Pricing

Risks in banking transactions impact banks in two ways: Firstly banks have to maintain necessary capital as per regulatory requirements. The cost of capital arises from the need to pay investor's in bank's equity and internal generation of capital necessary for business growth. Secondly, there is a probability of loss associated with all risks which need to be factored into pricing.

Risk Monitoring and Control

The key driver in managing a business is seeking enhancement in risk-adjusted return on capital (RAROC). Approach to risk management centres on implementation of risk and business policies simultaneously in a consistent manner. Risk management policies adopted at the corporate level is consistent with the broader business strategies, capital strength, and management expertise and risk appetite. Guidelines and other parameters used to govern risk-taking include detailed structure of prudential limits and risk taking functions. The banks establish an adequate system for monitoring and reporting risk exposures and assessing the bank's changing risk profile. The bank's internal control structure is essential to the process. Effective control of the process includes an independent review and the involvement of internal or external audits wherever appropriate.

Risk based supervision can reduce the adverse consequences of any financial crisis by taking into account the following aspects:

- Understanding the environment in which banks and banking systems operate;
- Understanding the risk profiles of individual banks and financial institutions;
- Understanding the risk profiles of products and services of individual institutions.

Risk in Banking Business

The banking industry has a wide array of business lines like commercial banking, corporate finance, retail banking, trading, investment banking and various financial services from the main business lines of banks. With in each lines of business there are subgroups and each subgroup contains variety of financial activities. The banking book includes all advances, deposits and borrowings which usually arise from commercial and retail banking operations. The trading book includes all the assets that are marketable, i.e., they can be traded in the market. Off balance sheet exposures are contingent in nature as banks issue guarantees, committed or back up credit lines, letter of credit etc., and banks face payment obligations contingent up on some event such as failure to meet payment obligations. In carrying all such banking operations, any mismatch between assets and liabilities results in different types of banking risk. The banking risk spectrum cover the following main risks: (a) Credit risk, (b) Market risk, (c) Liquidity risk, (d) Interest rate risk, (e) Basis risk, (f) Option risk, (g) Industry risk, (h) Business risk, (i) Country risk, (j) Sovereign risk and (k) Operational risk.

Credit Risk

Credit Risk is also known as default risk. It involves inability or unwillingness of a customer or counterpart to meet commitments in relation to lending, trading, hedging, settlement and other financial transactions. The credit risk depends on both external and internal factors. (A) The external factors are the state of the economy, wide swings in commodity/equity prices, foreign exchange rates and interest rates trade restrictions economic sanctions, Government policies etc. (B) The internal factors are deficiencies in loan policies/administration, absence of prudential credit concentration limits, inadequately defined lending powers for sanctioning of loan by officers/Credit Committees, deficiencies in appraisal of borrowers' financial position, excessive dependence on collateral and inadequate risk pricing, absence loan review mechanism and post sanction surveillance etc.

New capital accord (BASEL II) has set new approach for measurement of credit risk from regulatory perspective and prescribed regulatory capital charge for credit risk, market risk and operational risk.

Market Risk

Market risk is the risk arising out of unexpected change in market variables such as interest rate, currency, commodity & equity prices both on and off balance sheets item. As per RBI definition market risk covers both the banking book and the trading book. Basel committee's definition of market risk excludes banking book and include only the trading book. Market risk in the banking book is referred to by the Basel committee as interest rate risk. Market risk thus include (a) Interest rate risk both Indian rupee and other currencies in the banking book (b) Price risk in the trading book arising as result of interest rate, currency, commodity and equity price movement, (c) Liquidity risk of the institution whether it is funding or trading liquidity and (d) Credit spread risk unrelated to downgrade.

Liquidity Risk

The liquidity risk of banks arises from funding of long term assets by short-term liabilities, there by making the liabilities subject to roll over or refinancing risk. The liquidity risk in banks manifest in different dimensions:

(a) *Funding Risk:* need to replace net outflows due to unanticipated withdrawal/non-renewal of deposits (wholesale and retail);

(b) *Time Risk:* need to compensate for non-receipt of unexpected inflows of funds, i.e. performing assets turning into non-performing assets; and

(c) *Call Risk:* due to crystallization of contingent liabilities and failure of borrowers to pay.

Interest Rate Risk

It is the risk arising from the impact of the fluctuation of interest rates on the profitability as well of the assets and liabilities structure of the balance sheet. Deregulation of interest rates has exposed banks to the adverse impact of interest rate risk. Interest rate risk (IRR) refers to potential impact on Net Interest Income (NII) or Net Interest Margin (NIM) or Market value of equity caused by unexpected changes in interest rates.

Basis Risk

Market interest rates of various instruments seldom change by the same degree during a given period of time. The risk that the interest rate of different assets, liabilities and off-balance sheet items may change in different magnitude is termed as basis risk. The degree of basis risk is fairly high in respect of banks that create composite assets out of composite liabilities.

Option Risk

Significant changes in market interest rates create another source of risk to bank's profitability by encouraging prepayment of cash credit/term loan and exercise of call/put options on bonds/debentures and/or premature withdrawal of term deposits before their stated maturities. It is known that bank in India has traditionally been selling in built option while accepting deposit and granting loan.

Industry Risk

Industry risk analysis is concerned with SWOT profile of the industry within the economy *vis-a-vis* economic trends and the key success factors for the industry. The industry risk includes:

(a) Business cyclicality, earnings stability and diversify of earnings base.

(b) Economic parameters such as inflation, energy requirements.

(c) International competitive situation, demand projections and maturity of market of life cycle of the product.

(d) Basic financial characteristics of the business.

(e) Cost structure in terms of raw materials, labour, and plant capacity.
(f) Competitive structure.
(g) Ease of entry/exit.

Business Risk

This is defined as the inability of the business or project to service its debt in time. This inability strikes about inadequate income generation capacity of the business, which is affected by the following variables:

(a) Nature of business or the product it sales
(b) External economic or market environment
(c) Internal manufacturing organization
(d) Products mix.

Country Risk

In broad terms, country risk is that uncertainty which is created when funds cross international frontiers. Management of cross-border lending and international investment risk calls for country risk analysis periodically as comprehensive as possible. It is defined as risk of a foreign borrower failing to service his foreign currency debt obligations for reasons beyond the usual risks that arise in relation to lending. There are two basic differences between domestic and foreign loans. One is that repayment of international loans must route through exchange markets and therefore, lending banks should assess prospects for exchange rates and controls on capital flows. Another difference is that unlike in domestic loans, there is no established common legal system to act as an ultimate arbitrator to settle claims. It is because of these factors that assessment of country risk is critical for banks to safeguard their international exposures.

Sovereign Risk

If the borrower belongs to the public sector, the risk is usually referred to as "Sovereign Risk" Public sector comprise of all state owned agencies and institutions. While terming a borrower as public sector, there is an underlying assumption that the state will, ultimately, take responsibility for the financial obligations of the borrower concerned.

Operational Risk

Managing operational risk is becoming an important feature of sound risk management practice in modern financial markets in the wake of phenomenal increase in the volume of transactions, high degree of structural changes and complex support systems. The most important type of operational risk involves breakdowns in internal controls and corporate governance. Such breakdowns can lead to financial loss through error, fraud, or failure to perform in a timely manner or cause the interest of the bank to the compromised. Generally, operational risk is defined as any risk, which is not categorized as market or credit risk, or the risk of loss arising from various types of human or technical error. It includes legal risk but excludes strategic and reputation risk. The sources can be fraud, incompetence, transaction mistake, execution error, documentation error, people risk, exceeding limit, security risk, technology risk, system failure, programming error, telecommunication error, and product failure. Internal controls and the internal audit are used as the primary means to mitigate operational risk. Banks could also sets operational risk limits, based on the measures of operational risk. Insurance is also an important mitigation of some forms of operational risk. Risk educations for familiarizing the complex operations at all levels of staff also reduce operational risk. Under Basel Committee II guidelines, RBI has asked the bank to provide capital charge for operational risk equivalent to 15 per cent of their average gross income of previous three years.

Operational Risk as a Catalyst

The movement toward discovery of new techniques for managing risk was propelled, in large part, by emergence of operational risk as a focus of concern for the bank. When compared to credit risk (the risk of not being paid back) and market risk (risk evolving around investment decisions and broader financial market trends), operational risk-the risk of loss resulting from inadequate and failed internal processes, people, and systems or from external events-is uniquely difficult to evaluate. It includes internal and external fraud, money laundering, vandalism, customers information privacy, information security, physical security, business disruption, and system failures, process risk, and vendor management.

Managing Operation Risk with Six Sigma

The Six Sigma methodologies can help operational performance. When applied to a bank's operational risk management policy, it could add greater efficiency and reduce loss.

There is an opinion that operational risk as a stand-alone subject is not progressing and, to keep the stakeholders interested, risk practitioners are riding piggyback on programmes such as Six Sigma. Though operational risk management (ORM) is a challenge, it is an exciting subject area with depths that remain unexplored. IT is also an evolving subject and, like any subject in their infancy, it borrowers heavily from other related disciplines. There is a growing conviction that Six Sigma can be successfully applied in the banking industry to manage operational risk, thereby reducing the cost and harnessing the synergies of an existing Six Sigma implementation. Going by the number of banks that are already using Six Sigma, a practical implementation approach to integrate ORM and Six Sigma will not only benefit the risk management practice but the banking industry as a whole.

Six Sigma, Variation and Operational Risk

Six Sigma is a rigorous and disciplined methodology that uses data and statistical analysis to measure and improve a company's operational performance by identifying and eliminating 'defects' in processes. To achieve Six Sigma, a process must not produce more than 3.4 defects per million opportunities (DPMO). A defect in this context is defined as anything outside set specification. In other words, they are the process variation that is calculated by sigma level. The objective of Six Sigma implementation is to reduce variation and drives towards six standard deviation between mean and the nearest specification limit (upper/lower specification) in any process. A Six Sigma opportunity is the total number of chances for a defect. However, implementation of Six Sigma and arriving at zero defect state does not eliminate operational risk completely as operational risk is a function of four risk categories: people risk, process risk, system risk, and external risk.

Indian Banks-The Challenge Ahead

The risk situation in Indian Banks is no different from the bank world over. In fact, it is more complicated. The nationalized banks and SBI and its associates contribute more than 80 per cent of banking business. The RBI has advised banks to be ready to implement Basle II by March 2007. One consequence is that the bank will have to learn and adopt more sophisticated techniques of risk management in time bound manner. This has brought risk management and risk measurement into sharp focus. Each bank is not required to educated and train all officers/employees so that they are made to understand the process of generation of risk, its quantification, mitigation and management. Risk management, cutting across all hierarchical levels and activities in banks, has become part of every body job. While people at branch level are required to take calculated risks, the top-management level the risk is required to be monitored and managed. Further MIS is crore of risk management and has to be generated in timely and accurately. It is going to be a very big challenge for public sector banks having far flung manual branches. Thus, banks should attach considerable importance to improve the competency of their work force to identify, measure, monitor and control the overall level of risks by proactive management.

References

Sabnani, P. (2002), Risk Management by Banks in India, *IBA Bulletin* (July).

Salin l (1999), Risk Management of Financial Sector.

Sharma, H. S. (2003), Risk Management in Banks-Emerging Issues, Banking Finance (May).

Beck, U. (1992), Risk Society, Towards a New Modernity, Sage, London.

Eddie Cade, Managing Banking Risks Glenlake Publishing Company Ltd., Chicago.

Uyemura, D.G. and Deventer, D.R.V. (1993), Financial Risk Management in Banking.

45

Risk Management in Banks: An Overview

Dimpal Rani

The financial sector especially the banking industry in most emerging economies including India is passing through a process of change. As the financial activity has become a major economic activity in most economies, any disruption or imbalance in its infrastructure will have significant impact on the entire economy. By developing a sound financial system, the banking industry can bring stability within the financial markets.

Deregulation in the financial sector had widened the products range in the developed markets. Some of the new products introduced are LBOs, structured transaction, credit cards, housing finance, derivatives and various off balance sheet items. Thus new vistas have created multiple sources for banks to generate higher profits than the traditional financial intermediation. Simultaneously they have opened new areas of risk also. Many unknown issues that are intricately related to new products have exposed banks to various risks across the globe and India is no exception.

During the past decade, the Indian banking industry continued to respond to the emerging challenges of competition, risks and uncertainties. Risks originate in the forms of customer default, funding a gap or adverse movements of markets.

Measuring and quantifying risks is neither easy nor intuitive. Our regulators have made some sincere attempts to bring prudential and supervisory norms conforming with international bank practices with an intention to strengthen the stability of the banking system. Banks in general face the following risks: Liquidity Foreign Exchange Credit Market Interest rate Operational The industry has undergone drastic changes in the last three decades. Horizontal expansion of the financial markets, deregulation across the globe in financial markets and stiff competition have led the banks to multiply their activities. Increased activities in the industry have exposed the banks to more uncertainties and more risks.

'Risk Management in Banks' is broadly divided into six sections: Funds Management is a major activity of the banks. Liquidity management is an integral part of funds anagement. Banks mobilize the deposits and deploy funds in advances and investments. Banks also float funds through various subsidiary services extended to their clients.

There will be always a time gap between the availability of resources and their deployment. Hence banks will often swing between excess liquidity and liquidity crunch in their funds position. Liquidity management essentially deals with efficient handling of inflows and outflows of funds. Section-I discusses the liquidity management in banks in India and across the globe.

Cash Management is a subset of the entire funds management. The lead time is reduced in collection of cheques and other instruments by the banks, if they introduce efficient cash management services. From the bank's point of view it increases the fee based income. Cash management services is one innovative product introduced by the banks in the recent times. Section-II discusses the cash management techniques adopted by banks and corporate clients.

Credit risk is as old as money. When the default rate increases in the portfolio of the bank it may lead to its total collapse. To circumvent the credit risk, the system tries to design innovative products. Section-III discusses the credit risk management in banks.

The Basle committee defines the operational risk as "the risk of direct or indirect loss resulting from inadequate or failed internal processes, people and systems or from external events". This definition excludes operational risk but includes legal risk. Such operational risks can be broadly classified into four categories as information technology risk, human resource risk, loss to assets risk and relationship risk. Quantification of operational risk is a major challenge to the risk management group of the bank. Section-IV attempts to elucidate few issues involved in the operational risk management.

One of the core activities of the regulators is proper supervision of the system. The Basle committee had set certain guidelines for the bank supervisors. The Reserve Bank of India had set up an advisory committee under the chairmanship of M S Verma and the committee had submitted its report in May 2001. The committee recommended corporate governance, internal controls, risk management, loan accounting transparency and disclosures, financial conglomerates and cross border banking supervision. The supervisor should provide a safety net to the financial system. Section-V discusses the important issues of any risk management technique.

Section-VI consists of two case studies. It briefly discusses the risk management techniques to be adopted by banks.

Derivatives are the hedging instruments which help minimize the risks. But a 300 year old investment bank collapsed because of its exposure to derivatives. The Barings' collapse is a classic example of failure of supervision and incidence of human resource risk.

Section-I

Liquidity Risk Management

When economy is in recession, every one focuses on the performance of the manufacturing sector and other related corporate sectors. Actually economic slowdown creates a cumulative effect on the banking sector. The article *"Banks: Liquidity Management in Recession Times"* discusses the alternative investment areas the banks have when the credit off take is not significant. The liquidity in the financial markets largely depends both on the supply and demand sides. During the year 2007, there was a significant spurt in deposit growth because of various reasons like poor performance of mutual funds, UTI fiasco, failure of many NBFCs, stock market scams etc. With this back drop, the investors' confidence in banks has gone up. This has caused a gradual influx of deposits into the banking system increasing the supply side. The economic slow down both in domestic as well as international side resulted in a sluggish growth in the manufacturing and service sectors. Consequently, the credit off take in the banking sector was not at the desired levels resulting in low demand for funds. Low credit off take coupled with an influx of deposits created an excess liquidity in the banking system in 2001. The article discusses liquidity management to be adopted by the banks during tough times and the better ways to deploy the funds for higher returns.

Banks and primary dealers used to get refinance for their specific activities at a fixed rate. The RBI "de-regulated" the refinance facility and introduced the concept of Liquidity Adjustment Facility (LAF) in phases through its mid term review of Monetary Policy in 2001. Introduction of LAF will change the equation in money market functioning. As LAF is expected to develop a stable overnight rate, the market will be encouraged to take a view over a long period, which will help develop the rupee yield curve. The article *"Liquidity Adjustment Facility-Let's LAF for a While"* discusses the radical stand taken by the RBI to create liquidity in the banking system.

While the Indian banking system is experiencing high liquidity, the experience of the American banks is totally opposite. The percentage of US banks which are able to find at least two thirds of total assets with core deposits fell from 95 per cent to 75 per cent between 1992 and 2000. The recent survey (2001) of American Bankers Association found that the gap between deposit growth and loan demand had posed a full-fledged crisis for community banks. Core deposits in the American banking industry consist of checking, savings and money market deposits. The supply-demand gap between the deposit growth and deployment of funds always exists in the banking sector. The article *"Liquidity Drought"* discusses the trend of slow pace of deposit growth and the high demand for loans in the American banks. The American banks' experience was so bad that it led to a liquidity crisis. To improve the growth of the core deposits, the banks are innovating new products with a value proposition.

The liquidity of the banking system has drawn less attention compared to the importance given by the system to capital adequacy. The article, *"Banking System Liquidity-Developments and Issues"* reviews the development in the UK in the recent years in the light of a series of official initiatives introduced by the regulatory authorities. Maturity transformation and the provision of liquidity insurance are core banking businesses. There are two separate, but interrelated dimensions to a bank's liquidity to meet the short term needs borrowing from the market to meet any liquidity pressure; and selling high quality assets to the market. Hence, liquidity management depends on the business more than the structure of the balance sheet of the bank. The article discusses various strategies adopted by the bank for liquidity management analyzing the liquidity trends in the banking sector with reference to UK. A few of these issues are quite relevant to the Indian banks also.

Section-II

Cash Management

Funds Management is the most crucial issue. Banks will have to take prudent decisions relating to asset liability mismatches. Liquidity management is an integral part of the funds management. If the technology helps to reduce the lead time for collection and payment of cheques at banks, it not only helps the clients to increase their cash management but also helps the banks to increase their liquidity. The paper *"Cash Management: The Bank's Way"*, discusses the "Cash Management Services" (CMS) a new product introduced by some banks in India. The free float created by the CMS will help the tech savvy banks to improve their bottom line.

The sound payment system is a key element in maintaining financial stability. The article *"Recent Developments in the Payment System"* focuses on three topics: it reports on an international initiative to establish minimum standards for the national payment system with a special reference to New Zealand. It also analyzes the required structural changes in the industry and the prudential issues the Reserve Bank of New Zealand is currently engaged in. In India, we have the clearing system to settle inter bank transactions - twice or thrice a day depending on the volume of business. The tech savvy banks have introduced cash management services, reducing the lead time in payment settlements. The article discusses the changes that are taking place in the New Zealand payment system driven by international developments and technological changes and provides an insight into the cash management at tech savvy banks in our banking system.

Receivables management is a major treasury function in the corporate sector. If the lead time in debtor's receivables period is reduced, the corporates will be able to reduce their working capital requirements. The "Lockbox Banking" is one of the ways for a better cash management. But it should not lead to fraudulent encashment of cheques. Both banks and clients have to follow certain precautionary measures in their cash management system. The paper *"Is Lockbox Banking Right for You"* discusses the ways to curb fraudulent activity in lockboxes.

Section-III

Credit Risk Management

In the global scenario, the increased credit risk arises due to two reasons. Banks have been forced to lend to riskier clients because well rated corporates have moved away from banks as they have access to low cost funds through disintermediation. The other reason is the lurking fear of global recession. Recession in the economy could lead to low industrial output which may lead to defaults by the industry under recession culminating into credit risk. Hence, the markets are in search of new credit risk management models. Credit derivatives which were a new innovation in the market stood the real test in 1997 during the Asian financial crisis. Several European and US banks which were exposed to high risk areas in Korea, Philippines and Thailand were able to save themselves from losses as they could hedge themselves with credit derivatives. The papers *"Credit Risk Management-Models and Judgements"* and *"Use of Credit Derivatives"* discuss the critical operational issues in managing credit risk through credit derivatives.

In the recent times, we have witnessed runs on the banks-mainly the Urban Cooperative Banks like Madhavpura Coop Bank in Gujarat/Mumbai, Charminar Bank, a scheduled bank in Hyderabad and many others.

When the banks give the signals of distress, the depositors panic and run for their money. As per the existing rules, Deposit Insurance and Credit Guarantee Corporation of India (DICGC) guarantees the depositors' money up to one lakh rupees subject to certain conditions. Till now, the banks used to pay the insurance premium for the deposits they hold to get insurance coverage from DICGC. Now the committee set up by the RBI under the Chairmanship of J Capoor suggested that the risk premium is to be paid which is sensitive to the probability of the bank in question going bankrupt. The paper *"What Makes Banks Fragile"*, tries to compute the volatility of banks' assets and deposit insurance premium with an illustration and presents a view point of fixing higher deposit insurance premium if reserve requirements are to be phased out.

Section-IV

Operational Risk Management

The Basle committee formulated new rules on the capital adequacy, which are supposed to be introduced from 2005. The major issue of Basle II recommendations is the operational risk. Banks are yet to get clarity on the issues which are to be included in operational risk. System vendors have identified that a proper workflow and process automation would help reduce and detect errors. Apart from automating, right levels of audit and control are to be introduced to reduce operational risk. Increased operational efficiency of the system would reduce operational risk. The paper *"Operational Risk: Automate to Eliminate"* discusses how automation can play a role in mitigating operational risk.

The key factor in internet banking is the faith of the people on the regulations. But will it exist when they come to know that Bill Gates' credit card details were stolen by a hacker? Some of the new generation banks like ICICI Bank, UTI Bank, HSBC, HDFC, SBI, PNB Bank have introduced internet banking. The paper *"Banking on the Net: The Risk Factors"* discusses the operational risk related issues. To mitigate the operational risk in internet banking, multi-layer security like digital certification, encryption, two level passwords have been introduced. Once the right infrastructure is in place, relatively risk free internet banking will see a boom with more banks joining the activity.

To boost the sentiment of the stock market, the RBI recently had introduced margin trading. Of late, many banks have burnt their fingers in the stock market scams in one way or the other. In spite of strict monitoring systems, some of the banks have indulged in large lending to stock market operators in the recent past. As a consequence many heads have rolled in some of the leading private banks. Deregulation should not lead to "anarchy" in deployment of funds. Individuals make the system and the system fails to protect the interests of the stake holders of the bank. The debate *"Whither Bank Investment in Stock Market"* throws light on the risk and return, the banks expect from their investments in the stock market.

The core purpose of any central bank is to maintain stability in monetary and financial systems - be it the Reserve Bank of India in our country or Bank of England in the UK. The Asian crisis led to a lot of introspection by many of central banks across the globe. As a result, the Financial Stability Forum was created which meets semi annually bringing together central banks, finance ministries and regulators to discuss the issues of common concern and to develop policies in controlling risks of the international financial system. Two issues, crisis prevention and crisis resolution, are currently being debated in mitigating the risks in the banking sector. The first one is revision of the Basle Accord on capital adequacy ceilings and the other one is financial architecture and the respective roles of private and public sector banks in solving liquidity crisis, surveillance and crisis resolution. The work broadly considers the responsibility of surveillance in the UK shared by the Bank of England, Financial Services Authority (FSA) and Her Majesty's Treasury (HM's Treasury). The Bank of England articulates its role in financial stability by publishing Financial Stability Review from which this article has been reprinted. The article "*Crisis Management in Banks*" discusses the methods to be adopted in crisis prevention and crisis resolution in the global perspective and the role played by the Bank of England in some of the practical and conceptual issues.

Section-V

Financial Safety Net

The risks faced by a bank have interrelated components i.e., credit risk, environmental and financial risk, operational risk and strategic risk. The paper *"Risk Management by Commercial Banks: Time to Hammer out the Dents"* briefly discusses the role of the bank management to address these risks.

The new Basle accord talks about three pillars of the banking industry. They are capital adequacy, supervisory review and market discipline. The Basle accord is targetted at greater risk sensitivity in the industry. It is aimed to promote safety and soundness in the financial system with competitive equality. The new accord is a further improvement over the 1988 accord, which essentially dealt with the regulatory mechanism in capital adequacy. But how far this new accord is fool proof against the recent crisis witnessed by the banks in the emerging economics is an issue for debate. The article *"The*

New Basle Accord: More Questions than Answers" highlights the far reaching implications in the banking sector of the higher reliance on advanced credit risk management techniques. The success of the new accord which is supposed to come into force in 2005 is yet to be experienced.

Since mid 90s, the Federal Reserve has devoted particular attention to developing and implementing a program for supervision of the large complex banking organizations or LCBOs. These LCBOs are nothing but large banking organizations that have integrated an array of financial activities that extend well beyond traditional banking. During the six decades before 1999, the Banking Act of 1933 popularly known as "The Glass-Steagall Act" prohibited the US Banks from affiliating themselves with firms engaged in dealing and underwriting securities. During the mid 80s, the banking holding companies started establishing securities subsidiaries subject to certain conditions related to revenues and other limits without violating the Glass-Steagall Act. The Gramm-Leach-Bliley Act of 1999 facilitated the US banks to enter into securities trading and insurance underwriting activities through separate subsidiaries.

When the multiple activities are managed by the banking organization, supervisory responsibilities will also accrue on the part of the Federal Reserve. More so with regard to LCBOs. By paying special attention to LCBOs, supervisors aim to minimize significant adverse effects on the public, on financial markets and financial system as a whole in the US. The paper *"Risk-Focussed Supervision: Supervision of Large Complex Banking Organizations"* emphasizes that there is an absolute need for regulators to bring more efficiency to supervisory functions.

The decade of '90s has precipitated change in the financial markets due to mergers and acquisitions creating new challenges to supervisors who are entrusted with safeguarding financial stability. The traditional role of banks is intermediation, which reduces various transactional costs to individual borrowers and lenders in the financial markets. The process of technological innovation, disintermediation and increased competition has manifested in a marked increase in M & A activity in the banking industry. If we take the total M & A activity, about 4 per cent contributes to M & A activity in banks and non banks in the US whereas it accounts for 26 per cent in Europe. The M & A activity creates large banks. There are many arguments against large banks. How does a conglomeration increase or decrease the risk of the financial institutions? Many empirical results of the recent conglomerations have hardly led to any conclusion on reduction of risk in the combined entity after M & A activity. There are three organizational structures that constitute banking and non-banking activities.

Two of the models-German and British-follow the Universal Bank concept. The third one is the US model alternatively called as the bank holding company model. The US model talks about financial stability. The article *"Financial Consolidation and Conglomeration: Implications of the Financial Safety Net"*, discusses two elements of the financial safety net namely lender of the last resort and deposit insurance.

Section-VI

Case Studies

The Reserve Bank of India took up various measures to increase the liquidity in money markets. To facilitate the smooth transition of call money market, the RBI initiated various measures including liquidity adjustment facility. The case study *"Liquidity-A Gauge for the Market Health"* discusses few empirical evidences of liquidity.

One of the operational risks is human resource risk. A rogue trader ruined the 300 years old investment bank, 'Barings'. The paper *"Barings' Collapse - A Lesson for Operators in Derivatives"*, focuses on the dangers of exposed position in a trading activity. The functions of Front office, Mid office and Back office in a dealing room are mutually exclusive. Lack of a clear-cut management policy to distinguish these activities caused the collapse of 'Barings'. It should serve as an eye opener to the entire banking industry.

References

Reserve Bank of India (2004), *Report on Currency and Finance*, 2003-04.

The Economist (2006), "Special Report on International Banking", May 20-26, 2006.

McKinsey & Company (2005), *Indian Banking 2010: Towards a High Performing Sector*, New Delhi.

Reddy, Y. V. (2004), "Financial Sector Reforms: Review and Prospects", *RBI Bulletin*, December.

"Towards Globalisation of the Financial Sector in India", *RBI Bulletin*, January 2004a.

"Financial Stability: Indian Experience". *RBI Bulletin*, July 2004.

Finance & Development, IMF, September 2004.

46

Credit Risk Management in Banks

Md. Shahabuddin

Banking, basically being the business of financial intermediation, is synonymous with risk. Such risk has, however, become more in the context of the spate of economic reform measures exemplified in the lossening of controls and regulations as well as a strong urge of the country to align with the process of globalization. With the onset of globalization process and financial sector reforms, the fact that risk management is a matter of concern can hardly be overlooked. Whether a company is in the manufacturing sector or financial service sector, in running its daily operations it is bound to encounter a number of risks that need to be not only managed with a fair degree of efficiency. This, however, requires a risk management system that measures, controls and monitor these risks. The success of such a system presupposes a better understanding as to why do risks occur and how these should be managed.

In today's context, Indian banks have little idea about what is risk. When and where it occurs, how to measure it and how risk can be repelled or avoided. No doubt, such technical inadequacy at the industry level is, in a way, making the banking business in a market driven environment, more risky as there is every possibility that, in the absence of any appropriate risk measurement and containment tool, even normal level of volatility would tend to cause abnormal damage to the portfolio.

Among all the risks bankers are having, there is a measure of awareness only about the credit risk. This is because the institution of banking has its origin in lending business only and lending operations are as old as the banking institution itself. Therefore, to some extent, bankers are, by instinct, managing the credit risks, even through they may not be fully aware of the concept and contents of such risk. Besides, credit risk, due to the absence of any quantification method or measurement framework, has never emerged as a risk that could be expressed as a risk that could be expressed in specific numerical entity like other risks. In fact, all other risks, viz., market risk, interest rate risk, liquidity risk, exchange rate risk etc., could be measured and expressed in numerical terms, thereby facilitating two very important things: (i) risk element becomes known and, hence, chances of loss are predictable in the short and medium term and (ii) risk containment measures can be formulated. Lack of quantification method makes it virtually impossible to even hazard a guess as to what will be the quantum of potential/ future loss in normal circumstances in case a bank increases its lending by Rs.. 100. Once this potential loss is quantified and expressed in numerical terms, not only will it be possible to work out a risk containment framework but also facilitate the emergence of a comprehensive value-at-risk model for the credit portfolio at large. With this objective in mind, this paper attempts to explore the concept, definition and to model a workable quantitative framework so as to provide a tool for easy comprehension of credit risk and its application at every level of decision making process.

In the year 1988, the Basel Committee proposed a set of minimal capital requirements for banks. These became law in G-10 countries in 1992, with Japanese banks permitting an extended transition period. The requirements have come to be known as the 1988 Basel Accord. The 1988 Basel Accord primarily addressed banking in the sense of deposit taking and lending, so its focus was only on credit risk and under this approach banks were required to maintain a minimum capital covering certain percentage of its credit risk.

In the early 1990s, the Basel Committee decided to update the 1988 accord to include bank capital requirements for market risk and in April 1993, the Basel Committee released a package of proposed amendments to the 1988 accord. These guidelines together are known as Basel-I norms.

With a view to adopting the above framework on capital adequacy which takes into account the elements of credit risk in various types of assets and also to strengthen the capital base of banks, Reserve Bank of India decided in April 1992 to introduce a risk asset ration system for banks (including foreign banks) in India as a capital adequacy measure. The balance sheet assets, non-funded items and other off-balance sheet exposures are assigned prescribed risk weights and banks have to maintain unimpaired minimum capital funds equivalent to the prescribed ratio on the aggregate of the risk weighted assets and other exposures on an ongoing basis.

Recognizing the fact that financial crisis world over have revealed that weak financial systems and other supervision are the most important factors contributing to macro instability and the need to adopt international benchmarks for better acceptability and global presence the regulators have chosen to introduce the risk management system in banks. These measures are aimed at making Indian financial sector competitive, viable and resilient.

Accordingly the banking sector reform process was introduced by RBI including prudential norms, dismantling of interest rate structures, capital adequacy requirements, etc. Banks were advised to ensure capital adequacy at a minimum level of 4 per cent on the aggregate risk weighted assets including both fund based and non-fund based exposures by 31st March 1993 and 8 per cent by 31st March 1996. The minimum level of capital adequacy was increased to 9 per cent subsequently.

Concept of Risk

Before we go on to define the credit risk, it is necessary to define risk as a concept. Risk in simple terms for commercial entities, connotes the chances of damage that may be caused by an unforeseen event and its consequence on the profit and loss account of the organization. In the process of financial intermediation, banks use financial, physical, human, technological as also structural; resources to deliver banking products and services. Both sourcing of inputs as also generation of output are, however, conditioned to the financial environment in which banks operate. This environment is fraught with uncertainties.

Risk is essentially a group characteristic and it should never be equated with individual or isolated event. Risk iff perceived as a chance of default on a particular account or transaction, is always total or nil; but for a group of accounts/transactions may be anything between 0 and 100 on a scale of 100. Secondly, risk is not about total uncertainty. Risk is definitely different from uncertainty to the extent that risk can be expected, measured and managed while uncertainty remains altogether unknown and unmanageable. Therefore, risk may be defined as exposure on account of a particular group of transactions to the expected loss/variation/volatility which may adversely impact the profit and loss account. Various risks that banks are exposed to in running their day to day operations are: interest rate risk, market risk, credit risk, liquidity risk, exchange rate risk and capital risk etc.

Credit Risk

Of all kinds of risk that banks are exposed to, credit risk poses a major threat to the viability and sustainability of banks. If we surf through the major banking meltdowns around the globe and more recently the traumatic experience of Thai, Korean, Malaysian and Japanese banks, one point which emerges very strongly is that in almost all the cases bad loans were singularly responsible for such banking breakdowns. Indian banks, more conspicuous by their huge burden of non-performing assets in their books (about 20 per cent as of March 1997), are to put it mildly, hovering on the precipice of a crisis of sort.

Credit risk, in simple terms can be defined as the possible adverse impact on profit and loss account arising out of loan default i.e., non-payment or delayed payment. Whenever a bank enters into a transaction of loan/credit or alike where there is expectation of future income credit risk is created. Credit risk is merely a chance or probability of default; but not the default itself. Since risk is a group characteristic, it would be appropriate to evaluate the risk of an individual loan asset in relation to the other loan assets held by the Bank. Therefore, any attempt to determine the risk on a single borrower in isolated manner will be distorting.

Objectives of Credit Risk Management

The credit risk management can have different objectives at two levels namely Transaction level and Portfolio level.

At the transaction level, the objectives of credit risk management ideally should be:

- Setting an appropriate credit risk environment
- Framing a sound credit approval process.
- Maintaining an appropriate credit administration, measurement and monitoring process.
- Employing sophisticated tools/techniques to enable continuous risk evaluation on a scientific basis.
- Ensuring adequate-pricing formula to optimize risk-return relationship.

At the portfolio level, the objectives of credit risk management should bes:

- Development and monitoring of methodologies and norms to evaluate and mitigate risks arising from concentrating by industry, group, product etc.
- Ensuring adherence to regulatory guidelines
- Driving asset growth strategy.

If we closely analyze the above, we can observe that the transaction level pursues value creation and portfolio level pursues value preservation.

RBI's Concern

The RBI has already advised the banks to set up an independent credit risk management department to enforce and monitor risk parameters and prudential limits set by the Board or Credit Policy Committee.

Basel Accord II has proposed the adoption of a more risk-sensitive and balanced portfolio framework for the calculation of capital risk weighting and risk management. It is also intended to bring the current regulatory capital requirement more in line with the economic capital allocation approach. These two methods are categorized as: (i) Standardized approach (ii) Internal rating based approach.

Under the IRB approach, banks will be allowed to use their own internal estimates to determine the borrowers' creditworthiness to assess the credit risk. This approach adopts a detailed analytical framework based on a number of factors to calculate risk weightings. The more commonly used factors are probability of default, exposure at default, Loss given default.

The evaluation of credit rating is an imprecise process. Over a period, one should expected that the banks rating procedure should be compatible with ratings of capital markets elsewhere. Credit losses are not related to credit ratings. In other words, credit pricing, credit rating and expected loss are to be linked.

Determinants of Credit Risk

Various studies probing the causes of loans default in India have brought to the fore hundreds of reasons which contribute to the failure of loan. These encompass a wide range of factors from the insensitive dealing with the borrower by the bank (as in case of borrowers under Government sponsored schemes) to personal rift between the partners/directors (especially in the case of partnership firms or the closely held limited companies) to socio-political reasons (borrower in some of the regions show higher propensity to default due to some socio-economic factors). All these factors may broadly be grouped into two categories, viz.:

Endogenous Factors

- Weakening of borrowers credit standing due to financial mismanagement etc.

- diversion of funds from the established business to speculative areas
- wilful default
- managerial incapabilities.

Exogenous Factors:

- sudden changes in the Government Policies
- natural calamities
- new scientific/technological innovations
- political interference
- obsolete legal system & practices cases some borrower-specific unique factors are observable), we have only broadly put forth the factors that are very much common to a loan default. However, we assume here that all credit decisions are being taken in efficient market conditions and bank's loan appraisal system is ideal and near perfect. Needless to mention, in reality, such a condition is a almost impossible to obtain and hence, risk of a credit decision may be positively correlated with obsolete lending policies and practices as also bank personnels' attitudinal deficiencies. The focus of this paper, however, is not to probe into the various causation of loan default.

Need for Quantification and Measurement of Credit Risk

Having defined the concept of credit risk, the next logical step is to examine whether credit risk is measurable. Credit risk, in Indian context, is viewed as a qualitative aspect and is dealt with accordingly. Many people are reflexively used to talk about such risks without having any clue as to how to quantify the risk. The question, therefore, remains - how risky a credit account is? Is there any way by which credit risk can be expressed in terms of a numerical entity?

Credit risk evaluation is one of the basic functions of any lenders. However, this is becoming more and more complex due to multiplicity of factors contributing to the increase in credit risks and the difficulty in capturing the combined as well as individual contribution of all such variables in increasing or decreasing the chances of default. Fair amount of difficulty is also encountered in predicting the chances of default. However, one fact that emerges almost axiomatically is that the credit risk in the environment is increasing. Today's imperative is, therefore, to explore the appropriate risk measurement and risk containment tool to avert any possible disaster.

Much of the success of an effective credit risk management system will be hinged upon quantifying/measuring such risks. As is explained earlier, the risk on a credit transaction is equivalent to its chances of default. Chances of an individual borrower being defaulter is either zero or one (equivalent to the loss of total sum lent). In other words, the risk of an individual borrower is always total or zero.

Survey of Existing Risk Measurement Techniques

After surveying the existing literature on risk measurement, we have come across four techniques/methodologies which are described below:

1. In the absence of any standard measure, the application of capital adequacy rule under Basle Accord may be taken as a measurement of risk of a given commercial loan. But the risk weight as assigned under this approach to all commercial loan is too simplistic and standardised (all commercial loans carry 100 per cent risk weightage-in India loans backed by Government guarantees carry zero risk weightage) and, as such, does not make substantive difference between borrowers of different credit standing. To that extent, this approach acts as an anathema to assess the real riskiness of lending.
2. Another approach to affix the credit risk is through measuring expected loan losses on the basis of Altman (1993) approach, using a three step procedure. These steps are:
   - Estimation of default rates and losses associated with known credit standards since default rate

associated with particular rating grades can be reliably tracked over a considerable period.

- Objective Measurement of borrowers' credit quality i.e., consistent with those credit standards by applying credit rating process such as the ZETA risk control systems that combines corporate financial data into a unique index value for the company (Altman, Haldeman and Narayanan, 1977).
- Modelling the expected cash flow from each loan applying a present value calculation method and using an appropriate discount rate. If the present value of the loan is less than the amount to be advanced, the loan is unacceptable i.e., risker and falls beyond bank's risk taking capabilities.

3. The third approach for measuring expected loan losses, relatively a new one, is on the basis of the cost of holding a loan on a bank's balance sheet i.e., interest paid on deposits, loan origination and servicing cost, deposit insurance premium, proportion of funds required to be placed with the central bank as interest free deposits, the required return on equity, the required ratio of capital to total assets and the expected loan loss rate (Cumming, 1987). In an ideal competitive market, it can be argued that the average price of a loan will tend to equal its average cost (including a reward for capital employed) and, hence, the expected loan loss rate can be derived from the banks average lending margin compared against the tendency of average cost of holding a loan being equal to average price of a loan. Major drawback of this approach, is however, the analysis applies to the bank as a whole whereas any particular loan will differ from this norm as the default risk varies with a number of factors such as the size, industry, group, location and age of borrowing company. Both the expected loan loss per period and the accuracy with which

the default can be forecast will differ between loans. Another criticism against this approach based on lending margins and expected loan loss rates is that it does not fully reflect the uncertainty about how much of a loan may be repaid and the predictability about the timing of the losses over the life of loans. If losses are bunched in any one period, Banks may be exposed to the threat of insolvency. This necessities the importance of estimating the risk adjustment factor for a particular loan or working out an index by which marginal riskiness of a loan can be derived.

4. This brings us to the fourth approach, known as the beta value based risk adjustment (Davis, 1993) which seeks to estimate an appropriate risk adjustment factor for different types of loans by utilising Capital Asset Pricing Model (CAPM). For example, a bank's equity beta value measures the sensitivity of return on an equity investment in the bank to stock market wide changes (due to say, macro economic factors) and ignores risk factors specific to the bank (say, fraud). Higher the beta value, higher is the systematic risk. Since the beta value of portfolio is simply the weighted sum of the betas of the individual items, a bank's overall equity beta value depend, largely on the beta value of its own portfolio and this in turn depends on the beta value of the constituent loans both sector-wise and individual. If a bank makes a loan with a high beta value (say property related loan) this would mean the increase to total riskiness of the bank's loan portfolio and the appropriate measures of riskness of an individual loan will depend upon the deviation of its own beta value from mean beta value of the loan portfolio. This approach, complex as it is for its mathematical bias, is vulnerable to the non-availability of data and given the level of information generation and flow in our system, appears to be too sophisticated to be adopted by any Indian bank.

Credit Risk Measurement Model

The greatest difficulty in quantifying credit risk is to qualify the uncertainty ratio of how much of the loan may turn into loss due to default in loan repayment. There may be multiple reasons for default and some of which may once again be unique in case of a specific borrower. To capture all these factors in a single model will make an extremely complicated and unwieldy model-less user friendly and far less comprehensible. Further, uncertainty in case of an individual loan cannot be quantified independently of other assets held by the lender. Because, uncertainty value of repayment in case of a single borrower by itself is always total signifying a risk percentage of 100. It will, therefore, be appropriate to measure the propensity of default from the historical data in respect of a group of borrowers. Such groupings may be decided on the basis of activity, industry, segment, limit, borrower-group, region etc.

While factors of loan default are many as also widely variant, at present, there is hardly any easy method of measuring how all these variables are affecting the riskiness of a loan as also whether the riskiness of the loan portfolio is increasing or decrease in risk associated with credit. As the riskiness of loan has a positive relationship with loan default, it would be much easier to deduce and quantify the credit risk from the level of default cover created by a bank against the possible loss in case the loan account becomes irrecoverable. In banks' books, the best expression of such irrecoverability is linked to how much reserves bank has made in the form of write-off, provision, interest suspense etc., in covering the probable loss in future.

The easiest and most accessible indicator of such irrecoverabilities is reflected by the following information :

- Actual provision made against bad and doubtful loans.
- Actual write-off on account of NPLs
- Unrealized interest held in Suspense Account

This information is not only easily as certainable; but, due to the standardisation on account of mandatory application of uniform prudential norms recognition and asset classification across the industry, have become more acceptable numerators. Since there are acceptable norms for creating provision, higher ratio of such provision in the loan portfolio is undoubtedly indicative of higher loan failures. Again, within the overall loan portfolio, if in any segment, rate of provision and other reserves are found to be higher or lower in comparison to overall ratio for the loan portfolio as a whole, that particular segment of borrowers may be understood to be more risky or less risky depending upon the deviation of the ratio from the mean. While building up the model, the following assumptions are made to be the basis:

- Credit risk in case of the entire credit portfolio is bound to vary between 0 and 1. That is to say, if the entire loan portfolio is NPA (Loss Assets), the risk is 1. On the contrary, if there is no NPA, risk is 0. Similarly, in case of Sub-Standard Assets, the Credit risk varies within a bank of 10 per cent to 40 per cent i.e., ratio of provisioning and unrealized interest to total outstanding loan, contrary to the general perception, that substandard categories of advances do not significantly contribute to credit risk.
- Generally credit risk is misconstrued as total risk i.e., when a credit account is categorised as non-performing asset (NPA), it is generally believed that risk in the account is to the extent of 100 per cent. While this is true in case of loans classified as loss assets, what if the non performing loan is fully secured. Therefore, credit risk is not equal to the rate of NPA; but, of course, it is highly correlated to NPAs. And the degree of relationship increases with the tenure/duration of such advances as well as with the dilution of securities and so the degree of risk. Probability of loss is certainly higher in case the loan account is categorised as NPA. Even though the NPLs are directly and positively related to the riskiness of lending, risk in case of fully secured NPA account is very definitely less than that in case of a totally

unsecured NPA account. Because the chances of loss in case of the latter is higher than what it is in case of the former.

- Incremental credit risk moves up as asset quality moves down from Standard to Sub-Standard category then doubtful and then to loss. In order words, incremental credit risk is inversely related to the movement of asset quality.

Keeping in view this probabilistic characteristic of risk, we are trying to find out a basic risk factor index which would indicate the relative riskiness of a borrower in relation to a group of borrowers. Based on the above assumptions, the possible Risk Factor Index (RFI) of a bank's loan portfolio may be worked out as under :

$$RFI = \frac{IS + P + WO}{OL + WO}$$

where,

RFI = Risk Factor Index
IS = Cumulative Interest Suspense Balance
P = Cumulative Net Provision on NPLs
WO = Cumulative Write-off Of Loans
OL = Outstanding Gross Loans

Therefore, Cumulative Risk Factor Index at a given time (t) will be:

$$\frac{\text{Cumulative Interest Suspense (t) + Cumulative Provisions (t) + Cumulative Write-off (t)}}{\text{Outstanding Loans (t) + Cumulative Write-off (t)}}$$

or,

$$RFI = \frac{IS(t) + P(t)\,WO(t)}{OL\,(t) + WO(t)} \times 100 \qquad (1)$$

Since, the denominator is the gross outstanding loans, the risk factor index (RFI) in any situation will necessarily be more than zero but less than 1. From that angle the ideal credit risk management framework would aim at keeping the risk element i.e., RFI closer to zero. Credit Risk Index becomes 100 in case of portfolio consisting 100 per cent of loss assets. RFI in model I gives an indication of the amount of loss bank will suffer per Rs. 100 of its credit portfolio on a longer time horizon provided the risk environment remains stable.

Rationale of the Model

At this juncture it would be worthwhile to explain the rationale of determining the numerator factors because the accuracy of assigning risk value to the loan portfolio or borrower group will be dependent upon the accuracy of the attendant numerator factors. As is explained earlier the default indicator in any loan portfolio is best exemplified by the provision, write-off and non-performing loans over a period of time. Unrealised interest liability of the borrowers will also be a good indicator of default risks as the interest on non-performing loans are booked on realization basis only. Since loans of a bank under various sectors have been subjected to same set of regulatory and accounting norms, it makes sense to capture the cumulative position of provisions, write-off etc., in numerator factor as these are positively correlated with the default of loan. If for any particular year, the provisioning and write-off burden of a bank shows unusual increase, it may be due to change in regulatory framework or external environmental constraints. For example, recession in cement industry will increase the riskiness of the industry and any bank having substantial exposure to that industry will record higher RFI due to higher default rate in this segment. Again, there may be generic factors causing the NPAs, such as, stringent liquidity crunch which may cause the loan defaults across the segments to rise evenly. It may be remembered that strong liquidity problem in 1995-96 has debilitated the health of the many well run borrowing companies and there was across the board rise in NPAs in that year. Rise in interest suspense and provisioning amount fully reflect the qualitative downslide in loan portfolio. Therefore, if the overall provisioning, write-off and unrealized interest burden go up sharply due to very steep rise in any particular sectors, that is due to the increased riskiness in NPLs will subsstantively influence the risk factor index (RFI) indicating a deterioration of the riskiness. In such a situation, rise in risk factor indicator will signify to bank to cautiously expand in this area or the sector even if the credit scoring of a particular loan applicant is temptingly sound.

Incremental Risk Factor Index

While equation (1) gives the cumulative risk index of the loan portfolio, sometimes we may be interested in knowing the incremental risk factor, particularly to know the impact of both external and internal factors on the Risk Profile of Advances. Following the same logical explanation as given in Model I, the incremental Credit Risk Index can be defined as:

$$RFIi = \frac{\Delta IS(t_1 t_2) + \Delta P(t_1 t_2) + \Delta WO(t_1 t_2)}{OL\ (t) + \Delta WO(t_1 t_2)} \times 100 \qquad (2)$$

where,

Δ IS ($t_1 t_2$)	=	Incremental interest suspense balance
Δ P (t_1 t_2)	=	Incremental provision
Δ WO (t_1 t_2)	=	Incremental write off
OL (t)	=	Outstanding loan at the beginning of the period.

RFIi given in Model (2) will given the estimate of incremental loss bank is likely to suffer per Rs. 100 of its advances portfolio during a specific timeframe ($t_1 t_2$) say one year. Once the incremental RFI is worked out, further analysis may be undertaken to find out what are the causative factors that have led to the rise in risk and what are their individual contributions to rise in risk.

Using the same model, it may be found that the risk factor index of almost all the banks in the base year is very high, say, in the range of 20 per cent to 30 per cent. However, this is quite normal, because Indian banks are suffering from high accretion of NPLs during the past three decades and the reason for such a mess is too obvious to be repeated. Such excess baggage of NPLs being carried by the Indian banks on account of historical reasons would be distinctively reflected in the alarmingly high risk factor index value. But the model will be quite effective in tracking down the movement of risk, i.e., whether the credit risk is increasing or decreasing over a period of time and this may provide some lead as to how to monitor and control such increasing risk. Depending upon the period of interval, i.e., quarterly, half-yearly or yearly in deciding the time (t), there may be minor differences in the index. Ideally, this may be worked out on the basis of annual interval coinciding with the accounting norms existing in the country which may lend relatively more accuracy to the index so derived.

Uptil now we do not have any model, simple and easy to comprehend and which can be appropriately used in the Indian context. This model, at least, provides some pointers as to how to quantify the riskiness of lending in a specific segment as also track down the movement of risk over a period of time. However, this model may be suitably modified and further refined to enable it to gain higher accuracy as also to be usable in further analysis. For example, the RFI obtained with the help of this model can be used to test the relationship of various causative factors of loan default using statistical regression analysis so as to ascertain and measure up the contribution of a particular factor in increasing the credit risk, Further, relationship of default to industry, activity, borrower groups, limit, facility, sector, branch group, age group etc., may also be established and such analysis may be put to good use while designing risk management framework.

Once the RFI and RFIi is worked out across various segments as also on incremental basis, further analysis may be possible as to identifying the factors causing and increasing the incidence of NPAs i.e., risk propellers. Again, based on the experience, a set of preventive and protective factors to counter the incidence of NPAs, called the risk repellers, may be evolved and built into the loan appraisal system. With further refinement of the present model and with possible use of statistical tools, the impact of each and every propelling factor in increasing the credit risk on one hand as well as the effect of the repelling factors in diffusing the incidence of loan default on the other, could also be evaluated. Based on the analysis of segmentwise RFI and RFIi, different credit scoring models may be used in appraising fresh loan proposals in different sectors. For example, the credit rating model for a borrower in the property segment which is a high risk area may have to be significantly different from the credit rating model applicable to a borrower, say, in engineering segment. This will make the credit risk management framework more effective as well as more objective.

Application of the Model in Assessing Industry Level Risk

Apart form measuring credit risk index at the bank level, we visualize a situation where, using the same model, it may not be difficult to work out the inter-bank as well as the industry level Risk Factor Index (RFI). This would be possible, if RBI takes the lead in collecting and collating bankwise relevant information in this area and analyse the data with the help of this model. If we can stabilise this model and measure the credit at Industry level, its applicability could be easily extended to country-wise comparison. Once this is done, the true level of the credit risk will be visible. With the help of this Model, we could prove that even those countries, who boast of a less than 5 per cent net NPA level, are also carrying similar credit risk as Indian banks, because the written off loans are captured in our Model.

Advantages of Credit Risk Measurement Model

Now we have a risk measurement framework, a question naturally crops up is what is the use of this measurement model: The answer is simple. So long banks, operating in a controlled environment, had very little risk to manage. When everything gets managed by regulation, risk is almost dormant and invisible. With the central bank's role shifting from regulatory to a supervisory one, credit now requires fine management at the bank level without which the total operations may turn out to be the quicksand for any bank. Credit risk measurement is only the first step towards this end. Lending activity by itself gives rise to the chances of default. Contrary to the common expectation, this model will not wipe out such risk from the system totally. What it will deliver is a tool to differentiate between a good credit proposal and bad credit proposal. Needless to say, the improvement in the former will naturally reduce the overall riskiness of the credit portfolio. Measuring credit risk with the help of this model will primarily help banks in the following areas:

- Capturing the risk-proneness of various sectors as also identification of relatively more risky loan segments will be rendered easier. With this, is will be possible to evolve a risk-matrix across various activities, segment, regions, states, branch groups or even multi-segmental risk matrix may even by worked out.
- Movement of risk and its changing pattern across the board can also be tracked down so as to enable the lenders to formulate and adopt suitable risk containment measures.
- Data for this measurement exercise can easily be obtainable from the existing closing returns without creating any additional burden on the branches. Easy accessibility of information will increase the chances of applicability of this model at every decision making level with comfort. This is the most important aspect of the proposed framework as under the existing system, application of any new technique gets thwarted for lack of easy availability of data. The cost of collecting the data becomes too prohibitive and defeats the purpose of the exercise. However, under the proposed Model, implementation of this technique will not be difficult at all.
- The entire credit management system can be brought under a scientific framework - far removed from the intuition based on perception based management technique.

- This will minimise overall risk by dispersing of different risk value through a well planned diversification process. Credit risk measurement on the basis of activity, industry, sector, branch group, area, limit, facilities etc., would enable the management to reduce the probability of adverse selection. The model is not predictive in nature; but definitely preventive and pre-emptive. Credit expansion plan on the basis of loan portfolio analysis using this model will help reducing the overall riskiness.
- Measurement of credit risk will help in better profit planning at the corporate as well as other operational level. Since the credit risk is known, it will be easier for the banks to chalk out suitable plan for incremental business in terms of both quality and quantity so as to increase the marginal profitability of credit.
- This will also help banks to adopt more prudent accounting norms for creating healthy cushion against unpredictable financial shock. Better balance-sheet management will be facilitated.
- This model can be used as an effective tool for the management to find out the optimum risk absorption capacity or the risk appetite of a bank which will, in turn, enable formulation and adoption of compatible loan policy.
- Once the credit risk is measured, a suitable and scientific risk based pricing mechanism may be formulated. With the help of this model, bankers may evolve a risk-return trade-off matrix to price loans of different segments (risk-brackets). Discriminatory pricing system will not only increase the income level, but also will put a natural barrier to the addition to the high risk borrower groups.
- Lastly and more optimistically, the present model may provide a useful platform for further research and framing up of the value-at-risk model to measure, evaluate and indicate the maximum potential loss the

loan portfolio is likely to sustain over a particular period, given the determination of appropriate statistical assumptions to capture the volatility factors. This, being the subject of intense research and innovation, it is time that such techniques are experimented and put to greater use in mainstream banking.

Evolving a Credit Risk Management Framework

Evolution of a credit risk management framework presupposes that the top management has to have an appropriate perception of credit risk and its attendant impact on the profitability of the bank. Once the quantification mechanism of credit risk is established, it will be far easier for the top management to come out with a credit risk management framework so as to manage the risk in such a way that the return remains optimal within the preferred risk matrix. Dominant theme of any good risk management framework is to find out the right level of risk-return trade-off. This is factored by two things: (i) how risk savvy the management is and (ii) what is the existing risk level. Based on these two factors and other related assumptions with regard to various economic indicators, separate trigger points for targeted credit risk across different segments/sectors/regions may be fixed. With intermittent review of actual performance (actual segment-wise RFI) vis-a-vis the targeted risk bank, new trigger points may be fixed so that the overall risk of the credit portfolio can be kept within the desired direction. Credit management system based on the scientific risk measurement model will facilitate emergence of a more objective loan policy.

Pre-Requisites for Establishing a Credit Risk Measurement and Management Framework

Writing in the 1930s on the implication of uncertainty of inefficient market, Keynes, the renowned economist, made a shocking comment that those involved in taking financial decisions "know almost nothing whatever about what they are doing". He continued, "they do not possess even the rudiments of what is required for a valid judgment and are the prey of hopes and fears easily aroused by transient events". However, with tremendous innovation in communication technology, things have changed; and the world has become more uncertain than what it was in the 1930s. Hence, the need for possessing the requisite knowledge of the probability distribution of possible outcome has become extremely necessary.

- The imperative is to understand the inherent characteristic of risk, its definition and identification.
- Creating an awareness of about risk and its manifestation at different levels of management is also a must.
- The third important pre-requisite is to improve the necessary MIS capability. Creation of Comprehensive credit information system is essential.
- Last, but not the least, is to make a thorough use of the "Holy Trinity" of modern age, i.e., information, technology and research so as to analyse and constantly refine the risk quantification and control technique. Research supports for establishing the risk management system is a minimum must.

Perceiving credit risk is only half the way towards designing a credit measurement and management framework while research and analysis through better use of technology will complete the other half without which risk management will remain as uncertain as the risk itself.

Conclusion

Credit risk in the environment is increasing; and, so are the banking meltdowns. This is true around the globe. Fortunes of the banking industry the world over in the past decades as also in the present one has proved beyond doubt that there is a need for better and improved risk management technique.

References

Altman, E., Haldeman, R. and Narayanan, P. (1977), ZETA Analysis-New Model to Identify Bankruptey Risk of Corporations, *Journal of Banking & Finance*, June 1997.

Davis, E. P. (1993), Bank Credit Risk, Working Paper Series No. 8, Bank of England, April 1993.

Beattie, Vivien A. & Others (1996), Banks and Bad Debts: Accounting for Loan Losses in International Banking.

Godse, V. T. and Chakrabarty K.C. (1996), Risk Management, *IBA Bulletin*, March.

Harrison, David (1996), Art or Science? The Importance of Understanding Credit Risk-Chartered Banker, January.

Gupta, V. K. (2006), " Risk Management System in Banks", *The Indian Bankers*, May, 2006.

47

Relationship Banking in the Emerging Banking Scenario

Niru Kumari

A new approach to the marketing of bank services that is receiving growing attention in banks is "relationship banking". The emphasis here is on viweing the customer as a long term business relationship, rather than confining attention to the particular transaction. Banks make strategic plans to met the total banking requirements of the customers and expect repeat business from them. Banks takeon the role of all weather friends and establish a firm relationship wherein the customers confine all their banking transactions to them. For building up profitable customer relationships, it is inevitable on the part of the bankers, first of all, to know more about the customer and his banking needs and towards this end, banks need to prepare customer profiles. Building a long term profitable relationships with customers calls for systematic efforts. In order to ensure customer satisfaction, bank staff should guide the customers in making the right choice from among the available range of services and facilities.Conscious and continuous efforts on the part of the banker is a must for cultivating relationship banking with a customer, whether an individual or a corporate entity. The process of relationship banking follows five major steps:

Knowing thyself: This is an important prerequisite for relationship banking. The banker should have a thorough knowledge about his products and services. This helps the customer to develop confidence in his banker.

While knowing about one's products, it is desirable to know about the products of one's competitors as well. This would enable the banker to plan his sales strategy more effectively.

Presenting thyself: Presenting thyself is as important as knowing thyself. Banking is a service industry and service is identified with the person who meets it out. It is here, the customer first comes into contact. Not only his appearance, but also his attitude should be appealing to the customer. Proper dress code, immaculate surroundings, attractive interior decorations, ambience and courteous staff at the workstations are ways of presenting oneself to attract customers.

Understanding the customer: This is the most important part of relationship banking. Customer is the pivotal point around whom the entire gamut of banking revolves. He always deserves a patient listening. No matter how he reacts, the banker should remain calm, composed and pleasant. Every customer deserves to be treated with respect. The best way to show respect (especially in India) is to stand up and greet a customer.

Understanding and meeting the needs: Understanding the needs of the customer is an integral part of relationship building. The need of the customer gets revealed through conversation. Identification of common area of interest may help the banker to indulge the customer in conversation. This conversation would help the banker to understand the needs of the customer.

The bankers' duty is not to display what he has. This is equivalent to 'tell selling'. What is required is 'ask selling'. Tell sellijng is similar to order taking in a restaurant. There is a lot of difference between a bearer of a restaurant and a banker. The latter is expected to be more articulate and educated. He is expected to give expert advice to the customer.

Once relationship is cultivated and the needs of the customer are ascertained, the banker can slowly start making suggestions regarding his products/services that can meet the needs of the customer. The banker should be very honest and sincere in his approach. Then only he can win the trust of the customer.

Product development and technological adoption and upgradation are a must for meting out quality customer service. Banking has undergone a complete metamorphosis in the recent past due to technological innovation. The range of products/services in the shelves of technology-driven banks is unbelievably large now.

Follow up: Lastly, any amount of effort, in canvassing a customer, would be set at naught if proper follow-up is not done. Perhaps, this can be considered to be the singly major reason for the nationalised banks, especially SBI, losing customers. Correct name, full address, telephone number and other details viz. date of birth, names and details of family members etc. may be kept in the dossier for further follow up. Sending greeting cards on birhtdays, festive occasions, calling on customers at frequent intervals, wishing them success or congratulating them etc. are techniques in cementing the relationship.

No humen being is infallible, and a banker is a human being. But what is required is the mind to realise the mistake and relent. Never indulge in argument with a customer even if the latter is at fault. If the banker has committed a mistake, admkit it and apologise for it. Mostly this would salvage the situation. In worst cases, this approach can at least assuage the feelings of customer, if not undo the damage.

Some highly successful bankers go a step further in relationship building. They use the already existing strong relationships to cultivate and strengthen new ones. For example, therse bankers would already be having strong relationships with bureaucrats in customs, police, judiciary, education dept., hospitals, schools etc. These bonds are used to help other customers like arranging for spedy customs clearance at airport'seaport, getting admission in good schools for children, getting preferential treatment in hospitals and so on. Needless to say that such help from bankers can produce stronger and lasting relationship.

The advantages of relationship banking are manifold in the emerging banking scenario in India. Against the mounting competition, it works as a highly effective tool to widen the business opportunities through existing and potential clientele.

The major advantage of relatilonship banking is that it helps in retention marketing i.e. retention of existing customers by multiplying business relationships with them. Cross selling of products is the best and easiest way for multiplying business relationships. For e.g. a bank can multiply its relationship with a savings bank a/c holder by cross selling products like ATM, Credit Card and overdraft. ATM and Credit Card offer 24 hrs. banking whereas overdraft is a stadby arrangement.

Secondly, relationship banking helps in attracting new customers also. Generally new customers approach banks through three routes - those brought in by existing satisfied customers, those walk in, and those brought in by staff through concerted efforts. Each type of customer needs deft handling. In all the above three cases, the aim should be to cultivate relationship, not to conclude sale of one product/service. It is here the concept of 'soft selling' becomes more relevant. The idea is to slowly suggest to the customer the products/service of the bank after understanding his requirements. The approach should be 'soft' as distinguished from 'hardselling', normally resorted to be salesmen of consumer goods.In the latter case the aim is to just conclude one sale and move on to the next customer. It is totally product oriented. As opposed to this, the focus of soft selling is not on what the seller can give the customer, but on what the customer needs. Soft selling takes care of not only the present but the future also. This helps in relationship building.

Thirdly, the concept of relationship banking envisages better relationship between employees leading to team spirit and a tension free atmosphere within the organisation. Needless to say, this contributes to better productivity.

Relationshipbanking as a novel marketing technique, has not yet been fully assimilated in the Indian banking system. Barring the new private sector and foreign banks, majority of the banks, especially public sector banks (PSU Banks), have not yet started practising this consciously.

The success of foreign banks and new private sector banks should encourage the PSU Banks to introduce this technique in their branches. However, there are certain major issues that needs to be addressed befor this.

Firstly, the deployment of manpower in PSU Banks requires improvement. The edifice of relationship banking rests on the mindset and attitude of the person who metes out the service. Relationship building is an art and only talented and motivated people should be deployed for this. However, the oftrepeated complaint is that postings in PSU Banks are just a slot filling exercise resulting in a square peg sitting in a round hole. A detail profile of the personnel should be mainteained and updated. This should be referred to whenever key postings are made.

PSU Banks requires a jolt. Apart from testing candidates for their IQ (Intelligence Quotient), they must be tested for their EQ (Emotional Intelligence Quotient) as well. In a service industry where relationship building is very important, EQ has equal or ever more relevance than IQ.

Training in PU Banks has ben more of a skill imparting exercise. This should change. Participants should be given more training in relationship banking concepts. techniques viz. Ask selling, Soft selling, Cross selling should be taught with the help of case studies.

PSU Banks should evolve a system of rewarding monetarily and otherwise those who excel in the field of relationship banking. This would also plug the drainage of talented people from PSU Banks. It is a known fact that majority of foreign and new private sector banks could thrive by poaching on PSU Banks' human talent. Some of the best talents that left PSU Banks carried along with them some of the best customers also. Thus they lost on two fronts.

Lack of coordination between different entities within each group is another impediment in successfully practicing relationship banking. For example a PSU Bank will have different banking divisions or subsidiaries focussing on different target groups of customers. Cross-selling of products to these customers become easier and cost effective if there is fine co-ordination between the divisions/subsidiaries of the bank.

All said and done, it must also be noted that not all customers get carried away by relationship cultivation by banks. Many customers look at relationship building on a deal to deal basis. Benefit from each deal is what they look for, while cultivating relationship. Such customers are highly demanding and fickle. Winning their loyalty is an uphill task. However, many banks, especially the new generation banks, have been successful in wooing these customers not only through both product enhancement but making their products very competitive as well. Offers like gift vouchers, waiver of fee, home delivery, add on benefits etc. are introduced as product enhancements while offering various products at market competitive rates. Once a customer is brought to the fold of the bank, the focus is on him and the banks try to cross sell as many products as possible to him. Thus, we see a savings account customer (of a new generation bank) getting offers of insurance, mutual funds, credit cards, home loans, auto loans etc. in no time.

Lastly, a word of caution. Cultivation of relationship to serve organizational purpose is welcome. But relationship building cannot be pursued too far. The employee should know where to draw the line. In his over enthusiasm to cultivate relationship, he should not overdo it. In such cases, the organization's interests take a back seat leading to disastrous results.

Reference

Ford Philip (1989), Customer Services Marketing and the Competitive Environment, London, Pitman Publishing.

Peters Glen (1994), Bench Marking Customer Service, London, Pitman Publishing.

Puttaswamaiah, K. (1996), Customer Service in Canara Bank. Indiacators for Measurement, Bangalore, Canara Bank H.O.

Sarkar, Subrate (1990), Marketing of Bank Service to Corporate Customers (A Study of UCO Bank Customers in Calcuatta), Pune.

www. goodle.com.

48

Customer Relationship Management: Practice and Application in State Bank of India

Kumari Madhulata & P. K. Sinha

All service sector industries have realised that creating superior customer service is the key for their survival. Most offer across the industries are difficult to differentiate on the basis of offer quality, pricing, distribution or promotion for that matter. They all are saturated on the basis of certain parameters. The best quality offer with most competitive price and promotion with the greatest aggression have become the norm. The only point of differentiation left is the customer service and most of the industries are using it as a tool for competitive advantage.

Today many business such as banks, insurance companies and other service providers realise the importance of customer relationship management (CRM) and its potential to help them acquire new customer, retain existing ones and maximize their lifetime value. At this point, close relationship with customers will require a strong coordination between IT and marketing departments to provide a long term retention of selected customers.

CRM is a sound business strategy to identify the banks most profitable customers and prospects and devotes time and attention to expanding account relationships with those customers through individualized marketing, repricing, discretionary decision making and customized service all delivered through the various sales channels that the bank uses.

CRM Objectives in Banking Sector

The idea of CRM is that is helps businesses use technology and human resources gain insight into the behavior of customers and the value of those customers. If it works as hoped, a business can provide better customer service, make call centers more efficient, cross sell products more effectively, help sales staff close deals faster, simplify marketing and sales processes, discover new customers and increase customer revenues. It doesn't happen by simply buying software and installing it. For CRM to be truly effective, an organization must first decide what kind of customer information it is looking for and it must decide what it intends to do with that information. For example, many financial institutions keep track of customers' life stages in order to market appropriate banking products like mortgages or IRAs to them at the right time to fit their needs. Next, the organization must look into all of the different ways information about customers comes into a business, where and how this data is stored and how it is currently used. One company, for instance, may interact with customers in a myriad of different ways including mail campaigns, Web sites, brick and mortar stores, call centers, mobile sales force staff and marketing and advertising efforts. Solid CRM systems link up each of these points. This collected data flows between operational systems (like sales and inventory systems) and analytical systems that can help sort through these records for patterns. Company analysts can then comb through the data to obtain a holistic view of each customer and pinpoint areas where better services are needed. In CRM projects, following data should be collected to run process engine: (1) Responses to campaigns, (2) Shipping and fulfillment dates, (3) Sales and purchase data, (4) Account information, (5) Web registration data, (6) Service and support records, (7) Demographic data, 8) Web sales data.

CRM Practices

Realising the importance of retail segment in banking business and henceforth the importance of providing delightment with its service and delivery, the bank carved out a massive CRM programme. To facilitate services to the retail customers, the bank has even segregated branches into various segments depending on the types of customers it caters to such as corporate account group, treasury branches, SSI branches, commercial branches, NRI branch and network branch. For effective CRM in retail banking segment, the bank has separately created an exclusive Personal Banking Branch (PBB). There are 75 PBBs in india (SBI literature). The concept of PBBs are to offer all retail banking products right from Savings Bank accounts, Current account to home loan, car loan, personal loan, credit cards, mutual funds and insurance under one roof.

The CRM initiatives of SBI could be classified in the following heads:

Customer Relationship Schemes

1. SBI has carved out a separate section to look into retail segment known as Personal Banking Branch (PBB). The PBBs have uniform set of interiors with certain facilities across the country to make customer feel the same level of comfort with any of the bank branches in the country.
2. The concept of Relationship Managers (RMs) has been introduced in the PBBs. The PBBs have been asked to identify top 200 accounts of their branch based on their value and business with the bank and assign an exclusive RM to these accounts in a group of seven to ten accounts. These RMs are supposed to look after all sorts of requirements of these customers. They would be providing all services at one desk only. This arrangement is supposed to help the bank in serving the customers better and also to provide an opportunity to cross-sell and up-sell with the customers.
3. Every branch is supposed to form a Customer Relationship Committee meeting every month. This committee is to consist of staff members, five customers from various

customer groups–high net worth individual (HN) customers, pensioners, industrial loan customers, retail loan customers etc. These customers are called at the bank and are asked to lodge their complaints and offer their suggestions on various matters pertaining to bank services. A report and minute of the committee is prepared and follow up actions are reviewed in the subsequent meeting.

4. Every branch is supposed to organise one special customer relationship programme every quarter aiming at any of the customer issue coined in the Customer Service Committee meeting.
5. There is also a Customer Service Committee which consists of members of the staff. It meets once a month and discusses on the customer issues for betterment of customer service.
6. The corporate centre of the bank has a separate Customer Relation Cell. This cell is supposed to design programmes for various customer requirements and do all arrangements which can increase customer satisfaction with the bank.
7. The bank's local head office branches are also required to constitute a bank club/board club. The club members consist of staff and customers. These club members are supposed to work out on a strategy that could improve the bank's functioning and could provide better service to its customers. Once in half year, the CGM meets the elite and the HNI customers of the bank.
8. Pensioners, who constitute a large chunk of SBI customer group, are called for a meeting to bring out their grievances and suggestions to improve banking service, once a quarter.
9. To impart a feel-good factor among its customers, the bank also does community service banking for schools and colleges. Various programmes such as sports meet, college functions and honouring toppers are organised. Manager at local level can also offer certain scholarships and so on.
10. The bank has now even started sending seasonal greetings to its high-value customers. This is an attempt to induce personal feeling in their relationship with the bank.

11. It has been made mandatory by every branch, which has more than 20 staff strength, to set up a counter of "May I help you". It is supposed to help customers in all their requirements such as filling up a fixed deposit form, enquiry related to certain banking products and use of any type of service.
12. To attend customer's query over telephone only, the bank has started a helpline at all zonal offices. Any of the customer service requests is now attended over telephone only. This saves customer's time, money and harassment.
13. The members of the Circle Management Committee, Deputy General Manager and Assistant General Manager meet customers and other users once in a month in open forums at various centres to listen to their grievances and suggestions to improve the services of the bank. Advance announcements are made in the press before holding such meets.
14. The branch managers or managers of divisions should invariably call on customers at their workplace. In addition, all levels of staff should occasionally call on customers at appropriate levels at their workplaces, depending upon circumstances.
15. The CGM, DGM and branch managers meet the customers at the respective headquarters on the 15th of every month (or the next working day if 15th happens to be a holiday) for receiving their specific complaints/suggestions and resolving them at the earliest.
16. The bank is presently experimenting with this new concept of customer councils. With a view to promoting better interaction between operating staff and the customers, the bank has decided to set up customer councils at branches having a staff strength of 100 or more and at all intensive centres. Three to six customers are co-opted by the branch who, in the presence of Customer Service Committee, meet quarterly and identify areas of customer services and suggest steps to improve the same.

17. The bank became a member of the Banking Codes and Standards Board of India (BCSBI) in September 2006. It has thereby adopted BCSBF code of bank's commitments to customers as the Fair Practice Code for implementation at all its branches. It has also appointed Code Compliance Officers at all its offices. The bank places importance not only to redress customer grievances but also in identifying systemic/attitudinal issues, if any, that lead to a high frequency of complaints in particular areas and in rectifying them.

Complaint-handling Machinery

SBI looks at grievance redressal as very important for customer service and customer delight. For this, the bank has made several arrangement which are as follows :

1. *Complaint-cum-suggestion box:* A transparent glass window should be fixed at the bottom of the complaint-cum-suggestion box. Branch managers have made responsible for keeping watch on that.
2. *Display of notice:* It should be at a prominent place, indicating the five basic services that the customer should expect from the branch.
3. *Disposal of complaints:* All complaints, whether verbal or written, must be entered in the branch complaint book and acknowledged within 24 hours. The triplicate copy of the complaint format should be sent to the concerned controlling authority together with the branch comments as to the manner of disposal (so that the controlling office may have a proper monitoring). The complaint should be finally settled within a maximum period of 21 days, under confirmation to the controlling office.
4. *Complaint register:* It should be verified by the branch inspector. Suitable remedial measures should be initiated to avoid recurrence of complaints.
5. *Customer Service audit:* Format containing 25 core customer service areas, where customer service

evaluation and monitoring should be based, is to be sent to the controlling authority at the end of March, June, September or December.

Technology Initiatives

With increased competition and new business opportunities in the market place, it is imperative for SBI to introduce and absorb technology extensively and at a rapid speed to remain customer-friendly, efficient and competitive for existing services and business as well as perhaps more importantly, to be able to manage newer forms of business and services in an increasingly dynamic and global environment. The bank has adopted and is pursuing effectively its IT policy with the aim of achieving efficiency in operations meeting customer and market expectations and staying ahead in competition.

Few of the major technological initiatives undertaken by the banks to provide better and speedy services are as follows:

1. *Software Installation under Core Banking Project:* In major initiative set to revolutionise the banking industry in the country, State Bank of India has selected Tata Consultancy Services (TCS), Asia's largest global software solutions and consulting services company, to supply, customise and implement the prestigious Centralised Core Banking System.
2. *Centralised Core Banking System:* The B@NCS -24 to be implemented in SBI is a state-of-the-art core banking system which has been successfully implemented in 40 countries across the world in more than 50 banks.
3. *Branch Computerisation:* The bank's effort to improve efficiency and customer service through use of technology is reflected in the rapid pace of its branch computerisation. Out of the 14300 branches of SBI and associates in India, over 80% branches have been computerised. All specialised branches, such as overseas branches, NRI branches, personal banking branches, commercial branches and industrial finance

branches are now fully computerised". It provides the following services to the customers:

(i) Customer enquiry terminals in branches to answer queries on accounts
(ii) Neatly printed account statements and passbook
(iii) Speedy collection of instruments
(iv) Prompt execution of standing instructions.
(v) Extended business hours
(vi) Telebanking at select branches
(vii) Remote-log-in facility at selected branches
(viii) STEPS, to meet customer demand for faster remittances and speedier collection of outstation instruments.

4. *Automated Teller Machines (ATMs):* Today, the bank has, in a way, almost replaced a bank branch with ATMs. One can deposit cheques, drafts, cash etc. into any ATM and withdraw cash from it also. Besides, one can make balance enquiry, get mini statement, and enquire about different products of the bank. Banking through ATM has even become a mark of sophistication and fashion.

Other Customer Service Initiatives

SBI has introduced several other proactive customer service initiatives to make the banking pleasurable for the customers. They are:

1. *Arrival timings:* The staff is positioned 15 minutes before the commencement of banking hours at all offices/branches to avoid customers waiting needlessly.
2. *VIP ledgers:* Separate ledgers are introduced for VIP customers.
3. *VIP counters:* These are arranged at all the division branches.
4. *Maturity advices:* Maturity advices regarding term deposit receipts/short-term deposit receipts should be

sent to the customers without fail so that they can plan their investments accordingly.

5. *Documents:* Whenever a customer/party is required to sign any documents or a non-standard document, its contents should be made known to him beforehand. In the case of borrowal accounts, the arrangement letter should be invariably be delivered to the customers.
6. *Message to staff:* There is no substitute to the satisfaction derived from the "service with a smile" and this should be made clear to everybody.

Other Tech-based Offers

Most of the tech-based offer the bank has introduced are a result of greater application of web. Few of these are as follows:

1. State Bank Electronics Payment System (STEPS)
2. SBI Connect
3. Society for worldwide inter-bank Financial Telecommunication (SWIFT)
4. MICR Cheque Processing System
5. Video Conference

The Road Ahead

The State Bank of India at corporate level does understand the importance of a delighted customer in this hyper-competitive banking era and, hence, has given due importance to Customer Relationship Management practices in its overall marketing strategy. The bank while formulating its marketing strategy has tried to take cognizance of CRM and taken several initiatives in this regard. Even though the programmes sound to be very good, they do not meet to the objectives because of poor implementation of these programmes. SBI urgently needs to take the following actions for effective customer relationship.

1. Being a prominent player of mass banking, SBI should not try to please all customers with the same service facilities. It need to make clear customer segmentation

and design its customer service programmes accordingly-better customer service to profitable customers.

2. The bank has been laggard in the implementation of technology, but in the recent past, technology has taken the centre stage in customer services. Realising this, the bank has also started introducing ATMs, net banking and phone banking. The bank needs to see the working of its ATMs and other form of tech-driven banking as phone and net banking. As these forms of banking satisfy two customers faster but also leads to huge dissatisfaction in case of poor functioning of the system.
3. SBI has introduced the concept of Relationship Managers (RMs) in its Personal Banking Branches. This has been a good initiative, but it is not working very effectively as there is insufficient number of staff and they are mostly engaged with regular banking jobs. The bank should make arrangement of exclusive staff for relationship purpose, at least for high value customers.
4. SBI has designed several things for customer relationship such as a customer service committee, customer relationship programme and customer day. But due to the absence of their proper implementation, the bank has not been able to project itself as a customer-friendly bank. It should also take care that all these programmes are implemented on a consistent basis and do not become a one time phenomenon.
5. Though the bank has a standard grievance-handling mechanism, it is too complicated and rarely resolves the matter in a fixed timeframe. This could be corrected by introducing software which can automatically record a complaint/grievances/query and bring to the notice of the official concerned.
6. SBI does not have any policy for customer retention. The bank is even unable to monitor movements in

accounts, as the total number of accounts is very huge. An exclusive software can be very handy in customer retention as it may immediately inform the authority of any abrupt movements taking place in a particular account. This may help the bank identify the problem and check customer migration.

Conclusion

SBI employees need to change their approach of being in "sarkari naukari" (government job). Most of the bank officials do not even know of CRM and often ask "What CRM?". They need to realise that they work in an industry which is changing very fast and it is because of customers that their organisation and job survive. They need to inculcate the feeling that they all are for servicing the customers and it is not the customer, who is dependent on the bank.

References

Anderson, Alan R. and Authur Best (1977), Consumers Complain-Does Business Respond? *Harvard Business Review,* 55 (July-August), pp. 93-101.

Beckett-Camarata, E. J., Camarata, M. R., Barker, R. T. (1998), Integrating Internal and External Customer Relationships Through Relationship Management: A Strategic Response to a Changing Global Environment, *Journal of Business Research,* 41, 71-81.

Berry, M. J. A. & Linoff G. S. (2000), Mastering Data Mining: The Art and Science of Customer Relationship Management, John Wiley & Sons, Inc.

Cook, W.D., & Hababou, M. (2001), Sales Performance Measurement in Bank Branches, *Omega,* 29, 299-307.

Day, R.L. and M. Bodur (1978), Consumer Response to Dissatisfaction with Services and Intangibles, in Hunt, H.K. (Eds), Advances in Consumer Research, Association for Consumer Research, Ann Anbor, MI, 5, pp. 263-272.

Gitomer, J. (1998), Sales Secrets: Made a Mistake? How to Win Back Your Customers, *Amazon.com.*

Peppard, J., (2000), Customer Relationship Management (CRM) in Financial Services, *European Management Journal,* Vol. 18, No. 3, pp. 312-327.

49

CRM–A Vital Business Tool for Bankers

Jitendra Kumar Singh & Piyush Kumar Singh

We have been all along taking about public sector banks and private sector banks, technology banks and traditional banks, foreign banks and the new private sector banks as different entities that distinguish themselves. The time has now come to add a new classification: Banks, which believe in CRM and those who do not. Not that CRM is new to banks. But the way in which CRM has been rediscovered, with advanced technology to support, has added much needed value to the Relationship between the Customer and the Management (of Banks). The newly found CRM tries to elevate this Relationship to higher levels of functionality and fulfill ment that could not even be dreamt of in the past.

Whilst Banking Industry is observing tremendous changes, the focus is towards customer service. Nowadays more and more options are available to customers. The customer is aware of technology and the various service options. Due to these, there, is heavy competition between banks. Increased competition in the market has in the past few years propelled retail banks to focus greatly. In maintaining and increasing their customer base while improving customer service quality. In other words, customer relationship management (CRM) has become a major focus for the banks.

The paper is organized as follows:

Section–1 Outlines the principle of CRM.

Section–2 Discusses CRM as an important aspect of banking today.

Section–3 Conclusions

Section–1

Customers go through a defined process when purchasing. The complexity of the product, the customer's previous experience of the product of the situational context will influence the length of time needed to move through this buying process. The customer experience defines everything the customer feels, remembers, says and does about their interaction with organizations. Organizations position themselves to service customers through their product and service offering. This offering has to appeal not just to the immediate need but also to the emotional context within which the customer is operating. The organizations that remain adaptive and are able to tailor the experience to meet the changing emotional context of the customer will close the door to the competition. (Charley, Jonathan 2001).

Based on a thorough understanding of their customers, organizations need some well thought out customer strategies and individual customer action plans together with the ability to deliver responsive, tailored propositions. Cap Gemini Ernst & Young has identified 10 core principles in support of achieving enduring and profitable customer relationship that will enable organizations to spot the opportunities, ensure appropriate targeting and enable effective servicing.

The 10 principles of Customer Relationship Management:

1. *Value Segmentation:* based on customer needs, preferences, behaviors and economic potential, which provides the basis for resource allocation decision in marketing sales and service.

2. *Collaboration:* the customer is involved in the specification, design and/or delivery of a desired result.

3. *Institutional Memory:* when a customer interacts with your company, everyone in the enterprise is aware of prior interactions, outstanding issues and pending opportunities.
4. *Touch-point Alignment:* customers are able to do business with you through multiple channels, which are a aligned to customer need and value.
5. *Real-time Information Management:* employees have real-time access to the right information in order to make customer-based decisions and resolve issues immediately.
6. *Closed-loop Process:* integrated front and back office systems ensure that information and workflow carry through the entire enterprise to their logical conclusion, closing the customer loop and enabling continuous knowledge capture.
7. *Customer Scorecard:* employee performance requirements and measures are designed to drive specific customer behavior.
8. *Listening Post:* forums to facilitate information sharing and learning about your customers that helps your to do business with them, learn from each other and provide valuable customer input to your business.
9. *One and done:* solving customer needs first time.
10. *Total experience management:* mapping all of the touch-points between your and your customers and attempting to deliver a consistent quality experience as perceived by the customer.

Section–2

CRM-An Important Aspect of Banking Today

According to Peppers and Roges (1997), great service happens only when your relate to your customers "One to One". To do that, you have to identify your customers, differentiate them, interact with them, and finally, customize your products or services to meet their needs. This calls for customer relationship management (CRM), a tool in the hands of the Banker. Obviously a CRM strategy has numerous aspects, but the basic theme is for the (Firm) banker to become more customer-centric. This does not necessarily create a new revenue stream today or even tomorrow. How ever, it will add customer loyalty to the business's bottom line.

The traditional customer relationship management (CRM) approach based around the relationship manager can no longer be sustained without the application of CRM tools and techmoques, regardless of whether the organization is targeting the high net worth or the mass affluent customer segments of the market.

What can CRM add? The relationship manager is like a communication node between the customer and the organization, understanding customer's needs and preferences, and orchestrating the products and services to meet those needs. When life is simple, the relationship manager need only communicate with the customer to have a fully assimilated view of that customer's activities. The manager's brain is acting as the CRM tool for storing, processing and evaluating data leading to a customer strategy.

The dynamics and environment of today's organization are changing; creating a level of complexity and diversity that can no longer be handled by a single individual when interchanging with a customer. The latest downturn in the stock market will put increasing pressure on organizations to perform and give good cause for examining how CRM can achieve cost savings and enhance revenue.

If the relationship manager model is not to be compromised or needs increased levels of propel to support it, then CRM tools and techniques must be applied.

With many financial institutions now offering multi-channel access, customer relationship are becoming more complex to handle. As the Internet changes how people seek information, traditional customer service solutions are rendered inadequate. The challenge is how to deliver an equally high level of service across all channels.

This focus on CRM is in line with transition from transaction-based business model to a relationship-based model, concentrating on the acquiring, development and retention of profitable customer relationships. Until now, customers have been taken for granted. But, with growing population of Internet savvy and mere financially aware people with greater demands for increased value, the need to handle customer relationships effectively has increased, particularly as it is easy to switch between providers.

Developments in Information Technology, data warehousing and data mining have made it possible for Banks to maintain a one to one relationship with their customers. Simply, having relationship managers for select customers hoping to cross-sell products is not a welcome sign. Bankers in order to gain competitive advantage must fully integrate mission-critical business intelligence such as data warehousing and data mining into the CRM backbone. A key part of successful CRM is not only to engage with customers as much as possible but also to recognize their differing needs. In line with this, K V Klamath, CEO & MD, ICIC Ltd., observes 'Effective use of customer relationship information becomes the most valued and source for competitive advantage.'

Conclusion

Customer Relationship Management (CRM) has become an increasingly critical means of developing and maintaining customer loyalty while also helping business migrate to low value customer towards greater profitability. (Chu, McKinley & O'Neill, 2001). Bankers can now manage every single contact with the customer to build lasting relationships and glean information and insights about customer's needs and their buying behavior to design and develop services, which help create value for the customer as well as the bank. Although customized as well as off the shelf technological solutions to implement CRM practices. Those Banks developing close customer relationship will grow much more aggressively than their competitors will. Successful implementation of CRM requires a strategic approach, which encompasses developing customer-centric processes, selecting and implementing technology solutions, employee empowerment, customer information and knowledge generation capabilities to differentiate them, and the ability to learn from bestpractices. Mr. Swift says, "CRM should be integrated into everything a company does, everyone it employs, and everywhere it transacts." CRM is not technology interest; it is a business strategy to select and manage the most valuable customer relationships.

References

Bansal, Parveen (2001), *'Ignore CRM at Your Peril'*, The Banker.

Butler, Shahla (2000), 'Changing the Game: CRM in the e-World', *Journal of Business Strategy.*

Charley, Jonathan (2001), *'The Temperature is Rising...;* The Banker.

CRM Forum Resources, *http://www.crm-forum.com.*

Data Monitor's Report (2000), on *'Customer Relationship* Management in European Retail Banking'.

Gosney, Johd W. and Boehm, Thomas P. (2001), *' Customer Relationship Management Essentials;* PHI.

Macmillan, Keith, Money, Kevin and Downing, Stephen (2000), 'Successful Business Relationship', *Journal of General Management.*

Peppers, Don and Rogers, Martha (1997), 'The One to One Future: Building Relationships One Customer at a Time'.

Swift, Roland (1999), *'Accelerating Customer Relationships'*, Harper Collins.

Ray Mckenzie-The Relationship-based Enterprise.

David P. Snydler-Mind Read Your Customer.

Patrick Forsyth-Communicating With Your Customer.

William John-Successful Customer Care.

50

Customer Relationship Management in the Indian Banks

Ranjana Singh & Ajoy Kumar

In any commercial/service organization, customer is the centre point of all the activities around whom the entire organization pinpoints the entire gambit of operations. Customer satisfaction is the primary objective in the banking industry. Unless all the credit needs of the customers are not taken care of adequately by the bank, it is not likely that the bank may flourish to any extent. Relationship marketing sometimes is referred to as Customer Relationship Management, which is a relationship process which an organization can cultivate with its customer segments in such a way that it may benefit both the customer as well as the organization. The ever growing expectations of the customers, fast changing preferences and opportunities being made available to him as a customer have made him the king in the real sense. Customer satisfaction is a growing concern for the banks who want to grow in today's competitive world.

In order to cater to the customer needs to the fullest extent, the banks have to divide the entire lot of customers into various segments according concern to the activities in which they are engaged. A separate set of customers has got separate customer needs and necessarily separate nature of services are required by them. The customer segmentation could be as under:

(a) According to the nature activities : The segments may be Personal & Services; Small Industries; Small Business; Commercial; Institutional and Agricultural etc.

(b) According to Sector : The segments may be Public Sector or Private Sector.

(c) According to Constitution of the Customer: The segments may be corporate bodies, Co-operatives; Partnership / Proprietorship firms; Individuals, etc.

(d) According to the Size of the Customer's Activities: The segments may Retail Network or Commercial Network. It has been the experience that each and every set of customer has got its own priorities and separate treatment is to be given to a particular class of customer, meaning thereby that customer needs can not be generalized.

The concept of Customer Relationship Management is now gaining wide acceptance and is recognized as a powerful tool for business development and to have an edge over the competitors on account of the universal traits of the human behaviour. Various organizations had earlier focused on their products as the starting points and then looked around for the customer to sell them. The approach of Customer Relationship Management is somewhat different in the sense that it starts with the customer not in totality of customers because each customer is an individually to find out what he wants and design the products as per the needs of the particular set of customers and make the supply of it. In a nut shell, Customer Relationship Management is about growing enduring relationship with profitable customers.

In financial services, nationalized as-well-as new generation private and foreign banks have introduced private and foreign banks have introduced customer friendly products and services which could be listed as following:

- Account Statement,
- Automated Teller Machines (ATMs),
- Any where/ Anytime Banking,

- Credit Cards/Debit Cards/Smart Cards,
- Corporate Banking Terminals,
- Electronic Funds Transfer (EFT),
- Electronic Clearing Systems (ECS)
- Electronic Data Interchange,
- Home Banking,
- Internet Banking,
- Indian Financial Network (INFINET),
- Integral Payment & Settlement Systems (IPSS),
- Mobile Banking,
- Online Banking,
- Point of Sale Terminals,
- Real Time Gross Settlements (RTGS),
- Shared Payment Network System (SPNS),
- Tele–Banking,
- Universal Banking,
- 24-hours Banking,
- 24–hours Tall-free Customer Call Centres.

Role of Products and Services

The customers are coming in contact with the banks for their financial transactions as well as for use for use of various services and products by virtue of the banks operating in the financial service industry. Products or services are the vital link between the customers and the banks. It is also a very much necessary factor which is to be kept in view that each product has a particular life cycle which means that products will have to be updated on an ongoing basis to maintain their suitability as per customers' changing needs. A good product can not be expected to remain in demand for ever as customers' requirements go on changing with the change in economic, social, mental and political changes.

The Reserve Bank of India had taken certain steps and measures to redress the grievances of customers for better quality of service and a few of these are listed below:

- Setting up of Customer Service Committees,
- Observing Customers Meet Day,
- Setting up of Customer Service Centers,
- Observance of "Customers day",
- Setting up of several Expert Committees,
- Implementing Banking Ombudsman Scheme,

From the above, it is quite obvious that the matter has gained due attention of the Reserve bank of India as a regularity body for the Banking industry to redress the genuine grievances. The performance of the Banks has been subjected to the scrutiny and review by the Reserve Bank of India from time to time.

Strategising the Process of Customer Relationship Management in Banks

In the today's ever changing scenario, the Banks are facing the challenges of modernization and up gradation as well as maintaining quality to fulfill customers' expectations. They exhibit uneven strengths, efficiency, resources, problem dimensions and problem-solving capabilities. With a view to overcome the cut-throat and some times the unethical competition and to become more effective in the matters of Customer Services, it is very much imperative on the part of the Bankers to draw up certain strategies and frame work addressing the key issues concerning the quality aspects thereof. Some of these strategies and frameworks are summarized as following:

- E-CRM, that is, the Electronic-Customer Relationship Management, is fast emerging as an effective Customer Relationship Management strategy. It originated from the call centers and found its natural habitat on the 'World Wide Web' (www). An effective E- CRM model makes a judicious use through E-mail, chatting, call centers etc. Computer Technology Integration (CTI) is another emerging facility of reaching out to far-flung customers at comparatively lower cost. It can also be used to address the grievances of the customers by offering quick and prompt remedies to minor problems.

- The banks should be in a position to collect, store and assess all the information it will need in respect of each and every customer, it should be followed by appointment of highly motivated Relationship Manager who will identify each customer according to current and potential value. The Relationship Manager must develop long range and annual customer relationship plans. The annual relationship plans should state objectives, strategies, specific actions and required resources.
- The up gradation of the quality of human resources is of utmost importance as it is always the human being each and every project upon whom the success of any project depends. With greater role being played by technology in this very process, it is quite imperative that the skills of the employees be upgraded from time to time to equip them to meet the future challenges.
- It is also desirable to install the shops or more precisely Information Kiosks which can be accessed by the customers for getting account details, by keying in his account number and a password. It would also be possible for the customer to take a print-out of his transactions from the kiosks. Customer would be able to access information in respect of various products offered by the banks, opening of various types of accounts. This would reduce the burden on the staff as the customers will be in a position to obtain information on their own.
- Loyalty and customer satisfaction are the aspects strongly linked to Customer Relationship Management programme. Ensuring customer loyalty and satisfaction is basically the philosophy of training and taking good care of employees who in take care of the customers. Besides loyalty and satisfaction, communication is a vital aspect of any Customer Relationship Management.

- Taking advantage of computerization and technological up gradation, banks need to develop a comprehensive customer information system at branches so as to know the customers like age, qualifications, income level, tastes and preferences etc., should be created which will help in providing continuous feedback for anticipating customer needs.
- Quality Circles may be formed at the branches with more than say 10-12 staff members and they should be persuaded to take up at least one product month each month with a view to improve customer service, general efficiency or productivity of the branch staff. These should be properly recognized/appreciated by the Zonal Office/Head depending upon the quality of output and this should be done at the earliest possible so that the concerned employees feel elated and encouraged.
- The publicity campaign undertaken by the joint publicity committee has almost become a routine exercise and does not prove to be effective with the customer both in scope and scale as a customer identifies himself with a particular bank and not with a group of banks. It is necessary to allow the public sector banks the flexibility to pursue as imaginative publicity policy related to their bank level needs to reach their various prospective customers with the service products and effectively designed. The publicity campaign targets for the bank customer/ public in general can be undertaken by the Indian Banks Association.
- The efforts being made by the bank management cannot yield positive results unless the total involvement of the staff, down the line, is forthcoming. In view of the competition and threats being faced by the banks, the attitude of the staff will have to undergo a drastic change and their re-orientation towards the needs and expectations of the customers will have to

be brought about so that they display more care and concern for customers.

- Measurement of customer satisfaction through construction of Consumer Satisfaction Index (CSI) would be a novel idea in the context of the imperative for improvement in customer service. The idea of Customer Satisfaction Index (CSI) is to evolve a mechanism for a scientific assessment of the performance of Public Sector Banks in serving their clients.

Economic Benefits of Customer Relationship Management

There are some economic benefits of the Customer Relationship Management and a few of these are listed below:

(a) It is a fact that retaining profitable customers is very much cheaper than attracting new ones,

(b) Reduced marketing costs,

(c) Better use of database,

(d) Increased opportunity for cross selling of various products,

(e) Enhanced reliability of new customers introduced by the existing clients.

Conclusion

With the changing scenario in the banking industry, rather with the paradigm shift caking place in the present day, the concept of universa, banking has already started emerging. In the changing phase, the customer has become the key focus area of all sectors in the banking industry. The banks which provide value-added services and satisfaction to the customers will be bound to become winners. With the cut-throat competition, retaining market share still calls for adoption of Customer Relationship Management. The main focus should be on measuring profitability of each customer and not the products. There should a gradual shift relationship marketing by introducing this new approach in select branches and the in turn this should be expanded. As times get together, banks will have to focus on retaining their key customers. The customers are becoming increasingly more demanding and are looking for better and more convenient services. In such a scenario, the public sector banks have to play a pro-active role anticipating changes in customers demands and equip themselves to face the private banks and global challenges.

References

"Customer Relationship Management", by "Stanley A. Brown", Pricewaterhouse Coopers.

"CRM at the Speed of Light", by "Paul Greenberg", Tata McGraw-Hill.

"Customer Relationship Management", by Jagdish N. Sheth, Atul Parvatiyar, G. Shainesh, Tata McGraw-Hill.

Bank Technology News, April, 2001.

USA Today, June 1", 1999.

Uma Kapila, "Financial Sector Reforms", *AF Book News*, Vol. IX, No. 5, 2001, pp. 5-7.

Yogeshwar Kumar (2000), "Electronic Banking", *IBA Bulletin*, March Vol. XX, No. 5, pp. 10-13.

51

Role of Development Bank in Capital Market Integration

Murlidhar Mandal & Sumit Prasad

Capital Market is an intermediary in establishing relationship. Between the lender and the borrower. When this relationship integrates and intensifies with socio-economic consideration, to set a new trend in credit generation, the "Development Bank" emerges to play its role focusing on "Lower Transaction cost". Thus the Capital Market is considered imperfect in the absence of a development bank. The establishment of a development bank signifies a policy-induced financial interaction between the borrower and the lender. This chapter discusses the need for development bank, their innovation, definition, objective and role, the theoretical aspects outlined in this chapter are obviously intended to serve as a back-ground to the appraisals at the India experience in development banking. The present chapter also emphasises the role of Development Financial Institutions (DFIs) in capital formation and their support to Capital Market.

Development Bank–The Need

Need for development bank was very strongly felt in the country immediately after her independence to alleviate the gaps in the capital Market. Capital Market of the country was ill-equipped to provide long-term Financial assistance. The existing financial arrangements were found inadequate to cope with burgeoning financial requirement of U.P. and coming enterprises. Both Commercial Bank and managing agency houses were found insufficient to cope with the requirement of planned industrial development. Furthermore several malpractices important being, misuse of found, excess speculation and manipulation, high cost of promotion and finance and managerial concentration had emerged to discourage the interested investing public. There was also dearth of issue houses and underwriting firms, which sponsor security issues in the market.

A against the limited arrangement for supply of long-term financial facilities, there was a manifold increase in demand of long-term capital. Hardly a fraction part of the total requirement could be met by the existing. Financial institutions and for the rest, it became necessary to devies new institution with ample financial resources and more comprehensive function. The idea for development bank was contemplated as far back as 1918 when the industrial commission recommended and institution analogous to the Industrial Bank of Japan. The Central Banking Enquiry Committee 1931 also pin-pointed the gaps in the Indian Capital Market and strongly emphasised the need for development bank for economic development. The Committee also contemplated the possible establishment of an All-India industrial Finance Corporation. Towards the end of the Second World War, again the attention come to be focused on the problem of industrial finance in India. The problem indeed assumed not only a peculiar importance but also altogether new aspect. However, due to reluctance of British Government, the proposal for creation of development band could not see the light of the day–The question of establishing a development bank received the attention of our government immediately after liberation of the country.

Innovation of Development Banks in India and Capital Market

Historically, speaking, the idea of establishing of special institutions for industrial finance was put forth by central banking enquiry committee in 1931. The committee recommended for the creation of provincial industrial credit corporation and All-India institutions. For industrial financing both at regional and national levels very little action was taken on such recommendation till the beginning of 1945. In this regard, a detailed study was made by the Reserve Bank of India in May 1945 with an assumption that institution should be set up both at All-India and regional levels. The proposal for establishing an All-India institution went through several stages and modifications were made for broadening the institutions range of function.

On account of the constitutional change that took place, legislation for the establishment of Industry Finance Corporation of India (IFCI) was passed in February 1948. Accordingly, it was set up on 1st July 1948, which marked the beginning of the are a development banking in India. Its main objective is to provide medium and long term Finance to industrial concerns particularly in circumstances when normal banking accommodation are inappropriate or recourse of capital issue channels are impracticable. It was owned jointly by the Government of India, RBI and Financial Institution. But as a single institution, it failed to satisfy the capital needs of smaller concerns sprawling all over the country–First state level institutions was set up as Madras Institutional Investment Corporation now known as Tamil Nadu Industrial Investment Corporation Ltd. in 1949.

Accordingly, state Financial Corporation Act was passed in 1951, which empowered the state government to set up financial corporations in their province. In this regard Pubjab government took the lead in organising a financial corporation in 1953. Gradually, Financial Corporations were establishing in different states. At present there are eighteen SFCs functioning in deferent state up in India. Essentially SFCs were meant to supplement the work of the IFCI by making finance available to small and medium industrial units. The minimum amount of assistance for a single unit is Rs. 30 lakhs. The IFCI and SFCs functioned purely as industrial land mortgage banks organised on most orthodox lines. They concentrated more on organised on most orthodox lines. They concentrated more on traditional industries and more emphasis was laid on security rather than on prospect, which could not justify the expectation of solving the problem of Chronic shortage of industrial capital in India.

There was therefore, need or a more dynamic approach on the part of the development banks it the requirements of the private corporate sector were to be meet more effectively. Consequently, National Industrial Development Corporation (NIDC) was established in 1954 with a view to provide both Finance and entrepreneurship. It was to be primarily a development agency rather than a financial institution. At present it has been converted with the financing of the private industry.

For encouraging industrial development in private sector considerable provision of underwriting facilities were considered necessary in order to fill the gap in Industrial Financing. Accordingly, of the development bank called Industrial Credit and Investment Corporation of India (ICICI) was established in January 1955. It represents a landmark in the diversification of development banking in India. It was pioneer in many respects such as underwriting of as well as in the channelisation of foreign currency loans from World Bank to private sector. It was sponsored by World Bank in collaboration with the Commonwealth development finance company (CDFC) and other foreign institution.

Another milestone in the field of institutional structure of capital market was nationalisation of life insurance business in 1956 to form Life Insurance Corporation of India (LICI). The corporation came into existence with a vowed objective of helping the task of national development. Though a small proportion of its total resources are channeled into private sector it constitutes the largest source of finance in the country.

With a view to stimulating commercial bank to supply term-Finance Facilities to industrial concern Refinance Corporation of India Ltd., was established in June 1958 by RBI, LICI and some leading commercial banks. The object of this institution is to provide refinancing facilities to commercial bank and other financial institutions, giving medium-term loans. The most important development in the sphere of development banking in India, however took place in 1964, when Industrial Development Bank of India (IDBI) was established in July 1964. It was set up as a subsidiary of the Reserve Bank of India. It not only provides finance but also co-ordinates the activities of all the financial institutions. At present it is the 'apex' development bank in the country. In the meanwhile, the machinery of the state Industrial Investment Corporations (SIICs) and the State Industrial Development Corporations (SIDCs) were created to enable the financing system to meet the financial need of Five Year Plans. The main objective of SIICs is to subscribe directly to equity and provide loans to industrial units and promote and establish medium and large sized units themselves. The main function of the SIDCs is to give all help to entrepreneurs in regard to the supply of infrastructure facilities.

In 1971, consequent upon the financial re-orientation of the development banks resulting from a change in the strategy of development the Industrial Reconstruction Corporation of India Ltd. (IRCI) was set up.

Recent addition to the development banks are Industrial Reconstruction Bank of India (IRBI) and small Industries Development Bank of India (SIDBI). IRBI was established in 1985 under the IRBI Act, 1984 with a view to assist in rehabilitation of sick and closed industries units. It provides financial assistance to industrial units through term loans, underwriting of shares, bonds and debentures and guarantees for loans and deferred payments. SIDBI was set up as the Principal Financial Institution for Promotion, Financing and Development of Industry in tiny and small scale sectors and to co-ordinate the functions of institutions engaged in similar activities. It is a wholly-owned subsidiary of IDBI. It took over the financing activities relating to small scale sector from IDBI and commenced operations on April 2, 1990. The World Bank in co-operation with private sector and government and developing countries established such financial institution that worked to mobilise extend and domestic financial resources for relenting the development-oriented business ventures in under-develop countries. This was founded on the realisation that economic development required financing of specific projects in Agriculture, Industry and Infrastructure Facilities. Most of the other Financial Institutions at that time were not in a position to extend long-term financial assistance, especially for the purpose of fixed assets acquisition and transfer of technology from developed to developing countries. Thus, development banks differentiated from other financial institutions, in respect of shouldering up the challenging responsibilities of mobilising, administering and allocating long-term financial resources. Specialisation in the task of project appraisal and supervision aimed at reducing the transaction costs and thus is would lower down the cost of borrowing for an enterprise. Therefore, these development bank could recruit staff and expert knowledge in project appraisal and supervision. Their Technical Consultancy Services (TCSs) and Management Consultancy Services Centres (MCSCs) could be activated to meet the challenges on risky project in order to reduce the administrative cost and default risk projects in order to reduce the administrative cost and default risk of the enterprises. Against such a background the development banks successfully integrate the Capital Market and Functioned Efficiently and Safely.

Rationale of Development Banks

Although different terms like 'Term-Leading', 'Special Industrial Financing', Finance and Development Corporation, are used to describe the group of institutions under reference, the World Development Banks' would appear to be more appropriate and logical as it explains their rationale. In the first place, the conventional investment institutions own their origin and growth to the institutionalisation of personal saving, that is, mobilisation of savings through financial intermediaries and their channelisation to profitable investment outlets. Development Bank, in the contrast, have been conceived as gap-fillers. When availability of finance in general channels is inadequate the special machinery of development banks has been created to fill this gap. However, the ability of the Development Bank of Finance Development would depend on the extent to which funds are made available by their sponsors.

The second special features of Development Bank also distinguishes them from the ordinary investment institutions. The purpose for which funds are made available is different in the case of these two types of financial institutions. The accent of the Development Bank is on "development", so that their purpose is the provision of development finance invested in fixed assets whereas the conventional institutions, supply funds mainly to provide liquidity to the investments made earlier.

Capital Formation–The Role of Development Banks

As development banks make available the means to utilise savings generated in the economy, in a way they help in capital formation, which implies the diversion of productive capacity of the economy of making capital goods, thereby increasing future productive capacity. The process of capital formation involves three distinct but interdependent activities such as saving, financial intermediation and investment. However, a poor country may be, there will be a need for institutions which allow such saving as currently forthcoming, to be invested conveniently and safety and which ensure that they are channeled in the most useful purpose.

A well development financial structure will, therefore, did in the pooling and distributions of investable funds and thereby contribute to the capital formation of the economy. India capital market, although still considered to be underdeveloped, has been recording impressive progress during the post-independence period. Hence, to study the contribution of development banks in the capital formation of the economy, two parameters have to be used. They are:

(a) The ratio of financial assistance disbursed by development banks to the Gross Fixed Capital Formation in the private sector; and

(b) The ratio of financial assistance disbursed by development bank to the amount of Gross Fixed Formation of the economic.

The remarkable increase in the volume of assistance in absolute terms by them has led the development banks to grow into massive source of founds to corporate sector, as reflected in their share in financing industrial investment. During the period 1948-56, such assistance financed is about 4.1 percentage of gross fixed capital in private sector. It continues to below (around 5 per cent) during the period 1956-61 also corresponding to Second Five Year Plan, their share in financing industrial investment improved to 13 per cent during Third Plan Period (1961-66) and further to 19 per cent during 1966-67 through 1968-69 corresponding to the Annual Plan Period. The share of development bank in the capital formation of the economy increased considerably only after 1970.

Table 1
Role of Development Banks in Capital Private Corporate Sector during-1992-2005

Year	*Assitance Disbursed*	*Gross Fixed Capital Formation in Private Corporate Sector*	*(2) as % on (3)*
1992-93	2014.64	17183	11.72
1993-94	2374.30	19541	12.15
1994-95	2794.12	22172	12.60
1995-96	3737.61	26754	13.97
1996-97	4447.55	28006	15.88
1997-98	5137.50	36277	14.16
1998-99	6835.40	43663	15.16
1999-00	7321.10	8770	15.65
2000-01	9576.60	N.A.	15.01
2001-02	11448.10	N.A.	
2002-03	12832.09	10295	16.82
2003-04	14792.16	11435	17.60
2004-05	15876.24	13284	18.86

Source: 1. Report on Development Banking IDBI, Various Issues.
2. Report on currency and Finance RBI
N.B. – N.A. – not Available

Table 2
Role of Development Bank in Capital Formation in Indian Economy during 1992-2005

Year	*Assitance Disbursed*	*Gross Fixed Capital Formation*	*(2) as a % on (3)*
1992-93	2014.64	35769	5.63
1993-94	2374.30	29991	5.93
1994-95	2794.12	45508	6.14
1995-96	3737.61	54255	6.89
1996-97	4447.55	62052	7.17
1997-98	5137.50	72194	7.12
1998-99	6835.40	85669	7.89
1999-00	7321.10	102502	7.07
2000-01	9576.60	122573	7.81
2001-02	11448.10	136085	8.41
2002-03	12643.16	142156	9.23
2003-04	14769.25	154637	10.84
2004-05	17839.34	168395	11.34

Source: 1. Report on Development Banking IDBI, Various Issues.
2. *Report on currency and Finance RBI*

Reference

Srivastava, R. M. (1979), Management of Bank, Pragats' Prakashan, Meerut, p. 310.

Industrial Finance Corporation of India, Annual Report, 30th June, 1948.

Vicente, R. Jayme (1993), Challenges to Development Financing, *International Journal of Development Banking*, ICICI Publication, June, p. 21.

John Hicks (1965), Capital and Growth, Clarendon Press, Oxford, pp. 285-291.

Administrative Reforms Commission, Study them on Economic Administration Report, 1969.

Gupta, L. C. (1969), The Changing Structure of Industrial Finance in India, London, p. 85.

Economic Commission for Asia an Fur East, Mobilisation of Domestic Capital, 1953, p. 5.

Diamond, W. (1957), Development Banks, John Hopkins Press, Baltimore, p. 1.

Khan, M. Y. (1991), India Financing System, Theory and Practice, Vikas Publication House Pvt. Ltd., New Delhi, p. 2.

52

Urban Cooperative Banks in India: Issues and Challenges

Ajit Kumar Thakur

The urban cooperative banks occupy a significant place in the urban credit movement. The need for organization of urban cooperative bank was felt to provide helping hand to the weaker sections of urban community viz., small traders, artisans, salaried people, professionals and other people of small means.

The Urban Cooperative Banks (UCBs) are unique form of organisation. They are registered under the Cooperative Societies Act of the concerned state, which empowers the Registrar of Cooperative Societies to register and liquidate the societies. At the same time, these banks were converted into full-fledged banking system only after the extension of Banking Regulation Act' 1949 with effect from 01.03.1966, which ensures regulatory powers to the Reserve Bank of India (RBI) like issue of licence and controlling banking business. This creates a situatin of dual control of UCBs by both state and central governments.

Urban banks provide their members with a safe and sound institution to save and borrow at reasonable and affordable rates. These banks help to address the financial needs of under-served, predominantly low-income people. Today, urban co-operative banks (UCBs) are operative in a highly competitve market, on a level playing fields with commercial banks. They do so, successfully applying the co-operative principles underlying their business model, owned by members, their primary mission is to offer them the best services, as opposed to maximizing profit for shareholders.

Visualizing the importance of cooperatives in the development process, the first Prime Minister of India, Pandit Nehru, said that he wanted to "convulse" the nation with cooperatives. He had an abiding faith in the cooperative system, the objective of which was to give small traders, artisans, factory workers and others access to institutional credit, instead of them going to the moneylenders and then often meeting with disastrous consequences. By catering to the credit requirements of people with limited means in the urban and semi-urban centres, the urban cooperatives seek financial inclusion of people, who are economically disadvantaged and this is extremely important for the equitable growth of the country.

There has been a mushrooming growth of the number of banks and also the incidence of failure. Several UCBs have gone into liquidation, straining a large number of depositors. Even the RBI had to focus special attention on the growth and working of UCBs. As per the latest statistics available (end-June 2004), the financial position of 732 UCBs was not considered satisfactory. While the financial conditions of the 307 banks has deteriorated over the previous year. In about 529 banks, the financial condition has not been considered satisfactory; requiring the supervisory action in terms of ban on declaration of dividend. ban on opening of branches, etc. The financial condition of 203 banks got worsened to such an extent requiring drastic action in terms of imposition of directives. amalgamation, restructuring and liquidation. Thus, of the 2105 UCBs registered as per the RBI statistics, the financial condition of 1771 banks is either unsatisfactory or it has worsened; calling for drastic supervisory action.

The co-operatives have enjoyed special treatment from the Government of India, State Governments, Reserve Bank and other policy making bodies during the last 50 years. UCBs have been permitted to pay higher rate of interest on their savings' deposits at a rate not exceeding 1 per cent p.a. and on all term deposits at a rate for CRR and SLR for non-scheduled co-operative banks which are lower than those for commercial banks. Further, while the commercial banks have invested a major portion of their resources in Government and trustee securities, the non-shceduled co-operative banks keep some portion (10% to 15%) of their statutory liquid assets either with central co-operative banks or the State Co-operative Banks, which enable them to earn higher interest. Moreover, in order to encourage UCBs to finance SSI units in a greater measure, the RBI/NABARd have been granting concessional refinance to UCBs at 2.5 per cent below the bank rate. Likewise, income of co-operatives arising out of business of banking, as also, income arising out of credit facilities to members are exempted from tax under the Income Tax Act. But today, all these privileges, concessions, special treatment and monopoly powers of the cooperatives are being taken away one by one. Now, cooperative bank's income is taxable under Income Tax Act. In fact, under the new competitive pressures, inherent rigidities in UCBs to enhance their overall efficiency poses serious challenges. Since the operational efficiency of the UCBs is crucial in ensuring adequate and timely flow of credit to urban and semi-urban people for diverse purposes, intensive observation on their performance deserves serious consideration.

Review of Literature

The first ever study on the working of UCBs was made by the RBI in 1961. The study highlighted the fact that the UCBs were functioning quite satisfactorily and the government did not pay much attention to the development of non-agricultural sectors. The efforts of the RBI were strengthened by various study groups that touched upon the various aspects of the working of UCBs in the country. Mention may be made of the studies Varde Committee (1963). Damry Committee (1963), R.G. Saraiya Committee (1972) and Madhav Das committee

(1979) constituted by the RBI under the chairmanship of Shri K.Madhava Rao to review the performance of UCBs and suggest measures to strengthen them. The committee has gone into diverse aspects of the working of UCBs and made far-reaching recommendations.

Vidya Pitre (2003) has expressed that there was a paradigm shift in RBI's regulatory approach. An excessively regulated regime gave way to a thoroughly liberalized dispensation. Ramesh and Patil (1999) attempted to take an overview of the growth and working of UCBs in India for a period of 20 years (1974-94). R.B. Teli (2004) made a general review of the working of UCBs since the origin of the concept of UCBs. His focus had been mainly on the issues pertaining to operational performance, non-performing assets, and problems faced by the UCBs. He made a long list of suggestions that can improve the performance of UCBs. Katar Singh (2003) has raised the issue of governance in cooperative banks. He expressed an opinion that cooperative banks are based and managed on the principle of cooperation, self-help and mutual help.

Among those that focused their attention, one must refer to the addresses given by jagadish Capoor, Deputy Governor, RBI. Jagadish Capoor (2000) felt that financial and managerial weaknesses of a good number of cooperatives have been a matter of concern for quite sometime. Jagdish Capoor (2001) has dwelt extensively on certain regulatory issues related to UCBs' licensing policy, future set up of weak and unlicensed banks, application of capital adequacy norms, resolution of conflicts arising of dual control over UCBs, etc. In his address, he mainly focused on the agenda of reforms.

Encouraged by the research conducted at the national level, certain researchers have selected UCBs of their own states and localities. A significant number of studies conducted on UCBs, in fact, belong to this category. Studies carried out by Tridip Suhrud Suhrud, Avinash. V Raikar, Dr. S. S. Masali, K. G. Sevan, B. S. Rohilla and B. Ramesh and M.R. Patil are worth mentioning in this regard.

It is evident from the review of the existing literature that there has been enough focus on the issues concerning the performance of UCBs. Unfortunately, the rampant failures in this sector are still emphasizing the need for further in depth studies into the area. Besides the prudential norms of the RBI have been put in force only recently. The studies referred earlier have not focused much on this aspect, leaving scope for further studies in this area.

Important Recommendations of Various Commitees

The Indian urban cooperative credit movement is almost a hundred years old. During this long journey, the movement has passed through various phases of development. Various committees appointed by the RBI and Government of India gave lot of recommendations in order to tune up balanced growth of UCBs in the country.

Madhava Das Committee

The Committee constituted by the Reserve Bank of India under the Chairmanship of *Mr. Madhava Das* to evaluate the role and other working features of the Primary Urban Cooperative Banks in September 1977, submitted its report on 11th July'1978. The important recommendations of the Committee are:

1. Urban banks should do vigorous pioneering work in financing the small-scale industrial sector in close collaboration with the State Government departments dealing with small-scale industries.
2. Urban banks should solve unemployment problems by financing the educated unemployed, self-employed persons and professionals, such as; doctors, lawyers, chartered accountants, architects and engineers. This sector will include small shop owners, stallholders, fruits and vegetables' vendors, shoemakers, tailors, etc.
3. Provision of finance to small transport operators, such as pliers of cycles, scooters, rickshaws, taxis and vans.
4. Finance for small traders and shop-keepers
5. Urban banks can undertake the house finance to individuals, housing societies, housing boards, local bodies, slum clearance,etc.

6. Financing of consumer stores was also recommended to constitute a new and fruitful avenue for flow of credit from urban banks.
7. Urban banks may enter into participation/consortium arrangements with commerical banks.

Criterion of Viability

According to this Committee, the income earned by the urban banks should be adequate to cover the expenditure and leaves a certain amount of surplus to pay reasonable return capital. The Committee listed out the following methodology for retaining the viability of urban banks:

(i) Compute the margin available on raising the resources and deploying them

(ii) Compute the management and other expenditure

(iii) Find out the quantum of loan business which will meet the above expenditure

The Committee fixed the order of priorities for the lending of urban banks as:

1. Small scale and cottage industries
2. Schemes for gainful employment of educated unemployed
3. Self employed persons and professinoals
4. Small road and water transport operators
5. Trade and commerce
6. Housing shcemes
7. Consumption loans
8. Consumer cooperative societies.

The Registration and Licensing

The registration and licensing should be complementary to each other. There should be a team of officers of RBI, the State cooperative department and the state cooperative bank and a representative of promoters to study the viability of the proposals for registration. This joint body should also study the byelaws of the proposed bank in depth. (*Note:* The committee has prepared model byelaws for the guidance of urban banks).

Licensing of Existing Banks

There should be a separate cell in the Agricultural Credit Department to issue licenses to the existing bankers without further delay which prima facie satisfy the important requirement of Sections 11, 22 (3) (4) and 22 (3) (b) of the Banking Regulation Act. (*Note:* Section 11 refers to adequacy of capital. Section 22 refers to opening of branches).

Norms for Representation to Members of the Branches on the Board of Management

1. The representation may be based on membership and not on deposits or loan business
2. A certain number of seats on the Board may be provided exclusively for the Head Office
3. Every Branch in a group may get representation by rotation; and
4. The Director representing the area of the branch may probably be the Chairman of the Branch Committee.

Election of Branch Committees

1. The Branch Committees may be elected from amongst the members residing in the area of operation of the branch
2. The Branch Committee may be empowered to sanction loans up to certain limits by the Board of Directors.

Women Members

Urban banks may give representation to women members on the board of management and wherever necessary set up a separate section to cater for the needs of women members.

State Participation in Share Capital

The present practice of contributing to share capital of urban banks, which undertakes financing of small-scale industries is appropriate. The State Government may contribute to share capital of new banks organized especially in backward areas or weaker sections of the community. The retirement of Government Share Capital should not start earlier than seven years from the date of the receipt of the contribution and should be in a phased manner.

Deposits

The State Government should permit local bodies, quasi-government institutions and public trusts to keep surplus funds with urban banks which have earned 'A' or 'B' class in audit.

Training of Staff

The training should be for staff at different levels, i.e.:

(a) Chief Executive
(b) Key Personnel
(c) Junior Officers and
(d) Clerical Staff

The training should also be of different types:

(i) The course on cooperative banking and book-keeping
(ii) Orientation courses on resource mobilization, deployment of funds, diversification of loans portfolio, industrial financing, Banking Regulation Act, etc.

Marathe Committee

RBI had appointed the Marathe Committee (1992) to examine the licensing policy of new UCBs and accepted the recommendations of this committee and liberalized the licensing of USBs. As a result, during the period from May 1993 to June 2001, the RBI issued more than 800 licenses for setting up new UCBs. However, close to one-third of these newly licensed UCBs became financially weak within a short period. Similarly, branch licensing policy for UCBs have been liberalized w.e.f. 8.1.1996. Under this policy, over 3300 licenses were issued for opening new branches. At present, applications for banking license, including license for opening of new branches are not being considered by RBI. The issuance of fresh licenses would be considered only after a comprehensive policy on UCBs is put into place.

Narasimham Committee II

After the first phase of the reforms process was completed with the successful implementation of many of the recommendations of the first Narasimham Report, the Government constituted another higher-level committee under M. Narasimham to suggest further reforms for strengthening the foundation of the banking system. Accordingly, the Committee submitted its Report on 'Banking Sector Reforms' in April 1998.

While the first reforms committee did not examine any specific recommendation for co-operative banks as to the applicationof various norms, the second generation of reforms included the following specific references to co-operative banks:

- There should be no recourse to the scheme of debt waiver.
- Well run UCBs be permitted to expand their area of operation.
- Co-operative banks should reach capital adequacy of 8 per cent over a period of 5 years.
- Cooperative credit institutions to enhance their capital through subscription by members and not by Government.
- The UCBs should be brought within the ambit of the Board of Financial Supervision.
- The present duality of control over the cooperative credit institutions by State Government and RBI/ NABARD should be eliminated and all cooperative banking institutions should come under the discipline of B. R. Act by suitable amendments of the Act.

Performance of UCBs in India (1991-92 to 2003-04)

The UCBs in india have witnessed phenomenal growth during the last one and a half decades. From 1307 UCBs in 1991, the number of UCBs had risen to 2105 (number of reporting banks is 1917) in the year 2004. Deposits have increased by 12.8 times from Rs. 8600 crores to Rs. 1,10,250 crores, while advances have risen from Rs. 7800 crores to 67,900 crores i.e. 8.7 times during the above 15 years. With deposits of over Rs. One hundred thousand crores and credit of Rs. Sixty thousand crores as on 31st March, 2004, the UCBs in the country have emerged as an inseparable segment of the nation's banking sector.

During the year 2002-03, 39 UCBs were deregistered on account of their non-payment of deposit insurance premium to Deposit Insurance and Credit Guarantee Co-operation (DICGC). The incident jeopardized the financial interests of millions of small investors.

The number of scheduled UCBs had increased from 52 in 2002 to 55 in 2004 in Andhra Pradesh, Goa, Gujarat, Karnataka, Maharashtra and Uttar Pradesh. The minimum demand and time liabilities that a co-operative bank should have to qualify for inclusion in 'second schedule', had been enhanced to Rs. 250 crores from Rs. 100 crores through the Government of Indianotification dated October 30, 2003.

Table 1 shows the performance of UCBs in India with regard to the number of reporting banks, working capital, owned funds, deposits, borrowing and loans and advances for the period from 1998-99 to 2003-04. The number of reporting UCBs had increased from 1587 in 1998-99 to 1917 in 2002-04 except in the year 2000-01, which shows a declining trend. Owned funds and deposits constituted 88.91 per cent under the study period. It clearly indicates that the major source of working capital of UCBs depends on owned funds and deposits. Loans and advances showed continuous increase i.e., from Rs. 33169 crores in 1998-99 to Rs. 67,930 crores in 2003-04. It is also revealed from the table that the average annual growth rate of borrowing is 9.67 per cent only. It is apparent that the UCBs in India are self-reliant institutions. The other feature is that average credit-deposit ratio showed near 63.87 per cent nation at over a period of six years. It can be understood that UCBs in India are also concentrating on the deployment of their funds other than the traditional loans and advances.

Non-Performing Assets in UCBs

The prudential norms and assets classification ratios have aimed at bringing out the true picture of a bank's loan portfolio.

Table 1

Growth and Development Performance of UCB During the Period from 1998-99 to 2003-04

(Rs. in crores)

Year	*No. of Reporting Banks*	*Working Capital (Rs.)*	*Owned Funds (Rs.)*	*% of Owned Funds to W.C*	*Deposits (Rs.)*	*% of Deposits to W.C*	*Borrowing (Rs.)*	*% of Borrowing to W.C*	*Loans Out-standing (Rs.)*	*% of Loans Out-standing to W.C*	*C. D. Ratio*
1998-99	1587	67070	7314	10.91	52617	78.45	1041	1.55	33169	49.45	63.03
	(5.66)	(28.42)	(22.21)		(29.31)		(17.49)		(19.28)		
1999-00	1780	89957	9291	10.33	71094	79.03	1475	1.64	45916	51.04	64.58
	(12.16)	(34.12)	(27.03)		(35.12)		(41.69)		(38.43)		
2000-01	1685	102566	10936	10.66	81813	79.77	2071	2.02	53435	52.10	65.31
	(-5.34)	(14.02)	(17.71)		(15.08)		(40.41)		(16.38)		
2001-02	1809	109873	14847	13.51	84415	7683	1751	1.59	55282	50.31	65.49
	(7.36)	(7.12)	(35.76)		(3.18)		(-15.45)		(3.46)		
2002-03	1847	131542	8478	6.45	100666	76.53	1870	1.42	63635	48.38	63.21
	(2.10)	(19.72)	(-42.90)		(19.25)		(6.80)		(15.11)		
2003-04	1917	131812	12349	9.37	110256	83.65	1254	0.95	67930	51.54	61.60
	(3.74)	(0.20)	(45.66)		(9.53)		(-32.94)		(6.75)		
Average Annual Growth (%)	4.37	17.27	17.58	10.17	18.58	79.04	9.67	1.53	16.57	50.47	63.87

Note: Figures in parentheses indicate percentage of growth;
W. C.=working Capital Source : RBI- Urban Department, Central Office, Mumbai.

In a layman's perception, NPA formation in a bank is paradoxical. The severity of the incidence of NPA can be understood in relation to other variables like assets or advances. The ratio used to judge the extent of NPA problem of the bank is gross NPA / gross advances. Banks will try to show a lower net NPA figure irrespective of gross NPA magnitude because net NPA below a stipulated level has been made one criterion for the requirement for grading UCBs. It is argued that gross NPA is a better indicator than net NPA, since the former does not incorporate the endogenous provisioning process. This is because, banks make provision for NPAs according to their capacities. Hence, two banks with same gross NPAs may be able to show different levels of net NPAs. It can be seen from table -2 which shows that gross NPAs of reporting UCBs in India, have increased from Rs. 3,306 crores in 1999 to Rs. 11,922 crores in 2004, registering a 3.6 times increase over the period. The percentage of gross NPAs to total advances of UCBs in India, which was 11.07 per cent in 1999, raised to 21.90 per cent in 2002 and slightly reduced to 17.36 per cent in 2004. It was found that the level of NPAs of UCBs had jumped during 2001-02, because of difficulties faced by a few banks in Gujarat. High level of NPAs is an indication of poor credit management. It is to be noted that the gross NPA 'Percentage of total advances)' ranges between 11.07 and 21.90, on an average of 16.65 per cent over the study period. The rule of the thumb for percentage of gross NPAs to total advances are 10.20 per cent, which indicates moderate to severe problems. Though the average percentage of NPAs might have reduced, The table shows a higher percentage of NPAs during the study period. This is a major reason for failure of UCBs in India.

Analysis of Balance Sheet of UCBs in India (1998-99 to 2003-04)

Table 3 shows the details of liabilities and assets of UCBs in India for the six years period from 1998-99 to 2003-04 and macro mean growth rate for each type of liability and asset. It is clear from the table that all the components of liabilities as percentages show a flexible trend over the period whereas absolute terms of capital and deposit, have continuoulsy

Table 2
Non-performing Assets Position of Urban Cooperative Banksin India

Year	*No. of Reporting Banks*	*Gross NPAs (Rs. in crore)*	*Gross NPAs as % of total advances*
1999	1474	3306	11.07
2000	1748	4534	12.24
2001	1942	9245	16.10
2002	1937	13706	21.90
2003	1941	13647	21.00
2004	1917	11922	17.60

Source: RBI-Report on the Trend and Progress of Banking in India, 2002-03 and 2003-04.

increased over the priod. Deposits were the single largest portfolio on liabilites side. It was 84.65 per cent in 2003-04 as against 78.45 per cent in 1998-99, on an average of 80.26 per cent increase. Deposit is an important component which determines the profitability of the bank. Mobilization of deposits by UCBs over a period of six years is satisfactory. As regards the other liabilities, it remains more or less stable. Reserves of the UCBs in India showed a fluctuating trend over the period. Share capital of the UCBs also remains more or less stable and it forms 2.26 per cent of total liabilities. It is known that investment increases year-by-year and it is 34.34 per cent of total assets. Advances ranged from 49.45 to 53 per cent over the period. It takes the lion's share of total assets of UCBs on an average of 51.24 per cent.

It is also noted from the table that the macro mean of cash in hand and balance with banks constitute 1.08 per cent and 4.66 per cent under the study period. The annual growth rate of cash in hand and balances with banks was 10.8 per cent and 18.36 per cent respectively. It clearly shows that higher percentage of cash and bank balance with UCBs reflects poor management of funds, the reason being denial of direct access to the facility by RBI. In terms of the CRAR guidelines provided, the deposit balances kept with the RBI alone will carry zero risk weight; whereas the deposits kept with other banks, including natinoalized banks will carry a risk weight of 20 per cent. The RBI is operating in State Headquarters only.

Table 3
Liabilites and Assets of Urban Cooperative Banks in India (1999-04)

(Rs. in Lakhs)

Items	*1998-99 (Rs.)*	*1999-00 (Rs.)*	*2000-01 (Rs.)*	*2001-02 (Rs.)*	*2002-03 (Rs.)*	*2003-04 (Rs.)*	*Macro Mean (%)*	*Growth (%)*
Liabilities								
Capital	142100	196300	206600	248800	297900	326700	2.26	22.6
	(2.12)	(2.18)	(2.01)	(2.26)	(2.48)	(2.48)		
Reserves	589300	732800	887000	1235900	549900	908200	8.13	18.8
	(8.79)	(8.15)	(8.65)	(11.25)	(4.58)	(6.90)		
Deposits	5261700	7109400	8181300	8441500	10066600	11025600	80.26	16.4
	(78.45)	(79.03)	(79.77)	(76.83)	(83.83)	(83.65)		
Borrowings	104100	147500	207100	175100	187000	125400	1.55	8.2
	(1.55)	(1.64)	(2.02)	(1.60)	(1.56)	(0.95)		
Other Liabilities	609900	809800	774600	886000	906700	795300	7.88	6.6
	(9.09)	(9.00)	(7.55)	(8.06)	(7.55)	(6.02)		
Total	6707100	8995800	10256600	10987300	12008100	13181200		
	(100)	(100)	(100)	(100)	(100)	(100)		

Contd...

Items	*1998-99 (Rs.)*	*1999-00 (Rs.)*	*2000-01 (Rs.)*	*2001-02 (Rs.)*	*2002-03 (Rs.)*	*2003-04 (Rs.)*	*Macro Mean (%)*	*Growth (%)*
Assets								
Cash in Hand	78100	97600	111800	1195100	12800	128200	1.08	10.8
	(1.16)	(1.08)	(1.10)	(1.09)	(1.07)	(0.97)		
Balance with	294000	455400	448400	447400	660300	602200	4.66	18.36
Banks	(4.38)	(5.06)	(4.37)	(4.07)	(5.50)	(4.57)		
Investments	2279200	3056500	3519600	3785800	3927800	4822000	34.34	16.8
	(33.98)	(33.98)	(34.32)	(34.46)	(32.71)	(36.58)		
Loans and Advances	3316900	4591600	5343500	5528200	6363500	6793000	51.24	15.8
	(49.45)	(51.05)	(52.09)	(50.31)	(53.00)	(51.54)		
Other Assets	738300	794700	833300	1106400	928500	835800	8.69	4.0
	(11.03)	(8.83)	(8.12)	(10.07)	(7.72)	(6.34)		
Total	6707100	8995800	10256600	10987300	12008100	13181200		
	(100)	(100)	(100)	(100)	(100)	(100)		

*Note:*Figures in brackets ar percentage to total liabilities and assets.
Source:RBI-Urban Department, Central Office, Mumbai.

So the UCBs cannot make direct access to the services of RBI, where the banks are situated in other parts of the country.

Present Position

The number of urban banks grew from 1106 in 1966 to 1853 in 2006 showing 67.5 per cent growth. The membership grew to the extent of 2.5 crores with the share capital of Rs. 34.79 crores and the reserves of Rs. 9,082 crore. The deposits also grew from Rs. 153 crore in 1966 to Rs. 1,12,237 crores in 2006. Loans and advances also rapidly increased to the extent of Rs. 70,379 crore during the year 2006. The deposit wise classifications of UCBs reveal that there are 67 per cent small banks with depositsize of Rs. 25 crores and less around 22 per cent are medium sized banks with deposit size of above Rs. 25 crores up to Rs. 100 crores and remaining 11 per cent are major banks with deposits of Rs. 100 crore plus. The size of maximum deposit under this category ranges from Rs. 1000 crore to Rs. 4,000 crore in few cases.

Major Issues of UCBs in India

The major policy development of UCBs have been effective from the year 1992-93, ie., post prudential norms era. The sudden changes in the policy environment of both state and central governments concerning the operations of urban banking system have direct and indirect implications on the performance of UCBs. The following are some of the major issues of UCBs in India.

Competition

Nationalisation of major commercial banks in 1969 with the introduction of social control created a competitive environment for the UCBs, breaking its monopoly in the sphere of micro-credit. Subsequently, the introduction of financial sector reforms in 1991 and the opening up of the economy exposed the inherent adversities in the functioning of the UCBs. The UCBs operate in a highly competitive market, on a level playing field with commerical banks. They do so by successfully applying the cooperative principles underlying their business model. Owned by its members, their primary mission is to offer them the best services, as opposed to maximising profit for shareholders.

Mismanagement and Failure of UCBs

UCBs also have certain weaknesses. For instance, the weakness and instances of mesmanagement of the cooperative banking sector were highlighted when the Ahmedabad-based Madhavpura Mercantile Cooperative bank, with deposits of INR 1,200 crores went into liquidation in March 2001. This bank was one of the scheduled UCBs in the country. Out of total deposits of around INR 1,200 crores in the Madhavpura bank, almost INR 600 crores or more were from over 165 urban banks. This had brought about a situation whereby wrong doings of one bank affected other banks too.

Another significant incident, which took place in the history of UCBs sector in India, has seriously jeopardised the financial interest of millions of small investors during the year 2002-03. Thirty-nine UCBs in the country were deregistered on account of their non-payment of deposit insurance premium to deposit Insurance and credit Guarantee Corporation (DICGC), Mumbai for more than three consecutive periods.

The major crisis in UCBs can also be judged from the outflow of funds from DICGC. The DICGC paid INR 104.4 million to depositors of failed banks in the year 2004. The amount rose to INR 148.4 million in the subsequent two years; all the outflows of DICGC have been paid to cooperative banks only.

Political Interference

There are instances of gross misuse of cooperative funds for political ends, which has landed a good number of institutions in dire straits. Very often, elected boards and managements are superseded not for reasons of mismanagement or violation of law but on political considerations. These observations confirm that political interference in the cooperative sector always exists. The tendency of politicians to misuse the UCBs for their personal gains has many times landed the UCBs in trouble.

The autonomy and efficiency of UCBs have been eroded over a period of time due to political interference. The UCBs are run entirely with the public money and the Central/ State Government has no exposure to them. Political influence in the management of UCBs has an adverse impact on small traders. In order to depoliticize the system, there should be a legal prohibition on ruling and other political leaders holding office to become directors of cooperative banks.

Poor Credit Management

The gross NPAs of reporting UCBs (1853) in India have increased from INR 3,306 crores in 1999 to INR 13,871 crores in 2006, registering 4.2 times increase. The percentage of gross NPAs to total advances of UCBs, which was 11.07 per cent in 1999 rose to 23.40 per cent in 2005 and slightly fell to 1970 per cent in 2006. However, percentage of NPAs to total advances of UCBs at 19.70 per cent, as on 31st March, 2006 was quite high compared to the percentage as on 31st March' 1999 and also in comparison to that of commercial banks (3.3 per cent). The high level of gross NPAs of UCBs was on account of burdensome procedure of write-off of loans as also their inadequate profits to absorb such losses due to write-offs. High level of NPAs is an indication of poor credit management. This is a major cause of failure of UCBs in India.

Supervision and Regulation of UCBs by RBI

The RBI introduced Income Recognition and Asset Classfication norms for UCBs in 1993s. In terms of these revised accounting standards, income from NPAs could not be taken to 'profit and loss account' unless the income was realised. These norms prompted banks to pay attention to the quality of their assets. Two aspects of prudential regulation, which have assumed greater importance in the recent period, relate to capital adequacy and provisioning. The UCBs have been slack in relation to both these aspects. The following are some of the reasons: (a) High cost deposits (b) Lack of training for staff, (c) Low level of IT implementation, (d) High interest rates on advances, (e) Denial of incoem from other sources and (f) Non-adherence to the prescribed limits of loans.

The norms for the ratio of capital to risk weighted assets (CRAR) have been introduced in UCBs in a phased manner commencing from 31st March, 2002. The ability of UCBs to raise capital to meet CRAR norms is limited by certain peculiar features. The shares of UCBs are neither quoted in the stock market nor are the banks allowed to raise capital in the market. Members' shareholdings are linkled to the loan amounts and can be withdrawn once the loans are repaid. Members can redeem their shares in the capital resulting in fluctuations in the size of the capital. Managing this aspect is a challenge.

The norms of grading UCBs as weak and sick were modified in the year 2003. The UCBs are classified into four grades, namely; Grades I, II, III and IV instead of weak and sick with effect from 12.02.2003, on the basis of capital adequacy, asset quality, earnings, compliance with CRR/SLR requirements and adherence to RBI guidelines and directives. Grade I banks are only permitted by RBI to declare dividend to their members. This restriction will adversely affect the efforts of the UCBs for augmenting their capital.

A system of supervisory rating for UCBs, under the Capital Adequacy, Asset Quality, Management, Earnings, Liquidity and Systems (CAMELS) model has been introduced by the RBI. The rating system was initially being implemented for scheduled UCBs commencing from the year ended 31st March 2003. A simplified rating system was made applicable to non-scheduled UCBs with effect from 31st March, 2004.

In order to ensure adherence to the prudential standards by UCBs, the regulator's frequency of intervention increased, thereby affecting the cooperative character. In this regard, RBI intervention has indirectly infringed upon the functional autonomy covering areas like share-linkage, credit, investment, deposit and so on.

Absence of Professional Management and Governance

Professional management is essential for any banking system and hence, the RBI insists on it. But on many occasions, the state governments dissolve the elected boards of UCBs and depute government officials to manage the affairs of these banks. As the government officials do not posses adequate expertise in banking, the efficiency of the UCBs suffers.

Absence of Huuman Resorce Management

Human resource management (HRM) is one of the key factors defining the characteritics of a successful banking institution. Improving managerial skills within this sector is now a permanent challenge. Many UCBs are also seeking new ways to allow the involvement in the provision and governance of personal services. Employing and retaining skilled workersand specialists, re-training the existing workforce and promoting a culture of continous learning are challenges for the UCBs.

Lack of Technology Based Products

The number of customers unhappy with banking service in India is on the rise. This is brought out by the fact that the number of complaints received by banking Ombudsman shot up from 5,399 in 2002-03 to 8,246 in 2003-04, making an increase of 52 per cent. The process of globalisation requires banks to move towards global standards of customer service so as to effectively meet the growing demands by their customers. E-banking services offered by many banking institutions can be a strategic weapon against UCBs, threatening their very existence.

High Cost Deposits

UCBs receive deposits at very high rates of interest which leads not only to the erosion of funds but also affects the financial condition of the banks. It is to be observed that the average costs of deposits of UCBs are 8-10 per cent.

Non-Appraisal/Lack of Proper Appraisal of Loans

There is a lack of proper appraisal of laons in UCBs. Loans received are security based and not project based. It has been found that loans are issued without assessing the reapaying capacity of the borrowers and, are often more than the value of the property offered as collateral.

Lack of Training

A good number of misfits and unfits are found occupying the chairs of administration. Their inadequate knowledge and lack of training facilities, leads to ineffficiency.

Computerization

It has been found that many of the UCBs were not computerized. At some places, though computers have been installed, trained staff are not available.

Linking of Salary with Working Capital of the Bank

Previously the fixation of salaries was done based on the working capital of the banks (below 2 per cent of working capital of the banks), which does not indicate the financialstatus clearly. Hence, net interest income has been taken as the basis for fixing salaries.

Reduction of High Interest Rates

It is observed that high interest rates on advances are charged by UCBs. For a defaulting borrower, it is found that the interest rate was charged even upto 25 per cent, which has resulted in poor recovery of loans in UCBs and mounting of NPAs.

Denial of Income from Other Sources

Denial of income from other sources by the UCBs is also one of the reasons for low income of the bank. They should undertake non-funded business, like; issue of demand drafts, credit and debit cards, letters of credit, bank guarantee, increasing Safe Deposit Lockers, foreign exchange transactions (if RBI, permits), Insurance Agency, providing advisory and consultancy service to cottage and tiny industries, electronic transfer of money, etc. in order to increase their other income.

Non-adherence to the Proper Prescribed Limits of Loans

As per RBI guidelines, house mortgage loans should be issued within the limit of 15 per cent of the total deposit. It is noticed that the loans to this sector constituted more than 30 per cent in some banks.

Recent Development for UCBs

Considering very high rate of failures of UCBs in the recnt years, the government and the RBI have together initiated many steps, a few of which are enumerated as below.

RBIs Vision Document

The RBI formulated a draft vision document and placed it in the public domain in March' 2005. The salient features of the Draft Vision Document, which has been placed by RBI on its website, are as under.

- As per RBIs Draft Vision, the proposed operating framework for UCBs may be classified into two tiers- tier I: unit banks with deposits upto Rs. 50 crores; tier II: all other banks.
- To determine the deposit base, the fortnightly average of the NDTL reported in the statutory returns in the preceding accounting year, may be reckoned so that a stable and reliable basis is adopted.
- Different prudential norms were recommended for each tier of the banks, taking into view various factors, such as Asset Classification Norms, Provisioning Norms, and Norms for Investment, Borrowing, Capital Adequacy, Exposure Norms, Sensitive Sector Exposure, and Auditing of the banks.
- Enhancing professionalism and improving the quality of governance in UCBs by providing training for skill up-gradation as also by including large depositors in the decision making process/management of banks.
- A consultative arrangement for identifying weak but potentially viable entities in the sector and provide a framework for nurturing them back to health through a process of consolidation.
- To identify the unviable entities in the sector and provide an exist path for such entities.
- The strategy to deal with UCBs may need state specific approved one that involves the concerned State

Government, RBI and the UCBs operating in the state. A State Level Task Force on Cooperative Urban Banks (TAFCUB) could be set up in each of the 5 States with high concentration of UCBs.

- The guidelines on Merger and Amalgamations (M&A) of UCBs have been issued vide circular UBD NO (PCB) Cir. 36/09. 169.00/2004-05, dated February 2, 2005. In all cases of merger & amalgamation, the financial parameters of the acquirer bank, post merger, should conform to the prescribed minimum prudential and regulatory requirement for UCBs and the realisable values of assets has to be assessed through a process of due diligence. TAFCUB shall make suitable recommendations on M&A.

Memorandum of Understanding with State Governments

The working arrangement in the form of memorandum of understanding (MoU) between RBI and State Government/ CRCS to ensure that the difficulties caused by dual control are suitably addressed through such MoUs. In pursuance of the proposals in the draft vision document, state governments, having a large number of UCBs, were approached for signing a memoradum of understanding (MoU). Since June 2005, MoUs have been signed with eight state governments, viz; Andhra Pradesh, Gujarat, Karnataka, Madhya Pradesh, Uttranchal, Rajasthan, Chhuttisgarh and Goa, which together constitute 844 UCBs, ie, over 45 per cent of deposits of the sector. After signing of MoU, as per agreement, RBI constituted State Level Task Force for Cooperative Urban Banks (TAFCUB) which is six-member body with town representatives each from state government, UCB sector and the RBI. The constitution of TAFCUB is mainly concerned with the development of UCBs in the state on sound lines.

At the same time, some states have reservation on signing the MoU with the RBI. It is generally believed that if the state governments signed MoU with RBI, then that will minimise the role of the Registar of Cooperative Societies (RCS) of the concerned state and thereafter RBI will become the sole regulator of UCBs. It is the best way of eliminating dual control regime.

In order to achieve the objectives set out in the vision document, the RBI is bringing in a two-tiered regulatory and supervisory regime. Banks with deposits under INR 100 crores and whose operations are limited to a district, are considered to be more closely optimising the spirit of cooperative banking and, as such, are placed under simplified regulations to enable them to gain in strength. Gradually, over a period of three years, they can be brought at par with all other banks in terms of performance, strength and regulatory prescriptions.

The 'not-one-size-fits-for-all' approach of RBI will be effective only when there are uniform laws governing the management and operations of the cooperative institutions. Another difficulty encountered by the RBI in exercising 'two-tier approach' is lack of transparency and governance principle in the operations of the UCBs. The RBI and the national and state level federations of UCBs are struggling to gather information about the performance of UCBs. The information provided has discrepancies and only, 70 to 75 per cent of UCBs have reported their performance. As a result, it is very difficult to practice a two-tier approach by the RBI.

Merger and Consolidation

The merger process in UCBs sector has gathered momentum over the lost one year. The proposal of consolidation through the process of merger of weak entities with stronger ones in the cooperative sector, may not be a healthy process. Merger and consolidation process of a weak and a strong bank is not practicable because the financial burden of weak bank may adversely affect the financially strong one. It may also create conflict among the boards of directors of the merged entities.

Need for Strategic Transformation

The following measures are suggested for the development and improvement of UCBs in future:

Augmenting Capital

The capital of UCBs can be strengthened in the following three ways:

(a) Enhancing membership and motivating depositors to become 'A' class members, because they are contributing money to the bank for doing the business.

(b) Raising upper statutory limit of shared linked to borrowings.

(c) Increasing the face value of each share of the UCBs to INR 100.

Shuttling of Portfolios

As per the RBI direction, every UCB has to invest up to 10 to 15 per cent of their net demand and time liabilities (NDTL) in government securities for maintenance of their SLR. A bank can go for investment in government securities rather than parkingfunds in District Central Cooperative Banks (DCCBs), Scheduled Commercial Banks (SCBs) and increase their CRAR. The bank balance in DCCBs/SCBs will have 20 per cent risk weight, whereas the government securities have only 2.5 per cent of risk weight. Thus, a prudent banker can park funds in government securities and maintain the low risk assets and higher CRAR.

Reduction in High Cost Deposits

The share of fixed deposits in UCBs is more than three-fourth of their total deposits. Such a swing towards fixed deposits in the deposit-mix of the banks cannot be reckoned of profits, but also affects the financial condition of the banks. Special attention should, therefore, be paid by UCBs to mobilise savings and current deposits with a view to reducing the cost of funds. Due to high cost of deposits, the banks are unable to lend to the borrowers at a competitive rate, as they would incur loss, and in turn not being abve to capture good borrowers.

End of Dual Control

The earlier committees, like; Madhava Das Committee (1978), Marathe Committee (1992) and quite recently, Narasimham

Committee (1998) and High Power Committee (1999), have all suggested that there is a need to address the issue of duality of control on UCBs by carrying out necessary statutory amendments. It has also become a real challenge for the UCBs to maintain the cooperative character and, at the same time to do commercialy viable banking business. So, it is time, to put an end to the dual control of UCBs.

Removal of Political Interference

The autonomy and efficiency of UCBs have been eroded over a period of time due to undue political interference. Political influence in the management of UCBs has an adverse impact on small traders. In order to avoid political interference, there is a need to have suitable legal provisions prohibiting the office bearers of political parties from holding office of directors of UCBs. RBI or National Bank for Agriculture and Rural Development (NABARD) should prevail upon the government of India/state governments to bring suitable amendments in this regard to 'State Cooperative Societies Act/Banking Regulation Act, 1949'.

Similarly, guidelines should be issued in respect of situation when state governments would be justified in announcing waiver of interest and principal loans granted by UCBs. This will avoid instances of such announcements for political gains by the ruling parties, which affects the profitability of UCBs.

Increasing Income from Other Sources

The UCBs should undertake non-funded business, like; issue of demand draft, bank guarantee, increasing safe deposit lockers, foreign exchange transactions (if RBI permits), providing advisory and consultancy services to cottage and tiny industries, collecting electric bills, telephone bills, income tax, sales tax, custom duties in order to improve their income. Handling of government business would automatically increase the trustworthiness of UCBs.

System of Human Resource Management

In order to meet the global standards and to remain competitive, UCBs will have to recruit specialists in various fields, such as treasury management, credit and risk management, IT related services, HRM, etc., in keeping with the segmentation and product innovation. As a complementary measure, fast track merit and performance-based promotion from within would have to be institutionalised to inject dynamism in the workforce. Another important ingredient of HRM is reward and compensation, which at present, does not have any linkage to skills and performance. There is an urgent need to have the system of reward and compensation in place that will attract, recognise and retain the talent in UCBs on the lines comparable with other banks, particularly banks in private sector and the foreign banks.

Continued Existence of Cooperative

Apprehensions have been expressed that the cooperatives will not be able to face competition from the private sector. This fear is largely unfounded. First, cooperatives already have a head start in terms of their reach and infrastructure. Secondly, their area of business is such that, in most cases, private entrepreneurs/companies shy away from. For instance, one cannot imagine a multinational bank to open a branch in a remote place, however, profitable it may be, or suitably located.

Need for Autonomy

The interference of state government in the organisation and day-to-day functions of UCBs is a disturbing feature. Many times, this causes impairment to UCBs in governance and in management. The impairment in governance is deep due to various reasons: (1) Stay on elections in cooperatives in some states since May, 2001, (2) Interference in the form of superseding of Board of Directors and (3) Departmental interference in financial matters in various forms, like; directions on interest rates, interference in loan decisions, announcement of waivers etc. The functional freedom to UCBs is the need of the hour.

Awareness Programmes for Employees

A proper training to the employees in bank management enhances their knoledge, which is ncessary for the smooth functioning of the business of the banks. The role of employees for the success of banks is very important. Some employees do not have proficiency in their work. At the same time, some employees are not only worthy, but also honest and dedicated to their works. There has to be a commitment and involvement of every employee in the functioning of UCBs. They should appreciate the fact that their livelihood is based on the survival of their employer and collapse of the system would render them jobless. The political elements can switch over to other organisations and shareholders failure of a UCB, whereas the employees generally are left to fend for themselves. Hence, it is the basic duty of every employee of the cooperative sector to appreciate the above facts and work in the larger interest of cooperative banks.

Conclusion

The 100 years of existence of UCBs in India have clearly shown that the resource base of the bank is so strong, that it is able to run the business with its own funds and is truly financially independent. But, at the same time, UCBs are facing defferent problems. These include organisational, managerial, financial and operational issues and, unless these problems are solved on a war footing the very growth of the urban banking sector and integration of the economy will be a distant dream and will only be a wild-goose chase. It is not fair to treat the UCBs, which are catering to the needs of weaker of sections of the population at par with MNC banks, which do not have any social obligations.

UCBs are increasingly operating in highly copetitive market environment. The severe competition they face from nationalised banks, private sector banks, and foreign banks, poses a threat to the survival of UCBs in small towns. The ever-increasing incidences of overdues and consequent NPAs occasioned by poor recoveries of loans disbursed by the banks and inadequate human resources development have creppled their financial solvency, economic viability and profitability. As such, the problems faced by the UCBs need to be addressed urgently, not only to ensure future growth of these institutions, but also to secure orderly progress of the entire financial system of the country. In India, demand for quality service has been met with some degree of efficiency and equity; but in few cases, the customers' basic expectations are not satisfied. Although the UCBs have shown significant progress in attaining more just and inclusive financial services at local levels, there remains enormous practical and theoretical challegnes that demand multidisciplinary approaches and new strategies by those engaged in development.

References

RBI 2004-05, Report on Trends and Progress of Banking in India, p. 112.

Ibid, p. 110.

Devadasan, K., Dr. Resia Beegams, "Urban Banks in India- Is it Sheen or Want", *The Mah. Co-op. Society,* Vol. M84(I).

Ibid, p. 111.

RBI (1998), Report of the Committee on Banking Sector Reforms, p. 55.

S. B. Naik (2000), "Co-operative Bankin: The Deep Rooted Malaise", *The Hindu Business Line,* 15-05-2000.

T. V. Lakshminarayan (2001), "Madhavpura Bank Scam: Cooperative Banks Under Cloud", The Tribune, Chandigarh, April 14.

Co-operative Banking Tabloid, Vol. XIV, No. 10, March 6-12-2005, NAFCUB, New Delhi, p. 1.

RBI (2005), Draft Vision Documents for UCBS,, Text of the RBI's Documents placed on its website.

Co-operative Banking Tabloid, Vol. XIV, No. 26, June 25-July 2, 2005, NAFCUB, New Delhi, p. 1.

RBI (2005): Draft Vision Document for Urban Co-operative Banks, Text of the RBI's Documents placed its website.

42nd Annual Report of the Board of Directors of Deposit Insurance and Credit Guarantee Corporation for the year ended 31-03-2001, Mumbai.

RBI (2003-04), Report on Trend and Progress of Banking in India.

S. Venkitraman (1999), "Myth and Reality", *The Economic Times*, January 6, p. 9.

Gross NPAs Indicate Account Identified as NPA on Application of the Prudential Norms of Income Recognition and Asset Classification Specified.

Rajaraman, Indira, Vasishtha (1999), "Non-performing Loans of PSU Banks", *Economic and Political Weekly*, Vol. XXXVII, No. 2 (February).

RBI (2002-03), Report on Trend and Progress of Banking in India, p. 95.